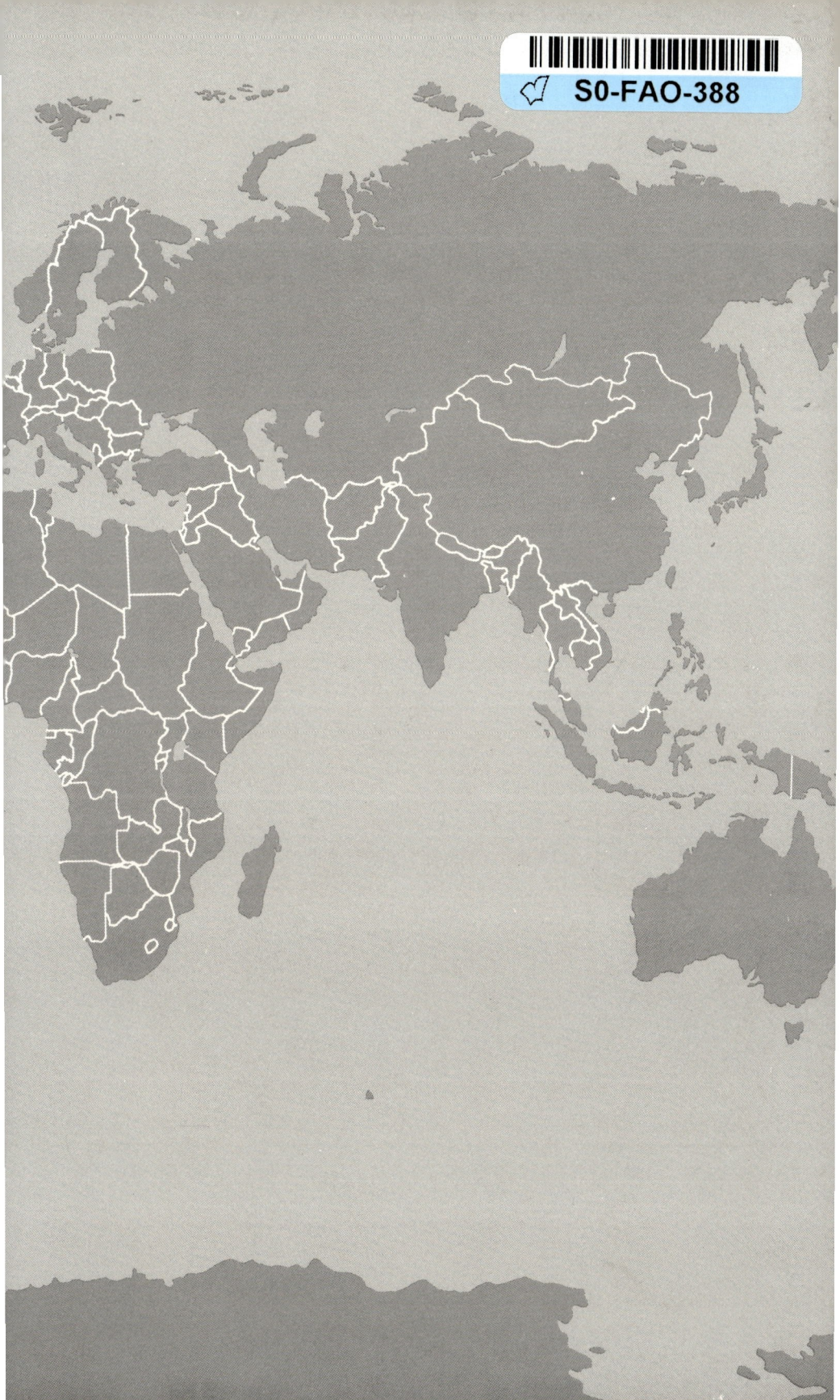

Saudi Arabia
a country study

Foreign Area Studies
The American University
Coauthors
Richard F. Nyrop, Beryl Lieff Benderly,
Laraine Newhouse Carter, Darrel R. Eglin,
Robert A. Kirchner
Research Completed May 1976

On the cover: The tall palm tree and the crossed
swords, adapted from the Saudi Arabia coat of arms,
by Lolita M. Grillo.

Third Edition, 1976; Third Printing: 1983

Copyright © 1982 United States Government as represented by the
Secretary of the Army. All rights reserved.

Library of Congress Cataloging in Publication Data

Nyrop, Richard F.
   Area handbook for Saudi Arabia.
   "DA pam 550-51."
   "One of a series of handbooks prepared by Foreign Area Studies (FAS) of the
American University."
   Supercedes 1971 ed. prepared by N.C. Walpole and others.
   Bibliography: pp. 347-369.
   Includes index.
   I. Saudi Arabia   I. Walpole, Norman C. Area handbook for Saudi Arabia.
      II. American University, Washington, D.C. Foreign Area Studies.   III. Title
DS204.W34 1977   953'.8'05   76-51268

Headquarters, Department of the Army
DA Pam 550-51
Supersedes 1971 edition

For sale by the Superintendent of Documents, U.S. Government Printing Office
Washington, D.C. 20402

Foreword

This volume is one of a continuing series of books written by Foreign Area Studies, The American University, under the Area Handbook Program. The last page of this book provides a listing of other country studies published. Each book in the series deals with a particular foreign country, describing and analyzing the economic, national security, political, and social systems and institutions and examining the interrelationships of those systems and institutions and the ways that they are shaped by cultural factors. Each study is written by a multidisciplinary team of social scientists. The authors seek to provide a basic insight and understanding of the society under observation, striving for a dynamic rather than a static portrayal of it. The study focuses on historical antecedents and on the cultural, political, and socioeconomic characteristics that contribute to cohesion and cleavage within the society. Paticular attention is given to the origins and traditions of the people who make up the society, their dominant beliefs and values, their community of interests and the issues on which they are divided, the nature and extent of their involvement with the national institutions, and their attitudes toward each other and toward the social system and political order within which they live.

The contents of the book represent the work of Foreign Area Studies and are not set forth as the official view of the United States government. The authors have sought to adhere to accepted standards of scholarly objectivity. Such corrections, additions, and suggestions for factual or other change that readers may have will be welcomed for use in future revisions.

William Evans-Smith, Director
Foreign Area Studies
The American University
5010 Wiconsin Ave., NW
Washington, D.C. 20016

PREFACE

The *Area Handbook for Saudi Arabia* is an attempt to provide a comprehensive study of the dominant aspects of the Saudi society and to identify the patterns of behavior characteristic of its members. The study results from the combined efforts of a Foreign Area Studies multidisciplinary team of researchers assisted by the organization's support staff. The team was supervised by Richard F. Nyrop, who wrote chapter 1 and coordinated the contributions of the other authors. Beryl Lieff Benderly wrote chapters 5, 6, and 7; Laraine Newhouse Carter wrote chapters 2, 3, and 4; Darrel R. Eglin wrote chapters 11, 12, and 13; and Robert A. Kirchner wrote chapters 8, 9, 10, and 14. The chapters represent the work of the authors and do not represent the official view of the United States government.

The authors wish to express their gratitude to individuals in various agencies of the United States government who gave of their time, documents, and special knowledge to provide data and perspective. The authors are also grateful to David L. Davies of the American Friends of the Middle East, Herbert R. Hengst of the University of Oklahoma, and James Knight of Aramco. Those individuals are not responsible for the work of the authors, however.

Sources of information used included scholarly studies, official reports of governments and international organizations, foreign and domestic newspapers, and numerous periodicals. Relatively up-to-date economic data were available from the Saudi government, and data on petroleum production, exports, and sales were available from Saudi and other reliable sources. Demographic data published by the Saudi government were less reliable and should be used with caution. Unless otherwise noted, weights are presented in metric tons.

The transliteration of Arabic words and phrases posed a particular problem. For many of the words—such as Muhammad, Muslim, Quran, and shaykh—the authors followed a modified version of the system adopted by the United States Board on Geographic Names and the Permanent Committee on Geographic Names for British Official Use, known as the BGN/PCGN system. In numerous instances, however, the names of persons or places are so well known by another spelling that to have used the BGN/PCGN system might have created confusion. For example, the reader will find Mecca rather than Makkah, Medina rather than Al Madinah, Qizan rather than Jizan, and Faisal rather than Faysal. A glossary is included for the reader's convenience.

Arab names are sometimes confusing to the Western reader, but they should be viewed as a sort of genealogical chart. The king's name—Khalid ibn Abd al Aziz Al Saud—means that he is Khalid, son of Abd al Aziz of the House of Saud. If the king deemed it important, he could recite his forebears back to the founder, Muhammad ibn Saud: Khalid ibn Abd al Aziz ibn Abd ar Rahman ibn Faisal ibn Turki ibn Abd Allah ibn Muhammad ibn Saud.

The Saudi government adheres to a lunar calendar, the Islamic hijra calendar, which has 354 days divided into twelve months. Moreover, the government's fiscal year begins midway through the hijra year. Conversions from the hijra year to a Gregorian date seem simple but are frequently complicated. To assist the reader the working of the hijra calendar is described in chapter 4, Living Conditions (see Patterns of Living and Leisure), and a conversion table is provided (see table A).

Table A. *Conversion of Hijra Years and Fiscal Years to Gregorian Dates*

Hijra Year (Muharram Through Dhu al Hijjah)	Gregorian Date Starts	Hijra Fiscal Year (1 Rajab Through 30 Jumada II)	Gregorian Date Starts
1380	June 25, 1960*	1380/81	December 19, 1960
1381	June 14, 1961	1381/82	December 9, 1961
1382	June 4, 1962	1382/83	November 28, 1962
1383	May 25, 1963	1383/84	November 17, 1963
1384	May 13, 1964*	1384/85	November 5, 1964
1385	May 1, 1965	1385/86	October 25, 1965
1386	April 21, 1966	1386/87	October 16, 1966
1387	April 11, 1967	1387/88	October 4, 1967
1388	March 30, 1968*	1388/89	September 23, 1968
1389	March 19, 1969	1389/90	September 12, 1969
1390	March 9, 1970	1390/91	September 2, 1970
1391	February 26, 1971	1391/92	August 22, 1971
1392	February 15, 1972*	1392/93	August 10, 1972
1393	February 4, 1973	1393/94	July 30, 1973
1394	January 23, 1974	1394/95	July 19, 1974
1395	January 13, 1975	1395/96	July 9, 1975
1396	January 2, 1976*	1396/97	June 28, 1976
1397	December 22, 1977	1397/98	June 16, 1977
1398	December 11, 1978	1398/99	June 6, 1978
1399	November 30, 1979	1399/1400	May 26, 1979
1400	November 19, 1980*	1400/1401	May 15, 1980

*Leap year.

COUNTRY SUMMARY

Saudi Arabia Country Summary Location Map

COUNTRY
Formal Name: Kingdom of Saudi Arabia.
Short Form: Saudi Arabia.
Terms for Nationals: Saudi(s) or Saudi Arabian(s); Adjectival forms—Saudi or Saudi Arabian.
Capital: Riyadh (Ministry of Foreign Affairs located in Jiddah).

GEOGRAPHY
Size: Approximately 864,000 square miles.
Topography: No rivers or permanent bodies of water. (See fig. 1 for regions.)
Climate: Hot desert climate, although coastal cities subject to high humidity.
Boundaries: Most boundaries not demarcated, some not defined.

SOCIETY
Population: Government data indicated 7 million August-September 1974, but most observers estimate about 5.6 million in early 1976, of whom an estimated 1.5 million were foreigners. About 95 percent live on 5 percent of land, under 50 percent rural.

Ethnic Groups and Languages: All Saudis are Arab Muslims, as are most foreigners. Arab official language.
Health: Data are inconclusive, but government hopes to lower infant mortality rate to 110 per 1,000 by 1980.
Literacy: Estimated at between 5 and 15 percent in mid-1970s.
Religion: Islam in the Wahhabi (see Glossary) interpretation of the Sunni doctrine—the official religion and the faith of over 90 percent of the Saudis.

GOVERNMENT AND POLITICS
Form: Monarchy. King also serves as prime minister.
Administrative Division: Six major and twelve minor provices.
Legal System: Law consists of the sharia (sacred Islamic law)—which includes the Quran, the hadith, and the Sunna—and of administrative decrees.
Politics: Political parties, interest groups, and similar organizations not permitted.
Major International Memberships: United Nations and many of its specialized agencies, League of Arab States (Arab League), Organization of Petroleum Exporting Countries (OPEC), Organization of Arab Petroleum Exporting Countries (OAPEC), and various Islamic conferences.

ECONOMY
Gross Domestic Product (GDP): In fiscal year (FY—see table A) 1975 oil contributed about 87 percent to GDP, agriculture less than 1 percent, construction about 3 percent, and industry, commerce, and services the remainder.
Petroleum: In early 1976 possessed an estimated 25 percent of world's proven reserves, was the largest oil exporter, and the third largest producer.
Foreign Trade: In February 1976 foreign exchange reserves about US$23.7 billion. Exports almost completely oil, which in 1974 amounted to 3.2 billion barrels worth over US$35 billion. Country imports almost everything except petroleum products, with valuation of about US$3.9 billion in 1974.
Currency: Saudi riyal—see Glossary.
Fiscal Year: See table A.

TRANSPORTATION AND COMMUNICATIONS
Railroads: One rail line operative, the Dammam-Riyadh run, 357 miles in length.
Roads: Approximately 6,200 miles of roads in 1975.
Ports: Four main ports, all badly congested; Jiddah and Yanbu on Red Sea, Ras Tanura and Dammam on Persian Gulf.
Airfields: Three international (Jiddah, Riyadh, and Dhahran) in ear-

ly 1976 plus seventeen smaller airports. Saudia only authorized domestic carrier.

Telecommunications: Inadequate system being expanded and improved as rapidly as possible by its owner, the government.

NATIONAL SECURITY

Armed Forces: As of early 1976, Royal Saudi Army—about 40,000; Royal Saudi Navy—about 1,500; Royal Saudi Air Force—about 5,550; Frontier Force and Coast Guard—about 6,500 combined. The paramilitary Royal Saudi National Guard had about 16,000 on active duty, an equal or larger number in reserves. Two army brigades of about 5,000 men each posted abroad, one in Jordan, the other in Syria.

Major Tactical Units: Royal Saudi Army and the National Guard organized in brigades and supporting battalions. Introduction of modern weapons into all branches matter of high priority in mid-1970s.

Major Equipment Suppliers: In early 1976 American firms continued to be the major source of supply for such sophisticated equipment as tanks, surface-to-air missile systems, and fighter-bombers. Saudi government has also purchased British and French equipment.

Military Budget: Twenty percent of government expenditures in FY 1975.

SAUDI ARABIA

TABLE OF CONTENTS

	Page
FOREWORD	iii
PREFACE	v
COUNTRY SUMMARY	vii

SECTION I. SOCIAL

Chapter 1. General Character of the Society 1

        2. Historical Setting 9
            Pre-Islamic Arabia—Muhammad and the Conquest of Islam—Arabia Before the Sauds—The House of Saud—The Reign of Abd al Aziz (1902-53)—The "Interlude" of Saud—The Reign of Faisal

        3. Geography and Population 45
            Boundaries and Administrative Divisions—Geographic Setting—Man-Made Features—Population

        4. Living Conditions 69
            Standards of Living—Public Health—Welfare

        5. Education and the Arts 91
            The Intellectual and Artistic Climate—Education and Society—The Organization of Education—The Educational Career

        6. Religious Life 113
            Islam—Islam and Society

        7. Social Systems 131
            Units of Organization—The National Society—The Individual, the Family, and the Sexes

SECTION II. POLITICAL

Chapter 8. Government and Politics 157
            Royal Family, Religion, and Politics—Governmental System—Legal System

        9. Mass Communications 193
            Government, Society, and Mass Communications—Survey of Mass Communications System—External Sources of Information

        10. Foreign Relations 205
            Relations with Middle Eastern and Islamic States—International Setting—Mechanics of Foreign Relations

		Page
Section III.	ECONOMIC	
Chapter 11.	Character and Structure of the Economy	219
	Structure of the Economy—Money—Banking—Public Finance—Labor—Planning	
12.	The Petroleum Industry and Foreign Trade	245
	Oil: The International Setting—Saudi Arabian Oil—Foreign Trade	
13.	Agriculture, Industry, and Domestic Trade	285
	Agriculture—Industry—Domestic Trade	
Section IV.	NATIONAL DEFENSE	
Chapter 14.	National Defense and Internal Security	311
	Armed Forces, Society, and Politics—Administration and Training of the Military—Foreign Influence and Military Posture—Internal Security	
Bibliography		347
Glossary		371
Index		375

LIST OF ILLUSTRATIONS

Figure		Page
1	Kingdom of Saudi Arabia	xiv
2	Ancient Arabia	12
3	Saudi Arabia, Simplified Genealogy of House of Saud with Order and Duration of Rule, 1976	26
4	Nineteenth-Century Arabia	27
5	Saudi Arabia, Administrative Divisions, May 1976	49
6	Saudi Arabia, Transportation, 1975	58
7	Saudi Arabia, Population Distribution in the Mid-1970s	65
8	Saudi Arabia, Educational Ladder, 1975	105
9	Saudi Arabia, Rites of the Haj	127
10	Saudi Arabia, Principal Tribes	135
11	Saudi Arabia, Major Amirs of the Royal Family, 1976	163
12	Saudi Arabia, Government Structure, 1976	176
13	Saudi Arabia, Organization of Judicial System, 1976	189
14	Organization of the United States-Saudi Arabia Joint Commission, 1974	213
15	World Oil, 1974	249
16	Saudi Arabia, Oil Fields and Facilities, 1975	261

LIST OF ILLUSTRATIONS—Continued

Figure		Page
17	Saudi Arabia, Government Organization in the Areas of National Defense and Internal Security, 1975	319
18	Saudi Arabia, Major Military and National Guard Installations, 1975	321
19	Saudi Arabia, Insignia of Officer Ranks, 1976	328

LIST OF TABLES

Table		Page
A	Conversion of Hijra Years and Fiscal Years to Gregorian Dates	vi
1	Saudi Arabia, Elementary, Intermediate, and Secondary Education, 1975 and 1980	106
2	Saudi Arabia, Postsecondary Education, 1975 and 1980	109
3	Saudi Arabia, Council of Ministers, 1975	179
4	Saudi Arabia, Major Publications, 1975	200
5	Saudi Arabia, Gross Domestic Product by Sector, Fiscal Years 1963, 1970, and 1975	222
6	Saudi Arabia, Summary of Accounts, Selected Fiscal Years, 1964-76	233
7	Saudi Arabia, Budget Allocations by Function, Selected Fiscal Years, 1966-74	236
8	Saudi Arabia, Employment by Sector, Fiscal Years 1967, 1970, and 1975	237
9	Saudi Arabia, Summary of Planned Financial Allocations by Sector, Five Year Development Plan (1970-75)	240
10	Saudi Arabia, Summary of Planned Financial Allocations by Function, Five Year Development Plan (1975-80)	242
11	Saudi Arabia, Oil Production, Revenues, and Exports, Selected Years, 1938-74	265
12	Saudi Arabia, Imports by Commodity Group, Selected Years, 1968-73	278
13	Saudi Arabia, Balance of Payments, Selected Years, 1968-74	280
14	Saudi Arabia, Production, Imports, and Consumption of Major Crops, Fiscal Years 1960-63 Average and Fiscal Year 1971	292
15	Saudi Arabia, National Defense, Strength and Overall Costs, Fiscal Years 1971-76	322
16	Saudi Arabia, Titles of Military Rank, 1976	329
17	Saudi Arabia, Chronology of Saudi Arabia-United States Military Relations and Saudi Arabia's Major Arms Purchases, 1943-76	334
18	Saudi Arabia, Arms Imports and United States Military Assistance, United States Fiscal Years 1950-75	336

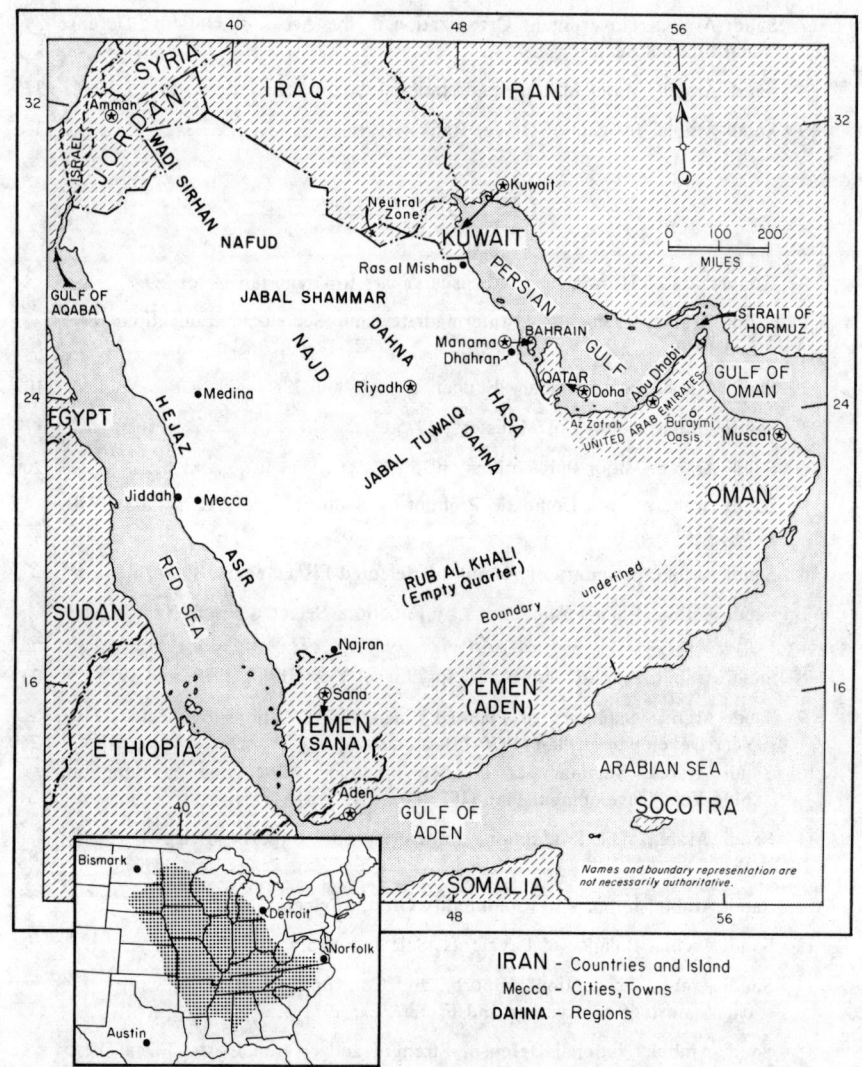

Figure 1. Kingdom of Saudi Arabia

SECTION I. SOCIAL

CHAPTER 1
GENERAL CHARACTER OF THE SOCIETY

When Abd al Aziz ibn Abd ar Rahman Al Saud established the Kingdom of Saudi Arabia in 1932, the foreign capitals then concerned with affairs on the Arabian Peninsula regarded the event as a minor curiosity. The general view of the new state was of an empty desert region ruled by a warrior family whose members were the dour adherents of a staunchly orthodox Islamic sect. The kingdom nevertheless possessed significance as the site of the two holiest cities of Islam —Mecca and Medina—and was of some interest to international oil companies as an area in which oil might be found.

Within four decades, however, the country had become the object of intense international interest and concern, and its leaders were accorded the deference and respect usually reserved to the chiefs of major powers. The literature on the kingdom—whether by journalists, academicians, or bureaucrats—invariably included a litany of superlatives to describe the society and its economic base. For example, as of early 1976 the country possessed the world's largest proven oil reserves and was the world's largest oil exporter. It was the third largest producer of oil (after the Soviet Union and the United States) but, with an estimated 25 percent of the world's reserves, had the capacity to be first in production. Its foreign exchange reserves were exceeded only by those of the Federal Republic of Germany (West Germany), and its Five Year Development Plan (1975-80) was on a per capita basis one of the most ambitious undertaken by any nation.

The country embraced about 80 percent of the Arabian Peninsula, but throughout its approximately 864,000 square miles there were neither rivers nor permanent bodies of water. Moreover the total population in early 1976 was not much above 5.6 million—of which an estimated 1.5 million were foreigners—making the country one of the world's least densely populated (see ch. 3). And the country is the only one in the world named after its founding and ruling family, the House of Saud, or Al Saud. The name in Arabic—Al Mamlaka Al Arabiya Al Saudiya—literally means the kingdom of the Arabs of the House of Saud.

The Kingdom of Saudi Arabia is sometimes described as an absolute monarchy; it might more aptly be described as an absolute monarchial system. The kingship derives an important element of its authority from the pervasive influence of Wahhabi Islam over all aspects of society; as the leader of the faithful the king enforces the moral and behavioral norms of this puritanical form of Islam, and he benefits from Islamic theories about the unity of secular and religious life. As long as the king adheres to and rules according to the sharia, he is in theory absolute. In practice, however, a king is selected by his peers and can be removed by the same process. He receives a mandate to rule, but that mandate can be withdrawn. In the words of a United States Department of State publication, "The powers of the King are not defined but practically are limited by the fact that he must retain a consensus of the Saudi royal family, the religious leaders (*ulema*), the chiefs of the important tribes, the armed forces, and the bureaucracy." Nevertheless, because the royal family is so intimately involved in and has such pervasive connections with the other "pillars" of the society and the governmental apparatus, the king as the chief representative and symbol of the House of Saud possesses extraordinary power.

Although the object of much scrutiny and informed conjecture, remarkably little is publicly known about decisionmaking within the House of Saud. In the aftermath of the assassination of King Faisal ibn Abd al Aziz Al Saud and the succession of King Khalid ibn Abd al Aziz Al Saud in March 1975, many foreign observers sought to identify factions or cliques within the royal family and to depict them as engaged in a power struggle. In a ruling group as large as the House of Saud there are numerous subgroups or factions, but an article by David Holden in the *New York Times Magazine* perhaps best described the Saudi political system in its title, "A Family Affair."

The House of Saud consists of the several thousand descendants of Abd al Aziz and his three brothers (see ch. 8). For the first twenty years after the death of Abd al Aziz in 1953 his sons and brothers held almost all the key government offices, but by 1976 several of the grandsons were assuming important positions as were a number of Western-educated technocrats who were not members of the royal family (see ch. 7). In early 1976 King Khalid's brothers, nephews, and cousins held important positions everywhere. A half brother, Crown Prince Fahd ibn Abd al Aziz Al Saud, was the first deputy prime minister and the "executive officer" of the government. Three of Fahd's brothers—Sultan, Turki, and Naif—served respectively as the minister of defense and aviation, the vice minister of defense and aviation, and the minister of interior. The military and police forces were controlled by these three men (see ch. 14). Another of the king's half brothers, Amir Abd Allah ibn Abd al Aziz Al Saud, was the second deputy prime minister and the commander of the Royal Saudi National Guard, an internal security paramilitary force of over 16,000 men. Three other half brothers of the king held important portfolios in the Council of Ministers; and a nephew, Amir Saud ibn Faisal ibn

Abd al Aziz Al Saud—a son of the late King Faisal—was the foreign minister. Other half brothers and nephews served as governors or deputy governors of provinces, vice or deputy ministers, and directors general of important government offices. In addition junior members of the royal family filled an estimated 1 to 2 percent of the approximately 168,000 positions in the civil service.

Members of the royal family also held many positions—some of them at senior rank—in the Royal Saudi Army (about 40,000 officers and men), the Royal Saudi Air Force (about 5,500), and the Royal Saudi Navy (about 1,500). The House of Saud remained keenly aware of the military coups d'etat that ousted monarchies in the neighboring Arab states of Egypt, Libya, and Iraq and of the coup attempts in such traditional monarchies as Jordan and Morocco. In the mid-1970s the government was spending the equivalent of billions of United States dollars to improve and modernize its armed forces, but at the same time the government also allocated very large sums to modernize the National Guard, which served as something of a counterweight to the regular military. Whereas any Saudi male could seek admission to the regular armed forces, the National Guard recruited its officers and men from a few noble beduin tribes that had close ties—often through intermarriage—with the House of Saud and were viewed by the government as particularly loyal and trustworthy (see ch. 7; ch. 14). Abd al Aziz had conquered most of these tribes in battle and had formed alliances with all of them. The shaykhs (tribal chiefs) accepted Abd al Aziz as the shaykh of shaykhs, and Abd al Aziz' successors have inherited this honorific. In the mid-1970s Abd Allah, as National Guard commander, was the chief liaison between the House of Saud and the important tribal shaykhs, although Khalid also maintained a close relationship with the shaykhs.

The relationship of the royal family to the senior ulama is also intimate and of long standing and in 1976 continued to be a highly interdependent one. The House of Saud and Wahhabism (see Glossary) entered Arabian history at the same time (see ch. 2; ch. 6). In about 1744 Muhammad ibn Abd al Wahhab, a religious scholar who preached a return to the orthodox practices of the days of the Prophet Muhammad, was expelled from his village because of his puritanical zeal. He sought and received refuge with Muhammad ibn Saud, the chief of a small region in the Najd (see fig. 1). The religious scholar and the warrior chief jointed forces with the avowed goal of conquering and purifying Arabia. Their early compact, which included taking the oath the Prophet had first used when he established his rule in Medina, was secularly strengthened when Saud married a daughter of Wahhab, the first of numerous marriages between the two families. King Faisal, for example, was the result of one such marriage.

The terms *Wahhabi, Wahhabite,* and *Wahhabism* are not used in Saudi Arabia. To the extent that a Saudi would go beyond a terse self-description of Muslim, he might use the phrase *al dawah ila al tauhid*, meaning the call to the doctrine of the oneness of God, to describe his faith. Opponents of the sect dubbed them Wahhabis. Just as the descendants of Muhammad ibn Saud constitute the Al Saud, the descendants of Muhammad ibn Abd al Wahhab are known as the Al ash Shaykh—the House of the Shaykh. In the mid-1970s many of the most senior ulama were members of the Al ash Shaykh, and three family members held portfolios in the Council of Ministers formed in October 1975 (see ch. 8).

During Wahhab's lifetime he was known both as *the* Shaykh and as the imam (see Glossary) of the faith. When he died, the successors of Saud assumed the title of imam. Although Abd al Aziz allowed the formal designation to lapse in favor of more secular ones—first sultan and in 1932 king—the term was still occasionally used informally, and the mystique of the imamate continued to be associated with the kingship. A formidable share of the religious leadership, in other words, remains fixed in the office and person of the king and the House of Saud. The king is quite literally the "commander of the faithful" to the over 90 percent of the Saudis who subscribe with no discernible reservations to Wahhabi Islam.

The Saudi bureaucracy is large—many observers assert that it is too large—and its work touches almost every citizen and foreign resident. In terms of decisionmaking, however, foreign observers viewed only a few senior technocrats as of importance. The official best known in the West was Shaykh Ahmad Zaki Yamani, the minister of petroleum and mineral resources. Because of the overwhelming importance of the production, export, and sale of oil to the Saudi and the world economies, Yamani enjoyed considerable international prestige and was an influential official of the government (see ch. 10; ch. 12). Other ministers, such as Minister of Planning Hisham Muhi al Din Nazir and Minister of Industry and Electricity Ghazi Abd ar Rahman al Qusaibi, also held highly responsible positions, were accorded great respect, and exercised great influence within the government. Several other ministers and many lesser technocrats were vitally important to the king and his advisers. But the position of the influential technocrats was somewhat anomalous. On the one hand the government needs them and many more like them to modernize and expand the economy. On the other hand an individual technocrat owes his position and his future to his continued good performance and the continued goodwill and approbation of the core group of the House of Saud.

As long as the Saudi economy continues to expand rapidly, a talented, industrious, and loyal secularly educated commoner can be certain of profitable employment and advancement. The best indication of the devotion and loyalty of this emerging modern middle class was that as of the mid-1970s almost all Saudis educated abroad returned home to work; this was in sharp contrast to almost all other developing nations, which have experienced extensive brain drains. Observers were uncertain, however, as to what happens when a commoner and a member of the royal family of comparable secular education compete for a job. As more members of the royal family receive secular and technical educations, the competition for jobs will increase. The family connection will presumably prevail, but results were impossible to predict in 1976.

The major formal institutions of the society—the royal family, the ulama, the military and paramilitary forces, and the bureaucracy—thus remain rooted in tradition and oriented to conservative procedures. A description of the Arabs by the late Joseph Schacht is particularly applicable to the Saudis: "The [Saudi] Arabs were, and are, bound by tradition and precedent; they were, and are, dominated by the past. . . . Whatever was customary, was right and proper; whatever their forefathers had done, deserved to be imitated." The dominant and central role of the royal family is at once sustained by and dependent upon basic beduin values (see ch. 7). In an article written in 1974 Harold W. Glidden observes that "ingroup solidarity (*asabiyah*), stemming originally from Arab tribal values, is probably the most salient characteristic of the mechanics of Arab society. It demands a high degree of conformity and therefore imparts a strong authoritarian tone to Arab culture and society."

Glidden also notes that, whereas societies based at least in part on the so-called Protestant ethic are often characterized as "guilt-ridden" or "guilt-oriented," the traditional Arab society is often described as "shame-oriented." According the Gidden, shame that "is intensely feared" comes not from the commission of an "act condemned by the value system" but from the "discovery by outsiders" of the act. "Hence there is an intense concern with and catering to outward appearance and public opinion that many observers have noted as being characteristic of the Arabs."

The royal family has nevertheless instituted many changes in the society, and it has accepted others. Slavery was abolished and modern telecommunications introduced despite strong misgivings by respected ulama. Strict public observance of the basic tenets of Islam is expected, but the private indulgence of various aspects of more permissive, Western-style social behavior is accepted. When Abd al Aziz died in 1953, only a few score Saudis had received secular educations abroad. By 1976 several thousand Saudis had been educated in the United States or Western Europe, had received technical training there, or had pursued secular studies in Western-oriented institutions in the Middle East. Thousands more were engaged in basically secular studies in the rapidly expanding Saudi university system (see ch. 5). The royal family was the prime mover in the rush to education in an attempt to produce Saudis to operate the growing socioeconomic system. But the impact on the basic social system of relatively large numbers of secularly oriented managers and technicians was something neither the royal family nor other observers could confidently predict.

The country's need for managers, technicians, and skilled workers remains enormous and immediate. The 1975-80 development plan identifies the necessity of importing some 500,000 workers. The skills required range from doctors and teachers through truck drivers, electricians, and crane operators to computer technicians and engineers. Personnel who possess such skills usually insist not only upon high salaries or wages, which the economy can easily afford, but also upon housing and other related facilities either in short supply or not available (see ch. 4; ch. 11). For example, the King Faisal Specialist Hospital and Research Center in Riyadh was probably as technically advanced and sophisticated as any in the world. The level at other hospitals was far less impressive, however. Despite such major government efforts as the construction of fifteen public hospitals between 1971 and 1975, large areas of the country lacked adequate or even minimal medical attention. The infant mortality rate, especially among the estimated 10 to 30 percent of the population that was nomadic, was extremely high. The goal of the development plan is to reduce the infant mortality rate to "no more than 110 per 1,000" by 1980 (see ch.4).

By 1976 the government was spending more money than the economy could absorb on a variety of social welfare, agricultural, commercial, industrial, and defense-related projects (see ch. 4; ch. 13; ch. 14). The five-year development plan that was approved in May 1975 calls for government expenditures about the equivalent of US$142 billion during the 1975-80 plan period. In addition to schools, hospitals, and housing, the plan envisages the creation of an industrial complex based on petrochemicals; the establishment of other industrial plants such as cement, iron, and steel works, using the country's vast supply of natural gas; the erection of huge desalinization plants; and various agricultural projects (see ch. 11; ch. 12; ch. 13). In addition to a shortage of manpower, seriously inadequate port and transportation facilities will continue to hamper the implementation of the plan. In late 1975 and early 1976 the country's few ports were gravely congested and, despite crash construction programs, the problem cannot be quickly resolved (see ch. 11).

Nevertheless in early 1976 the Saudi economy gave every indication of continued rapid growth. The experience of the early 1970s, when as a result of the sharp increases in the price of oil the gross domestic product (GDP) grew at the rate of nearly 55 percent a year, will probably not be repeated. Future growth will be more modest but still very substantial. In any event the government will continue to earn more than enough money to finance its development projects. In a prepared statement to a United States House of Representatives committee in February 1976, a senior Department of State official observed that the Saudi government "has maintained [oil] production levels which are well beyond its economic needs." That is, even if the world demand for oil were drastically reduced for some reason and Saudi exports fell sharply, Saudi Arabia would still be able to finance its economic and military modernization programs.

The Saudi oil economy is of recent vintage. Abd al Aziz sold an oil concession to an American oil firm in 1933. The company discovered the first commercially exploitable field in 1938 and exported the first oil in 1939. World War II hampered the expansion of production and export facilities. It was not until the late 1940s that the oil company—by that time the Arabian American Oil Company (Aramco), jointly owned by four American oil companies—started making fairly large payments to the government. During the 1950s and 1960s the payments increased substantially as exports increased and as new and huge fields were discovered with almost monotonous regularity.

The massive leap in government receipts took place in 1974 and 1975 when Saudi Arabia joined with its fellow members of the Organization of Petroleum Exporting Countries (OPEC) in several sharp increases in the price of oil (see ch. 12). In February 1976 the country's foreign exchange reserves totaled US$23.74 billion, about US$5,600 for every Saudi citizen, despite extensive foreign loans, grants, and investments, large purchases of military and industrial hardware, and the acquisition of 60 percent of the ownership of Aramco. In April 1976 Saudi and Aramco officials confirmed that Saudi Arabia would soon be the sole owner of Aramco, probably sometime later that year.

Nations usually are considered powerful only if they have agricultural wealth and industrial and military might. Saudi Arabia is deficient in all three categories, not only in absolute terms but also in comparison with its neighbors. Given its soil, terrain, and climate, the country is not likely ever to be self-sufficient in food; and given its scarcity of raw materials other than oil and its small population, it will not be able for at least several decades to achieve industrial or military strength.

First and most obvious is its oil, which it can deny to the world market albeit to its own eventual ruin. Second, and equally obvious to the managers of the international money markets, is the present and future wealth derived from the sale of oil. In the mid-1970s a large proportion of the government's foreign exchange holdings was in short-term deposits in foreign banks. Although the Saudis have behaved with considerable caution and circumspection in their foreign investments and deposits and have never publicly threatened to use their fiscal power in a capricious or vindictive fashion, they possess that power. According to knowledgeable observers, a sudden withdrawal of Saudi deposits would seriously disrupt the international money market and might cause the collapse of many West European and American banks. As journalist David Holden observed, "The [Saudi] money machine becomes a juggernaut, menacing everything in its path. The task of the House of Saud is to drive it so that they do not destroy their people or themselves."

The Saudi economy also constitutes a major market for the industrialized nations. Because of the Saudi government's strong antipathy for communism, its major trading partners have been Japan, the countries of Western Europe, and the United States. The excellent reputation of Aramco within Saudi Arabia resulted in an early, close, and continuing relationship between the Saudi and the United States governments. Private American research organizations were intimately involved in the drafting of the development plan, and United States government officials have long served as advisers on countless industrial, construction, and military projects. The regular military forces and the paramilitary National Guard were largely equipped with weapons and matériel purchased from American firms, and American military advisers—supplied both by the United States Department of Defense and by private American firms—have long been active in the country.

In several statements on national policy, senior Saudi officials have emphasized that they wish to continue and to expand the past close relationship with the United States government and the American business community. They have indicated, however, that they feel no sense of dependence on the United States and that they are prepared to take their business elsewhere. The Saudi statements were made in response to questions raised in the United States Congress about the impact on American business firms of the Arab boycott of firms that did business with Israel or that had Jews as principals in the firm. The issue was a highly emotional one in both countries, but officials of both governments were confident in early 1976 that it would not damage a long and fruitful relationship.

CHAPTER 2

HISTORICAL SETTING

The position of Saudi Arabia as the world's largest oil exporter makes its internal changes of critical interest to the rest of the world. But the assassination of King Faisal ibn Abd al Aziz Al Saud in March 1975 aroused little consternation in either the Arab or the Western worlds as to the future stability of the young nation. The kingdom of Saudi Arabia did not always have such an optimistic future. In the days before the discovery of oil its future was of concern only to those nations that had territorial interests in the immediate area and to Muslims who wished to make the pilgrimage to Mecca in relative safety.

Faisal's father, Abd al Aziz ibn Abd ar Rahman Al Saud, established the state through a combination of tribal conquest and diplomatic maneuvering over a period of twenty-five years, and in 1932 he proclaimed the creation of the kingdom of Saudi Arabia. Saudi Arabia was named after the House of Saud (Al Saud) and was ruled by its first two monarchs as if it were a tribal confederation (see ch. 7). Abd al Aziz was a political and religious leader of some genius, but the administrative complexities that accompanied the discovery of oil, the introduction of various aspects of Western technology, and the sudden acquisition of considerable wealth made the last years of his reign difficult and inefficient.

His successor, Saud ibn Abd al Aziz Al Saud, was gifted neither with the political perspicacity of his father nor with administrative prowess. When in 1964 Faisal ascended the throne in place of his deposed brother, he faced the onerous task of transforming the nearly bankrupt nation with a legacy of tribal attitudes and methods into a modern state while placating the opposing forces of religious conservatism and modernization. By the year of his death Faisal had managed to take steps to ensure that the vastly increased wealth of his country would be directed toward long-term industrial and social welfare programs that would eventually benefit all sectors of the society and would secure Saudi Arabia as a permanent and important power in the Arab world and in the international community. Faisal accomplished this without seriously offending tribal sensitivities and at the same time retained the traditional religious base of his family's power and the conservative orientation of the society.

Although Saudi Arabia was founded in the twentieth century, its heritage was 1300 years old, and its methods, those of the nomadic beduin, were even more ancient. In the eighteenth century a local leader in the Najd, the Saudi homeland in north-central Arabia, Muhammad ibn Saud, had aligned himself with a local religious leader, Muhammad ibn Abd al Wahhab, who wished to revive the spirit and practices of Islam as it was in the seventh century A.D. Saud and Wahhab acting together offered conversion or the sword, basically the same method used by Muhammad, the Prophet of Islam, in his conquest of Arabia. Intermarriage cemented the Saud-Wahhab alliance, and a series of descendants kept the movement alive, however feebly, until Abd al Aziz decisively established his rule in the twentieth century. David Hogarth, a British specialist on Arabia, predicted in 1925 that Abd al Aziz's domination outside the Najd, would probably not last more than a decade and certainly would not survive his death. Although Abd al Aziz was a sagacious ruler, Hogarth's prophecy almost certainly would have come true were it not for the discovery of oil a decade later.

Western powers have only had economic reasons to be interested in Saudi Arabia since the 1930s, but to the world's Muslims the area has always been important because their two holiest cities are located there: Mecca, the city that holds its most important shrine, the Kaabah; and Medina, the city where the Prophet established his first community and laid the foundation of the Islamic nation (see ch. 6). Despite this the area remained isolated, unknown, and little visited. The Arabic name for the Arabian Peninsula is Jazirat al Arab, the "Island of the Arabs." T.E. Lawrence described the land, particularly the interior, as a factory of Arabs and Arab values, kept pure by isolation. The nomads have been portrayed by other writers as people of marvelous imagination, energy, and dedication to ideas. The idea of material permanence was alien to them because one could carry little in the desert. Nomads came to value products of the mind—religion, language, lineage, and relationships. This was their legacy to Islam and to the rulers of Saudi Arabia.

Historically the homeland of the beduin has been capable of vitalization by only two forces—religion and economics. When Arabia was enlivened by one or the other of these factors, the effect was always noteworthy, and the repercussions were felt and responded to by the world around it. After periods of economic or religious greatness Arabia receded in men's minds. Settlements that had been built up dwindled or vanished. The people migrated from Arabia or disappeared into the desert. The harsh terrain and climate of the peninsula soon effaced or concealed any visible changes that had been made. Because outsiders could get Arabia's products by ship, they rarely attempted to penetrate the interior; thus Arabia bears little mark of peoples that colonized along the coasts. In a similar manner foreign pilgrims who were unable to return home because of financial difficulties were quickly assimilated into the culture.

The strength of the indigenous culture and its ability to endure despite change and to overwhelm any new influences around it had been apparent since the founding of Saudi Arabia. Present-day Saudis are eager to have all the benefits of modern technology but insist that foreigners respect Saudi value systems. Saudis perceive themselves as leaders of the Arab world just as the beduin perceive themselves as the only unspoiled and "true" Arabs and therefore a model for all others.

Modern technology has largely ended the migrational patterns of the beduin, and many more of them will become urban dwellers. The upper classes will become increasingly dependent on western luxuries. Many observers believe, however, that the basic values developed by the people for over a millennium will endure.

PRE-ISLAMIC ARABIA

The Civilizations of Prehistoric Arabia

Archeological investigations of pre-Islamic Arabia are still in an embryonic state, and the results are hypothetical and controversial at best. Through the middle of the twentieth century few people had the physical endurance or the survival techniques crucial to investigate the area. Scarcity of water, the difficulties of desert transport, and until the 1940s hostile tribes made systematic research a heroic undertaking. Further, little was known about present-day Arabia beyond its coastal settlements. Initial archeological discoveries were often the accidental finds of explorers anxious to investigate this isolated land and map its interior.

The first three known Arabian civilizations were coastal settlements (see fig. 2). The oldest evidence of civilized man in northern Arabia are artifacts found sixty miles to the north of Dhahran on the coast of the Persian Gulf. Dated to 5000 B.C. they are identical to those of the Al Ubaid culture of Mesopotamia, the first people to cultivate and settle the Fertile Crescent (the valley of the Tigris and Euphrates, an arching crescent from near present-day Kuwait to modern Israel) and the ancestors of the Sumerians, the first known people to develop a high culture. If Al Ubaid culture originated in Mesopotamia, then civilization reached Arabia from the north. If, however, Arabia was the parent site, then the first known agriculturists in the Middle East were migrants from Arabia. This would substantiate the Sumerian myth that agriculture had been brought to Mesopotamia by a fish-man from the Persian Gulf.

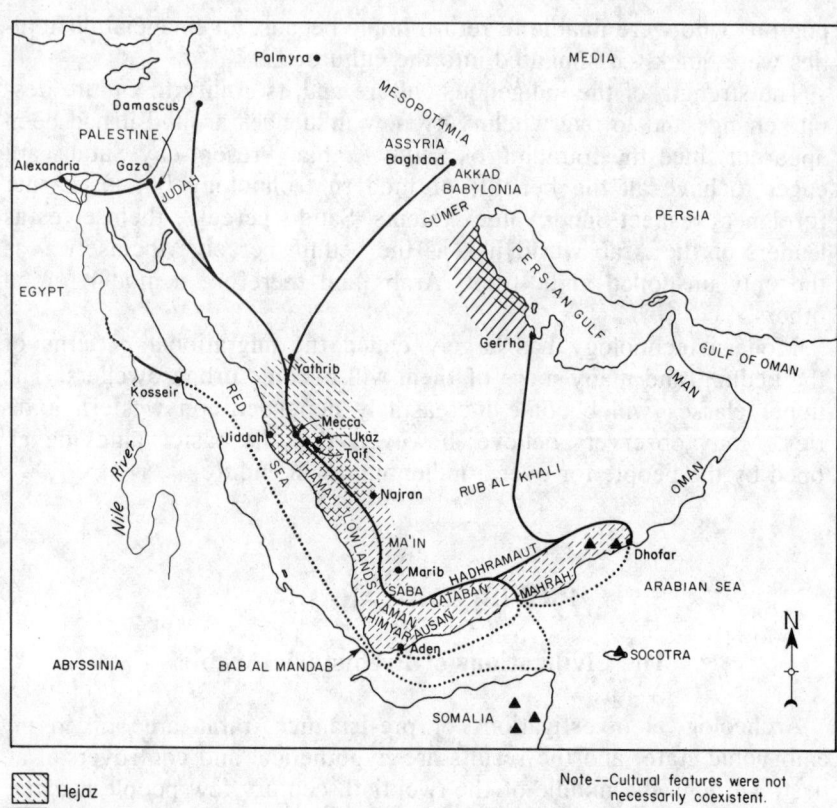

Figure 2. Ancient Arabia

From about 4000 to 2000 B.C. the civilization called Dilmun dominated 250 miles of the eastern coast of Arabia from present-day Kuwait to Bahrain and extended sixty miles into the interior to the oasis of Hufuf. At its zenith in 2000 B.C. Dilmun controlled the route to the Indies and was the trading link between the civilizations of the Indus Valley and those of Mesopotamia. The Mesopotamians regarded Dilmun as a holy place and its people as extraordinarily blessed. At Oman and Abu Dhabi remains of another civilization were found that might be related to Dilmun.

Arabia was only sparsely peopled in the interior. Until about 3000 B.C. inland Arabia was sufficiently verdant to support both cereal agriculturists and herding peoples in the north and hunting and gathering societies in the south. As climatic conditions changed and the desert slowly encroached upon land that formerly had supported both animal and human life, the inhabitants were faced with three choices: to cling to the inland oases, to move to the coasts, or to leave Arabia entirely. Those who made the third choice and migrated to the north, northeast, and southwest are the only ones who left a historical record.

The Migrations

In the middle of the fourth millennium B.C. a pattern emerged that proved disastrous to the material advancement of the peninsula but that benefited the rest of the world immeasurably. Approximately every thousand years either because of population pressures caused by inadequate food and resources or because they were following wild herds, major migrations of Semitic-speaking people from the Arabian Peninsula insinuated themselves into the more hospitable lands around them. In about 3500 B.C. two parallel migrations occurred: one by the western route northward to the Sinai Peninsula and into Egypt, where the immigrants mixed with the indigenous people to produce the historical Egyptians; the other by the eastern route to Sumer where they amalgamated and became known as Babylonians. The Egyptians made important innovations in irrigation, mathematics, and architecture and developed the world's first solar calendar. The Babylonians developed the world's first known law code and were also adept at mathematics and astronomy.

In about 2500 B.C. there were further migrations from the peninsula to the Fertile Crescent. These migrants merged with the indigenous people and became the Canaanites and the Phoenicians (collectively, the Amorites). Both peoples devised alphabetical scripts; the Phoenicians developed a commercial empire based on navigational routes that linked the Mediterranean with northern Europe for the first time. Between 1500 and 1200 B.C. some migrants settled in Syria and were among the ancestors of the Aramaeans or modern Syrians. The others settled in southern Syria and Palestine and were among the forebears of the Hebrews. The Aramaeans provided some of the biblical authors their language, which was also to be the language of Christ. The Hebrews developed ethical monotheism.

Each of these groups merged with and absorbed certain characteristics of the peoples of the areas into which they moved, but they retained Semitic languages. Few, however, were able to withstand the eventual invasions of other non-Semitic peoples and the eventual adulteration of their culture.

Arabia Felix

If Arabia seemed virtually resourceless to its inhabitants, other more technologically advanced peoples found it very alluring. Sometime in the third millennium B.C. peoples of Mesopotamia and Egypt discovered that the area of southern Arabia uniquely possessed two highly desirable gum resins: frankincense and myrrh. Egyptian records survive detailing expeditions to Punt (Somalia and the Bab al Mandab) to collect the resins that were grown only in Dhofar and its colonies of Somalia and the island of Socotra.

Frankincense, an essential element in certain pagan rituals, was burnt as an offering to the gods. It was used lavishly in cremation services and, in Egypt, for embalming. For the funeral of Nero's wife an entire year's harvest was reputedly consumed. Myrrh was the foundation of many cosmetics and perfumes and was also used medicinally. Although myrrh was always expensive, the demand far exceeded the supply, so that workers were minutely examined upon leaving the harvesting much as they are in diamond fields.

For almost two millennia foreigners dominated and controlled this trade until descendants of Arabian migrants, attracted by the products from southern Arabia, returned from eastern Jordan and southern Iraq to their ancestral homeland. These colonists from the Fertile Crescent had benefited from the diaspora of their ancestors into Mesopotamia. They were familiar with the institutions of urban life and brought with them irrigation techniques, metallurgical and ceramic skills, an alphabetic script, a complex religion, and a developed art. They arrived in southern Arabia in two waves: one before 1500 B.C. and one at about 1200 B.C.

The immigrants possessed a common culture, and the kingdoms of Saba (Sheba), Qataban, Hadhramaut, Ma'in, Himyar, and Ausan—the area known as Arabia Felix—were formed into a confederation of states during the first millennium B.C. Each kingdom enjoyed periods of prosperity and prominence. Although internecine warfare was rife, apparently they felt secure enough from outside forces, because of their relative inaccessibility, to have unfortified towns. They shared a common religious system based on an astral triad and initially were ruled by a *makkarib* similar to the Mesopotamian priest-king.

Eventually this position became secularized. Under the *malik* (king) were prominent *qayls* (chieftains) who controlled the *ash'b* (sedentary tribal units). Unlike the northern tribes, whose allegiance was based on blood ties, those of the *ash'b* were commercial and labor oriented.

A huge and complex commercial network comprising both land and sea routes was established by the people of southern Arabia. In addition to their own exports they became the middlemen for trade from India and the Horn of Africa. Customers of the Arabian market assumed that all the goods were products of Arabia, thus the designation of the area by ancient writers as Arabia Felix—happy or prosperous Arabia. Among the items of trade were pearls from the Persian Gulf, spices necessary to preserve as well as to flavor food, textiles and swords from India, Chinese silk, slaves, monkeys, ivory, Ethiopian gold, and ostrich feathers.

The southern part of Arabia was the only area of the peninsula that was agriculturally self-sufficient. The people of Arabia Felix imported only luxury items for their own use, never foodstuffs. This was possible because they capitalized on the potential of their area by the use of an ingenious irrigation system. Not having rivers to exploit, they designed their system to catch the runoff waters from the infrequent rain that would seasonally flood the wadis. Dams were used to direct the water to irrigation canals. The famous Marib Dam irrigated over 4,000 acres.

The Indian Ocean trade was carried to Arabia by ships and from Aden was transported largely overland to the markets of the western Mediterranean coast, Mesopotamia, and Egypt. Navigation on the northern part of the Red Sea was dangerous because of monsoon winds; therefore goods to Egypt were usually transported halfway by sea and then transferred to overland caravans. Caravan cities, colonies of southern Arabia, developed along these trade routes and became the nuclei for the important cities of the Hejaz in the medieval period. The use of the camel as a carrier and the development of such caravan cities as Mecca, Yathrib (modern Medina), Palmyra, and Petra formed part of the legacy of the southern Arabians to the north and eventually enabled the north to succeed to mercantile supremacy. Because demand for luxury items grew, prices rose, trade routes increased, and the transportation of these goods became organized under stricter control. Increased trade became possible because of the more effective use of the camel, which had originally been domesticated by the southern Arabians as a dairy animal.

In the fourth century A.D. the civilization of Arabia Felix began a slow but inevitable decline. The southern Arabian monopoly was challenged, and indigenous people of the caravan cities and distribution points began to assert their own control over trade tolls. In the third century B.C. the Ptolemaic merchant marine had reopened the Nile-Red Sea Canal and had begun actively to compete for trade. When the Romans captured Egypt in the middle of the first century B.C., they continued and intensified this competition. Petra, Palmyra, and northwest Mesopotamia were incorporated into the Roman Empire. A matter of even greater significance occurred early in the Roman period when Greek shippers plotted the vagaries of the monsoon winds and successfully traveled to India and back to Alexandria, discovering in the process that many of the products thought to be of Arabian origin were in fact from other lands.

The core of the market, which was frankincense and myrrh, was retained by Arabia until the demand eventually evaporated when Christianity was made the religion of the Roman Empire by edict in A.D. 325 and cremations and pagan rituals, in which large amounts of frankincense were used, were banned. This edict created further difficulties when Christian missionaries entered Arabia in 356. Judaism was well established in the south by that time. Brought to Arabia Felix by refugees after the destruction of Jerusalem by Titus in A.D. 70 the Jews quickly made converts there because the Arabians' traditional enemies, Byzantium and Abyssinia, were Christian countries. By the fourth century there were numerous Judaized Aramaeans and Arabians. For example, the last Himyarite king was a Jew.

Religious rivalry led to hostility and eventually to a massacre of Christians at Najran. The Christians sought help from Constantinople, which in turn requested the Abyssinians—their Christian allies closest to Arabia—to intervene. In A.D. 570 an Abyssinian protectorate was established in southern Arabia, but the protectorate was replaced in 575 by a Persian satrapy. Persian help had been requested by Jewish and pagan Arabians who regarded a Zoroastrian presence less of a threat than a Christian one. When the Persian satrap embraced Islam in 628, thereby opening the area to influence from the north Arabians, Arabia Felix became effectively absorbed into their cultural orbit.

The Hejaz on the Eve of the Islamic Conquest

Muslims refer to the period before the revelation of Islam as the jahaliyah, or time of ignorance, and feel that knowledge of this period is of little use to them in understanding Islam. Nevertheless jahaliyah is a religious and not a historical concept, i.e., it refers to religious ignorance of the one God. Islam was able to take root quickly and acquire the allegiance it needed to forge a far-flung empire because the place of its revelation, the Hejaz, had been ripened for such momentous activity by contributions both from its indigenous people, the north Arabian beduin, and from the dying civilization of the south, Arabia Felix. The Hejaz legacy from the south included the domesticated camel with which they could expand into the interior, a trade route to support their rudimentary cities and, most important, a diverse religious atmosphere occasioned by the presence of Judaized Arabs, Christians, and Zoroastrians, who as merchants made their influence felt along the trade route.

This bequest to the atmosphere that produced Islam was far eclipsed, however, by that of the beduin who, besides providing the conquest with its raw material of warriors, imbued it with beduin spirit. Northern beduin values and culture, and not those of the sophisticated high culture of the south, remain the leitmotiv of Islam and those implied in the term *Arab* (etymologically, Arab means the desert or its inhabitants, and in the Quran the word *a'rab* is used to describe the beduin). The desert inspired the prophets of the three monotheistic Semitic religions—Judaism, Christianity, and Islam—but the cities produced them. Mecca, the city that produced the Prophet of Islam, was the most important city of the Hejaz and the matrix in which northern and southern elements interacted.

By A.D. 500 members of the Quraysh tribe had established themselves as leaders of the caravan city of Mecca and were attempting with some success to coerce the surrounding tribes into an organization to serve Meccan trading interests. Mecca was equidistant from the incense-producing lands of the south and the consumers of the north; and even though trade had diminished, it was still significant. It was also as far from the Byzantine Empire as it was from the foreign conquerers now residing in the south. An annual truce of four months when there would be a cessation of all tribal hostilities had been mutually agreed upon by the northern Arabian tribes. Three months were for religious observances and one for trading. The existence of many sacrificial altars and sacred shrines, particularly the Kaabah, and of the Ukaz fair, then the site of an annual poetry contest and fair a few miles southeast of Mecca, made it a natural meeting place for beduin tribes and the logical place for them to exchange commodities and ideas (see ch. 6).

Two other cities of the Hejaz were more climatically favored than Mecca: Taif and Mecca's sister city, Yathrib, both of which were to figure prominently in the Quran. Taif, the summer resort of aristocratic Meccans, was as rich agriculturally as Mecca was barren and rocky. Taif, 6,000 feet above sea level, produced a variety of fruits, nuts, and flowers as well as the grapevines that supplied the Hejaz with wine. Yathrib, 300 miles north of Mecca and situated on the spice route, developed from a date-palm oasis. The four major tribes that resided there were the pagan Aws and Khazraj and the Judaized Banu Nadir and Banu Qurayzah, who were the city's leaders. Although more richly endowed by nature, neither Taif nor Yathrib approached Mecca in wealth or influence.

The trading wealth that accrued to Mecca was a consequence of neither its position as a cultural center nor its geographical location but rather the result of the Meccans' control of the spice trade by force. The Quraysh originated in northern Arabia and had close contacts with tribes on the periphery of Byzantine control. They had experience with desert trade and were familiar with camel warfare. The Quraysh offered protection to the caravans, assuring them that in exchange for tribute they would be minimally harassed and sometimes guarded by tribes along the route. The tribes received payment for their cooperation and services. A delicate monetary balance was necessary to make it profitable for the Quraysh to pursue this activity, to keep the cooperation of the increasingly extortionate tribes, and to accomplish all of this while ensuring the caravaners a comfortable profit margin.

The beduin of north Arabia became a potentially dangerous power after they invented a kind of camel saddle that enabled them to sit securely above the camel's hump, thus giving the rider efficient control over the camel and an advantage over an enemy. The beduin were expert riders, and when furnished with sword and spear their appearance alone encouraged merchant cooperation. Camel breeding increased with the twin incentives of guarding or raiding and the transportation of goods.

The camel, although necessary for survival in the interior, is in most instances inferior to the horse as a war animal because it does not gallop or maneuver easily. The monetary success that came from camel breeding, raiding, and guarding enabled the major tribes to begin the slow (because expensive) acquisition of the Arabian horse and to breed it specifically for military purposes. The horse rather than the camel became the animal of the conquest, but its chief importance in pre-Islamic society was that its care forced owners to keep in close contact with civilization to procure grain and clean water. Horses became a prime target in intertribal raids.

In addition to herding, hunting, and camel and horse breeding, the beduin had early developed among themselves a survival system more immediately productive than their pastoral pursuits. This was the *ghazw*, a guerrilla battle involving raiding and plundering. The object was to capture as many animals as possible from another tribe but without bloodshed, thus avoiding the eventual paying of a blood price. In the period before Muhammad was able to leash this energy, the history of the beduin, called by Arabs the *ayyam al Arab* (the days of the Arabians), is a catalog of constant warfare and a testimony to the difficulties of uniting these people into an effective force. Disputes occasioned by waterhole or pasture rights immediately provoked action by a people who were chronically hungry and who accepted warfare with an almost happy fatalism as the modus vivendi.

These engagements provided the raw material for heroic tales and poems. The total artistic expression of the nomads was through their language, a medium not dependent on a permanent locale or wealth for its production. Poetical expertise was highly valued and was reinforced at Ukaz (see ch. 5). Perhaps developed from the rhymed prose of the *kuhhan* (oracles and soothsayers), or from the rhythmic song of the camel driver, poetic expression reached its zenith with a *qasidah*, a particular kind of ode that some literary historians consider unsurpassed as an ode form. The form of the *qasidah* was rigidly conventional as were its themes, which embodied the corpus of beduin values (see ch. 7). Chief among the values was *muruah* (manliness). The components of *muruah* were courage, loyalty, and generosity. Basically *muruah* expressed the capability of a leader to do what was necessary for tribal survival in a manner considered civilized. The hero also possessed *ird* (honor and the avoidance of shame) and *hamasah* (fortitude and enthusiasm), and he was aware of his genealogy.

The fascination of these people with the spoken word took an additionally important form in the utterances of messianic prophets who were numerous and popular in the century before Islam. These prophets offered no theological ideas other than that a messenger would soon come from God to help the people. Along with the Hanifs, who were early monotheists, they did encourage monotheistic worship, which was becoming more popular in Mecca (see ch. 6). The Hejaz was thus prepared for someone who combined in his person the qualities of warrior, poet, and prophet, which the beduin had come to value, particularly if that person could offer an alternative to the precarious economic life-style of internecine wars and raiding that was, in the long run, mutually costly.

MUHAMMAD AND THE CONQUEST OF ISLAM

Such a combination of qualities was to be found in Muhammad, the Prophet of Islam, who was born in A.D. 570 into the prosperous Quraysh tribe. His own position within the tribe was not an especially happy one. Orphaned at the age of six, he was raised by his grandfather and after his death by an uncle, Abu Talib. As a youth he accompanied his uncle on caravans to Syria and became practiced in trade. At twenty-five he married a wealthy widow of his tribe, the forty-year old Khadijah. He worked with her in the trading business, and this auspicious change of luck gave him the leisure to contemplate his life and that of his fellow Meccans. Perhaps his own impoverished beginnings made him sensitive to the moral malaise of Mecca. When nomads adapted to a sedentary commercial life, tribal solidarity was weakened, and strong members gave little protection to the weak and poor members of their tribe. Widows, who were always numerous, were often forced into prostitution instead of remarrying into the tribe or being supported by it. Wealth had made the tribes less generous than they had been when poor, and there were no urban institutions to replace humane tribal mores.

About 610, when he was nearly forty, Muhammad began to seclude himself in a cave outside Mecca and one evening there received the first of a series of divine revelations from the angel Gabriel. After a period of self-doubt he began preaching the messages he received first to his extended family and then to his tribe. Initially his message was relatively innocuous: there was only one God, who had created all things, and there was a day of judgment after which all men would be assigned to paradise or to hell. Exclusive of his wife and a few friends he was generally scoffed at as a harmless but unbalanced religious enthusiast.

Gradually his approach changed from *rasul* (prophet) to *nadhir* (warner). The punishment of evildoers and those who refused his message was painted more luridly, and the uproar he was raising became serious enough for members of his tribe to oppose him firmly. Abu Sufyan, who represented the Umayyad—the most influential branch of the Quraysh—began to harass Muhammad and his converts because of the danger of Meccan economic life that Muhammad's gospel posed. Income from the pilgrimage to the many gods of the Kaabah was secondary only to the profits of trade. If monotheism became prevalent, who would make the pilgrimage? Trade itself would be disrupted if faith as Muhammad suggested, replaced blood as a social bond because the administration of trading interests was regulated through tribal leaders and was organized according to the geographical position of clans. Although generosity was a tribal value, what would be the results if the poor believed Muhammad's teaching that they had a right to partake of the wealth around them?

The Quraysh had good cause for anxiety. Exclusive of converts within Muhammad's clan, the Hashim, the first Muslims were those dissatisfied with the status quo either because of tribal laws inappropriate in an urban setting or because of the intensely competitive commercialism in Mecca. Younger brothers and younger sons of merchants were in a reduced state because of tribal primogeniture. Foreigners and outlawed tribesmen who did not have clan protection were in an extremely vulnerable situation since there were no civic protective institutions. Tribesmen whose clans were not in the first order of economic importance resented the monopolistic practices of the wealthier clans. As his father's posthumous child, Muhammad too had been hurt by tribal laws because he had not been able to inherit. The Hashim was a weak clan, and Muhammad had felt the indignities of a low position.

Pressure was placed on Muhammad's uncle, Abu Talib, to excommunicate him from the clan. Although Abu Talib had not converted, as a member of the Hashim he was eager to support any movement that might dilute the power of the wealthier clans, and he knew that if he excommunicated his nephew, he would be delivering him up to certain death. When this approach failed, the Prophet's clan was blacklisted from business or social relations with the other Quraysh. Prevented in Mecca, Muhammad tried to win converts in Taif but was rejected and physically ousted from Taif; he campaigned among the various tribes at the Ukaz fair of 620.

The only major tribe to show interest at the fair was one from Yathrib. After a series of conferences between Muhammad and the tribe's leaders, Muhammad and his converts were invited to live in Yathrib. The tribal leaders thought Muhammad might be able to mediate among them and to settle some long-standing blood debts. The hijra (see Glossary) to Yathrib was a well-planned quiet migration of 200 people who left in small groups (see ch. 6). It was a very dangerous undertaking since their clans could not protect them once they left the city. Sixteen years later the caliph Umar designated July 16, 622, when Muhammad left Mecca, as the starting point of the Muslim calendar and era.

In Yathrib, whose name would be changed to Medina—the city of the prophet—Muhammad was welcomed as a powerful shaykh. In this new security he was able to assess his position, stabilize his leadership, and make practical political plans for Islam's infant *umma* (community of believers), who were the nucleus of the Islamic state. The most pressing problem was economic support for the *muhajirun* (emigrants). They were boarding with Medinese *ansar* (supporters), but in two years their assets were depleted. Using the device most familiar to them they began to raid and plunder the caravans. Not only did raiding provide economic relief, but it also damaged the Meccans who controlled the trade. Early raids were unsuccessful because Muhammad's Medinese opponents alerted the Meccans. The first successful raid was accomplished by guile during the month of holy truce—when guards were fewer—by twelve men operating under sealed orders. Although reactions were mixed because the holy truce had been violated and because of fear of blood vengeance, Muhammad continued to organize raids.

A plan was devised to strike at the caravan of Muhammad's major antagonist, Abu Sufyan. Abu Sufyan had received intelligence that there might be trouble and had secured 900 reinforcements from Mecca. Eighty-five miles south of Medina at Badr the 300 Muslims attacked. The overconfident Meccans were vanquished, and Islam was established as a militant polity. A year later Abu Sufyan defeated the Muslims at Uhud, but Islamic warriors already had won a reputation as highly disciplined warriors who were contemptuous of death. Under the banner of Islam, raiding and warring were legitimized as jihad, or holy war. Warriors could not lose: if they died, they went to a sensual and verdant paradise; if they were victorious, they received plunder. Encouraged by their victory at Uhud the Meccans, allied with beduin and Abyssinian mercenaries, besieged Medina with a force of 10,000. The Muslims had only a third of that number and, preferring military innovation to foolhardiness, dug a trench around the city. There had been only twenty Muslim casualties when the Meccans departed a month later in disgust at the shamefulness of the Muslims in avoiding open combat.

The fact that half of the major tribes of Medina were Jewish had an important effect on the early development of Islam. Muhammad had apparently hoped that by incorporating Judaistic elements into Islamic practice the Jews might recognize him at least as a prophet to the Arabs and possibly might view Islam as the fulfillment of their religion, as Muhammad believed it was. When the Jews made it clear that they could not consider a non-Jew a prophet, Jewish-Muslim relations deteriorated. Islam became more exclusively Arabian and more specifically beduin in its orientation; the *qibla* (direction of prayer) was changed from Jerusalem to Mecca; a muadhdhin called people to prayer, as opposed to the trumpet and gong; and *dhimmis* (People of the Book)—Christians, Jews, and Zoroastrians—were accused of having obstructed the divine plan.

Within Medina religious differences were fed by political rivalries. Abd Allah bin Ubayy, the potential prince of Medina, had strong support in several Jewish clans. If Muhammad's hegemony increased, any influence to be gained by supporting Ubayy would be threatened. Muhammad, knowing that the Meccans would try an all-out offensive after their defeat at Badr, tried to weed out his enemies and spies in Medina and strengthen his political hold there by increasing allegiance to his cause.

A squabble between Muslims and a Jewish clan was taken up by Muhammad, who besieged the clan and finally expelled them from Medina. During the battle at Uhud a Jewish contingent under Ubayy had abruptly left the Muslim side, which no doubt contributed to the Muslim defeat. In 625 the Jewish clan that controlled the date palms was expelled. At the seige of Medina the remaining Jewish group leagued with the Meccans and planned a rear assault as soon as the forces at the front were engaged. After the siege the Muslims attacked the clan, which had returned to their fortified mud enclave. The women and children were sold, and all the men were killed. Exiled Jewish clans of the earlier disturbances had fled to the Khaybar Oasis to the north. When the Muslims captured Khaybar and exacted as tribute a percentage of agricultural production, all Jewish resistance in the Hejaz was effectively quelled.

The unsuccessful siege of Medina proved to be a greater victory than Badr in winning Meccans to the Islamic side. Meccan trade to the north had been virtually destroyed by Muslim raids, and now Meccan prestige was weakened when they could not dislodge Muhammad with a force three times as large as his. Muslim forces continued to harass any caravans foolish enough to venture out of Mecca, but on the whole, Muhammad, aware of his superior position, initiated a policy of conciliation toward the Meccans, preferring to have a team of astute businessmen with excellent administrative abilities on his side than a conquered and dead city.

In 630 the city submitted to Muhammad. Meccan contingents were critical in subduing other tribes of the Hejaz. Many outlying tribes rushed to pledge allegiance or make treaties of various kinds. Acceptance of Islam became a requisite to alliance with the Muslims. The political result was that a federation of tribes was formed with Mecca functioning as the area of central authority.

When Muhammad died in 632, the Hejaz, the Najd, and areas on the southern and eastern shores of the Arabian Peninsula were under Islamic rule. Immediately after his death, the wars of *ridda* (apostasy) began. Southern tribes were reluctant to pay zakat (annual alms tax) to Medina and resented the rising power of the Hejaz, and many powerful tribes reverted to their previous situation. Exclusive of

Hejazi and Najdi tribes, for the most part only weak ones remained Muslim. Religious conversion of tribes outside the Hejaz had been nominal, and Islam had not become an integral part of tribal life during Muhammad's short ministry. Powerful peninsular tribes joined after the conquest showed signs of success. Abu Bakr, the first orthodox caliph, subdued much of Arabia before the conquest in the north began. Muhammad had unified the tribes, but expansion with its economic benefits was necessary to keep their energies directed away from each other.

ARABIA BEFORE THE SAUDS

Arabia had become unified, but ironically it had to be virtually emptied to ensure unification. Like the great migrations of the past, Arabia in the immediate post-Muhammad period once again fed its people into the surrounding areas. Peasants were easier to control than refractory tribes, and the social structure and agricultural assets of the conquered land outside the peninsula encouraged permanent settlements that were necessary in any case to secure Islamic rule. Thus Islamic politics moved from Arabia to Damascus, and in the period between the ministry of Muhammad and the rise of the House of Saud, Arabia became an economic backwater.

Nevertheless because Arabia was considered the homeland of the Arabs and because Islam's two holiest cities were there, it could not be ignored. Pilgrims who made the haj had to be afforded some protection. Furthermore control of the holy cities gave a ruler instant prestige. The political unit that kept the Hejaz secure was usually Egyptian based, and Egypt was also the source of much of the Hejazi food supply. Islamic rulers in Damascus paid off religious leaders in Arabia who might cause trouble. Arabia became a frontier zone from which political rivals could emerge. During the various struggles for religiopolitical supremacy in Damascus and later in Baghdad, Mecca and Medina became sites for the opposition, and both cities were virtually destroyed in the tumult that ensued. For the most part social organization in Arabia continued as it had before Muhammad's unification (see ch. 7).

Sometime around 1450 the Saud clan moved from the Qatif Oasis to the Najd and established modest date-palm plantations. They also supplied pilgrimage caravans with camels, food, and water. Gradually the Saud clan prospered, and branches of the clan spread to other parts of the Najd. Wealth was difficult to accumulate, and tribes could be devastated in hours by local tribal raids and by the constant forays of the Sharifians, the rulers of Mecca since the tenth century and distant descendants of the Hashim. The Sharifs ruled by virtue of their thralldom to the Mamluks of Cairo (Turkish rulers from 1257 to 1382) and regulated the religious life of Mecca and Medina. As long as the Mamluks received their share of the trade profits, they did not interfere with Sharifian policy.

Interest in the Hejaz quickened however, when the Portuguese began to compete for Red Sea trade at the end of the fifteenth century. Except in the south the tribes of the interior had not benefited from the centuries-old seagoing trade, but they felt the results of threatened Mamluk profits. The Mamluks established defensive divisions in southwest Arabia and, accustomed to luxury, made the people of the Hejaz and particularly those of Jiddah pay heavily for it.

The Portuguese proved to be a lesser menace to the region than the Ottoman Turks, who conquered Egypt and Syria in 1517. Ottoman domination of the region lasted until 1669 when the Bani Khalid tribe, which had settled in the area, ousted their reduced forces. Control of maritime routes passed to the Dutch and then to the British. The Sharifians, continually flexible, prospered as they had always done and ruled as local despots.

THE HOUSE OF SAUD

Wahhabi Islam

Islam was still strong in the Hejaz but weak or nonexistent elsewhere in Arabia. Animistic practices had been resumed in the interior and integrated into Islamic rituals. Although developed by desert people, Islamic tenets and values needed an urban setting in order to flourish. Islam presumed a settled life or at least access to one. The Najd, although perforce inhabited mostly by tribes on the move, did possess some settlements where rudiments of Islam were taught. Uyaynah, not far from the main Saudi settlement at Dariyah, was one of these. In 1703 Muhammad ibn Abd al Wahhab, a religious prodigy, was born in Uyaynah into the Banu Sinan tribe. His religious enthusiasm was encouraged by his family, who were experts in Islamic law, and they sent him to study at a number of Islamic cities noted for theological learning.

Apparently Wahhab's enthusiasm early progressed to fanaticism because he was expelled from Basra for his extreme criticism of local religious practices. He preached a return to the orthodox practices of Muhammad's day and particularly condemned any devotion that detracted from the oneness of God. His interpretation of Islam was primarily based on the works of the strict Hanbali scholar Taki al Din Ahmad ibn Taimiya (see ch. 6).

His reception at home in Uyaynah was as cool as the Prophet's had been in Mecca. Finally at the instigation of the Bani Khalid, who were Shiites, he was expelled from his village in 1744 (see ch. 6). He eventually sought physical protection at Dariyah with Muhammad ibn Saud, who was impressed with Wahhab's views and became his ally.

Together they planned a jihad to purify and, in the process, conquer Arabia. A procedure that had been successful in the seventh century might work again. A series of intermarriages, the most important being Saud's marriage to Wahhab's daughter, cemented the relationship (see fig. 3).

By Muhammad ibn Saud's death in 1765 most of the Najd was Wahhabi (see Glossary). Wahhab renewed the alliance with the dead shaykh's son, Abd al Aziz (1765-1803), and together they took the city of Riyadh. Expansion out of the Najd was blocked in all directions by enemies who felt less threatened by the religious doctrine than by the political manifestation that accompanied it. To the east the powerful Bani Khalid harried the Wahhabis with unremitting raids. To the southwest the Sharifians banned any Wahhabis in the holy cities. Farther to the southwest the Ismailis—Shiites like the Bani Khalid—began to invade the Najd (see ch. 6). From the north Muntafiqis, an Iraqi tribal confederation, attacked. Many Muntafiqis, however, converted and joined the Najdi forces.

By the time of Wahhab's death in 1792 Wahhabis had established suzerainty south to the Rub al Khali (Empty Quarter). Gradually the south and east accepted the movement, and Hasa (particularly the oases of Qatif and Hufuf) was compelled by the sword. In 1801 Karbala, a Shiite holy city in present-day Iraq, was attacked, the tomb of Hussein stripped of its jeweled encasing, and the surrounding area looted (see ch. 6). When Abd al Aziz died in 1803, the march between the Najd and the Hejaz was more Wahhabi than Sharifian, and Wahhabis were firmly established at the Buraymi Oasis.

Control of the Hejaz was of paramount importance to secure the newly conquered area. Mecca was taken in 1801 and Medina in 1805, and both cities were cleansed of anything perceived as a religious infraction. Hookahs and tombs of saints were attacked with similar ferocity. Sharif Ghalib was authorized to continue administering the area, and Saud (1803-14) attempted to sort out the chaos of the conquest by standardizing governmental procedures in the widely scattered territories. Sharia law (the sacred Islamic law), was reintroduced where necessary and safeguarded by qadis in villages and qadis and muftis in towns and cities. Tribal feuds were regulated by mediators of the central Wahhabi authority. The area was pacified under the watchful eyes of district governors and deputies stationed in moated forts outside captured towns.

Nineteenth-Century Arabia

The government of the Ottoman Empire in Constantinople, although uneasy about the Saudi movement, had largely ignored requests from the pasha in Baghdad to put down the insurrection, underestimating its importance. The loss of the holy cities, destructive

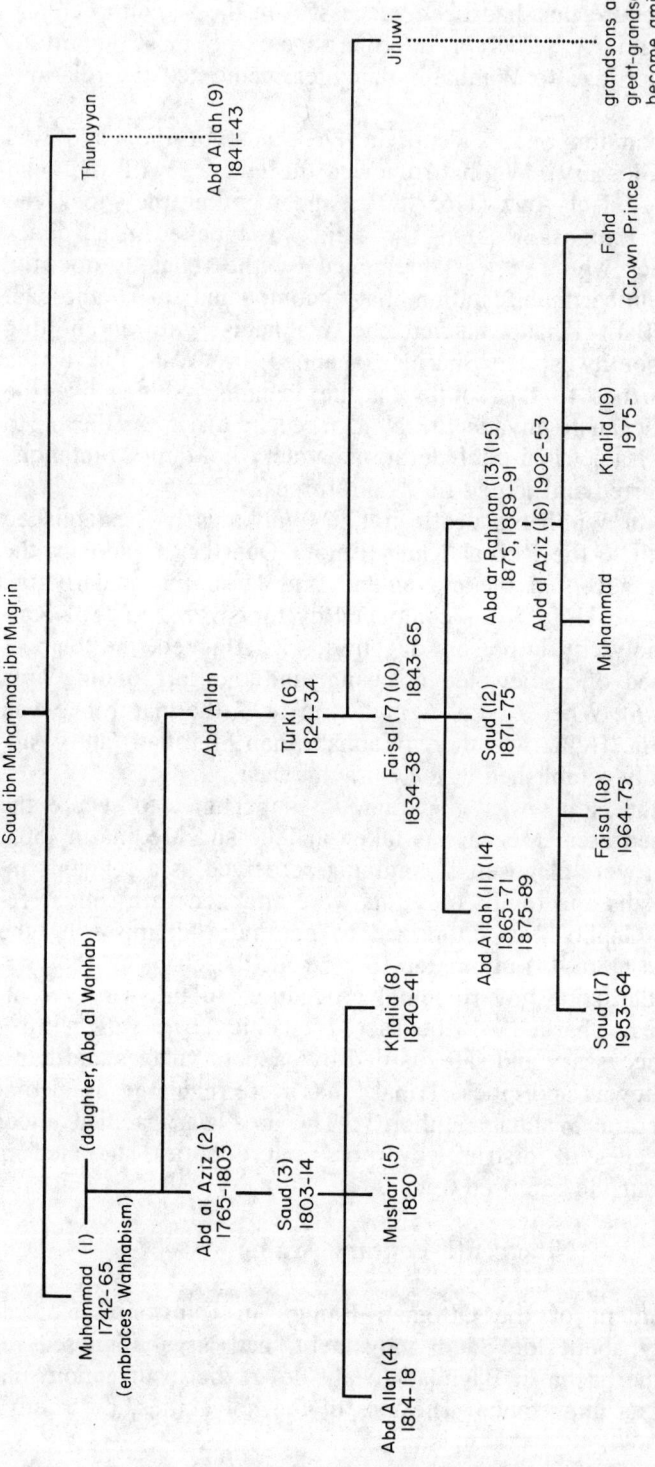

Figure 3. Saudi Arabia, Simplified Genealogy of House of Saud with Order and Duration of Rule, 1976

of both prestige and income, made a reprisal imperative. The Ottoman government asked its viceroy in Cairo, the formidable Muhammad Ali, to crush the upstarts. The viceroy's son, Tusun, led the first advance in 1816. Modern weapons at first proved ineffectual against tribal tactics in the desert, although Mecca and Medina were taken. Muhammad Ali, surprised at the Saudi military competence, assumed command. In the end the Saudi defeat came from within. Abd Allah (1814-18) retreated to Dariyah after his father Saud's death in 1814 (see fig. 4). Ibrahim, another of Muhammad Ali's sons, battered the town until it fell. Dariyah was razed, and Abd Allah paid with his head in Constantinople for his cowardice.

The Saudi clan was not deterred. Abd Allah's uncle, Turki ibn Abd Allah (1824-34), organized troops to oust the Egyptians who had occupied the Najd. Settling in Riyadh after the destruction of Dariyah and establishing Riyadh as the Saudi capital, he harassed the Egyptian

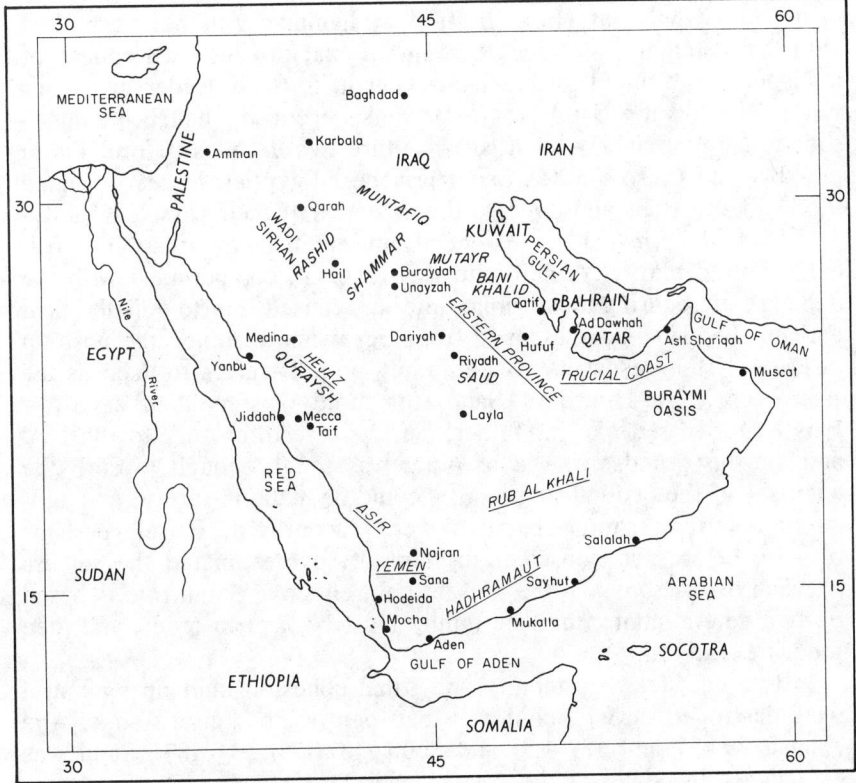

HEJAZ — Regions
RED SEA — Geographical Features
SAUD — Tribes
Mecca — Cities, Towns
IRAN — Countries and Island

Figure 4. Nineteenth-Century Arabia

garrison to the point of mutiny, causing them to be transferred to the Hejaz. Turki protected the integrity of Saudi-Wahhabi rule and warned oppressive governers that they would be dealt with severely if they forgot that the establishment of true Islamic rule was the reason for the movement, not political oppression of subject peoples. Successive exploitation and occupation of Arabia by foreigners had made Turki sensitive to the fact that justice alone could legitimize this conquest in the name of religion. Wahhabism had become a nationalistic movement, though the concept had not been articulated by its leaders.

Once again internal dissension ravaged the movement when Turki was assassinated in 1834 by a rival within the family. Turki's son, Faisal (1834-38 and 1843-65), quickly picked up the reins of government. Faisal was as intelligent as his father, but internal problems diluted his potency against foreign powers. The rulers in Qatar and Bahrain, sensing the Saudi family troubles, revolted as did the ferocious Bani Khalid of Hasa. In 1834 Muhammad Ali, having broken with the Ottomans, decided to bring Arabia into his own sphere of influence and brought forth a rival claimant to Saudi leadership as his wedge. Khalid ibn Saud (1840-41), Faisal's cousin, had been imprisoned in Egypt since Abd Allah's capture two decades before. Faisal now became Cairo's token Saudi prisoner. Egyptian forces occupied the Najd and Hasa and directed the activities of their vassal, Khalid.

Muhammad Ali had overextended himself in many areas. The British rebuffed him in Yemen, and this reversal, compounded with the difficulty of securing the Arabian interior, caused him to quit the field in 1840. In 1843 Faisal escaped from Egypt and resumed the position of leader. The present-day Saudi family proudly refers to itself as the House of Faisal-House of Saud, for more reasons than ancestry. Faisal endeavored like his father, Turki, to restore order to the land and like his grandson, Abd al Aziz, was tough enough to curb the excesses of the beduin. Pilgrimages could be made in safety, and agricultural and mercantile pursuits were encouraged. Faisal, perhaps because he was so conscientious himself, overestimated the selfless altruism of his sons. To the present day, effective Saudi rule is based on two determinants: first the family must be kept in order, and then the tribes (see ch. 8).

In two decades the stability and tribal cohesion built up by Faisal were destroyed through civil wars between two of Faisal's sons, Abd Allah (1865-71 and 1875-89) and Saud (1871-75). By 1871 Saud was established in power at the cost of anarchy throughout the territory. Famine was rife, and even weak tribes became uncontrollable. The Ottomans, who had repossessed the Hejaz after Muhammad Ali's death in 1844, sniffed carrion and easily occupied Hasa and imprisoned Abd Allah, who foolishly had sought support from them. Abd Allah escaped from prison and gained power again for a period of several months, after which power was returned to Saud. At Saud's death in 1875 Abd ar Rahman (1875 and 1889-91), the younger brother of Saud and Abd Allah, announced his accession. Abd Allah regained power after one year and ruled until his death in 1889 when Abd ar Rahman once again assumed leadership.

The Saudi preoccupation with the warring sons and brothers had distracted them to the point that they were unprepared to withstand the growing power of the Rashidis, who had been established by the Sauds in Hail to govern the northern province of Jabal Shammar. Muhammad ibn Rashid, an able administrator and general, had much of the Najd under his control when Faisal's youngest son, Abd ar Rahman, was finally forced out of Riyadh. Exiled, he eventually settled in Kuwait with his family, among whom was his eleven-year-old son, Abd al Aziz, founder of the modern state of Saudi Arabia. Rashid was succeeded by a son of greater vision and lesser administrative abilities; his harsh rule alienated tribes in his domain and facilitated the eventual reconquest.

In the nineteenth century in addition to the dynamics of tribal rivalries and occupation by foreign Muslim powers, Western interest in Arabia quickened because of the British desire to safeguard its Indian trade by retaining control over Arabian ports and coastal areas. French interest was aroused by French mercenaries who had fought with Muhammad Ali, and by the 1850s both France and Great Britain had consulates in Jiddah. Through the nineteenth century the British had been reluctant to interfere in landward political affairs. Arabia had already benefited from British interest in the Middle East when British forces stymied Muhammad Ali's activities in Yemen. A plethora of British protectorate treaties limited the future expansion of the Saudis into south Arabia. Such British alliances were actually advantageous to the Saudis because they prevented Saudi forces from dissipating their strength, although they never perceived them as such.

THE REIGN OF ABD AL AZIZ (1902-53)

In 1902, at the age of twenty-one, Abd al Aziz ibn Abd ar Rahman Al Saud, called by his tribesmen the patronymic Ibn Saud, recaptured Riyadh with a force of less than fifty men in a dramatic dawn raid. Abd ar Rahman, aware that his son would be a more effective leader, quickly abdicated his title of amir in favor of his son but retained the title of imam (see Glossary), which ceased to be used after his death because his son preferred secular titles. His leadership legitimized, Abd al Aziz engaged in successful battles with the Rashidis and their Turkish allies from Hasa and reestablished Saudi rule in the Najd. Abd al Aziz was forced to acknowledge Ottoman suzerainty of the area, however, because Hussein, a Hashimite installed as Sharif of

Mecca by the Ottomans in 1908, had captured one of Abd al Aziz's brothers and was holding him hostage. As soon as the boy was released, Ottoman control of the Najd was extinguished. By 1913 the Turks were eliminated in Hasa, and the territory from Kuwait to Qatar was under Saudi control.

The Creation of the Ikhwan al Muslimin (Muslim Brethren)

Abd al Aziz realized very early that allegiance to the House of Saud as a secular power was not sufficient to retain volatile and fickle tribesmen. The suprastructure needed was supplied in a revival of Wahhabism in which Abd al Aziz was an ardent believer. Beduins, forced by nature to be ascetic, responded eagerly to imposing asceticism on others. A hijra (agricultural oasis settlement; pl., *hujar*—see Glossary) had the triple purpose of breaking down tribal allegiance (by settling a variety of tribesmen in each settlement), inculcating the tribesmen thoroughly with Wahhabi precepts, and providing reserves of ready warriors.

By 1912 there were 11,000 Ikhwan al Muslimin, the term used for both the settlers and the organization, settled on oases. In 1916 all beduin tribes were ordered to join the Ikhwan and pay zakat (see ch. 6). Tribal shaykhs were required to attend the school of Islamic law and religion at the mosque in Riyadh and were encouraged to remain in the town and become part of Abd al Aziz's court. By depriving the Ikhwan of a resident tribal leader, Abd al Aziz hoped to transfer all such allegiance to himself, his movement, and the House of Saud.

World War I

Alliances of some Arabian power groups with the Ottomans and of some with the British ultimately favored the full conquest of Arabia by the Sauds. The Rashidis allied themselves with the Ottomans, and Sharif Hussein, wishing to be recognized as an independent sovereign, allied himself with the British. The British, aware of but consistently underestimating Abd al Aziz's growing power, attempted to enlist him in the general Arab revolt against the Ottomans. This would have meant subordinating himself to Hussein, which Abd al Aziz adamantly refused to do, and would have weakened his forces, which were as yet unready for a major foray in the Hejaz against the Ottomans. A series of negotiations between the British and Abd al Aziz culminated in 1916; the British recognized Abd al Aziz as amir of the Najd and Hasa and gave him a subsidy both to encourage his efforts against the Rashidis and to discourage an all-out offensive against Hussein.

In 1916 Hussein with the assistance of T.E. Lawrence ousted the Turks from the Hejaz, unwittingly smoothing the way for his enemy

Abd al Aziz. Bolstered by Ikhwan forces, by 1917 Saudi control was extended to the outskirts of Hail, the Rashidi capital. Abd al Aziz refrained from attacking the Hejaz and contented himself with consolidating the surrounding areas.

The Taking of the Hejaz

After World War I, as a result of British and French support, Hussein's sons, Abdullah and Faisal, were established as kings of Transjordan and Iraq. When Abdullah and Faisal began to negotiate with the Rashidis, Abd al Aziz was forced to take decisive action to avoid being encircled by Hashimite powers. In 1921 the Ikhwan seized Hail, and Abd al Aziz married the widow of Saud ibn Rashid, who had been murdered a year before by a cousin. He adopted her children, made peace with her relatives, and thus forestalled any further Rashidi alliance that would be in conflict with his own.

A series of successful Ikhwan border raids on Transjordan encouraged Ikhwan forces to invade the interior without orders. They seized the caravan city of Jawf and massacred the inhabitants of Turayf but were finally driven south by British Royal Air Force bombers. Abd al Aziz, infuriated at being placed in a compromising situation with the British, killed the Ikhwan survivors.

Abd al Aziz proceeded to negotiate with the British resident minister in Iraq, Sir Percy Cox, over disputed frontiers with Iraq and Kuwait. Borders were fixed, and neutral zones, the cause of much friction in the future, were agreed on (see ch. 3; ch. 10).

Abd al Aziz could now concentrate his efforts on the Hejaz where Hussein, a self-proclaimed king, was making himself generally unpopular by levying exorbitant taxes on the citizenry but allowing a decline of public services. The Ikhwan, obsessed with desire for the Hejaz because the holy cities were there, grew impatient and unruly. In 1924 they carried out a massacre at Taif, after which the citizens of Jiddah, not given to senseless heroics, surrendered. Abd al Aziz carefully marshalled his forces for the decisive attack on the Hejaz and had one of his sons, the amir Faisal, conquer Asir as a precaution. Hussein, in an attempt to gain prestige, declared himself caliph of all Muslims. Aware that after this outrage the Ikhwan could no longer be restrained, Abd al Aziz led them in battle. Mecca and Medina fell without massacre; the Ikhwan were content to destroy and plunder all religious manifestations deviant to their belief. The most zealous Ikhwan were quickly ordered to remote areas in the interior, and in 1926 Abd al Aziz was proclaimed king of the Hejaz.

The British wished to support Abd al Aziz, but first disagreements over frontiers shared by the Saudis and British allies and protégés had to be settled. A series of negotiations between Abd al Aziz and Sir Gilbert Clayton was finalized in the Treaty of Jiddah in 1927, which recognized Abd al Aziz's authority from the gulf to the Red Sea and set limits on his expansion. In the same year Abd al Aziz was crowned king of the Hejaz and Najd and its dependencies.

Frontier agreements were complicated by the ever-eager Ikhwan, who were unenthusiastic about agricultural pursuits and refused to be dissuaded from raiding Iraq. Additionally Ikhwan extremists were discontent with the introduction of such modern devices as motor vehicles, aircraft, telephones, and telegraph. The denouement came with an Ikhwan revolt and the crushing of dissident Ikhwan at the battle of Sibila in 1929. Many *hujar* were abandoned, and veterans were transferred to the new army. After a period of consolidation, in 1932 Abd al Aziz proclaimed that the realm was to be called the Kingdom of Saudi Arabia, this establishing in no uncertain terms that in the Saudi-Wahhabi affiliation the secular arm would predominate.

Toward a Modern State

Abd al Aziz was aware that the legitimacy of his rule was based on the Wahhabi interpretation of Islam and that his role, as perceived by the ulama (religious scholars) was to preserve a divine nomocracy in Arabia. At the same time he had become familiar enough with the great powers to realize that a continuation of extremist religious policy would hinder the introduction of modern technology. If Arabia wished to survive, it had to modernize or face the consequence of the eternal Arabian cycle of tribal upheavals and conquest by foreign powers. The urbanized Hejazi, for example, viewed the Saudi force as another group of foreign invaders and certainly not the most sophisticated they had experienced.

Within the Hejaz Abd al Aziz began to walk his diplomatic tightrope between the forces of modernization and religious conservatism. In 1929 the Committee for Encouragement of Virtue and Discouragement of Vice, based on long-standing Wahhabi practice, was formed to eradicate religious sloth and such spiritually dangerous practices as smoking, drinking alcohol, and singing. At the same time, the Organic Instructions of the Hejaz were formulated, which guaranteed existing governmental institutions. The 1926 legislation established the important principle that secular law could supplement and complement the sacred law of the sharia (see ch. 8). Abd al Aziz called a pan-Islamic conference in Mecca in 1929 to regulate pilgrimage affairs. This was an important bit of public relations to assure other Arab leaders that the holy cities were not in the hands of wild and uncouth tribesmen.

Government

Power had two fonts: the secular political power of Abd al Aziz and the religious authority of the ulama, the mutawwiun (missionaries), and Abd al Aziz (see ch. 8). On the secular level Abd al Aziz began the formation of his first formal governmental system in the Hejaz. Major cities were administered by local and experienced administrators, but the most senior officials were Najdi.

The country as a whole fell into four divisions: the Najd was ruled by the crown prince, Saud; the Hejaz by Amir Faisal with the special rank of viceroy; Hasa by Abdullah ibn Jiluwi; and Asir by Amir Turki. These last two positions indicate Abd al Aziz's keen understanding of tribal politics and his cleverness in dealing with them. Jiluwi was a cousin and a longtime intimate and colleague, but he was also a powerful potential rival. Amir Turki was a nephew and a member of the still-powerful Sudairi clan (see ch. 8). Abd al Aziz's dedication to the extinction of tribal rivalries was so fervent that he personally entered into over twenty dynastic marriages.

Ministers of foreign affairs and finance were appointed in 1931 and 1932 respectively, a minister of defense in 1944, and a minister of interior affairs in 1951. In October 1953, shortly before his death, Abd al Aziz appointed the Council of Ministers under the leadership of the prime minister, Crown Prince Saud. Existing departments were made ministries, and new ones were created. The head of each ministry was a member of the council. The council had neither legislative nor executive authority. It made recommendations to the king, who alone had the power to enact law. Most of the ministries were originally established in the Hejaz but during the mid-1950s were transferred to Riyadh, establishing without question the location of the heart of the kingdom. The earlier ministerial experience within the Hejaz helped bring about the cultural integration of that area with the Najd.

Aware of the need for a modern military force, Abd al Aziz brought in advisers from various Arab countries. Because he feared political control by outsiders and also reactions from religious leaders, he tended to rely heavily on support from his sons and a peninsular Arabian, Shaykh Abdullah Sulaiman, who became minister of finance.

The system was patrimonial, but Arabians were most familiar with this kind of rule. Abd al Aziz's tact, personal charm, sense of justice, and deep concern for his people mitigated the effects of his absolute monarchy. He functioned as a tribal leader and held a majlis (see Glossary) every week when any citizen could approach him for help. When it became clear that great distances prohibited certain citizens from coming directly to him for assistance, he responded with a curious mixture of tribal and modern ingenuity. Instead of delegating authority, which might seem a logical solution, he expanded the postal service and telegraph systems so that citizens could continue to reach him directly. He was infuriated when he found that messages were being censored or kept from him entirely and commanded severe penalties for the offenders.

The holding of the majlis, an ancient tribal custom, was not altogether an altruistic device. Beduin shaykhs perceiving him as first among equals expected him to listen to their counsel and display in their meetings tribal leadership values developed almost a millennium before. In the old days generosity meant the sharing of one's food with the wayfarer; in the new kingdom of Saudi Arabia it meant job patronage and large sums of cash. A value necessary for survival in the desert was inappropriate in this new setting and brought the kingdom to the verge of economic ruin.

Fiscal Policy

The pattern of traditional paternalism exercised in government was extended to fiscal policy. All income from the state was the private purse of its ruler and was doled out almost as quickly as it came in. Great Britain had been forced to end its subsidy because of its own economic slump after World War I. In the late 1920s income was chiefly from provincial taxes and the pilgrimage trade. Abd al Aziz was eager to make educational and health services available to his people as well as to expand the primitive transportation and communication systems. Automobiles, airplanes, and the wireless telegraph existed, but the numbers were inadequate for the need.

Almost in desperation for funds and going against the nearly xenophobic feelings of the ulama, the king in 1923 granted the first oil exploration rights to a British firm. Additional exploration rights were granted to secure more funds, and among these grants was one in 1933 to the Standard Oil Company of California. After the discovery of large oil fields in the Jabal Dhahran region, the Arabian American Oil Company (Aramco) was formed (see ch. 12). Largely because of World War II, development of the fields was relatively slow, and the annual oil revenues received by the king did not exceed US$4 million until after 1944. By 1948 the kingdom's annual revenue was about US$85 million and because of oil increased geometrically each year thereafter.

Internal development proceeded slowly. Social services were initiated, experimental agricultural projects were set up, the nation began to acquire the paraphernalia of a modern state, and new industries in addition to the ever-burgeoning oil companies were begun. But Abd al Aziz was "the state"; and as his health declined, his tribal methods of ruling proved inadequate to control a nation of vast wealth. Millions of riyals were wasted in graft, corruption, and conspicuous consumption by certain members of the royal family.

Social Climate

By the time of Abd al Aziz's death in 1953 the only contented people in the kingdom seemed to be the more grasping members of the royal family and the foreigners who were cashing in on oil and on sales to the government and the royal family. For Abd al Aziz money had only been something to spend. In 1930 he nonchalantly and arbitrarily had chosen the rate at which his new nickel coins would be exchanged for a riyal. The king became less placid, though no more able, as his lack of administrative abilities became evident even to himself. H. St. John Philby, certainly his most loyal non-Arab friend, wrote in 1934:

> Things at present are in a frightful muddle and everyone seems to be robbing the king and the government just as fast as they can and the King is helping them splendidly. . . . He can't bear to be argued with and he always smothers anything anyone else may have to say in a torrent of words.

Joseph Malone quotes a Lebanese contractor made wealthy in Saudi Arabia who referred to the last years of Abd al Aziz's rule as "the good old days, when the old king didn't know the difference between a thousand and a million."

Members of the royal family who had been educated abroad returned shocked and disgusted at the waste and at the slow pace of change. To the religious leaders change was happening all too fast, and modernization and the presence of foreigners were having precisely the effect they had predicted. The effect was most noticeable among the royal family where religious laws could not reach.

Saudi workers at Aramco viewing the educational, health, and recreational facilities made available for American and other foreign workers resented religious leaders who would not permit them access to the Aramco facilities and the fact that their government did not provide similar benefits for them. Economic discontent culminated in a strike of Aramco workers in 1953. Based on the report of a royal commission that investigated the strike, the leading spokesmen of the workers were jailed and unionization forbidden.

Abd al Aziz made a last effort to regain popularity for the royal family when he agreed to attempt to expand the state by occupying the Buraymi Oasis, an area covered under the Treaty of Jiddah of 1927 (see ch. 10). The adventure was ultimately unsuccessful, and Saudi Arabia's prestige lessened considerably, especially in the Western world. Much of the Arab world viewed Saudi Arabia even less favorably than did the West. A council of ulama in Cairo, aware of the ever-growing economic disparity between the royal family and the rest of the country, criticized Abd al Aziz's regime, saying that his state had been created in the name of God but was little more than a collection of masters and slaves.

THE "INTERLUDE" OF SAUD

All of the problems of Abd al Aziz's reign but few of his personal qualities were bequeathed to his son and successor, Saud (1953-64). Saud's first administrative assignment in the new kingdom had been the governorship of the Najd, and this may have contributed to his disastrous rule as king. Governorship of the Najd did not require learning new ways to approach the problems of governing. Saud relied on his father's charismatic leadership and cash to maintain tribal loyalty in the Najd and relaxed to enjoy the fruits of royal privilege and royal income.

Not having the qualities expected of tribal leaders, yet knowing no alternative, upon his accession to kingship Saud secluded himself from the citizen body and relied heavily on his advisers, many of whom, including native Saudis, were only concerned with the personal acquisition of wealth and power. Saud paid huge sums to maintain tribal acquiescence to his rule in return for recruits for an immense palace guard, the White Army (see ch. 14). Revenues could not match Saud's expenditures for the tribes, the Buraymi expedition, subsidies to the revolutionary movement in Algeria, and his personal follies. By 1958 the riyal had to be devalued nearly 80 percent, despite annual oil revenues in excess of US$300 million.

Dissatisfactions grew over wasteful expenditures, the lack of development of public projects and educational institutions, and the low wages of the growing labor force. Citizens were becoming aware of the dual culture emerging everywhere in Saudi Arabia. In the Eastern Province foreign Aramco workers lived in suburban comfort not far from beduin settlements as poor as they had ever been. Desert democracy had vanished and had been replaced by class justice; the royal family, foreigners, and westernized administrators received treatment different from the rest of the population. Privileged classes had been unknown in the early days of Abd al Aziz's reign; his first palace was made of the same sun-dried mud bricks that the peasants used, shaykhs and beduin herdsmen called each other by their first names, and the clothing of rich and poor was highly similar.

Dissatisfaction came from many sources, chief of which were a few of the more liberal princes and the sons of the rising middle class educated abroad. The rising discontent found an outlet in the nation's first daily newspaper published in 1953 (see ch. 9). Saud's first response to the dissatisfaction was to issue a *fatwa* (royal decree) in April 1955 requiring the return of all precollege Saudis being educated abroad. Refusal would incur loss of citizenship. In an effort to discourage the formation of critical attitudes, college students abroad were forbidden to major in law, political science, or related areas. In 1956 native Aramco workers called a second strike. The strike featured nationalistic and anti-imperialistic slogans reflecting resentment of foreign exploitation of Saudi resources. Saud issued a *fatwa* in June 1956 forbidding further strikes under penalty of dismissal.

There were some positive accomplishments. In 1954 ministries of commerce and industry and of health were created largely at the instigation of Crown Prince Faisal, whom Saud appointed prime minister as well as foreign minister. Appropriations were increased for urban planning, communications, schools, roads, and the needs of pilgrims. The power of the Council of Ministers was increased under Faisal's direction, but many of his plans were vitiated by Saud and by some of their less responsible brothers who held important ranks. Essentially all domestic and foreign control remained with Saud.

In foreign relations Saud followed the inclinations of his father and promoted Arab unity by demanding the liberation of Palestine in cooperation with Gamal Abdul Nasser of Egypt. Saudi Arabia's ties with Egypt had been strengthened by a mutual defense pact in October 1955. Together Nasser and Saud assisted in financing an effort to discourage Jordan from joining the Western-sponsored Baghdad Pact. When the French, British, and Israeli forces invaded Egypt in 1956 as a result of Nasser's nationalization of the Suez Canal, Saud granted the equivalent of US$10 million to Egypt, severed diplomatic relations with Great Britain and France, and placed an embargo on oil shipments to both countries.

American-Saudi relations also declined during the early years of Saud's reign. The leasing of the Dhahran Air Base to the United States was criticized by nationalists as a concession to American imperialism. In 1954 the United States Point Four mission was dismissed. Even the deferential Aramco management experienced controversy with the Saudis over the transport of oil in Greek tankers, which Aramco considered a violation of their concession agreement.

A major reorientation of Saudi policy began in 1957 after Saud's successful visit to the United States. In a conference with President Dwight D. Eisenhower, Saud gave support to the Eisenhower Doctrine and agreed to a five-year renewal of the lease of the Dhahran Air Base.

But as Western relations improved, those with Egypt worsened. Egypt and Saudi Arabia had been drawn together because of their mutual interest in securing Arab independence from non-Arab foreign intervention. Beyond that point all similarity of objectives vanished. Nasser had deposed a king in Egypt and was encouraging revolutionary attitudes in other Arab countries. His notions of Arab unity and economic socialism were abhorrent to Saud and to many Saudis who wished to preserve an independent and capitalistically oriented kingdom. Further, the Egyptians trafficked with the Soviet Union, from whom the Saudis had declined an arms offer and to whom they denied diplomatic recognition because of their hatred of communism. The presence of large numbers of Egyptian military attachés and teachers in Saudi Arabia caused fear among the Saudis that, at the very least, unacceptable views would circulate. Saudi officials were aghast when Syria and Egypt merged in 1958 to form the United Arab Republic. Yet the shock generated by news of the union paled before the subsequent disclosures of an alleged conspiracy by Saud to subvert the venture and to assassinate Nasser. The embarrassed senior members of the House of Saud urged Saud to relinquish power to Faisal.

On March 24, 1958, Saud issued a *fatwa* giving Faisal executive powers in foreign and internal affairs, including fiscal planning. By 1959 as a result of Faisal's initiation of an austerity program, which included a reduction of subsidies to the royal family, the budget had been balanced, currency stabilized, and embarrassing national debts resolved. Faisal increased the powers of the Council of Ministers and assumed a neutral position in Arab politics.

The reductions in the royal household budget incensed Saud and his circle; and a dispute, arising out of Saud's desire to give full control of a Hejaz oil refinery to one of his sons, made Faisal's position increasingly precarious. In January 1961 Faisal and his Council of Ministers tendered their resignations.

Saud assumed the post of prime minister and made another brother, the progressive Amir Talal, minister of finance and economy. A new cabinet was formed composed of many Western-educated commoners. There was much talk of innovative governmental moves, but none materialized. Talal, concluding that Saud had misrepresented his intentions to engage his support, departed for Cairo, taking several air force officers and their planes with him. Saud reacted passionately and accused Nasser of being an ally of the Zionists and of trying to destroy Islam. When civil war broke out in Yemen in September 1962 and Egyptian forces arrived to support the revolutionaries against the Saudis who supported the overthrown royalist government, the destruction of the Saudi monarchy seemed a distinct possibility (see ch. 10).

Faisal had been restored as deputy prime minister and foreign minister in March 1962 to substitute for Saud, who was in the United States for medical treatment. In October 1962 Faisal was urged by the ulama and many princes to accept the kingship, but he declined, citing his promise to his father to support Saud. Instead Faisal again became prime minister, named Amir Khalid deputy prime minister, and formed a government from among his supporters. He took command of the armed forces and quickly restored their loyalty and morale.

The following month he announced a ten-point plan for reform. Projected changes in the government included promises to issue a constitution, establish local government, and form an independent judiciary with a supreme judicial council composed of secular and religious members. He pledged to strengthen Islam and to reform the Committee for Encouragement of Virtue and Discouragement of Vice (see ch. 6). Progress was to be assured by the regulation of economic and commercial activities, and there was to be a sustained effort to develop the country's resources. Social reforms would include provisions for social security, unemployment compensation, educational scholarships and, most important, the abolition of slavery (see ch. 7). Consultations between Faisal and President John F. Kennedy led to promises of United States support of Faisal's plans for reform and of Saudi Arabia's territorial integrity. Diplomatic relations were reestablished with Great Britain and France, and debts to them were repaid.

Faisal's projects and the budgetary allowance necessary to modernize the armed forces for their engagement in Yemen meant that the king's personal income had to be cut. In March 1964 a *fatwa* endorsed by the royal family and the ulama reduced Saud's powers and his personal budget. The White Army was placed under the Ministry of Defense and Aviation, and the royal court was abolished. The response from Saud, who had been on an extended and expensive tour of Europe with a large entourage, was outrage. Saud tried to garner support for a return to power, but the royal family and ulama held firm. On November 2, 1964, the ulama issued a final *fatwa* on the matter. Saud was deposed, and Faisal was declared king. This decision terminated almost a decade of external and internal pressure to depose Saud and assert the power and integrity of conservative forces within the Saudi family.

THE REIGN OF FAISAL

Faisal ibn Abd al Aziz Al Saud (1964-75) was the first king of Saudi Arabia to comprehend the enormity of the task of modernization and to accept total responsibility for achieving it. His first two official acts were protective, directed toward securing the nation from potential internal and external threats that could thwart development. In the first month of his reign Amir Khalid ibn Abd al Aziz Al Saud, a half brother, was designated crown prince, thus assuring that the succession would not be disturbed by the kind of family power politics that had nearly destroyed Saudi hegemony in the past. Amir Sultan, as minister of defense and aviation, was given a fiat to modernize the army and establish an air defense system to protect the nation and its petroleum reserves from foreign invaders.

Funds to the King Abd al Aziz University in Jiddah were substantially increased, and the College of Petroleum and Minerals was opened in Dhahran. Faisal felt that, although undesirable, foreign influence was unavoidable as long as the population remained undereducated and unable to assume the country's many demanding positions. Faisal reorganized the Central Planning Organization to develop priorities for economic development (see ch. 11). The result was that oil revenues were spent on investments designed to stimulate growth.

Continually troubled by the spread of revolutionary ideas generated by foreign Arab leaders, especially by Nasser, Faisal called an Islamic summit conference in 1965 to reaffirm Islamic principles against the rising tide of modern ideologies. During 1965 Faisal traveled to Turkey, Pakistan, Iran, Morocco, and Tunisia—countries with close ties to the West—to interest other leaders in the conference. Nasser denounced Faisal's conference proposal, which Nasser referred to as the Islamic Pact, as a political maneuver aimed at uniting "reactionary" Muslim states against the modern and necessary forces of revolutionary socialism. Faisal continually insisted that his only aim was to encourage Muslim countries to assist and support one another.

Both Faisal's and Nasser's assessments of the situation were correct. Saudi Arabia had emerged in the 1960s having the revenues usually associated with nations that had undergone a sophisticated developmental process over a period of centuries. Yet Saudi Arabia remained a model of the medieval Islamic state, and Faisal had internalized the attitudes proper to a ruler of such a state. He understood his primary role, enunciated a millennium before, as protecting and securing the Dar al Islam (territory under Islamic rule) and the well-being of the Muslim community (*umma*). His duties also included safeguarding and supporting the sharia (body of Islamic law) within his land. Finally, he was to be a benevolent ruler who would strive to increase the well-being of his subjects without placing them in moral danger.

Faisal's dedication to these ideals had its roots in his upbringing in the house of his maternal grandfather, a direct descendant of Abd al Wahhab, the eighteenth-century initiator of the revival of religious orthodoxy in Arabia (see The House of Saud, this ch.). Faisal was raised in a spartan atmosphere, unlike that of most of his half brothers, and was encouraged by his mother to develop values consonant with tribal leadership. Faisal's religious idealism did not diminish his secular effectiveness. For him political functioning was a religious act that demanded thoughtfulness, dignity, and integrity. Respect for Faisal increased in the Arab world based on the remarkable changes within Saudi Arabia, Faisal's excellent management of the holy cities, his reputation as a stalwart enemy of Zionism, and his rapidly increasing financial power.

Faisal proceeded cautiously but emphatically to introduce Western technology. He was continually forced to cope with the insistent demands of his westernized associates to move faster and the equally vociferous urgings of the ulama to move not at all. He chose the middle ground not merely in a spirit of compromise to assuage the two forces but because he earnestly believed that the correct religious orientation would mitigate the adverse effects of modernization.

Under Faisal's reign a massive educational program was initiated (see ch. 5). Expenditures for education increased to an annual level of approximately 10 percent of the overall budget. Vocational training centers and institutes of higher education were built in addition to the more than 125 elementary and secondary schools built annually. Women's demands, increasingly vocalized, led to the establishment of elementary schools for girls. These were placed under religious control to pacify the many (including members of the royal household) who were opposed to education for women.

Health centers multiplied, and at least one was among the best in the world (see ch. 4). Faisal instituted many qualitative changes in the governmental structure, but it remained highly centralized and basically autocratic. By 1970 there were fourteen ministries, the Council of Ministers with two deputy prime ministers, and the Juridical Institute (see ch. 8).

Regional affairs within the peninsula, with the exception of Yemen, were primarily concerned with boundary disputes. Faisal made much progress, but at his death Saudi Arabia still possessed more unsettled than settled frontiers (see ch. 3). In August 1965 a final determination of boundaries was reached between Saudi Arabia and Jordan. Saudi Arabia received a net gain of 580 square miles, mostly at the southeast corner of Jordan, that facilitated the administration of Saudi Arabia's Northern Province.

In 1965 border delineations with Qatar were also agreed upon. The Continental Shelf Agreement with Iran in October of 1968 established the separate rights of Iran and Saudi Arabia within the Persian Gulf (called the Arabian Gulf in Saudi Arabia), and an agreement was reached to discourage foreign intervention there. Faisal greeted with seeming equanimity the new government formed in July 1970 in Oman by the son of the deposed sultan but tightened Saudi Arabia's security in the area. The formation of the United Arab Emirates did not receive official recognition until the settlement of the long-standing Buraymi Oasis dispute (see ch. 10).

Saudi Arabia's largest problem within the peninsula remained the settlement of the Yemen crisis. In August 1965 Faisal and Nasser agreed at Jiddah to an immediate cease-fire, the termination of Saudi Arabian aid to the royalists, and the withdrawal of Egyptian forces (see ch. 10). In 1965 at Harad in Yemen, Saudi Arabia and Egypt sponsored a meeting of Yemenite representatives from the opposing sides. The conference became deadlocked, and hostilities resumed after the promised Egyptian troop withdrawals. The royalists claimed extensive victories. The Egyptians announced that they would not withdraw their remaining troops and were incensed at what they believed was Saudi reintervention. Egyptian aircraft bombed royalist installations and towns in southern Saudi Arabia. Saudi Arabia responded by closing its two Egyptian banks, an action countered by Egypt's sequestration of all Saudi Arabian property holdings in Egypt.

Saud, then residing in Egypt, made a personal gift of US$1 million to the Republic of Yemen and made broadcasts from Sana, Yemen's capital and from Cairo, stating his intention to return to rule "to save the people and land of Saudi Arabia." A series of terrorist bomb attacks against residences of the royal family and American and British personnel led to the arrests of a group including seventeen Yemenis accused of the sabotage. They were found guilty and were publicly beheaded in accordance with the law (see ch. 8). Egyptian and Saudi disagreements over the area were not resolved until the Khartoum Conference of August 1967.

In the aftermath of the June 1967 War between Israel and various Arab states, the disputes between Arab states had to take a secondary position to what the Arabs called the "alien threat" of Israel. Faisal's influence at Arab conferences continued to increase, his position strengthened by the enormous revenues with which he could make good his commitments and by his irreproachable reputation as a pious Muslim. Faisal's pan-Islamic pronouncements, vague in the first two years of his reign, took concrete form after the June 1967 War when an Islamic nation, Jordan, received a direct threat to its existence and that same "infidel power," Israel, seized and retained Jerusalem, the third holiest city of Islam.

At the Khartoum Conference Saudi Arabia, Libya, and Kuwait agreed to set up a fund equivalent to US$378 million to be distributed among countries that had suffered from the 1967 war. The Saudi contribution would be US$140 million. Jordan and Egypt were both in desperate financial positions. The monies were intended not only to ease this situation but also to buttress their political bargaining power. Egypt could no longer continue expensive commitments to the war in Yemen, and Nasser and Faisal agreed to a compromise proposed by Sudan for financial and economic pullouts in Yemen. Military aggression against Israel was not mentioned, but the conferees agreed neither to recognize nor to make peace with Israel and to continue to work for the rights of the Palestinians.

A fire in the Al Aqsa Mosque in Jerusalem on August 21, 1969, prompted the Islamic Summit Conference of September 1969 in Rabat, Morocco. Representatives agreed to intensify their efforts to ensure the prompt withdrawal of Israeli military forces in the occupied lands and to pursue an honorable peace. No definite proposals were made, but the conference had a salubrious psychological effect on its participants, who shared their anxieties over the increasingly disturbing situation with Israel.

Saudi Arabian oil revenues continued to multiply. In addition to the 25-percent increase in production in 1971, gains resulted from the raising of posted prices by the Organization of Petroleum Exporting Countries (OPEC) at the Tehran meeting in February 1971. At the Beirut meeting of OPEC in March 1972 the idea of gradual nationalization of oil companies had been introduced.

Faisal, having increased his economic power, in July 1973 threatened to reduce oil deliveries if the United States did not seek to equalize its treatment of Egypt and Israel. The threat was realized during the October 1973 War between Israel and three Arab states when the Organization of Arab Petroleum Exporting Countries (OAPEC) imposed a general rise in oil prices and an oil embargo on major oil consumers who were either supporters of Israel or allies of its supporters (see ch. 12). The embargo was a political protest aimed at securing Israeli withdrawal from occupied Arab territory and recognition of the rights of the Palestinian people.

At an Arab conference held at Algiers in November 1973 Saudi Arabia agreed with all the participants except the representative of Jordan to recognize the Palestine Liberation Organization (PLO) as the legitimate representative of the Palestinian people. Jordan's King Hussein refused to participate but was encouraged by Faisal to attend the follow-up conference in October 1974 in Rabat. At this meeting Hussein gave his reluctant agreement to the proposal that the PLO should be the negotiators with Israel over the establishment of a Palestinian entity in the territory newly occupied by Israel. In return Saudi Arabia promised Hussein US$300 million a year for the next four years.

Faisal's preoccupation with the Arab-Israeli conflict and the rash of revolutionary regimes near Saudi territory made him slow his pace in the development of domestic programs. Faisal's failing health, overwork, and age began to tell in his assessment of national priorities. His character judgment, however, never failed him, and those he chose—men like Amir Sultan, Amir Fahd, and Shaykh Ahmad Zaki Yamani—carried out many of his plans after his assassination on March 25, 1975. The circumstances of Faisal's death were ironic. He was shot by a nephew, a member of the royal family whose dynasty Faisal worked so diligently to secure. The assassination occurred at a majlis, which Faisal had insisted on retaining (see ch. 8).

* * * * * * * * * * * * *

Useful sources for pre-Islamic Arabia include Geoffrey Bibby's *Looking for Dilmun*; Gus W. Van Beek's "The Rise and Fall of Arabia Felix" in *Scientific American*; and Irfan Shahid's article in *The Cambridge History of Islam*. W. Montgomery Watt's *Muhammad: Prophet and Statesman* is an account of Muhammad's ministry from a secular point of view. The effect and importance of the camel to the development of Arabian economic life is discussed in Richard W. Bulliet's *The Camel and the Wheel*. Richard Bayly Winder's *Saudi Arabia in the Nineteenth Century* offers a complete account of the House of Saud during that time. In *Philby of Arabia* Elizabeth Monroe offers an intimate view of the reign of Abd al Aziz, and the book is particularly enlightening for the king's response to the problems of modernization. For the reign of Faisal, Gerald de Gaury's *Faisal, King of Saudi Arabia* remains the most complete study. (For further information see Bibliography.)

CHAPTER 3

GEOGRAPHY AND POPULATION

The Kingdom of Saudi Arabia occupies approximately 80 percent of the Arabian Peninsula, an area roughly equivalent to the United States east of the Mississippi. Saudi Arabia possesses more undefined than defined boundaries, and as a result the exact size of the country is unknown. The Saudi government estimate is 865,000 square miles. Other reputable estimates vary between 864,000 square miles and 869,774 square miles. Less than 1 percent of the total area is suitable for settled agriculture, and population distribution varies greatly among the towns of the eastern and western coastal areas, the densely populated interior oases, and the vast, almost empty deserts.

In early 1976 reliable data on the population were not publicly available. The Saudi government asserted that in September 1974 the population was slightly over 7 million, but most foreign observers considered the Saudi figure too high. Many analysts estimate that in early 1976 the population was about 5.6 million, of which between 1 million and 1.5 million were foreigners. The estimates of other reputable observers were as low as 4.7 million, of which only about 3.2 million were Saudis. The problem of making an accurate population count is complicated by the fact that perhaps one-third of the population lives a nomadic or seminomadic existence and that privacy in matters relating to the family is highly valued among Muslims.

The Arabian Peninsula is a unified plateau sloping slightly toward the east, with a major fault line along the Red Sea coast. In the extreme west a line of rugged mountains parallels the Red Sea coast and forms the watershed for the peninsula. East of this range the land is relatively even; the gradual drop toward the Persian Gulf is broken only by the escarpment of the low Tuwaiq mountains (Jabal Tuwaiq), which extend along a west-facing crescent north and south of Riyadh.

Most of the surface is sand covered, forming the great deserts of the Nafud, the Dahna, and the Rub al Khali (Empty Quarter) (see fig. 1). Outside these deserts the surface is gravel or, in limited areas in the west-central portion, consists of jumbled beds of lava. The climate of most of the peninsula is debilitatingly hot and dry. In Saudi Arabia only the Asir highlands along the Red Sea receive enough rain to permit a degree of nonirrigated cultivation (see ch. 13).

Transportation systems have been steadily improved but as of 1976 remained inadequate to serve the country's economic and human needs. An ambitious project was designed for ports, airports, and roads in the Five Year Development Plan (1975-80).

BOUNDARIES AND ADMINISTRATIVE DIVISIONS

External Boundaries

Saudi Arabia is bounded by eight countries and three bodies of water. On the west the Gulf of Aqaba and the Red Sea form a coastal border 1,100 miles long that extends south to the Yemen Arab Republic [Yemen (Sana)]. The border with Yemen (Sana), which follows a mountain ridge for approximately 200 miles inland from the Red Sea to the vicinity of Najran, has been demarcated since 1934 and is one of the few definite and clearly defined borders with a neighboring country. The Saudi border running southeast from Najran, however, is still undetermined.

To the north Saudi Arabia is bounded by Jordan, Iraq, and Kuwait. The northern boundary extends 850 miles from the Gulf of Aqaba on the west to Ras al Mishab on the Persian Gulf. Saudi Arabia and Jordan agreed in 1965 to boundary demarcations involving an exchange of small areas of territory that gave Jordan needed additional lands near Aqaba, its only port. In 1922 Abd al Aziz ibn Abd ar Rahman Al Saud (reigned 1902-53) and British officials representing Iraqi interests signed the Treaty of Mohammara, which established the boundary between Iraq and the future Saudi Arabia. Later in the year the two parties agreed to the creation of the diamond-shaped Neutral Zone of approximately 2,702 square miles adjacent to the western tip of Kuwait in which neither Iraq nor Saudi Arabia would build permanent dwellings or installations. Beduin from either country could utilize the national resources of the zone. In May 1938 Iraq and Saudi Arabia signed an additional agreement regarding the administration of the zone. In April 1975 an agreement signed in Baghdad fixed the borders of the countries; this was followed in July by an agreement setting up the formal division of the Neutral Zone.

In December 1922 a convention was signed regulating Saudi Arabia's boundary with Kuwait. In an effort to avoid territorial disputes, another diamond-shaped neutral zone of approximately 2,227 square miles directly south of Kuwait was agreed upon. The agreement was not finalized, however, until 1963, and in 1966 the zone was divided between Kuwait and Saudi Arabia, each country to administer its own half. In the mid-1970s resources, including the production of oil, continued to be shared equally.

Saudi Arabia's eastern boundary follows the Persian Gulf for 200 miles from Ras al Mishab to the peninsula of Qatar, whose border with Saudi Arabia was determined in 1965. The seven small states of the United Arab Emirates south of Qatar bound the remainder of the Persian Gulf area.

The state of Oman, occupying the largest part of the southeastern coast of the Arabian Peninsula on the Gulf of Oman and the Arabian Sea, borders a significant portion of Saudi territory. The Buraymi Oasis, situated near the conjunction of the frontiers of Oman, Abu Dhabi (one of the states of the United Arab Emirates), and Saudi Arabia has occasioned much dispute among the three states since the Treaty of Jiddah in 1927. In 1974 Abu Dhabi agreed to a compromise, which included Abu Dhabi's sovereignty over six villages in the Buraymi Oasis and the sharing of the rich Zararah oil field between Saudi Arabia and Abu Dhabi. In return Saudi Arabia obtained an outlet to the Gulf of Oman through Abu Dhabi.

Saudi Arabia is bounded in the south by the People's Democratic Republic of Yemen [Yemen (Aden)] lying along the Gulf of Aden and the Arabian Sea. The periphery of Saudi Arabia's vast Rub al Khali desert roughly demarcates Saudi territory from Qatar in the east in an arc to Yemen (Aden) in the south. Exclusive of Qatar and the Buraymi Oasis there are no definite boundaries for the whole of this area.

Saudi Arabia's maritime claims include a twelve-mile territorial limit along its coasts. The Saudis also claim many small islands as well as some seabeds and subsoils beyond the twelve-mile limit. Maritime boundaries with Bahrain, the island state off Saudi Arabia's northeastern coast, have been agreed upon. Claims with other Saudi neighbors along the Persian Gulf, including Iran, are in an almost constant state of negotiation and adjustment. Saudi Arabia does have oil fields seventy miles offshore in an area between the town of Dammam and the Saudi-Kuwait border.

The idea of a sovereign state with clearly defined boundaries is a new one in the Arabian Peninsula. Before the unification of the Kingdom of Saudi Arabia in 1932 boundaries were either those claimed under the aegis of foreign powers, most particularly Great Britain, or those based on tribal de facto possession. For the tribes the most desirable areas were those that possessed waterholes, grazing lands, and fertile oases. To outsiders with untrained eyes there were few geographical clues to distinguish one area from another. Although seasonal tribal migrations were the norm, each member of a tribe knew the territorial limits of his tribe or clan. Tribal members also knew that to trespass on another tribe's grazing lands or to utilize its waterholes invited almost certain armed attack and probable death.

By the beginning of the twentieth century the largest tribes of the interior had begun to coalesce around rudimentary settlement centers, usually oases. When Abd Al Aziz began the conquest of his future kingdom, he concentrated on the territory of the interior tribes. Moving concentrically from the Saudi homeland in the Najd, he subdued the major tribes before he moved against the more urbanized Hejaz. Expansion to the north was limited by Abd Al Aziz's negotiations with the British, and the limitation was enforced on one occasion by the British Royal Air Force. Qatar, Oman, Muscat, and the area around Aden were also under British protection, and Abd Al Aziz was anxious for British acceptance of his suzerainty over the greater part of Arabia. Additionally, with the exception of Yemen, he enjoyed good relations with the leaders of those areas at least until the discovery of oil. As a result of the Treaty of Taif in 1934, which ended for a period the Saudi conflict with Yemen, Saudi Arabia annexed the Najran area. Later conflicts with Yemen did not affect territorial boundaries (see ch. 10).

The discovery of oil in disputed areas continues to make border demarcations a matter of long-term arbitration. Saudi Arabia's boundaries with the countries to the east were proclaimed unilaterally by Great Britain in 1955 after various attempts at international arbitration failed. As might be expected Saudi Arabia's acquiescence was more formal than real. In the past Saudi Arabia has even repudiated signed treaties through various legal loopholes because Islamic law—formerly Saudi Arabia's only legal code—does not correspond in many cases to international law. (Abd al Aziz was fond of giving gold watches to foreign geographers. On the backs of the gifts were carefully engraved maps of Saudi Arabia depicting frontiers far different from those supposed to be in effect according to treaty.) National boundaries continue to be accepted lightheartedly by beduin whose seasonal migrations may make them residents of three different countries in a year.

Internal Divisions

Saudi Arabia is internally divided into eighteen administrative divisions or provinces, each ruled by a governor appointed by the central government (see fig. 5). Six of them are considered major provinces and in 1976 were ruled by governors who were members of or related to the royal family (see ch. 8).

GEOGRAPHIC SETTING

Geologic Structure

The Arabian Peninsula is an ancient massif composed of stable crystalline rock whose present geologic structure was developing concurrently with the formation of the Alps. Geologic movements caused the entire mass to tilt eastward and the western and southern edges to tilt upward. In the valley created by the fault, called the Great Rift, the Red Sea was formed. The Great Rift runs from the Mediterranean

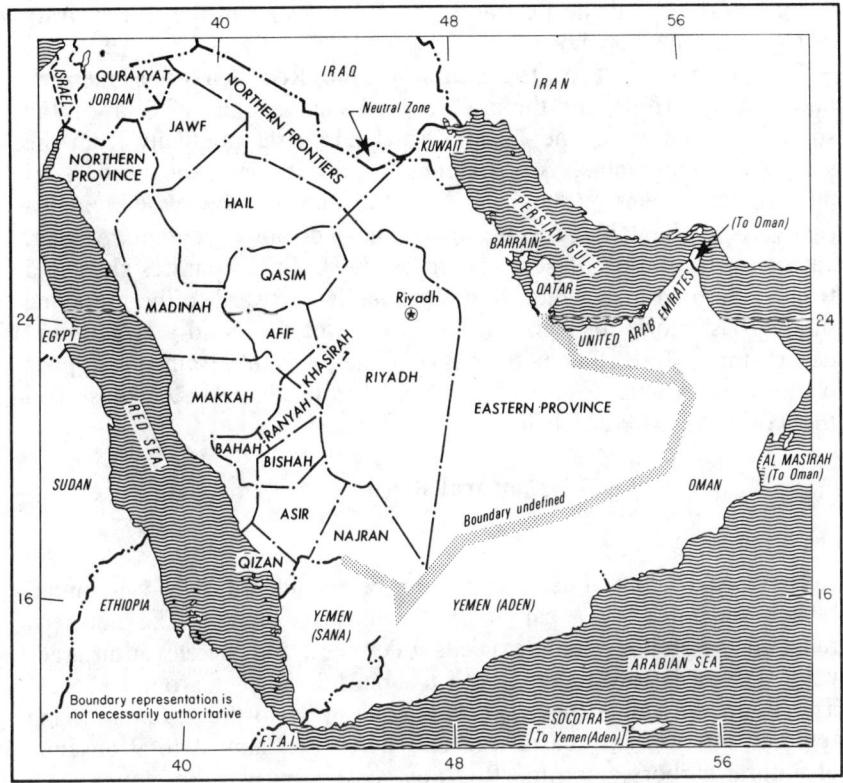

Figure 5. Saudi Arabia, Administrative Divisions, May 1976

along both sides of the Red Sea and southward through Ethiopia and the lake country of East Africa, gradually disappearing in the area of Mozambique, Zambia, and Southern Rhodesia. Scientists analyzing color photographs taken by American astronauts on the joint United States-Soviet space mission in July 1975 have detected a vast fan-shaped complex of cracks and fault lines extending north and eastward from the region of the Golan Heights. These are believed to be the final portion of the Great Rift and are presumed to be the result of the slow rotation of the Arabian Peninsula counterclockwise in a way that will in approximately 10 million years close off the Persian Gulf and make it a lake.

On the Peninsula the eastern line of the Great Rift fault is visible in the steep and, in places, very high escarpment, which parallels the Red Sea between the Gulf of Aqaba and the Gulf of Aden. The eastern slope of this escarpment is relatively gentle, dropping to the exposed shield of the extremely ancient landmass that existed before the faulting occurred. A second lower escarpment, the Jabal Tuwaiq, runs roughly north-south through the area of Riyadh. East of this escarpment the shield is covered by layers of sediment increasing

49

in thickness toward the Persian Gulf. Oil is found in the lower strata of these sedimentary layers.

The northern half of the region of the Red Sea escarpment is known as the Hejaz and the more rugged southern half as Asir. In the south a coastal plain, the Tihama Lowlands, rises gradually from the sea to the mountains. Asir extends southward into the borders of mountainous Yemen (Sana). The central plateau, the Najd, extends eastward to the Jabal Tuwaiq and a short distance beyond. A long, narrow strip of sand desert known as the Dahna separates the Najd from eastern Arabia, which slopes gradually eastward to the low-lying sandy coast along the Persian Gulf. North of the Najd a larger sand desert, the Nafud, isolates the heart of the peninsula from the steppes of northern Arabia. South of the Najd lies the largest sand desert in the world, the Rub al Khali.

Natural Regions

Hejaz and Asir

The western coastal escarpment can be considered as two mountain ranges separated by a gap in the vicinity of Mecca. The northern range in the Hejaz seldom exceeds 7,000 feet, and the elevation gradually decreases toward the south to about 2,000 feet around Mecca. The mountain wall is rugged, dropping abruptly to the sea and having few and intermittent coastal plains. There is an almost total absence of natural harbors along the Red Sea coast. The western slopes have been stripped of soil by the erosion of infrequent but turbulent rainfalls that have fertilized the plains to the east. The eastern slopes are less steep and are marked by wadis that mark the courses of ancient rivers and still lead the rare rain down into the plains. Scattered oases, drawing water from springs and wells in the vicinity of these wadis, permit some settled agriculture. Of these the largest and most important is Medina.

South of Mecca the mountains are higher, exceeding 8,000 feet in a number of places; some peaks reach nearly 10,000 feet. The rugged western face of the escarpment drops rather steeply to the coastal plain, the Tihama Lowlands, which averages only about forty miles in width. Along the seacoast is a salty tidal plain of limited agricultural value, backed by potentially rich alluvial plains. The relatively well-watered and fertile upper slopes and the mountains behind are extensively terraced to make possible the maximum use of the land. An average of about twenty inches of rainfall a year permits the cultivation of grain, coffee, *qat* (a mildly narcotic plant), fruits, and vegetables (see ch. 13). The top of the mountain ridge is covered in places by narrow strips of the only natural forest in the country, mainly juniper. Luxuriant undergrowth gives these strips—many only a few dozen feet wide—the character of a tropical rain forest.

The eastern slope of the mountain range in Asir is gentle, melding into a plateau region that drops gradually into the Rub al Khali. Although rainfall is infrequent in this area, a number of fertile wadis, of which the most important are the Bishah and the Tathlith, make oasis agriculture possible on a relatively large scale. A number of extensive lava beds (*harrat*) scar the surfaces of the plateaus east of the mountain ranges in the Hejaz and Asir and give evidence of fairly recent volcanic activity. The largest of these beds is Khaybar, north of Medina.

The Najd

East of the Hejaz and Asir lies the great plateau area of the Najd, the birthplace of the country (see ch. 2). This region is mainly rocky plateau interspersed by small, sandy deserts and isolated mountain clumps. The best known of the mountain groups is the Jabal Shammar, northwest of Riyadh and just south of the Nafud desert. This is the home of the pastoral Shammar tribes, which under the leadership of Muhammad ibn Rashid were the most implacable foes of the Sauds in the nineteenth and early twentieth centuries. Their capital was the large oasis of Hail, now a flourishing urban center.

In conformity with the peninsula as a whole, the plateau slopes toward the east from an elevation of about 4,500 feet in the west to about 2,500 feet at its easternmost limit. A number of wadis cross the region generally in an eastward direction from the Red Sea escarpment toward the Persian Gulf. There is little pattern to these remains of ancient riverbeds; the most important of them are the Rumma, the Surra, and the Dawasir. Rainfall in the region averages less than four inches a year, and several years may elapse between rains. When rain does occur, it may be torrential and cause the wadis to flood, in some cases doing serious damage to settlements and making travel impossible until the water disappears into the gravel and sand base.

The heart of the Najd is the area of the Jabal Tuwaiq, an arc-shaped ridge whose steep west face rises between 400 and 800 feet above the plateau. Many oases exist in this area, which is one of the most densely populated in the country. The most important of these oases are Buraydah, Unayzah, Riyadh, Al Kharj, and Aflaj. Outside this oasis area the Najd is sparsely populated. Sabkah, large salt marshes, are scattered throughout the area.

Northern Arabia

The area north of the Nafud desert is geographically a part of the Syrian desert. It is an upland plateau with a surface of dark-colored rock and gravel and scored by numerous wadis, most trending northeastward toward Iraq. This area, known as Badiet ash Sham, is covered with grass and scrub steppe vegetation and is extensively used for pasture by nomadic and seminomadic herders. The most significant feature of the area is the Wadi Sirhan, a large basin as much as

1,000 feet below the surrounding plateau that is the remnant of an ancient inland sea. For thousands of years some of the most heavily traveled caravan routes between the Mediterranean and the central and southern peninsula have passed through the Wadi Sirhan. The most important oases in the area are Jawf and Sakaka, just north of the Nafud.

Eastern Arabia

East of the Dahna lies the rocky Summam plateau, about seventy-five miles wide and dropping in elevation from about 1,300 feet in the west to about 800 feet in the east. The area is generally barren and has a highly eroded surface of ancient river gorges and isolated buttes.

Farther east the terrain changes abruptly to the flat lowlands of the Persian Gulf coastal plain. This area, about 100 miles in width, is generally featureless and covered with gravel or sand. In the north is the gravelly Dibdiba plain and in the south the Jafura sand desert, which reaches the gulf in the vicinity of Abqaiq and Dhahran and merges with the Rub al Khali at its southern end. The coast itself is extremely irregular as sandy plains, marshes, and salt flats merge almost imperceptibly with the sea. As a result, the land surface is unstable; water rises in places almost to the surface, and the sea is shallow and full of shoals and reefs for an extended distance offshore. Only the construction of long moles at Ras Tanura has opened the Saudi coast on the Persian Gulf to seagoing tankers.

Eastern Arabia is sometimes still called Hasa after the great oasis of that name, one of the most potentially fertile areas of the country. Hasa, the largest oasis in the country, actually comprises two neighboring oases, including the town of Hufuf.

The Great Deserts

Three great deserts isolate the Najd from north, east, and south as the Red Sea escarpment does from the west. In the north the Nafud—sometimes called the Great Nafud because *nafud* simply means desert—covers about 25,000 square miles at an elevation of about 3,000 feet. Longitudinal dunes—scores of miles in length, as much as 300 feet high, and separated by valleys as much as ten miles wide—characterize the Nafud. Iron oxide gives the sand a reddish tint, particularly when the sun is low. Within the area are several watering places, and winter rains bring up short-lived but succulent grasses that permit nomadic herding during the winter and spring.

Stretching more than 400 miles south from the Nafud in a narrow arc only about thirty miles wide is the Dahna, a narrow band of sand mountains also called the river of sand. Like the Nafud, its sand tends to be reddish in color, particularly in the north where it also shares with the Nafud the longitudinal structure of sand dunes. The

Dahna also furnishes the beduin with winter and spring pasture, although water is scarcer than in the Nafud.

The southern portion of the Dahna curves westward following the arc of the Jabal Tuwaiq. At its southern end it merges with the Rub al Khali, one of the most forbidding sand deserts in the world and, until the 1950s, one of the least explored. The topography of this huge area, covering more than 250,000 square miles, is varied. In the west the elevation is about 2,000 feet, and the sand is fine and soft; in the east the elevation drops to about 600 feet, and much of the surface is covered by relatively stable sand sheets and salt flats. In places, particularly in the east, longitudinal sand dunes prevail; elsewhere sand mountains as much as 1,000 feet in height form complex patterns. Most of the area is totally waterless and uninhabited except for a few wandering beduin tribes.

Climate

With the exception of the provinces of Asir and Qizan on the lower western coast, Saudi Arabia has a desert climate characterized by extreme heat during the day, an abrupt drop in temperature at night, and slight and erratic rainfall. Because of the influence of a subtropical high-pressure system and the many fluctuations in elevation, there is considerable variation in temperature and humidity. The two main distinctions in climate are between the coastal lands and the interior.

Along the coastal regions of the Red Sea and the Persian Gulf the desert temperature is moderated by the proximity of those large bodies of water. Temperatures seldom go above 100°F, but the relative humidity is usually over 85 percent and frequently 100 percent for extended periods. This combination produces a hot mist during the day and a warm fog at night. The prevailing winds are from the northern quadrant and, when they blow, make the coastal areas more bearable in the summer and even pleasant in winter. A southerly wind is invariably accompanied by an increase in temperature and humidity and by a particular kind of storm known in the Persian Gulf area as *kauf*. In late spring and early summer a strong northwesterly wind, the *shamal*, blows; it is particularly severe in eastern Arabia and continuous for almost two-thirds of the period. The *shamal* produces sand and dust storms that can decrease visibility to a few feet.

A uniform climate prevails in the Najd, Qasim Province, and the great deserts. The average summer temperature is 112°F, but readings of up to 130°F are common. The heat becomes intense shortly after sunrise and lasts until sunset, followed by comparatively cool nights. In the winter the temperature seldom drops below 32°F, but the almost total absence of humidity and the high wind-chill factor make a bitterly cold atmosphere. In the spring and autumn temperatures average 85°F.

The region of Asir is subject to Indian Ocean monsoons, usually occurring between October and March. An average of twelve inches of rainfall occurs during this period of an annual total of twenty inches. Additionally, in Asir and the southern Hejaz, condensation caused by the higher mountain slopes contributes to the total rainfall.

For the rest of the country rainfall is low and erratic. The entire rainfall may be the product of one or two torrential outbursts that flood the wadis and then rapidly disappear into the soil to be trapped above the layers of impervious rock. This is sufficient, however, to sustain forage growth. Although the average is four inches per year, whole regions may not experience rainfall for several years. When this occurs, as it did in the north in 1957 and 1958, entire areas are devastated, and the majority of pastoral animals are lost.

In the absence of permanent rivers or bodies of water, the rainfall, groundwater, and very scarce surface water must supply the country's needs. In eastern Arabia and in the Jabal Tuwaiq regional artesian wells and springs are plentiful. In Al Kharj and Hasa a number of large, deep pools are constantly replenished by artesian springs as a result of underground water from the eastern watershed of the Jabal Tuwaiq. Such springs and wells permit extensive irrigation in local oases. In the Hejaz and Asir wells are abundant, and springs are common in the mountainous areas. In the Najd and the great deserts watering places are comparatively fewer and scattered over a wide area. Water must be hoisted or pumped to the surface; and even where water is plentiful, its quality may be poor.

Modern technology has located and increased the availability of much of the underground water. Arabian American Oil Company (Aramco) technicians have determined that very deep aquifers lie in many areas of northern and eastern Arabia and that the Wasia, one of the largest of these, has more water than the Persian Gulf.

The Saudi government, Aramco, and the United Nations Food and Agriculture Organization (FAO) have made separate and joint efforts to exploit underground water resources. In the past improperly drilled wells have reduced or destroyed any good they might have served by leaching the lands they were drilled to irrigate. Successive agricultural projects, many of which were designed primarily to encourage beduin settlement, have increased water resource exploitation (see ch. 13). A national policy for the conservation and management of water resources is being developed and implemented by three government agencies: the Ministry of Agriculture and Water, the Ministry of Municipal and Rural Affairs, and the Water Desalinization Organization.

Soils and Vegetation

The soil in certain areas is fertile when irrigated, but irrigation requires considerable effort, both technological and financial. Irrigation must be carefully handled, particularly around oases, to avoid exacerbating the problem of salination, which is already severe in eastern Arabia. Sporadic flooding and overwatering in the absence of sufficient drainage systems cause the deposit of salts, lime, and potassium on the surface by the percolative effect produced by extreme surface heat and a raised groundwater level.

Desert marls (alkaline formations) permit limited agricultural production with such salt-resistant crops as the date palm when the surface is not crusted by surface saltpans. Marls are most prominent in the Hejaz, where in extreme cases crusty saltpans or limestone pans prevent any vegetative growth.

Sand-covered areas are suitable for agriculture if sufficiently irrigated and drained. One factor that most seriously limits their use is the susceptibility of dunes to shifting in high winds. This mobility, often reaching forty feet a year, makes the dunes a grave threat to oases, particularly in the Eastern Province. Government countermeasures include planting millions of eucalyptus trees and tamarisk shrubs against the dunes, erecting sand fences, and spraying the windward side of the dunes with asphalt or oil to stabilize them.

A heavy sand-gravel soil, found in the Najd and in parts of the Eastern Province, produces a luxuriant but ephemeral vegetation after rains. Although not suitable for cultivation, it produces excellent forage for grazing.

Loam soils, which have good agricultural potential when properly irrigated, are found predominantly in the highlands of the Najd. When additional sand is mixed with a clayey loam, the soil becomes highly productive. The wadi banks contain alluvial soils that are rich and fertile sandy loam soils. They are intensively cultivated, mainly for cereals and vegetables (see ch. 13).

Despite the great difficulties attending the development of an agricultural industry in a desert country, Saudi Arabia continues to invest enormous sums of money in what is the least efficient part of its economic program. The government wishes to be less dependent on imported foodstuffs, and agricultural settlements appear to be the most congenial solution to the problem of settling the beduin (see Population, this ch.).

Indigenous Flora and Fauna

With the exception of the provinces of Asir and Qizan, Saudi Arabia is botanically located in the North African-Indian floristic zone, a desert belt extending 6,000 miles from the west coast of Africa to the Indus Valley. Areas within this zone share distinctive botanical features that have been modified by the life-styles of the different peoples within them—some depending on grazing, others on farming. Plants are small in size and either are succulent or are active only in the brief rainy season. The number of naturally occuring species is small. The perennial vegetation used for pasture by the beduin includes a sedge and a grass, both common in the eastern coastal sands. Farther inland *arfaj*, a small shrub, and *rimth*, a salt-producing bush, sporadically cover many hundreds of miles.

Few desert plants are comestible by humans. Desert truffles, herbs, and the seeds of the mesembryanthemum are among the ones used by the beduin. Frankincense and myrrh, the basis of the area's wealth in ancient times, now grow wild in the south. Desert flowers appearing after the sporadic rains are mostly dwarf varieties of the iris, chamomile, lily, and scarlet pimpernel. In the southwest highlands of Asir, which are in a different botanical zone, forests of wild olive trees and juniper cover some of the higher slopes.

The late and minimal impact of man upon the ecosystem of Saudi Arabia has led to the survival of many desert animal species almost extinct elsewhere. Two notable exceptions to this are the oryx *(wadayhi)* and the three Arabian subspecies of the gazelle: the *rim, ifri,* and *idm*. These animals are virtually extinct but in the mid-1970s were seen occasionally at the rim of the Rub al Khali. Small numbers of ibex exist in the upper regions of the mountains, and a few baboons survive in the Asir highlands. Wolves, hyenas and, more rarely, striped cheetahs range throughout the peninsula. Jackals are common around settled areas. Small mammals include the ratel, fox, mongoose, coney, porcupine, jerboa, gerbil, and *jird* (sand rat).

The ostrich was last sighted and apparently killed, in the early 1950s, but eagles, hawks, falcons, vultures, owls, and ravens abound. Species favored by the beduin as food are the *qata* (sand grouse), stone curlew, quail, and *darajab* (coursers). Flamingos, egrets, and pelicans are found on the Persian Gulf coast and the white-cheeked bulbul and the two-striped lark *(umm salim)* in the oases.

Snakes are common throughout the peninsula; but only the sand viper is venómous, and its bite is usually not fatal. The *dabb*—a twenty-inch, heavy, spiny-tailed lizard—is valued as food by the beduin. Geckos; the carnivorous *waral*; lacertids; agamids; the shiny, sand-swimming skink; and the pink, legless lizard are found everywhere in the interior.

Mosquitos are common along the coast, but the malaria-carrying mosquito has been under control since 1942. Saudi Arabia is one of the world's major breeding grounds for locusts. The government has been working with neighboring states and international agencies since 1942 in an attempt to bring this very serious problem under control. The dung beetle, scorpion, red rain mite, and the hairy shabath, an enormous but harmless spider, can be found inland and along the coasts.

More than 200 species of fish exist in the Persian Gulf. Of greatest commercial importance are the sawfish and king mackerel, and of those caught by trolling, the grouper and the *jihabah* (a kind of tuna).

Mineral Resources

The government's interest in decreasing its economic dependence upon oil has engendered extensive geologic exploration for other mineral resources. The Arabian Shield, an immense area of igneous and metamorphic rock in western Saudi Arabia, had by 1975 yielded the largest and most varied deposits. Four areas within the shield have been identified as having mineral deposits commercially worth exploitation: the Jabal Sayid area (192 miles northeast of Jiddah); the Al Naqrah area (300 miles northeast of Jiddah); the Lamar area (114 miles southwest of Riyadh); and the Wadi Shuwas area (192 miles southeast of Jiddah). All of these areas contain deposits of copper ore variously estimated at between 3 million and 20 million tons. In the Lamar area deposits of zinc and gold have been located as well. As of 1975, however, the qualities of the ores had not been assayed.

Gold is being sought in the Mahd al Dhahab area 360 miles northeast of Jiddah, near the sites of several precious metal mines. Between 1945 and 1954 one of these ancient gold mines was financed by an American company and worked by the Saudi Arabian Mining Syndicate but with little profit.

Sulfur, phosphate, and rare earths have been found in the shield in addition to a major deposit of low-grade (30 to 40 percent) iron ore east of Jiddah. The Wadi Fatima and Jabal Idsas also have iron deposits but in relatively minor amounts.

Salt, gypsum, and marble have been produced in small quantities since 1965. Large quantities of such nonmetallic minerals as barite, fluorite, magnesium, asbestos, talc, high-purity glass sand, rock salt, ceramic clay and, most important, limestone (for cement production) have been found.

French, Japanese, and American geologic teams dominate the effort to explore and produce Saudi Arabia's potential mineral wealth, but there is a major effort to train more Saudis for the field. In 1974 twenty-two Saudi geologists, of whom twelve were on location, worked under the supervision of officials from the Ministry of Petroleum and Mineral Resources.

MAN-MADE FEATURES

Roads

Aware of its critical importance in both economic and political terms, the government has pursued an ambitious policy of road development since 1955. In 1955 there were less than 150 miles of paved roads compared with approximately 6,200 miles of primary and secondary paved roads in 1975. Overall planning of road construction before 1963 was haphazard, and construction was so inferior in quality that several road links had to be rebuilt after a short period of use. Quality has improved consistently since 1963. In 1975 virtually all the major trunk roads connecting major population centers had been completed at a cost of approximately US$455,000 per mile (see fig. 6). There is a systematic maintenance program for 90 percent of the major roads. Traffic has increased by approximately 12 percent a year since 1970 and is expected to increase by 15 percent annually during the implementation of the Five Year Development Plan (1975-80), the second development plan.

Road construction and maintenance are under the jurisdiction of the General Roads Administration of the Ministry of Communications. The roads are designed and their construction supervised by

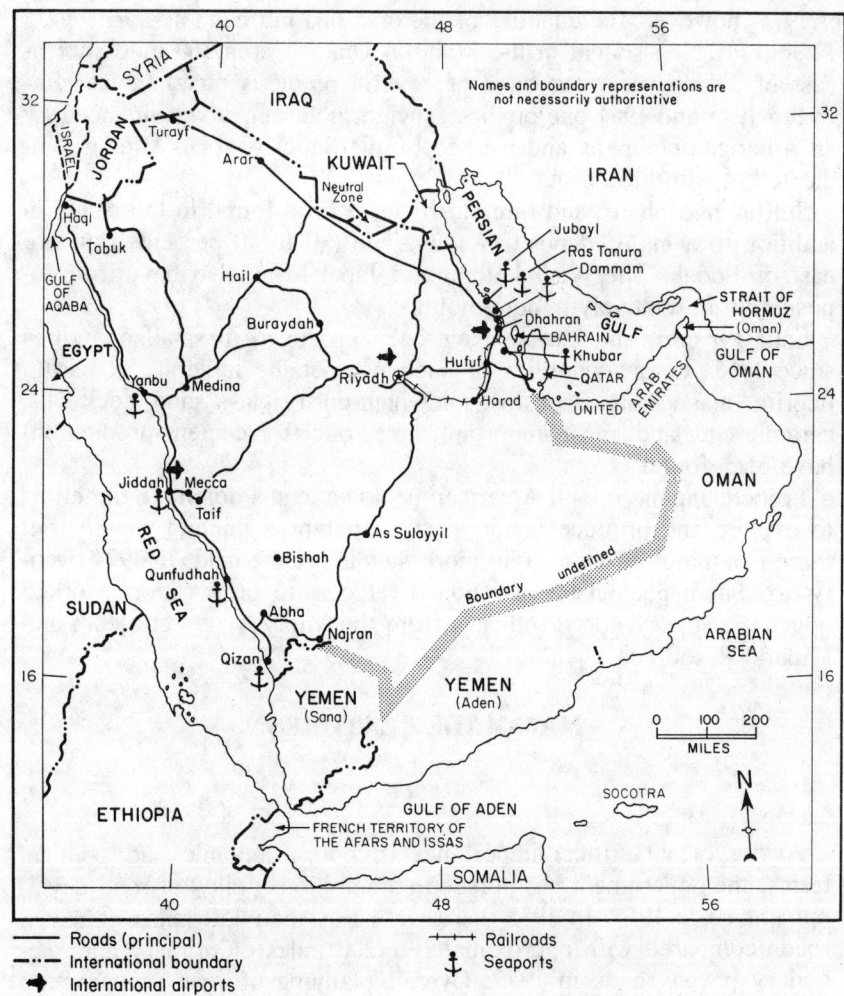

Figure 6. Saudi Arabia, Transportation, 1975

hired consultants; they are constructed by contractors selected by tendering on an international basis. Initially both consultants and contractors were foreign, but by the 1970s a few Saudi firms participated.

Roads are built mainly according to American standards; widths vary from twenty to thirty feet, and the roads are constructed to support loads of sixteen tons. The legal axle load limit is thirteen tons but is not enforced, and consequently road rehabilitation is required well before the usual time. There is a forty-ton maximum limit on road vehicle weight.

The improvement in road networks and in road maintenance has encouraged the importation of motor vehicles. In 1974 the total number of registered motor vehicles was approximately 200,000, and the annual rate of increase in vehicle importation reached 15.5 percent that year. The most spectacular increase has been in the number of passenger cars, approximately one-third of which are used as taxis. In the absence of public mass transportation, taxis and privately owned buses provide important service both in and between cities.

Under the Five Year Development Plan work is to be completed on 36,000 miles of principal roads, 4,500 miles of secondary and tertiary roads, and 7,000 miles of earth-surfaced roads. In addition it is expected that work on 8,000 miles of primary, secondary, and paved tertiary roads will be started. In order to maintain the roads a program of recruitment and training of Saudi citizens is to be undertaken. Expenditures for the entire plan are estimated at US$4 billion.

Railroads

Of the two railroads in the kingdom, only one, the Dammam-Riyadh line, remained in operation in 1976, and its future was questionable. The line extends for 357 miles from the eastern port of Dammam. It passes through Dhahran, Abqaiq, Hufuf, Harad, and Al Kharj to Riyadh and has 100 miles of subsidiary lines. Aramco built the single-track, standard-gauge railroad at the request of Abd al Aziz; at its completion in 1951 it had cost the equivalent of US$52.5 million, which the Saudi government had paid by 1960 in yearly, interest-free installments. Since 1963 the railroad has been owned, operated, and managed by the Saudi Government Railroad Organization. The original purpose of the railroad was to move imported freight from the port to internal distribution centers; the passenger trains run during the day and freight at night. In 1974 the line carried 145,000 passengers for an average journey of 253 miles each and 43.5 million tons of freight for an average haul of thirty-six miles, a figure that is low because some inland depots are less than twelve miles away.

Current revenues from the line were barely meeting operating costs in 1975, and the government was subsidizing it in order to pay for replacements and to offset losses. Observers concluded that the railroad would lose at least half its freight in 1976 when a new pipeline from Khurais to Riyadh became operational and changed the pattern of petroleum transport. In 1975 freight to Riyadh was being refused because of a shortage of freight cars and the long delays caused by difficulty in the initial loading, especially those caused by further loading and unloading in customs. As a result much freight, more suitable for rail carriage, was transported by road from the yard in Dammam to decrease delivery delays. A freight car earned SR200 (for value of the riyal—see Glossary) for a run from the port of Dammam to the city of Dammam, although it could be earning SR690 for the full run to Riyadh with an almost imperceptible difference in operating costs. The Five Year Development Plan has committed itself to the study of the function and performance of the railroad in relation to the national transport system. Several alternative strategies for the line's future have been proposed, the most important of which were that rail and port operations be separated, that freight to Riyadh become the primary objective, and that passenger service be discontinued because fares sufficient to meet costs would be three times that of an express bus service and twice the taxi fare.

The other railroad in existence, defunct by 1976, was the Amman-Medina line; popularly known as the Hejaz Railway, it was constructed by the Turks from 1904 to 1908 to connect Medina with Amman, Jordan, and Damascus, Syria. The line was used primarily to transport pilgrims to Medina. Military sabotage under the leadership of T.E. Lawrence during World War I rendered the line inoperative, but it resumed partial service from 1918 until 1924, when it was finally abandoned. Proposals have occasionally been made to revive the railroad and reestablish the link with Jordan. Plans to rebuild it were actually initiated in 1964 and consultants and contractors chosen. Ultimately the cost was considered exorbitant in relation to the need (Jordan and Saudi Arabia have different rail gauges), and the project was abandoned.

Airports

Air transport development is considered to be second in importance to roads in minimizing the vast distances between population centers. Because the terrain is so inhospitable to ground travel and so expensive to build on, airport development has obvious advantages. Of the twenty airports that were served on a regular schedule in 1975, three were international (Jiddah, Riyadh, and Dhahran). The twenty airports varied in facilities from asphalt and concrete runways to unlighted dirt landing strips. Fifteen of the airports had been or were scheduled to be significantly improved; the five others will probably be abandoned as lacking potential. The Civil Aviation Department in the Ministry of Interior had the responsibility for all activities related to construction, operation, and maintenance.

In 1973 there were approximately 350,000 international and 200,000 domestic passengers. It was estimated that by 1990 international passenger departures would reach a total of 2 million and domestic boardings 4.5 million. Haj passenger and teacher passenger traffic, which was nonscheduled revenue traffic, was expected to grow from 180,000 in 1973 to about 400,000 in 1979. International air freight carried by Saudia (the national Saudi airline) was expected to grow by 23 percent annually through 1979 and by 17 percent and 14 percent annually through 1984 and 1989 respectively.

The Five Year Development Plan includes extensive plans for renovation of existing airports and construction of new ones. Many programs are planned in aviation safety and control and in ground service improvement, particularly the expansion of training activities for Saudi nationals.

Saudia was in 1975 the only carrier authorized to provide domestic service and made a number of international stops as well. Established by the government in 1945, Saudi is a separate corporate entity—an autonomous agency of the Ministry of Communications. Because it is the national airline, some of its services were initiated without a profit motive, and it was not until 1973 that a very slight operating profit was achieved. In 1970 Saudia's operating losses amounted to more than SR77 million. Government subsidies amounted to between SR60 and SR70 million from 1970 to 1972 in addition to government payments of SR20 to SR25 million on long-term debts in 1971 and 1972. In 1975 Saudia was still beset by the operational problems caused by its very rapid growth, but implementation of the objectives entailed for it in the five-year plan, as well as the introduction of wide-bodied jet aircraft in 1975, should make it an international airline of importance by 1980.

Seaports

The four main ports are Jiddah and Yanbu on the Red Sea and Dammam and Ras Tanura on the Persian Gulf. The kingdom relies heavily on importation of foreign goods, and most of these enter through the ports, airfreight shipments being negligible. The demand for port facilities was created by the discovery of oil in the 1930s, and in the mid-1970s Ras Tanura, probably the most important oil facility in the world, continued to be used primarily by oil tankers. Jiddah is the oldest and still the most important commercial port in the kingdom. Centuries before a major port structure (piers with two berths each) was built there in 1947, Jiddah had been the principal entry point for foreign pilgrims.

Dammam is the largest general cargo port on the Persian Gulf and the second largest in the kingdom. Constructed by Aramco and operated by it until 1953, in the mid-1970s it continued to handle virtually all materials imported for the oil industry and most goods destined for use in the eastern and central regions. Both Jiddah and Dammam continued to experience serious congestion problems in 1976 even though modern berths and facilities had been constructed almost continuously since 1965. Improvements begun in 1965 at the Yanbu port eased the situation slightly, particularly because of the incentive of the cancellation of certain duties on cement imports unloaded at Yanbu instead of Jiddah. Of the 3 million tons of cargo passed through the nation's ports in 1973, two-thirds were handled by Jiddah and Dammam alone.

In addition to Ras Tanura and Dammam, two other ports on the Persian Gulf, Jubayl and Khubar, both embryonic in terms of service in 1975, were scheduled for expansion to minimize demands on Dammam. The demand for cargo through Dammam was predicted to grow from 1.3 million tons in 1973 to 7.4 million tons in 1980. Dammam's handling capacity per berth was 160,000 tons a year in 1974, which could be increased to 260,000 tons before 1980 if various improvements were introduced, most important of which was a mechanized handling scheme.

Under the five-year plan the small port of Qizan on the Red Sea will be expanded to include two new berths. In 1973 Qizan handled 40,000 tons of dry cargo, and an increase to 150,000 tons by 1980 was expected. Development plans for Jiddah and Yanbu are understandably more extensive. Jiddah's cargo demand in 1973 was 1.4 million tons. An increase to 6.2 million tons by 1970 and 16.2 million tons by 1990 is anticipated. Twenty-four cargo berths and three berths for passenger ships will be required to meet this increase. In early 1976 only twelve berths were available, and two of the oldest of those were scheduled for removal. Under the five-year plan a total of SR745 million will be invested in the port of Jiddah.

In 1975 experts proposed that Yanbu handle half the 200,000 pilgrims expected to arrive by sea in 1980 and that a third berth be constructed to handle the expected increase in cargo imports from 270,000 tons in 1973 to 310,000 tons in 1980. During the implementation of the five-year plan SR45 million will be invested in Yanbu.

POPULATION

Size and Growth

Population estimates both from international organizations and from official Saudi sources continued to vary widely in the mid-1970s. The first official Saudi estimate, in 1956, was 6,036,400 inhabitants. The first official census was conducted in 1962 and 1963, but the results were officially repudiated. In 1962 and 1963 the Central Statistics Department undertook a comprehensive survey of five major cities: Jiddah, Mecca, Medina, Taif, and Riyadh. Government statisticians using the results of this survey and of later investigations arrived at an estimated population figure of 3.3 million, which the government subsequently found unacceptable. In February 1976 the government released a brief statement on a census conducted between August 19, 1974 and September 16, 1974, showing the total population to have been 7,012,642. The International Bank for Reconstruction and Development (IBRD, commonly known as the World Bank) estimate for 1974 was between 5 and 5.5 million.

In traditional Islamic society the recording of births, or even the celebrating of birthdays, was unimportant and nonexistent. This situation has created problems throughout the nation's history for those involved in census taking in Saudi Arabia. For this reason a general census that would yield social breakdowns of the population is still a difficult task, and without an accurate census estimates are almost impossible to derive. In the mid-1970s the task of government demographers was considerably facilitated by increased recording of births, which had been strongly encouraged by the government during the previous decade.

Author Joseph Kraft reported in an article in *The New Yorker* that during his visit to Saudi Arabia in late 1975 he had been told by a respectable source that the total population was about 5.6 million, of which about 4.3 million were native Saudis. Ramon Knauerhase in his book *The Saudi Arabian Economy* estimated 3.75 to 4 million with "an absolute upper limit of 4.5 million persons in 1974." Still other sources suggest a total 1975 population of about 4.7 million of whom perhaps 1.5 million were foreigners.

For reasons that were not always discernible the Saudi government has been reluctant to use such low population figures publicly. The collection of census data is complicated by the geographical mobility of the beduin, who probably from between one-third and one-half of the population. The lack of clear definition of national boundaries—which in itself complicates data collection—is exacerbated by certain beduin migrations across national frontiers, making their citizenship unclear.

Estimates of annual population growth rates vary between 1.7 and 3 percent. Foreign workers are estimated officially to be approximately 1 million in number, and there may be many more. The majority of these, particularly the non-Saudi Arabs, have a status equivalent to that of permanent resident. Although the government has very tight immigration laws, the "guest workers" may be considered to be part of the permanent population.

Characteristics: Age, Sex, and Ethnic Composition

Official Saudi estimates indicate and annual birthrate of approximately 2.75 percent and a death rate of twenty per 1,000. Although the Saudi birthrate appears to be high by any estimate, this is counterbalanced by an unusually high death rate. The beduin make the most substantive contribution to mortality statistics. Among the migratory beduin infant mortality is estimated at approximately 60 percent. The reported ratio of women to men among the beduin drops sharply after age seventeen; this is largely a function of the high death rate of women in childbirth, but it also reflects the conservative social orientation of much of the male population, which makes them reluctant to give information on the number of women living in their households (see ch. 4; ch. 7).

The increase in medical and sanitary facilities since about 1960 has increased the life expectancy from age thirty in rural areas, as of 1963, to an estimated forty-five for the total population in 1974. The population is probably one of the youngest in the Middle East. In 1970 the Central Planning Organization estimated that almost half the population was under fifteen years of age.

The Saudis are relatively homogeneous ethnically and are primarily from indigenous Arab tribes (see ch. 7). In the Hejaz there is a slight admixture of Turks, nonpeninsular Arabs, and non-Arab Muslims as a result of religious pilgrimages in the eighteenth and nineteenth centuries. The concentrations of non-Saudi Arabs are highest in the cities associated with the pilgrimages: Mecca, Medina, and Jiddah. The populations of these three cities swell considerably during the pilgrimage month, and many travelers remain. Yemeni refugees entered Asir in large numbers after the September 1962 coup d'etat, but significant numbers of them have since dispersed to more urbanized or industrialized centers.

Distribution and Settlement

Because more than half of the country is considered wasteland and less than 1 percent is suitable for settled agriculture, the estimated average population density of five persons per square mile is misleading. Estimates of population density in some oasis settlements exceed 2,000 per square mile. The government has given high priority to developing its physical infrastructure to minimize communication and transportation difficulties among its widely scattered towns and villages.

Population is concentrated in a few major cities and three population belts (see fig. 7). In the west the population is densest on the coastal plain that extends from north of Medina to Taif, Mecca's summer resort; in Asir and Qizan there is an additional small band of

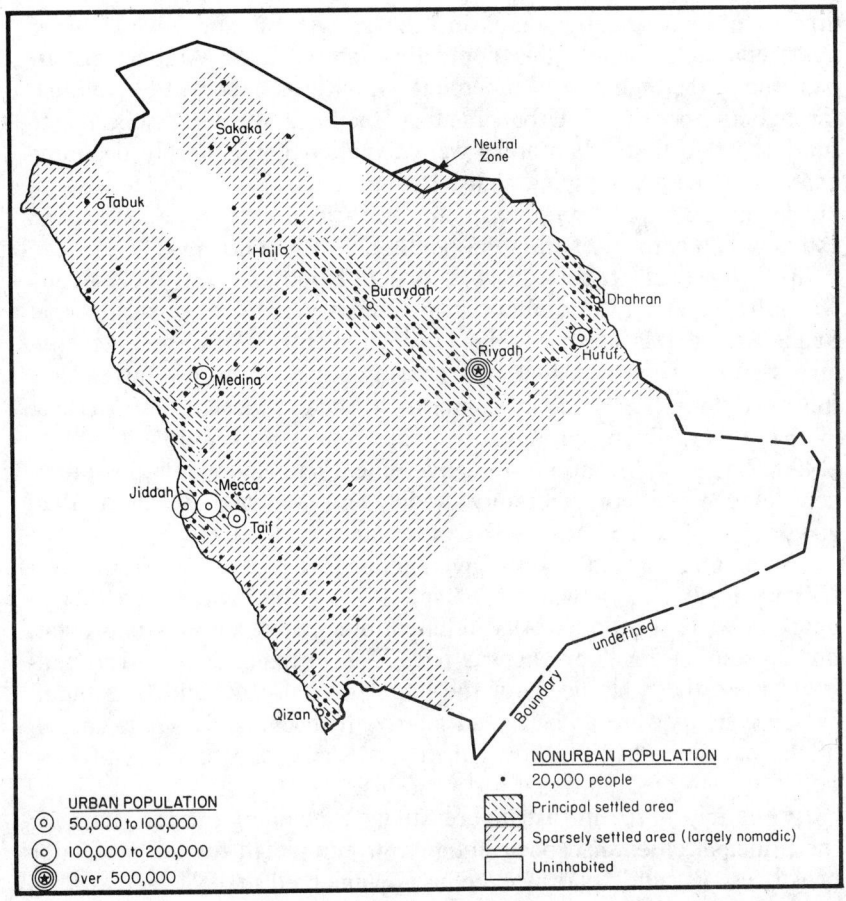

Figure 7. Saudi Arabia, Population Distribution in the Mid-1970s

settled agricultural areas running south to the Yemeni border. This belt includes Jiddah and the Hejaz oases. The second population belt is in the Najd, beginning near Hail and stretching south along the Jabal Tuwaiq past Al Kharj. The cluster of oases in this area has given stimulus to larger settlements, the most important of which is the royal capital of Riyadh. The eastern belt begins on the coast of the Persian Gulf at Ras Tanura and extends south and west to Harad, an important agricultural settlement. The oases of the Eastern Province are included in this area as are the agricultural center of Qatif, the administrative center of Dammam, the commercial center of Khubar, and the Aramco headquarters town of Dhahran.

Urban Centers

In the mid 1970s Saudi Arabia was in the early phase of a major demographic transition because of its late urbanization. The rural to urban shift was greatly increasing the growth of cities, which were not prepared to handle this population influx. Saudi Arabia was urbanizing at the high rate of 6 percent, which was expected to continue throughout the 1970s. Urban medical facilities were far superior to rural ones, so that urban areas were experiencing a sharply declining death rate and a continuing high birthrate, thus contributing to a spectacular urban population growth. In 1974 urban centers comprised an estimated 26 percent of the total population of the country.

In 1976 Riyadh reportedly had a population of over 700,000 and was growing at a rate of about 10 percent a year. This suggested that Saudi Arabia was experiencing the phenomenon of the primate city, an urban disproportion that was causing Riyadh to grow faster than the next three largest cities combined—Jiddah, Mecca, and Medina, in that order. Even approximate population figures were difficult to obtain, however, because of the government's tendency to repudiate or conceal census data. Certainly Jiddah and Mecca have more than 200,000 people each and Medina approximately 150,000.

The number of settlements given municipal status rose from fifty-four to eighty-five between 1970 and 1975. Public parks were developed, flood prevention works initiated, and public utilities improved, but substantial development was needed in virtually every urban center to meet the basic needs of the population already settled in them. Water systems were archaic, and many streets remained unpaved. All of the old cities had outgrown their city walls, and new towns were not built with the traditional fortifications.

By the mid 1970s infrastructure studies, including master plans for the principal cities, had been initiated or completed for the six major provinces. Riyadh's plan was being implemented in 1974, and studies and final designs for Mecca, Medina, Jiddah, and Taif were expected to be implemented in 1976.

Rural Settlements and Villages

In 1974 there were approximately 3,084 villages or settlements of basically three kinds: natural, accidental, and planned. The older villages whose sites were originally determined mainly by the availability of water—or in the mountains by the occurrence of natural defenses offered by the terrain—are natural settlements. In modern times natural settlements that are not helped by government agricultural or water projects may not survive, and whole villages are frequently abandoned for either the city or for accidental or planned settlements.

Accidental settlements are those generated by technological improvements that were not originally intended to promote human habitation. For example, since 1950 seminomadic herders attracted by the water available at pumping stations along the Trans Arabian Pipeline (Tapline) have informally established a number of settlements in northern Arabia. The government does not encourage this kind of settlement because it is basically unproductive. In many cases, however, the beduin prefer these to official settlements because beduin can be more mobile when they are not committed to a specified project. The towns of Arar, Al Qaysumak, and An Nuayriyah have developed as a result of these encampments.

Many planned settlements have been developed, but they vary considerably in terms of success. These settlements are designed with the combined motive of encouraging the beduin to settle permanently and of exploiting areas with agricultural or water resource potential. The expansion of the oases of Hufuf, Harad, and Al Kharj has been very successful in terms of both agricultural production and permanent settlement (see ch. 13).

Beduin Settlement

Estimates of the beduin population vary considerably; non-Saudi estimates are invariably higher than official Saudi figures. Some observers claim the beduin number to be as high as 50 percent of the population, others claim a figure as low as 15 percent. One of the difficulties in estimating, even roughly, how many beduin there are is the lack of a firm definition of what constitutes a beduin—the lack of clear distinctions among seminomadic, fully nomadic, and settled. A further difficulty experienced by the demographer is that certain beduin who may appear to be permanently settled either in projects or in urban squatter towns sometimes abruptly assume a fully nomadic or seminomadic life style (see ch. 7).

Some observers, including Saudis, view the beduin as the principal obstacle to the unity of the state and perceive them as disruptive and unproductive citizens. Actually even those in a fully nomadic state are productive in that they make a significant contribution to the nation's animal protein supply. Most domesticated animals are owned by beduin and live by desert grazing. Nevertheless the beduin tendency toward overstocking and therefore to overgrazing has led to soil erosion and widespread pasture degradation.

Many tribes do not identify themselves with the state, and tribal loyalty remains the principal point of self identification. The government has initiated several kinds of projects intended to suppress tribal identification and to integrate the nomads into the political, social and economic life of the country.

The initial phase of any settlement project is work undertaken by social specialists who are trained in beduin mores. These educators, who spend three months working with the tribes in their summer camps, provides a kind of combined mobile school and medical service. In addition to teaching the children they speak to the men about the concept of the state and how the beduin can contribute to the state's well-being by accustoming themselves to work they have traditionally disdained. They attempt to convince the beduin to settle in one of the government projects, because, to force them to do so would ultimately be counterproductive. Beduin volunteers are sent to centers as close as possible to areas they have habitually frequented, and every attempt is made to keep tribe and family together. The beduin most commonly choose agricultural settlements. This appears to be the kind most congenial to them and is fortunately the one capable of absorbing the greatest number of people. The final objective is to make the agricultural settlements permanent and self-sufficient. The principal areas for the settlements are in the Najd and Hasa, both of which are rich in oases.

Pastoral projects that have been initiated at Wadi Sirhan, Jawf, and Sakaka involved collecting rainwater in dams and reservoirs, digging wells, and constructing silos for forage. Directed by the FAO, shepherds are taught basic irrigation techniques, rudimentary veterinary science, flock maintenance, and the rearing of livestock. Saudis of nonbeduin origin are used as instructors. It is anticipated that such animal products as dairy products, wool, meat, and skins will eventually be produced. Semipermanent fishing settlements have also been encouraged. Many beduin settle around oil industry centers and refineries. In 1974 approximately 10,000 beduin worked for Aramco. Some beduin are assimilated, but many return to the desert when land conditions improve.

The second generation of settled beduin adapt and are assimilated very easily. Highly motivated, some occupy important positions and are an encouragement for other beduin to settle. In spite of all the programs, however, it appears that it will take at least two generations before the beduin abandon their traditional life-style.

* * * * * * * * * * * * *

Ramon Knauerhase's *The Saudi Arabian Economy* contains a wealth of information on the topics presented in this chapter and on their political implications. The *Aramco Handbook* is also excellent as a general guide. For a more detailed account of the geography of the region, W.B. Fisher's *The Middle East: A Physical, Social, and Regional Geography* is unsurpassed. (For further information see Bibliography.)

CHAPTER 4

LIVING CONDITIONS

Saudi Arabia in many ways remained an underdeveloped country, but the standard of living had been substantially improved for the majority of the population during the country's first Five Year Development Plan (1970-75). Employment or paid training programs were available to all who wished to work, and welfare programs were generous for those who could not. Greater importation of food and its subsidy by the government ensured that the Saudis were among the best fed of all Middle Eastern nations.

Extensive programs planned to improve living conditions were frequently frustrated, however, by an underdeveloped physical infrastructure and the same problems encountered in expanding other segments of the economy: a shortage of skilled manpower and a small human resource pool made more critical because only a minuscule number of women worked; a lack of knowledge of managerial and organizational techniques; and severe port congestion that reduced to a trickle the movement of necessary supplies and construction materials into the country (see ch. 11). The sharp inflation of prices in the mid-1970s engendered the most distress for the Saudis in need of housing. In early 1976 land in the country's capital, Riyadh, was more expensive than land in Manhattan, and less than 50 percent of the needed dwellings existed. Housing was the principal social welfare problem in the country.

Although underpopulation caused severe problems to economic development, it was helpful in other ways. Virtually all citizens had access to a variety of health services, all of which were free. Further, public health projects were able to eradicate smallpox and cholera and had almost eliminated malaria.

STANDARDS OF LIVING

Nutrition and Diet

A dramatic increase in imported foodstuffs has substantially improved the diet of most Saudis. In 1975 two-thirds of the total food supply was imported, and much of the imported food was subsidized by the government. The average Saudi diet in 1975 contained about 2,500 calories per day, an increase of 300 calories since 1972, and by 1978 it was expected to reach 2,800 calories per day. During the early 1970s Saudi Arabia experienced food shortages at various times, particularly during the drought in adjacent countries in the 1972-74 period, which killed many animals destined for markets in Saudi Arabia. By 1975, however, Australia had become the major source of live animal imports, and future meat imports appeared secure. Although imported tinned and dried meats were also available and were slowly becoming more popular, they were distrusted by the native population, who feared that religious proscriptions regarding the manner of slaughtering animals might not have been observed.

Camels, sheep, and goats are raised domestically for meat, but local forage conditions limit their numbers. In 1975 some beef was produced at experimental cattle farms (see ch. 13). The Saudis did not appear to enjoy beef very much, but this may reflect their uncertainty about how to prepare it for consumption. Saudi beef was neither grain fed nor aged and therefore was extremely tough and stringy.

Saudis enjoy chicken, and poultry farms established in the 1960s and 1970s have made it available throughout the kingdom. Vegetables, melons, and dates grown on experimental farms have increased local supplies in the interior. Although rice is grown in the kingdom, Saudis prefer the long-grained Basmati rice imported from Pakistan, which is as cheap as domestic rice because of government subsidies. Fish, once available only along the coasts, is available in large towns of the interior and, although not a preferred food, is slowly becoming more popular. City inhabitants enjoy a wider variety and choice of foods than rural dwellers, but even rural dwellers appear to have a quantity and variety sufficient to ensure a balanced diet.

Breakfast for most Saudis is a light meal consisting of heavily sweetened and often spiced tea, a small piece of bread, and sometimes cheese, yogurt, or eggs. Lunch, usually taken in early afternoon, is a very heavy meal. Mealtimes for the employed may change, however, as a result of a government experiment begun in late 1975 to have a working day unbroken by a four-hour lunch period; civil servants finished their work at 2:30 P.M. and thus ate their main meal much later than was usual.

People of means almost always serve more than one meat, and lamb is the most popular. Although typical Middle Eastern dishes involving such ground or diced meats as kibbe are eaten, most Saudis prefer a whole animal stuffed and roasted or boiled and heavily but piquantly spiced. On special festive occasions baby camels are eaten. Rice and bread are consumed in quantity, and the main purpose of cooked vegetables, although they are gaining favor, is to sauce the dish. A fresh salad usually accompanies the meal. Fruit is the preferred dessert, but such traditional Middle Eastern highly sweetened pastries as baklava and *konifa* are becoming more common. Beverages are not consumed during the meal, but tea or coffee or both are taken afterward. Dinner, eaten late in the evening, is a lighter version of lunch.

Although the intake of animal protein by rural dwellers was slightly lower than that of townsmen, in all parts of the kingdom there was a higher consumption of meat and vegetables than in the past. Completely nomadic beduin, in spite of having greater access to markets, appeared in 1976 to be consuming their traditional diet of dairy products, breads, and dates, supplemented whenever possible by meat and fruits other than dates. The favorite beduin dish is *kuzee*, a whole stuffed lamb served on a bed of rice. Beduin and those of beduin origin consider camel's milk the beverage best for one's health. Lighter and slightly sweeter than cow's milk, it supplies an important part of the daily protein intake. Babies profit from the Islamic injunction that they be breast-fed for at least one year and ideally for two.

The value Saudis derive from the meat that is available is greater than it would be in the West because virtually the whole animal is consumed. The marrow sucked from large bones and cartilage on bones and from the nose and ears of sheep supply calcium. Gristle and fat are considered quite delectable. The consumption of pork is forbidden to Muslims, as is the flesh of any animal dead of natural causes and of all carrion-eating animals.

Most Saudis have little idea of nutrition or of the concept of a balanced diet. Many projects included in the second Five Year Development Plan (1975-80) were designed to introduce such subjects to the population. Most observers agreed, however, that the Saudi citizen of 1976 was generally well fed and suffered only minimally from diseases caused by vitamin deficiencies. This situation was noteworthy considering that only a decade earlier chronic food shortage was a serious problem and the diet of the population inadequate by Western standards in vitamins, proteins, and total caloric intake. The new abundance had its drawbacks, however; carbonated sodas, sweetened chewing gum, and other empty calorie foods were widely available. Dental health, previously very good because of the absence of such foods and the inability to purchase quantities of sugar, was gradually deteriorating.

Clothing

The usual mode of dress for all men and boys is the *thaub*, a long sleeved, high-necked, A line garment. Usually the *thaub* is made of white cotton, but ones made of khaki-colored synthetics and wool are also worn during the winter months. The *bisht*, a long outer cloak of white, brown, or black depending upon the season, is worn over the *thaub*. The black *bisht*, worn mostly in winter, is made of wool manufactured in Hufuf. Both the *thaub* and the *bisht* are tailored locally. The traditional head covering for men is the square white silk *hujra* or *shma*, usually held in place by doubling the black cordless agal. (Only the first three kings of Saudi Arabia wore agals threaded with gold.) The square cotton checkered kaffiyeh is worn, usually in red and white, because black and white is the headgear pattern of the religious police (see ch. 6). Sandals or Western footwear are worn, depending upon personal taste and the weather conditions.

Where traditional dress would be cumbersome or dangerous, particularly in industrial settings, Western clothes are worn. Saudis do not consider it chic or becoming to wear Western dress, and the politically astute civil servant invariably wears the *thaub*. Shaykh Ahmad Zaki Yamani, for instance, always wears traditional dress in public, although he often wears Western casual clothes at home.

Women wear embroidered long dresses clasped at the waist by a *hazam*, a metal belt made of tin, silver, or gold, depending upon the wealth of the family. The *abayah*, an opaque black voluminous cloak with batlike dolman sleeves, is worn over the dress and completely covers the wearer from the head to the toes. Full face veils are always worn in public and at home in the presence of any man who is not a close relative. The kind of veil varies according to locality and family custom. A double thickness of black silk quite difficult to see through is most common. The burqa, a veil with eye cuts, is also worn, as is a leather mask that is extremely uncomfortable.

There are some tribal women who are not used to veiling, but most wear a veil when in settled areas. An immodest public appearance is immediately censured by the religious police. Rich women, particularly if they are young, may wear Western designer clothes under their cloaks, but the *abayah* ensures complete anonymity. Whereas men's clothing appears to be well suited to the climate, the light-absorbing *abayah*, increasingly made of synthetics, is not. Girls wear Western-style uniforms in school but after the age of nine usually wear the *abayah* and veil in public.

Housing

In 1976 inadequate and insufficient housing was the most serious social problem experienced by the citizens. A major shift from the country to cities had caused severe overcrowding in most urban areas, particularly in Riyadh, which was reported to have a population of over 700,000 in early 1976. During the period between 1970 and 1975 approximately 75,000 standard or better than standard urban dwellings were constructed compared with an estimated need for new houses and replacements of 154,000 units. Further, thousands of people were faced with the eventual loss of their meager investments in shanties whose locations did not conform to urban growth patterns.

Although government housing for the poor was in various stages of planning or completion housing difficulties for all economic groups were increased in 1976 by inflated costs of construction labor and materials. Land speculation, particularly for desirable areas near the center of Riyadh, had prompted many people of middle incomes to build around the outermost perimeter of town, where such amenities as sewage lines, electricity, and water supply were extremely sketchy. Houses and apartments tended to be hastily assembled, and tenants were frustrated by collapsing plumbing lines and by improper wiring that caused shocks and failures when an appliance was plugged in. (An unstandardized electrical system was strained further when the government subsidized electricity rates by 60 percent, thus increasing the demand.)

The ability to finance the construction of houses became the preserve of the few. In the absence of available mortgages houses were paid for out of savings or income. The government, aware of the critical nature of the housing problem, had a multitude of projects planned for execution between 1975 and 1980, but observers concluded that considerably more than five years would pass before housing became even minimally adequate.

New houses are commodious to provide sufficient space for extended-family living. Generally two storied and built after Western models, they incorporate features of traditional Middle Eastern housing. In homes of the middle or upper economic classes there are two living rooms, one where strangers may be entertained without inconveniencing the women of the house and one that serves as the *haram* (see Glossary), for family and visiting women friends. Although the center courtyard of traditional Middle Eastern housing has been abandoned as too expensive and space consuming, houses are surrounded by high walls to protect the privacy of the family and to enable the women of the house to take fresh air without endangering their modesty. Most middle-income and upper income housing is designed with central air conditioning, and many traditional homes are being renovated to accommodate air-conditioning units. Saudis are becoming increasingly dependent on such appliances and view life as a hardship without them. Families with moderate incomes are easily able to afford air conditioning and, because electricity is subsidized, use is quite inexpensive.

Around principal cities there are tent communities and shantytowns that are constructed of tin, packing crates, and cardboard; the cardboard houses are covered with polyethylene in inclement weather. Although the houses are an embarrassment to the government, observers point out that many of the beduin who settle there find them quite comfortable compared with their previous situations. In such old urban settlements as Mecca and Medina the houses are frequently of mud brick and are clustered irregularly along winding, narrow streets. Such an arrangement does not facilitate vehicle traffic but is well suited to the climate, because it both cuts off the biting winter winds and shelters the streets and fronts of the buildings from the sun.

In the villages the construction materials and designs for housing vary considerably from one region to another. In parts of Asir where African influence is most apparent the people use reeds for the construction of huts resembling beehives. In mountainous regions houses are built of both cut and uncut stone. In desert areas most houses and walls are of bricks made of mud mixed with straw and palm; available woods are used for beams and doors, which are often intricately decorated. The house of the average poor family is a one or two storied structure of two rooms, one of which may also house family livestock.

Consumption Patterns

In the past, Saudis possessed few material goods and attached relatively little importance to them. Oil wealth has engendered conspicuous consumption of those things that can be bought, but to a certain extent Saudis are detached from material possessions. Nonetheless gold and jewelry—traditionally valued by Arabs as investments—are bought in staggering quantities. Although many domestic interiors are kept very simple—low cushions, tables, and rugs being the only furniture—many upwardly mobile Saudis are accumulating Western furniture, particularly in the gilded Louis XV style popular in other parts of the Middle East. The development of a domestic aesthetic is slow, however, and most houses, even of the well-to-do, lack wall decorations and other embellishments.

Radios, television sets, stereo systems, and audiocassette players are considered highly desirable and are the principal means of passive entertainment given the absence of public cinemas, nightclubs, and even restaurants. Laborsaving devices are imported and are in high demand among the wealthy but generally out of the reach of all but the well-to-do. Importing and consuming alcohol are forbidden by law, and the few Saudis who do drink smuggled liquor do so discreetly. The smoking of tobacco, once forbidden by law, seems to be increasing by those who can afford it, but some social disapproval is attached to it, particularly by the older generation.

Cost of Living

The cost of living had increased almost geometrically in the early 1970s, an increase precipitated by an infusion of cash into an underdeveloped economy. Observers placed inflation in 1973 at 20 percent and in 1974 and 1975 at anything from 28 to 40 percent. The government hoped eventually to supply all basic human needs free or at nominal prices, leaving a high level of disposable income for those things regarded in most of the world as luxuries. In 1974 public employees received wage and salary increments ranging from 30 percent for the lowest paid to 15 to 28 percent for the medium to high brackets. In November 1975 there was an across-the-board increase of 12 percent.

In addition to keeping salaries level with inflation, the government aimed at reducing state-imposed increases in the cost of living: the road tax was abolished, the excise on petroleum products was eliminated, customs tariffs were reduced, and the import surcharge was eliminated. The list of subsidized goods—flour, rice, and sugar—was extended to include imported lamb carcasses, milk and dairy products, vegetable oils, and medicines. In fiscal year (FY) 1974 these goods cost the state approximately SR800 million (for value of the riyal—see Glossary).

In July 1974 the Real Estate Development Fund was established to finance up to 70 percent of the cost of houses constructed for personal use, plus a 20-percent rebate on their building costs, and to finance 50 percent of the cost of houses built for investment. In late 1975 the government froze rents and gave security of tenure to renters. Loopholes in the bill, however, enabled unscrupulous landlords to evict hundreds of tenants.

Patterns of Living and Leisure

Saudi Arabia uses the lunar Islamic calendar initiated in the late seventh century A.D. by Umar ibn al Khattab, the second caliph. The first year was that of the Prophet's flight—the hijra from Mecca to Medina in A.D. 622. Muslim dates are followed by the notation A.H. (anno hegirae). The year has 354 days in twelve lunar months, a month being the time between two new moons, approximately twenty-nine and one-half days. Months alternately contain twenty-nine and thirty days and, to adjust for a slight overlap, an additional day is added eleven times every cycle of thirty years, making eleven leap years of 355 days for every nineteen normal years. Months thus have no fixed relation to the season but make a complete circuit every thirty-three Gregorian years (see table A). The months are: Muharram, Safar, Rabi al Awwal (Rabi I), Rabi ath Thani (Rabi II), Jumada al Ula (Jumada I), Jumada al Akhirah or ath Thanayah (Jumada II), Rajab, Shaban, Ramadan, Shawwal, Dhu al Qadah, and Dhu al Hijjah.

Each day is reckoned to begin at sunset. For example, what would be Sunday night in the West is considered Monday evening. Friday is the sabbath, and people usually work Saturday through Wednesday. There are three official national holidays, two of them religious and one secular. The Feast of the Breaking of the Fast (Id al Fitr, the little feast) takes place during the first three days of Shawwal, after Ramadan, the fasting month (see ch. 6). Fasting is a religious obligation, and much hardship is endured when Ramadan occurs during the hot months. Abstinence from food, water, smoking, and sexual contact for all but a few specifically exempted or excused is expected from that time in the morning when a white thread can be distinguished from a black one to that time after sunset when it cannot. During Ramadan the usual patterns of living are suspended. Ramadan "breakfasts" are occasions for feasting far into the night with family and friends. Those who can, sleep as late in the day as possible.

The second religious holiday, the Feast of the Sacrifice (Id al Adha, the great feast), begins the tenth day of Dhu al Hijjah, the haj month, and lasts four days. The holiday commemorated Abraham's obedience to God in his willingness to sacrifice Ishmael, his son by Hagar (see ch. 6). The only secular holiday is National Day, which commemorates the unification of the country—by King Abd al Aziz—under the name of the Kingdom Saudi Arabia in September 1932. That is the only day not determined by the Islamic calendar. The date for the holiday is the first day of the month of Libra in the solar zodiacal calendar. Usually it falls close to September 23. Solar calendars are used only by farmers who must make exact calculations about the seasons.

In Saudi Arabia work does not have the intrinsically high value placed upon it by Western societies. Most work activities whether in the home or on the job are taken at a leisurely pace. Any quickness of activity is perceived as haste and certain to cause carelessness and, because "haste comes from the devil," is studiously avoided. In the absence of public entertainment most leisure activities are centered in the home. Domestic duties consume most of the day even for a woman with servants. Spare time activities for such women include gardening, watching films or television at home or at the homes of friends and, perhaps most preferred of all, visiting with other women. Men's leisure activities, although larger in scope, are similar to those of women. There is a small café society in Saudi Arabia, but meeting in cafés is largely the amusement of Palestinians and Syrians. Enormous amounts of money are spent by Saudis on touring other countries. For both sexes amusements abroad are richer than those available at home, and women particularly enjoy the freedom to shop unconfined by the veil or *abayah*.

Some older Saudi men, particularly those of recent beduin origin, including the present king, continued to take delight in the classic Arabian exercises of horseback riding, hawking and, when they had access to water, swimming. Sports of Western origin were for the most part the province of the younger generation.

The government was anxious to encourage this interest in sports and in 1973 created a directorate general within the Ministry of Labor and Social Affairs, the Supreme Council for Youth Welfare, to oversee sports and cultural affairs. The country sent a track-and-field team to the Munich Olympic Games in 1972 and in 1973 and 1974 participated in other international events including soccer tournaments in Tunisia, Egypt, and Kuwait; swimming competitions in Egypt and Kuwait; track events in Morocco and Algeria; and a weapons competition in Lebanon. In 1975 fifty-three sports clubs were subsidized by the government, and nine national societies were recognized for soccer, basketball, volleyball, bicycling, handball, table tennis, swimming, weaponry, and track and field. In the years 1975 to 1980 the government planned to expand sport facilities significantly and to encourage such extracurricular cultural activities in school as acting and painting. The government also was attempting to stimulate public service among the young by setting up associations similar to American 4-H clubs. The country desperately needed manpower, and it was felt that participation in such volunteer activities as helping to eradicate illiteracy, repairing mosques, filling in swamps, and fencing land would have a wholesome effect on the youth of the country.

PUBLIC HEALTH

Sanitation and Water Supply

Although considerable progress was made between 1970 and 1975, safe water supplies and sewage networks in urban centers remained sufficiently unsatisfactory to be considered a major health hazard. The sewage network built by the Arabian American Oil Company (Aramco) in Khubar and Damman was perhaps the best in the kingdom in the mid-1970s, although even it was being severely taxed by unexpected demand. The system in Jiddah may have been one of the worst, having capacities seriously below the level needed. Cesspools and septic fields are the most common means of waste disposal; although the government has begun construction of water-flushed sewage pipelines, most sewage is untreated. Water supplies were erratic in all parts of the country. Many new houses have piped-in water, but even in those houses water meters to measure and therefore regulate use are absent. In 1974 many people, particularly those living in the older sections of towns, obtained water from public faucets or had tanks deliver water to their houses. In rural areas people remained very dependent on wells and the springs of oases for their water supplies, which were frequently brackish or contaminated. Wells near pumping stations along the Trans Arabian Pipeline (Tapline) have become an important new source of relatively clean water for the beduin (see ch. 3).

Plans to improve both sewerage and water supplies were extensive. Their implementation would require foreign contracting and large numbers of foreign workers, to which not all members of the government were completely reconciled (see ch. 7; ch. 11).

Incidence and Treatment of Disease

Morbidity statistics and data on which to base estimates of the incidence of disease continued to be conspicuously absent from the public record in Saudi Arabia in early 1976. In addition to observations reported by reliable nongovernmental sources, the extent of unhealthiness may be gauged from one of the objectives listed in the Five Year Development Plan: "Introducing a network of Mother and Child Care Clinics with the aim of reducing the infant mortality rate to no more than 110 per 1,000 births and improving mother and child care generally."

Saudis lacked knowledge about the disease characteristics of their country, and there was widespread ignorance of basic hygienic practices and home health care. Flies proliferate, and certain Islamic ritual hygienic practices, such as washing parts of the body before prayer, may actually spread disease when infected mosque pools are used for ritual washing.

As recently as the mid-1950s most Saudis believed in the supernatural origin of disease. By the mid-1970s the majority of Saudis appear to have accepted the germ theory of disease causation enthusiastically, primarily because of the vigorous efforts of Aramco and government agencies. Since disease has been removed from the realm of the supernatural to that of the empirical, Saudis have tended to reason that all medical problems, however slight, have a cure. This occasionally caused ill will when a physician did not immediately produce a remedy. Hypochondriasis was common and, where physicians were available, they were troubled incessantly by patients with minor complaints. Saudis were gradually becoming accustomed to the treatment of women by male physicians. Gynecological examinations provoked no resistance among Saudi women, contrary to what might be expected, because the entire experience was so totally out of the range of the normal.

The belief in the supernatural origin of disease from the evil influence of jinn has not entirely disappeared, however. Among the Shia of the Eastern Province, blue beads of ward off the evil eye were universal. In other parts of the country amulets were sporadically encountered. Moreover, when modern medicine proves ineffective, even the most sophisticated and educated townsman may consult a *harma*, a woman with knowledge of healing magic. The touching of various parts of the body with a stick heated in fire was considered particularly efficacious for fever. Many of the traditional remedies, such as mercury for venereal disease, senna as a purgative, and copper sulfate crystals for trachoma, are of real therapeutic value.

Malaria

Malaria, transmitted by the bite of the anopheles mosquito and characterized by periodic attacks of chills and fever, was previously endemic throughout large areas of the country. In 1955 there appeared to be a 100-percent incidence in certain areas. Concerted efforts by the World Health Organization (WHO), Aramco, and the Saudi government had by 1975 isolated malaria to only periodic outbreaks in the Asir Valley, parts of the Tihamah Lowlands, and the Qatif, Jabrin and Khubar oases. Inadequately planned irrigation and agricultural projects, however, frequently provided new areas for infestation. Antimalarial teams were encountering increased immunity of the Saudi *Anopheles stephensi* and *Anopheles pharaoensis* to both dichloro-diphenyl-trichloro-ethane (DDT) and dieldrin. In 1976 ten malaria control stations existed, and eleven were planned.

Trachoma

Trachoma, a highly infectious eye disease, was endemic throughout the country. A chronic contagious conjunctivitis marked by inflammatory granulations on the eyelid surface, trachoma produces photophobia, pain, and excessive tearing. It was estimated that 70 percent of the population suffered to some degree from the disease, thought to be carried by flies. Trachoma is easily cured if treatment is begun early, and basic hygiene substantially decreases its incidence. Aramco's trachoma research center at Dhahran has been influential in educating the local population to identify and seek treatment for the disease.

Respiratory Diseases

Tuberculosis was widespread and among the most serious disease problems in the country. An antituberculosis immunization campaign was being carried out in 1976 throughout the kingdom, including an X-ray and tuberculin test program for the entire population. Although detection and treatment improved during the first plan period, incidence rates have increased slightly with the population's rural to urban shift. The most concentrated areas of infection were the shantytowns rapidly developing around major urban centers. Pulmonary tuberculosis is the predominant form among settled and coastal peoples, and visceral kinds and nonpulmonary lesions are most common among the beduin.

Insanitary conditions, crowded living quarters, insufficient diet, and inadequate sheltering contribute to lowering resistance to the disease. In 1976 the kingdom possessed two tuberculosis clinics and twelve chest disease dispensaries. During the implementation of the five-year plan the number of tuberculosis clinics will be increased to eight and of chest disease dispensaries to ten. This number of facilities, however, appears to be inadequate considering the prevalence of the disease, which seems likely to increase until living conditions are substantially improved. Aramco, which provided beds in company hospitals for treatment of the disease in Eastern Province, reported only seven cases in a total patient population of 80,000 in 1975, thus demonstrating the efficacy of its tuberculosis program in that one locality.

Enteric Diseases

Amoebic and bacillary dysentery and other intestinal disorders remained prevalent. The inadequacy of sanitary facilities, the abundance of flies, and casual food and meat preparation contributed substantially to the problem. The effects of diarrhea and gastroenteritis were most severe among infants and children, and almost half of the infant mortality rate was attributed to intestinal ailments, which caused rapid dehydration and electrolyte imbalance. Rehydration facilities were available at the four mother and child welfare clinics that existed in 1976 and at some other medical facilities. Twenty mother and child clinics that were expected to be completed by 1980 should improve the situation.

Parasitic diseases, seldom fatal but always debilitating, may afflict as much as 50 percent of the population. Bilharziasis, also called schistosomiasis, was the most serious parasitic disease to affect the country. Formerly thought to occur only in Asir, it had been identified in other areas, and in 1975 eight control stations were opened, one each in Riyadh, Arar, Abha, Najran, Asir, Jayzan, Mecca, and Medina. It did not, however, occur east of the Arabian Shield (see ch. 3).

The disease is caused by a blood fluke whose intermediary host is a snail. It is contracted by wading or bathing in an area where the snails have had contact with human excrement. Drugs potent enough to destroy the fluke in a human host are extremely debilitating, and the treatment is long term. The chance of reinfection is high, however, unless the snails are destroyed. Because alluvial poisons are nonselective and pollutive, the government has been induced to experiment with biological controls.

Roundworms infected as much as 15 percent of the population. They thrive in agricultural areas, where their eggs are spread through irrigation canals.

Venereal Diseases

Congenital and contracted syphilis and gonorrhea, formerly found only in coastal towns, were quite common everywhere by the 1970s. Bejel (*bajlah* in colloquial Arabic), an attenuated nonvenereal form of syphilis, has long been endemic in the Arabian Peninsula. Caused by a spirochete closely related to that which transmits yaws, bejel may be contracted through the habit of eating with the fingers from shared dishes. In other cases flies that alight on food are the vectors. The initial lesion usually occurs in the lower gums.

Although bejel sufferers test positive for syphilis, it was understood that transmission of the disease was nonsexual, and it evoked no stigma, whereas syphilis and gonorrhea were regarded with great social horror. Although condoms were available and might be utilized in extramaritial relations, the infrequency of their use in the home and the reluctance of many women to consult physicians made prevention, early detection, and cure of venereal disease quite difficult and thus increased the incidence of congenital syphilis. The government has established the Venereal Disease Control Demonstration Center at Mecca and diagnostic laboratories throughout the country. Sex education studies did not form part of the high school curriculum.

Other Diseases

In the mid-1970s a mild form of sickle-cell anemia was found to exist in the country. Smallpox, cholera, and the plague—the traditional killers often associated with the haj—have been completely eradicated. Relapsing fever, a variable acute epidemic disease marked by recurring high fever lasting five to seven days and transmitted by the bites of lice and ticks, remained a problem throughout the country in the mid-1970s, as did dengue fever, an infectious virulent epidemic disease transmitted by mosquitoes and characterized by fever, rash, and severe joint pain. Additionally Saudi Arabia appeared to have the highest rate of esophageal cancer in the world.

Birth Control

Birth control devices were available from pharmacies, but their use was officially forbidden by the government, which has a strong interest in increasing the population and which issued the decree after the 1974 census. Large families continued to be considered highly desirable. The rhythm method appeared to be the most frequently used birth control method and the only one officially endorsed by the Islamic religious leaders in Saudi Arabia. Judging from the severity with which the religious leaders of Al Azhar University (the renowned school of Islamic jurisprudence), in Egypt attacked the practice as universal in all Arab states, *azl* (coitus interruptus) also appeared to be practiced. *Azl* is strictly prohibited by Islamic law as being unnatural and psychologically unsettling. Abortion is a major crime in Islamic law, and there was no evidence of its practice in Saudi Arabia.

Government Medical Facilities

Services relating to human health and nutrition are offered to the population through a number of government channels, the most significant of which is the Ministry of Health. In 1974 the Ministry oversaw sixty-two hospitals with a total of 7,734 permanent beds, 215 dispensaries, 372 health centers, and 3,934 nurses. The health programs operated by other government agencies employed an additional 517 doctors and 1,464 nursing and technical staff, many of whom were working in mobile health units for the beduin.

Progress in health services has been uneven and hampered by a number of factors, the most critical of which continued to be the lack or skilled manpower at all levels. In the mid 1970s organization and management difficulties also existed because of both the lack of skilled manpower and the lack of integration of the preventive, curative, and educational components of the health system. There was insufficient information and research on the health characteristics of the country and on the appropriate form and size of an effective health system. There was a low level of enrollment and output in the country's training schools: in the 1970-74 period only 152 female nurses and 357 technical assistants graduated from the nursing schools and health institutes.

In 1976 many of the physicians and virtually all of the female nurses were foreign, and this situation was unlikely to change for many years. The country will have two fully functional medical colleges by 1979, one at the University of Riyadh and the other at King Abd al Aziz University. In 1976 King Abd al Aziz University had 258 male and thirty female medical students. It was hoped that this number would be raised to 597 men and 214 women by 1976. Saudi female physicians generally trained for pediatrics, gynecology, and obstetrics and in those fields were not subject to the strong social opprobrium affecting nurses who treated male patients.

As of 1976 the government's most impressive medical service was the King Faisal Specialist Hospital and Research Center in Riyadh, regarded by many physicians as the most complete and sophisticated medical center in the world. Contrary to popular opinion, the center treated all Saudi citizens regardless of social background. The medical technology system was designed to free hospital staff from as much routine administrative and test procedure as possible in order to give them maximum time for patient care. The center had fourteen computer systems, the most important of which was the hub of the medical information storage and distribution network. Other systems performed chemical tests in minutes that would take hours to perform manually; controlled radiotherapy and nuclear medicine procedures; monitored intensive care patients; scheduled patients; and plotted the most efficient deployment of staff, sounding an alarm the moment a maldistribution developed.

Such technological exploitation minimized human error and enabled the center to overcome some of the severe restrictions otherwise imposed by the shortage of medical staff. In every department equipment was the most advanced available in the world, in some cases designed specifically for the center. Some of the technology under development has influenced work in the United States, Great Britain, and France, an extraordinary circumstance for a country that has had secondary education for only twenty years.

Private Facilities

Aramco was the principal nongovernmental source of medical facilities. In 1976 Aramco had a 110-bed hospital and had plans to add 150 more beds. In addition it maintained smaller clinics throughout the Eastern Province. Aramco's medical facilities were designed to operate at no cost to employees and their dependents, a population of 80,000 in early 1976. Aramco's medical teams provided health education, well baby clinics, vermin control, and sanitation inspection and operated research centers for indigenous diseases. The importance of Aramco's medical service as a model for both action and procedure cannot be overemphasized.

In 1976 six small private hospitals existed, mostly to serve foreign residents: five in Jiddah and one in Khubar. The government wished to encourage additional private medical facilities and was prepared to lend 50 percent of establishment expenses.

Saudi Red Crescent Society

The Saudi Red Crescent Society was formed in 1962, modeled after the International Red Cross and Red Crescent associations. The society provided first-aid, ambulance, and emergency medical services—principally during the haj season and on highways where traffic accidents were numerous. Through a general center in Riyadh the society operated a first-aid training institute, three branch offices, eight health centers, twenty-seven round-the-clock first aid centers, and 120 ambulances.

Operating funds came primarily from the government budget and were supplemented by contributions from private individuals and *awqaf* (sing., *waqf*—see Glossary). Policy was formulated by the Board of Directors, which included the deputy ministers of finance and national economy, interior, and labor and social affairs, among others. In 1976 the society was beset with problems relating to insufficient skilled manpower, outmoded equipment, and inadequate emergency supplies.

During the period of the Five Year Development Plan (1975-80) a study of the society's operations was to be undertaken to improve its efficiency. Planned were thirty new first-aid centers for emergency treatment of accident victims, five new clinics in the haj area, a mobile hospital unit, and a radio network. A public relations office was to be established to publicize the society's work and needs and to attract and recruit more technical and administrative employees. Volunteer first aid workers were urgently needed, particularly during the haj season. The society hoped to organize training programs for youth groups and to establish Red Crescent societies among them.

Health and Living Conditions Among the Hajis

The haj to Mecca and Medina is the largest regular gathering of human beings in the world and one of the most varied considering the pilgrims' nationalities, languages, cultural habits, ages, and professions (see ch. 6). As such it poses a yearly challenge to health authorities and administrators responsible for the visitors' living conditions. In 1975 a total of 894,573 non-Saudi Muslims made the haj; the average number for the previous decade was 1 million a year. Approximately 500,000 Saudis also make the haj annually.

During the 1975 Haj 138 pilgrims were killed and 151 injured when fire broke out in one of the tent camps at Mina. Despite the concerted and continuing efforts of government agencies to improve conditions for the pilgrims, fatalities are not surprising considering that many pilgrims are elderly and that the religious rites, exhausting to perform at any age, are made especially enervating by religious enthusiasm, the heat, and overcrowded conditions.

The special High Committee for the Haj, headed by the governor of Mecca, coordinates the activities of the many agencies concerned with providing services to the hajis. The Ministry of Pilgrimage Affairs and Awqaf supervises the daily administration of the haj in Jiddah and the holy cities, but virtually every government agency is involved. The consulates of the Ministry of Foreign Affairs work around the clock to process visa applications. Agencies within the ministries of communications, interior, health, and information as well as such private organizations as the Saudi Red Crescent Society devote a full month to haj affairs.

The overriding concern of the administrators is to ensure that the haj does not serve as a breeding ground for communicable diseases. The haj has frequently generated pandemics, particularly after the advent of modern transportation—such as steam navigation and railroad trains—which did not allow any contagion to run its course, as had been possible in caravans and sailing ships. In the 1865 world cholera epidemic 15,000 of the 90,000 hajis died in Arabia, and 60,000 Egyptians subsequently died when the disease was carried home by pilgrims.

As a result of international concern over this epidemic, which eventually ravaged Europe and the United States as well as the Middle East, health and quarantine procedures came under international control. In 1957, however, WHO ceded all its responsibilities and those of preceding organizations to the Saudi government. Smallpox and cholera injections have been required of hajis since 1927. With the completion of the Jiddah Quarantine Center in 1956 more rigorous control of the hajis was effected. No pilgrim is admitted to the country without inoculation papers, and any sign of epidemic illness either among the passengers or in their country of origin requires a stay of five days in the Jiddah Quarantine Center.

The quarantine center, virtually a city in itself, comprises 150 buildings in a total area of 56.3 acres. It includes two hospitals—a 105-bed surgical hospital and a 200-bed isolation hospital—administrative offices, steam sterilizing rooms, public baths, laundries, and bacteriological laboratories. From the sixth to the fourteenth day of Dhu al Hijjah three field hospitals—two at Arafat and one at Mina, with a combined capacity of over 500 beds—screen serious cases and are fully equipped for general curative medicine and most general surgery. In addition to the field hospitals twenty health centers equipped for outpatient medicine are erected in the Arafat-Mina Muzdalifah area. Each health center has a physician, a pharmacist, four male nurses, eight assistants, and three clerks.

The health centers and field hospitals handle most of the heat prostration cases. The number of fatalities from heat prostration depends upon the season in which the haj falls. For approximately seventeen years it occurs in the summer (April through September) and for the next seventeen in the cooler months. In the 1950s the haj fell in summer with the result that 454 pilgrims died in June 1959 of heat-related illness. Because the haj falls a little earlier every solar year, the number decreased after that: 377 died in 1960, and there were 194 deaths in 1961, thirty four in 1962, and none in 1965, when the haj was in April. The haj will fall in the summer months again in the 1980s.

In addition to disease detection special teams of health inspectors under the supervision of the Directorate General for Inspection attempt to ensure that there is adequate ventilation in the tent cities. The provision of adequate sewage disposal in the tent cities and the health control and supervision of the pilgrims' hostels and the homes of *mutawwifun* (the pilgrims' guides) are also under its supervision.

The Ministry of Health works with Meccan municipal authorities to supervise the sacrificial slaughtering of over 500,000 sheep, goats, and camels that occurs from the tenth through the twelfth of the haj month. In 1975 only one slaughterhouse as Mina was designated for the sacrifice. According to Islamic law the pilgrim may take up to one half of the sacrificed animal for his own use, and the other one half must be distributed to the poor. Disease control authorities require that the pilgrim take only as much of the animal as he and his family can consume by the end of the haj.

The logistics of the sacrifice made it impossible for the rest of the meat to be distributed to the poor. During the 1975 haj the remaining parts of the animals were covered with lime and disinfectant and pushed by tractors into large pits. Saudi authorities, sensitive to complaints that this practice violated the spirit of Islamic law, were considering various plans by which the meat could be frozen and redistributed at a later time, although the cost of such an undertaking would be more than the value of the meat. In 1975 Zamzam water from the Well of Hagar, in great demand during the haj season both as part of the ritual and as a souvenir for home, was placed under more stringent health control so that disease would not be unwittingly carried out of the country (see ch. 6).

Saudi health authorities are aided by the Saudi Red Crescent Society, which operates dispensaries and first-aid stations during the haj season, and by medical delegations from twenty-three countries from which substantial numbers make the haj. Health awareness and guidance are propagated among pilgrims and citizens alike during the haj season through publications, posters, and such local information media as the press, radio, and television.

The government has proposed various improvements for haj conditions to be implemented during the five year plan. In 1975 a British Lebanese consortium was engaged under contract to design public health and services systems costing the equivalent of about US$740 million for the benefit of the 3 million pilgrims the government expected in 1977.

Transportation studies will be undertaken to arrange the separation and flow of vehicular traffic within the *haram*. Mass transportation systems will be considered because of the danger and traffic jams caused by private vehicles. The number of automobiles moving between haj locations totaled between 60,000 and 70,000 in each year between 1970 and 1975. Motorcycles, trucks, and buses add to the confusion. In 1976 a Swedish firm was planning a closed circuit television traffic surveillance system for the *haram* in Mecca to monitor traffic.

The Haj Affairs Directorate regulates the haj service industry, which supplies lodging and sets up special markets, post offices, and mosques for the pilgrims (see ch. 13). The government is attempting to standardize housing and to set price controls on merchandise offered to the pilgrims in an attempt to offset the frequently inflated prices that prevail during the haj season. New housing projects will be designed, and areas within Mina will be leveled to provide more living space for pilgrims. The five-year plan estimated that physical infrastructure development for the haj might require up to SR5 billion over the plan period.

WELFARE

Traditional Welfare

The belief that it is incumbent upon the more fortunate members of a social group to assist the less fortunate is deeply ingrained in the

Arab consciousness. Even before the emergence of Islam in the seventh century, which made care of the poor a religious obligation enforceable by law, able family members through the medium of the extended-family system usually cared for and protected the aged, the ill, the handicapped, the widowed, and the orphaned. Generosity, even to the limits of self-impoverishment, was expected, especially of kinsmen.

Under Islam the traditional pattern was enlarged: a Muslim was obligated not only to his family but also to the entire Islamic community. Almsgiving, one of the five pillars of Islam, was institutionalized as an annual tax (zakat), and the proceeds were used primarily for charitable purposes (see ch. 6). Almsgiving is not conceived of as gratuitous generosity but as the duty of the donor and the right of the recipient.

The practice of King Abd al Aziz and King Saud of treating the entire Saudi nation as a tribe of which they were the shaykh and of distributing purses to tribal leaders reinforced the idea that the wealthy had a moral obligation to support the poorer members of society. Varying amounts of this money filtered down to tribesmen, who expected the shaykhs to assume a certain responsibility for their welfare.

Zakat has survived in the country, although it has not been rigorously collected since the government began receiving large revenues from oil. Another traditional source of welfare is the waqf, an endowment left by the donor to be used for charity in perpetuity after his death or the deaths of his heirs. In 1976 *awqaf* were benefiting only a small segment of society.

Governmental Programs

The Ministry of Labor and Social Affairs has since 1962 offered a range of programs oriented toward the social development of individuals and groups as well as more conventional forms of welfare for individuals in special need. The ministry's activities were divided into two groups—social security and social affairs—which included social welfare institutions, rehabilitation for the physically and mentally handicapped, assistance to and regulation of agricultural cooperatives, and planning and research relevant to social programs within the kingdom.

Social Security

Social security provided pensions to people over the age of sixty, to those partially or completely disabled, to orphans, and to women without support. Grants-in-aid were made to persons affected by natural and social calamities. The social affairs agency had ministry offices in Riyadh, three regional offices (Jiddah, Riyadh, and Dammam), and forty-six branch offices. In 1976 the maximum annual payment for a family of seven people was SR5,400, comprising a basic rate of SR1,080 for the family head or supporter plus SR720 for each additional member. In 1974 approximately 110,000 people received pension benefits, and 3,700 received grants. By 1977 the government plans to have introduced such new, noncontributory assistance projects as child allowances payable to limited-income families with children, death allowances payable to widows of pensioners, and housing allowances payable as lump sums to tenants who have lost their accommodations through no fault of their own.

Social Welfare

Social welfare provided various kinds of institutional care. In 1975 twelve institutions cared for 1,218 orphaned children. At that time four social orientation institutes cared for 211 nondelinquent problem boys, and three probation homes accommodated twenty nine delinquents or first offense juveniles. The expansion of institutional facilities for delinquent and problem boys represented an important change of attitude in Saudi society; boys previously subjected to the harsh punishments incorporated in sharia law were given social guidance and vocational training. The five social welfare institutes cared for 149 elderly, and there were seven offices for beggar control.

The office of social welfare supervised a foster and alternate care program for foundlings and infants separated from their mothers. In 1974 this program cared for 555 children. Administrators hoped eventually to use private benevolent societies to seek out adoptive parents for these children. Another social welfare function was the encouragement of private benevolent societies. In FY 1974 subsidies to thirteen societies amounted to approximately SR450,000.

A department under the social affairs agency was formed in 1974 to provide rehabilitation services and training to the mentally and physically handicapped. In 1975 only forty two people were served under the program, but five vocational rehabilitation centers and three social rehabilitation centers were expected to be implemented during the 1975-80 plan period.

Community Development

Through seventeen community development centers serving eighty-three communities, governmental services were coordinated with local efforts to improve the welfare of the community by emphasizing the concept of self-help. The majority of community development centers were located in rural areas. Training for community development personnel was undertaken jointly by the Ministry of Labor and Social Affairs and the United Nations at a center at Dariyah, which had a staff of forty-seven Saudis and seven United Nations advisers.

A typical community development center included a health clinic and operated programs in literacy, public hygiene, libraries, cooperative activities, and agricultural extension. Cooperatives were registered and regulated by a department that also offered technical and financial assistance in the establishment and initial operational stages of cooperatives. In 1974 there were eighty-three registered cooperatives with a membership of 27,560. The government's policy has been to discourage the formation of consumer cooperatives except in remote rural areas. The government considered community development centers to be important vehicles with which to foster social stability under circumstances of rapid social change.

Social Insurance

Since 1973 the Social Insurance Law has provided several kinds of protection for workers regardless of nationality, sex, or age: disability, old age, and death benefits; benefits in cases of occupational injuries and occupational hazard diseases; benefits for temporary disability because of sickness and maternity; family grants in cases in which the insured has several dependents; unemployment compensation; and protection for the self-employed. The social insurance project operated on a contributory basis; that is, the organization's revenues comprised contributions from both employers and employees (although only employers contributed to the occupational hazards program) as well as investment revenues and government subsidies.

* * * * * * * * * * * * * *

The Saudi *Development Plan 1395—1400 (1975—80)* contains discussions of the country's problems relating to living conditions, welfare programs, and plans for the future; it includes a wealth of statistical data, which must, however, be used with great caution. David Long's dissertation, "The Hajj Today: A Survey of the Contemporary Pilgrimage to Makkah," contains an excellent description of living conditions among the hajis. Pearce Wright's extensive article in the *Times* (London) is a detailed description of the King Faisal Medical Center and has useful essays on the health problems of the country. The article "Saudi Arabia" by Richard Johns et al in the *Financial Times* (London) examines the standard of living in 1974 Saudi Arabia. (For further information see Bibliography.)

CHAPTER 5

EDUCATION AND THE ARTS

Not since the seventh century A.D., when it harbored the intellectual and spiritual revolution of the rise of Islam, has Arabia been a leader of Middle Eastern thought. Shortly after establishing the political power of the Islamic community the leaders and many of the followers quit the peninsula to establish capitals in more hospitable climes (see ch. 2). Receiving little intellectual stimulus except that offered by the annual influx of pilgrims, Arabian art and thought stagnated in the traditional religious centers of Mecca and Medina in the Hejaz (see ch. 6). In other parts of the peninsula much of the pre-Islamic culture reasserted itself. Islamic civilization, meanwhile, spent its creative powers embellishing monuments and refining thought outside the land of its birth.

The puritanical Islamic movement that established and continues to dominate Saudi Arabia has for the most of its history been actively inimical to artistic endeavor and encouraged only certain forms of traditional religious scholarship. Saudi Arabia only recently began to feel tremors of the confrontation with the West that shook the great centers of Islamic culture and learning to their foundations in the nineteenth century, and it feels them in somewhat different form than did Beirut and Cairo. Traditional poetry, the art form that has dominated Arabian life since pre-Islamic times, remains the major aesthetic outlet of the people. Infiltration by the more modern, Western influenced literary forms and subjects prevalent in neighboring Arab countries began as recently as the 1950s. Elements of Western culture, particularly technological and administrative subjects, have gained considerable prominence and prestige in the schools and universities but generally remain unintegrated into the value system of the people.

Saudi leaders as early as King Abd al Aziz ibn Abd ar Rahman Al Saud perceived that certain forms of Western knowledge were needed if the country were to exploit and control its vast oil resources. By the 1950s a strong commitment to mass public education had become a cornerstone of national policy. Education, however, was intended to serve the interests of religion and the royal family; the schools were to bring the instrumental advantages of Western progress while retaining the purity of traditional culture.

Even within these constraints the establishment of modern schools was a marked departure from Saudi practice despite the very high percentage of the curriculum devoted to religion. An even more radical step was the establishment of public schools for women. In order to assuage conservative opinion women's education takes place within a separate school system entirely distinct from that for men and under the authority of a religious leader. A third government-supported system of religious schools trains males for the ulama (body of religious authorities).

The Five Year Development Plan (1975-80) makes explicit the government's total commitment to education. An extremely rapid expansion of facilities would bring schooling to the vast bulk of Saudi youth by 1980. Most analysts question the probability of the plan's goals being met, however, especially in view of the severe personnel shortage that makes the country depend heavily on foreign teachers. Nevertheless Saudi Arabia's educational achievements merit admiration. Although the general level of literacy is still among the lowest in the Arab world, some of the government's educational institutions, for example the University of Petroleum and Minerals, have achieved a notable academic standard in a relatively short time.

In the mid-1970s less than a generation had passed since the beginnings of mass education in Saudi Arabia, and the social and cultural results were still unclear. Some authorities have expressed doubt, however, that the government will be able to maintain in the long run the apparently unstable combination of mass modern education and strict adherence to traditional thought. For the foreseeable future, however, there appears no likelihood that the dissident intellectual class so prominent in other Arab states will develop in Saudi Arabia. The nation's inherent social conservatism combines with the tremendous shortage of trained manpower to assure every graduate of at least a good job and in many cases a position of some prestige and authority.

THE INTELLECTUAL AND ARTISTIC CLIMATE

For the vast bulk of the Saudi people intellectual and artistic expression retains forms in use for centuries, whether study of the Quran or traditional, time-honored poetic styles. Since only 5 to 15 percent of the population is literate, according to government estimates, written materials exert far less influence than oral traditions from pre-Islamic times. Some literary work in more modern forms has been undertaken in the country, but the practitioners are generally foreigners, and their efforts receive less encouragement, either official or popular, than more traditional work. Even television, introduced into the kingdom during the 1960s, is used in part to support traditional modes of thought (see ch. 9). At the time of the United States moon landing, for example, special televised talks by members of the ulama reconciled this phenomenon with the teachings of the Quran.

In Arabic lands, as in Semitic cultures generally, verbal expression is the highest form of art. Plastic and decorative arts in Arabia have traditionally remained within the constraints of Islamic law, which forbids representations of the human form and other animate objects. Although decorative work using intricate geometric compositions was long practiced, the Wahhabi (see Glossary) strictures against ornamentation have tended to suppress this activity. For this reason, as well as because of a lack of building materials adapted to elaborate ornamentation, architecture has traditionally been simple, consisting mainly of unadorned mud-brick structures. Wahhabi influence had a similar effect on music and dance, although these forms retain some vigor, especially among the beduin. It is likely that rapid cultural change bears as much responsibility as religious restrictions for the loss of the folklore of the desert (see ch. 7).

Although other art forms have been little cultivated in the territory of Saudi Arabia, the literature produced there remains one of the glories of Arabic-speaking peoples everywhere. The century preceding Islam was the classical or heroic age of Arabian literature, producing works still venerated today. Arabic poetry as now known appeared about A.D. 500, showing a uniformity of language and sophistication of technique that implied a long prior period of development. Classical poetry grew out of tribal society and expressed that society's profoundest values and mores. The poet served to express the life of his tribe rather than his own inner life and functioned as a propagandist in the psychological struggle among tribes.

The artistry of classical poetry inhered in the use of language rather than in the choice of subject matter. Based upon but not identical with the language of everyday life, poetic usage was uniform from Iraq to Egypt and from Syria to Yemen despite differences in the vernaculars of these regions. Even a minimal understanding of Arabian poetry therefore depends on an understanding of the Arabic language. Rich in synonyms, rhythmic, highly expressive, and poetic, Arabic can have a strongly emotional, almost hypnotic, effect on its speakers and listeners. The emotional attachment of Arabic speakers to the beauties of their language is far greater than that of most peoples to their native tongues, and poetic eloquence has long been the most admired cultural attainment and sign of cultivation in the Arab world. In villages and among nomadic tribes as well as among literate city dwellers, Arabic speakers have long striven to display in their speech an extensive command of traditional or classical phrases and locutions. The speaker and writer traditionally strove for an elaboration and circumlocution in both spoken and written forms that often strike Westerners as flowery or verbose. Beauty of expression has long been valued above factual accuracy; only among the technically educated has this preference begun to shift.

One of the more widely spoken languages in the world, Arabic is the mother tongue of 100 million people from Morocco to the Arabian Sea. It is related to other Semitic language, such as Aramaic, Phoenician, Syriac, Hebrew, various Ethiopic languages, and the Akkadian of ancient Babylonia and Assyria.

Throughout the modern Arab world the language exists in three forms: the classical Arabic of the Quran and early literature; the literary language developed from the classical and known as modern standard Arabic, which was virtually the same structure wherever used; and the local form of the spoken language. All educated Arabs tend to be functionally bilingual—in modern standard Arabic and their own dialect of spoken Arabic. Even uneducated Arabic speakers can usually comprehend the general meaning of something said in modern standard Arabic, although they cannot speak it themselves and often have difficulty understanding it precisely. Classical Arabic is known chiefly to scholarly specialists; many men have memorized Quranic phrases by rote but cannot be said to have mastered the classical form.

Within the same region a city dweller speaks slightly differently from a villager and a tribesman differently from either. Even within villages, quarters often display some differences. Each variety of the language has some different sounds and different ways of expressing ideas, and the vocabulary includes words fitted to the specific way of life of its speakers. Grammatical structure differs as well.

Like other Semitic languages, Arabic is based on the triconsonantal root. In this system a group of three consonants carries the essential germ of meaning of the word; various standardized combinations of vowels transform the root to specific meanings. For example, the root *krj* generally concerns going, emerging, protruding. Thus *karaja* means he went out; *kuraj*, a skin eruption; *kirrij*, a graduate of a school or university; *makraj*, a place of exit; *ikraj*, an act of removal; and *karij*, outward. Various classes of roots exist, each of which must be modified by a different set of vowel combinations to produce an array of meanings. Within a class, however, the same system of vowels is applied to a number of roots.

This structural system gives Arabic great concision while allowing extreme subtlety in the use of multiple meanings and overtones. The patterned vowels also afford tremendous rhyming possibilities. Fine Arabic poetry fully exploits these features of the language. In addition to displaying excellent word choice poetry must have rhyme and meter, the meter being determined by length of vowels rather than, as in English, by stress. So great are the formal opportunities for virtuosity in Arabic verse that form rather than content has long dominated as the criterion of excellence. Formal perfection rather than integrity of meaning has traditionally marked good poetry, and this tendency remains strong even in the late twentieth century.

Several poetic forms arose during the classical period or shortly thereafter, of which the *ghazal*, or love lyric, is prominent. To most people, however, the greatest form of Arabic poetry is the *qasidah*, a form of ode that reached its zenith in the century preceding Islam. A *qasidah* consists of fifteen to 120 couplets, all with the same rhyme and meter and intended to be chanted or sung. Each line consists of the same or very similar sequences of vowels; the superimposition of different roots produces lines with various meanings. The possibilities for subtlety, allusion, and wit based entirely on form are obviously enormous in the hands of a master of the language.

Rhyme and meter rather than content unify the poem. The individual couplet or *bayt* (literally, tent) stands apart from the others, a unit of meaning complete in itself. The eminent Islamicist Bernard Lewis has likened the couplets to "strung pearls," each independent and all "interchangeable." The *qasidah* follows a set progression of ideas or themes, beginning as the poet, traveling with companions, comes upon a place where he was happy with his beloved. He recalls nostalgically the joy they shared before her tribe moved away. He then praises his mount, either camel or horse, and the life in his own tribe. This section often includes praise for his tribal leader or patron. Within this rigid framework the poet showed his ability and won admiration by the brilliance of his variations rather than by originality of subject matter. William Polk and William Mares, writers on Islamic literature, state, "Perhaps the best Western equivalent is not in literature but rather in the plastic arts. What differentiated Michelangelo from his lesser contemporaries was not his choice of materials or subjects but rather the virtuosity of his handling of themes common to his contemporaries and successors."

Great odes and the men who composed them enjoyed tremendous prestige, even veneration. The most famous works in the *qasidah* form are the seven so-called golden odes in the collection known as Muallaqat, or the "suspended" odes. These poems, winners at the great poetry contest held annually at Ukaz, were said to have been written in gold and hung from the wall of the Kaabah shrine (see ch. 6). The Ukaz poetry fair was an event of considerable importance, and the people came from the whole surrounding area to listen and compete. At a Ukaz fair, for example, the Prophet Muhammad met the Yathribi leaders who later accepted him into their city (see ch. 2).

The classical period also saw the rise of rhymed, unmetered prose, or *saj*. In this medium the greatest work is the Quran, the holy scripture of Islam, believed to be the literal word of God and the most perfect example of expression in Arabic. The influence of the Quran on Arabic language, literature, and thought is incalculable. It provided an inviolable model for prose expression and thus strongly affected the development of the language.

The same conservatism and regard for past examples of perfection have dominated literary expression in Arabia. For fourteen centuries the *qasidah* remained the most admired form of poetry. Poets followed the dictates of Khalil ibn Ahmad (died A.D. 791), who compiled the sixteen accepted meters. The themes and meters of the classical age continued to recur. Arabia has proved the most culturally conservative region of the Muslim world. In other Arab countries social change altered the nature of society and thus outmoded the forms of expression suited to past social realities. Poetry of a more personal nature, often using freer, Western-inspired meters and rhyme schemes, began to appear in these countries along with novels, short stories, and essays.

Although these trends have developed slowly in Saudi Arabia, they are nonetheless visible among the modern educated and those influenced by foreigners. In the 1970s poetry remains the major literary outlet both of the ordinary people, who retain traditional, mostly oral forms, and of the modern educated, who write of modern themes in both traditional and consciously Western forms. Such subjects as the Palestine dispute, social change, and even some social criticism are explored in poetry. Journalism, essay writing, the novel, and the short story have also begun to develop. Modern literary criticism, for example, appeared in 1926 when two books on local literature were published. The 1920s and 1930s were a period of polemics and disputes expressed in very derivative articles. By the late 1940s and early 1950s, however, a more mature, objective criticism had emerged, concentrating on aesthetics, structure, and logic and emphasizing evidence rather than authority in presentation. All these developments were made possible by the establishment of printing in the kingdom under King Abd al Aziz. Previously poetry had been essentially oral; written works, such as those of Muhammad ibn Abd al Wahhab, the founder of the country's dominant religious sect, had circulated in the form of manuscripts.

Despite the wish of the government to prevent it, foreign cultural influence appears to be spreading. Traditional music is losing popularity in the face of records, tapes, and radiobroadcasts of Egyptian and Syrian popular singers and folksingers from the Persian Gulf. Amateur theatrical groups composed of foreigners reportedly exist. Art exhibits were first held in the 1900s, and art classes were offered in many schools. In a 1970 exhibit most of the artists represented were foreign Arabs, but some Saudi artists also showed works. Critics stated that the Saudi work, which eschewed representations of people or animals, emphasized calligraphy despite the inappropriateness of the chosen media. Although the Saudi artists had not reached a high artistic standard, their interest in Western artistic forms was significant in itself. Some newly wealthy Saudis have also begun to acquire art works by old masters of the West, although the acquisitions may be as much in the form of financial investment as in the collection of art objects as art. The strict religious injunction against representation of humans or animals has begun to break down. The Saudi post office, for example, has issued stamps in honor of the late King Faisal that depict his face in prayer.

Far more important inroads of nontraditional thought have been made by the technology of the West introduced to exploit the huge oil holdings. The government had committed itself to mastering the techniques of engineering, administration, and finance that would permit it to gain full advantage of its wealth. A growing class of Saudis has had lengthy exposure to these subjects and the instrumental, inquisitive values they represent. The government thus tacitly expanded the realm of permissible knowledge far beyond the traditional limits of the Quran.

Observers have noted, however, that the new knowledge and values have thus far not disturbed the traditional values of most educated Saudis. Although many of them would like faster social change, few reject the essential rightness of their religion, its teachings, and the values it represents. Some observers speak of the ability of the educated to compartmentalize their knowledge, mastering modern subjects while retaining traditional values. Intellectually and artistically Saudi Arabia remains one of the most conservative of the Arab societies. Whether the penetration of modern thought and the expansion of modern education would one day change this situation could not be predicted in early 1976, but the change was only barely discernible.

EDUCATION AND SOCIETY

The history of Saudi education before 1950 is not clearly known. The earliest educational organizations that retain influence in modern Saudi Arabia were established from the seventh century A.D. onward to teach Islam and the Quran. At first private teachers received students in their homes. Eventually, however, the custom developed of giving lessons in a special room devoted to that purpose, often within the precincts of the community mosque; the school was known as the *maktab* or *khuttub* from the Arabic root "to write." The training offered in these schools consisted almost entirely of reading and reciting the Quran and emphasized rote methods and a reverence for tradition and orthodoxy. In substantial parts of the country these were the only educational institutions.

For students who wished to pursue their studies beyond this elementary level an informal network of scholarly lecturers offered instruction in more advanced aspects of Quranic and legal interpretation. Such teachers generally offered lectures in mosque courtyards to anyone who wished to listen; educational centers of this kind were known as madrasahs. Students would join a teacher at will and stay with him as long as they wished. Thus masters gathered groups of disciples, some of whom acted as teaching assistants and repeated the lectures for those who had not grasped them the first time. During question and answer periods students were able to pursue points of interest and simultaneously bring themselves to the attention of the master. Rather than depending on organized diploma-granting schools, individual masters certified their students as having reached a certain level of proficiency.

The holy pilgrimage cities in the Hejaz were natural magnets for devout and learned Muslims, many of whom remained to study after their haj had been completed. For a number of centuries the only semblance of intellectual life in the country was in these centers of religious learning. Although the early Muslim period had encouraged wide-ranging intellectual investigation, rote learning and orthodoxy gradually became dominant. Professor Joseph Szyliowicz, a historian of education, writes: "Although knowledge was highly valued and its quest always considered important. . . its very importance led quickly to precise definition and the view that what lay beyond was not proper for study. Freedom of thought was never a central value of Muslim society and culture—rather the emphasis lay upon acquiring as much of the accepted wisdom as possible."

This situation continued well into the twentieth century. At the outbreak of World War I the Hejaz, by far the most developed sector of the country, had Muslim schools and mosque circles as well as a small, primitive educational system established by the Turks and a few private schools, some teaching modern subjects. Of the seventy-eight state elementary schools that existed in 1915, some did not survive the war, and the number of replacements was small. In all these schools religion was the major subject, although some taught modern subjects as well. The Najd area, meanwhile, had no organized system of education at all until the establishment of the *hujar* (agricultural settlements—see Glossary) by the Wahhabi movement.

Soon after the founding of the state of Saudi Arabia, the government undertook to organize the educational facilities into a new system. The ulama opposed this project, however, and their opposition, along with a lack of funds, prevented the new Directorate of Education, a component of the Ministry of Interior, from making the hoped-for progress. The first Saudi government elementary school for boys was established in 1925, but not until 1939 did government elementary schools offer a full range of subjects. In 1927 the first public secondary school was founded, a semireligious institution called the Saudi Elmi Institute that was intended to train elementary teachers. Located in Mecca, this institute had a faculty recruited in Egypt.

The first secondary school teaching a full modern curriculum, the School of Abroad Preparation, was founded in 1937-38 to prepare students for higher education in Egypt and Beirut (see table A for comparison of Hijra and Gregorian calendars). This school also used Egyptian teachers. A few excellent students of the Saudi Elmi Institute were also sent abroad for advanced training. Since few of these foreign-educated Saudis went into teaching on their return, more modern influences did not penetrate the educational system. The educational system continued to expand gradually. In 1930 there were only an estimated 2,300 students in the whoe country; by 1949 the number had risen to approximately 20,000. Not until 1949-50 was an institution of higher learning, a faculty of sharia (religious) law, founded. A teachers college was established in 1951.

The modern period of Saudi education began with the establishment of the Ministry of Education in 1953. Nevertheless A.L. Tibawi, an authority on Muslim education, states that "the traditional system with its spirit, methods, and even curriculum survived in the modern Saudi system as nowhere else in the Arab world." In the mid-1970s an entire religious school system, also supported by the government, existed side by side with the schools of the ministry. Public elementary schools for girls, which are run by an entirely separate authority, were not established until 1960. Female education in the 1970s, extending to the university level, remained completely segregated from that of males. Although the government wished to reduce the 99-percent illiteracy among women, the idea of girls' schools faced stiff opposition from the ulama and other conservative elements. Girls' education only got under way because the government decided that it would be "compatible with the country's religious position and Arab tradition" and because the girls' schools are run by a religious functionary.

From a modest base Saudi educational facilities grew during the 1950s, 1960s, and 1970s into a complex system embracing institutions from preschool to graduate school. By the 1970s students were only sent abroad to study subjects unavailable at home (see The Educational Career, this ch.). This growth reflects oil wealth and the government's ambition to transform the kingdom from a poor, backward desert state to a prosperous, industrial, albeit Islamic and conservative, nation.

In contrast to most Arab countries Saudi Arabia faces the problems of abundance rather than of poverty. The major obstacle to the rapid development of the society is the critical shortage of trained Saudi manpower. Unlike most developing countries, which must contend with the dissatisfaction of large numbers of unemployed intellectuals and university graduates, Saudi Arabia literally cannot produce graduates fast enough to meet its needs, especially in technical fields (see ch. 11). Although some observers believe that a future excess of liberal arts graduates is possible, in the mid-1970s the government exercised the policy of hiring all graduates of both local and foreign universities. Saudi Arabia has experienced almost no brain drain since it began sending students abroad; virtually all return. Observers ascribe this unusual phenomenon to several factors, including the availability of desirable jobs, the strong ties of family obligation, and the fact that all students abroad are closely supervised by government offices established in each country where Saudis study. The abundance of good jobs has even been cited as a factor in the high dropout rate at preuniversity levels.

The five-year plan issued in 1975 foresees the educational system's nearly doubling in five years, from 600,000 to 1 million elementary-school children and from 12,000 to 31,000 university students. The success of these ambitious plans depends in large measure on the availability of teachers. The country has depended heavily on foreign teachers ever since the 1920s; this dependence continued into the mid-1970s and would doubtless continue for many years. At the elementary level the teaching staff in 1975 was almost two-thirds Saudi, and the country was reportedly moving toward self-sufficiency in the production of new teachers; the academic preparation of many teachers was admittedly inadequate, however. At higher levels the balance shifted, Saudis filling about one-third of the positions on intermediate school faculties and less than one-fifth of those on secondary school faculties. Saudi citizens, however, dominated administration at all levels and outnumbered foreigners two to one on the faculties of religious schools. The largest number of foreign teachers were from Egypt and Jordan, and Palestinians were next; most Arab countries were represented. At the secondary level most Saudi teachers were concentrated in the humanities and social studies. In higher education many non-Arab foreigners—primarily Americans and British—worked as teachers.

Foreign teachers are generally contract employees who live in Saudi Arabia during the school year and return to their home countries during vacations. Government policy has long sought to replace the foreigners with Saudi teachers, both as an economy measure and to ensure a faculty attuned to the students' home values and culture. Two main factors militate against this outcome, however. First, the planned expansion of education far outstrips the country's ability to produce new teachers and, even if achievements fall short of the planned goals, the percentage of foreign teachers, at least at the secondary level, will probably rise. Reversing this long-term trend will take many years. Second, efforts to recruit young Saudis into the teaching profession have not met with notable success.

The opportunities for well-trained young men are so great that teaching, which is less well paid than other comparable government work, is a relatively undesirable profession. Foreign teachers, in fact, are much better paid than Saudi teachers. Three-fourths of the students interviewed in one survey had not even considered teaching as a possible career. Other unattractive features of teaching include the possibility of being posted to a distant or rural school, the relative difficulty of the work as compared with most other government jobs, the limited promotion potential, and the low social status of the profession. Most Saudis preparing for teaching careers are studying the humanities or social studies; they enjoy less promising career prospects than the much sought after science graduates. The stipends received by students in teacher training schools are lower than those of students in more technical fields, students at the prestigious University of Petroleum and Minerals receiving the highest. Only women, whose career prospects are strictly limited, view teaching as a relatively desirable profession. Saudi Arabia is one of the few Arab countries in which women constitute more than half of those training to be elementary-school teachers.

A further serious obstacle to the spread of education is a shortage of buildings. In rural areas the vast distances and sparse populations of much of the country and the nomadic habits of as many as a third or more of the people complicate the provision of schoolrooms. In the mid-1970s more than half of the twenty-three educational districts had fewer inhabitants than square miles. Quite apart from the problem of providing teachers in isolated localities or migratory camps, the government had yet to solve the problem of providing facilities and supplies. In urban areas, especially Riyadh, overcrowding because of rapid population growth had caused many classes to be held in rented space designed for other purposes. In the city of Riyadh, for example, 75 percent of elementary schools and nearly 50 percent of intermediate and high schools used rented buildings in 1974, usually residential villas unsuitable in design for school use. In the surrounding district the percentage of rented space was even higher. General demand for buildings had far outstripped supply in Riyadh for a number of years, and education suffered accordingly. Even alteration of existing structures for school use is difficult; construction practices produce a high percentage of interior bearing walls, making modification of existing partitions very difficult. Serious crowding was also reported in Mecca and elsewhere. It is likely, however, that the planned school construction program, which foresees the building of 100 classrooms a week for five years, will help alleviate this problem.

In early 1976 it was close to impossible to comment on the place of education in Saudi Arabian society. Foreign observers regard all Saudi population statistics as suspect, and the data issued by the government educational authorities suffer from a number of deficiencies as well (see ch. 3). A United States government study of Saudi Arabian education commented in 1975 on the "insufficiency of reliable information and statistics . . . on the socio-economic backgrounds of families of children and their aspirations." One can merely surmise the probable social origins of students. Although students of all social backgrounds are found at all levels of instruction, it appears likely that most students who proceeded beyond the first few grades and probably a high proportion in those grades as well were from privileged, urban families. Observers state that in rural schools the larger age-spread within each grade, the higher percentage of repeaters in each grade, and the higher percentage of dropouts indicate a general pattern of inferior performance by rural students. Such factors as distance and the lost value of young people's work militate against school attendance, and it is not known to what extent subsidies to students overcome these problems.

One of the few things known for certain about rural students is that most of those who do complete school leave their native regions to seek advanced training or suitable employment in cities. Whether this is viewed as a drawback in the close-knit families of Saudi Arabia can only be guessed by foreign observers. In general even postelementary training has little economic value for the student who intends to remain in one of the poorer sections of the country, such as the southwest.

The city schools were generally very crowded, although the dropout rates were probably high there as well. Observers believe that the privileged classes of the population took disproportionate advantage of the postelementary facilities. It has been suggested, for example, that most students in the religious schools came from upper middle-class backgrounds. The two model schools run by the government were reportedly heavily patronized by the royal family and the wealthy. The sociology of female enrollment was, if anything, even less known in the mid-1970s than that of males. Some observers believe that girl students generally come from urban families of middle-class or higher standing. It has been suggested that education increases the marriageability of a girl, but this is probably true only in certain modern-educated circles. Modern education has been identified with members of the privileged class ever since Abd al Aziz sent some of his children abroad to study.

THE ORGANIZATION OF EDUCATION

Education in Saudi Arabia falls almost completely under the control of the central government. In early 1976 various educational functions fell under different authorities, however, with the result that the government supported three parallel but wholly separate school systems, two model schools, and a system of higher education and subsidized private schools as well. Boys' modern education between kindergarten and age eighteen was the responsibility of the Ministry of Education, which executed general educational policy as well. The General

Directorate of Religious Institutes and Colleges supervised a system of religious schools enrolling boys from age twelve through eighteen. Girls' education from kindergarten to age eighteen was controlled by the general directorate of girls' education, which was headed by a male religious figure and was responsible to the king. Although by law autonomous institutions, the universities fell under the authority of the Ministry of Higher Education. The Ministry of Labor and Social Affairs supervised vocational training in a number of skilled trades, and other ministries supervised advanced training institutes in various fields. The Ministry of Defense and Aviation ran schools for military dependents. National educational policy generally was enunciated by the Supreme Council for Education (see ch. 8).

The Ministry of Education was the country's largest ministry, having over 50,000 employees in the 1970s, nearly 30,000 of whom worked at the ministry itself in Riyadh. Although the country was divided into twenty-three educational districts with district superintendents responsible for day-to-day operations, very little actual authority resided in the hands of local officials. Curriculum development and text selection took place in the ministry. Knowledgeable observers have criticized the high degree of centralization characteristic of the ministry, which they believe hampers efficient operations. The ministry desires to upgrade the administrative skills of its staff and has systematically sent staff members to the United States for training. Although foreign training has led to a desire for change and reform in the individuals who have experienced it, it is not clear that this desire has become widespread in the ministry.

Certain administrative complications arise in the general directorate of girls' education because of the requirement of female seclusion. The head of the directorate, being a man, does not visit the schools under his authority while students are present. He communicates with his female subordinates by telephone or in writing. As far as is practicable, the government attempts to run an entirely segregated female school system. Although in some places the first two or three grades may be coeducational, at the age of nine girls are required to wear the veil in public and withdraw to female schools. They travel to school in specially chaperoned buses and are instructed entirely by female teachers in schools run by female administrators; the only exception is some religious instruction given by blind male teachers.

The division of Saudi schools by sex and function has been blamed in part for the lack of facilities in many rural areas. The Ministry of Education, for example, will not build a school in a locality if the potential enrollment falls under a certain minimum. Because only boys count toward the total, however, the size of the settlement necessary to support a school is considerably larger than if both boys and girls could enroll.

THE EDUCATIONAL CAREER

Saudi Arabian schools follow the three-cycle sequence of education adopted in 1958 by all members of the League of Arab States (Arab League): six years of elementary school beginning at age six, three years of intermediate school, and three years of secondary school. Standardized certificate examinations control movement between the cycles. A number of different options in modern academic, modern vocational, and religious training are available, but these vary by sex (see fig. 8). In the mid-1970s all public schools and the universities were free, and all students received cash subsidies, the amount of which varied according to the curriculum. Observers believe that the higher stipends offered for scientific and religious studies were significant in attracting students to these fields.

Because of the total lack of reliable population statistics available to foreigners in the mid-1970s, the number of young people in various age-groups was not known, and it was therefore impossible to state with any certainty the percentage of Saudi youth enrolled in school. The problem was further complicated by the probability of high absenteeism, especially in rural areas. It was therefore impossible to determine with any accuracy the percentage of Saudi youths who actually attended school. One authority estimated in 1970 that about 33 percent of the boys and 20 percent of the girls of the appropriate age were enrolled in elementary school, 9 percent of the boys and 3 percent of the girls of appropriate age were enrolled in secondary school, and 1.3 percent of the boys and 0.2 percent of the girls of appropriate age were enrolled in higher education. Although enrollment ratios doubtless increased between 1970 and 1975, some authorities believe that some of the true figures may be even lower than those cited. They estimate that only about one-sixth of elementary-age girls may have been in school in 1975.

The five-year plan calls for rapid increases in the numbers and percentages of each age-group enrolled (see table 1; table 2). It foresees the enrollment of 100 percent of the boys aged seven and eight and 90 percent of the boys aged six by 1980. It further foresees the enrollment of 50 percent of the girls aged six to twelve, of 80 percent of female elementary graduates in intermediate school, and of 50 percent of intermediate graduates in secondary school. Observers regard these outcomes as highly problematical, however.

Regardless of the future envisaged by the plan, in the mid-1970s attendance at school for any significant length of time was probably the experience of less than 50 percent of Saudi youth. Because of the continual increase in the size of the lower grades, it was difficult to calculate with certainty the likelihood of a student's advancing to the upper grades; when present-day secondary students were in the early

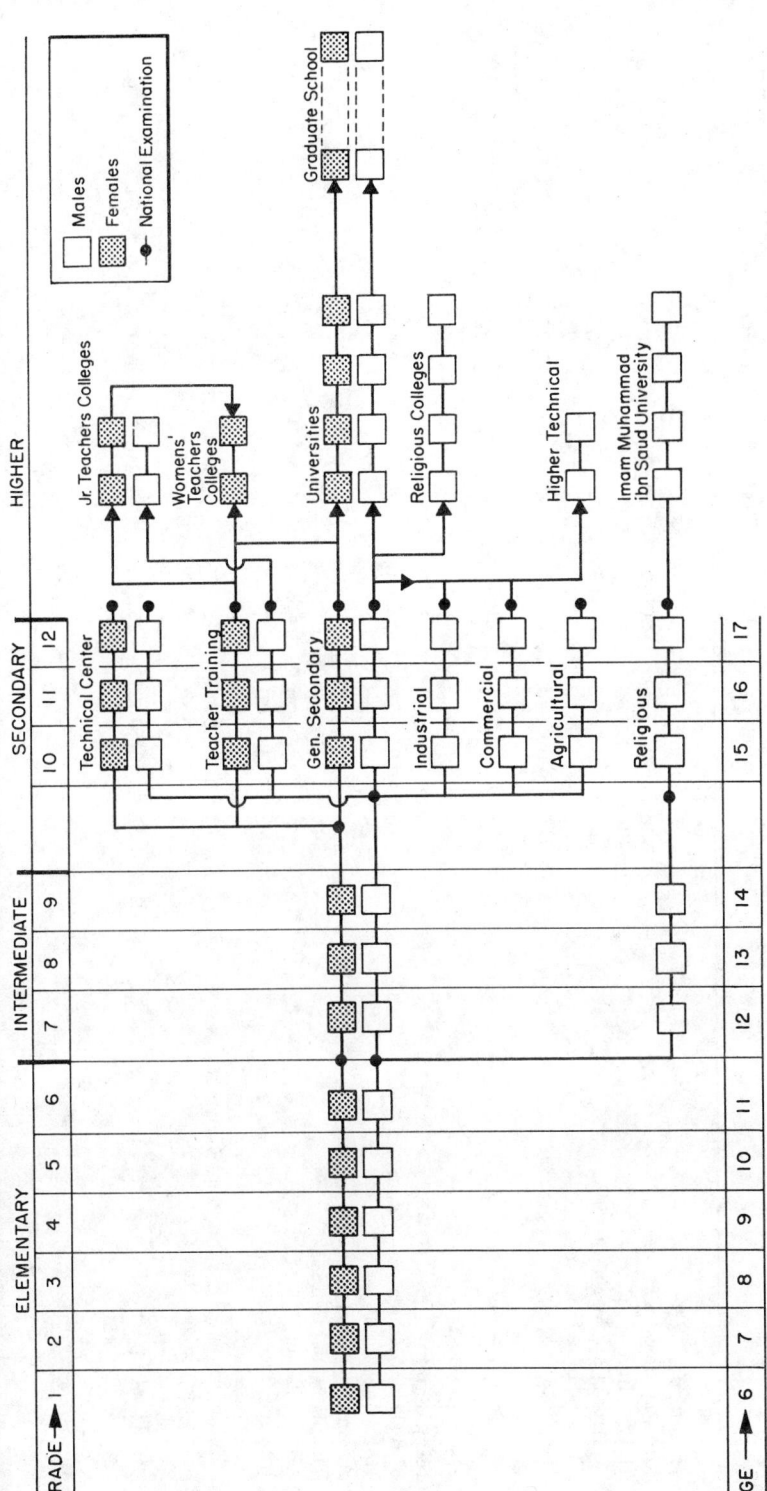

Figure 8. Saudi Arabia, Educational Ladder, 1975

Source: Based on information from Saudi Arabia, *Development Plan 1395-1400 (1975-80)*, Springfield, Virginia, 1976; and Abdelkader Madani Alaki, "Industrial-Vocational Education in Saudi Arabia: Problems and Prospects," Tucson, 1972.

Table 1. Saudi Arabia, Elementary, Intermediate, and Secondary Education, 1975 and 1980

Educational Program	Enrollment		Graduates			Schools	
	1975[1]	1980[2]	1975[1]	1980[2]	Plan Total	1975[1]	1980[2]
Elementary:							
Ministry of Education	401,348	677,458	30,906	58,283	225,835	2,063	2,908
Holy Quran	2,306	8,687	111	481	1,549	7	23
Al Amma Model School	662	750	99	117	501	1	1
Thaghr Model School	921	840	113	136	712	1	1
Elementary (girls)	214,641	353,428	18,545	38,464	145,773	827	1,534
Total Elementary	619,878	1,041,163	49,774	97,481	374,370	2,899	4,467
Intermediate:							
Ministry of Education	70,270	127,136	14,495	27,886	108,036	372	596
Holy Quran	128	950	18	139	535	4	4
Al Amma Model School	353	600	88	188	715	1	1
Thaghr Model School	455	420	134	133	671	1	1
Adult (evening)	6,570	16,290	1,498	3,834	15,169	47	115
Intermediate (girls)	34,061	70,200	7,177	17,401	65,826	93	233
Religious Institutes							
Imam Muhammad ibn Saud University	8,107	13,098	1,628	3,287	13,113	37	39
Islamic University	466	1,358	135	298	971	2	2
Total Intermediate	120,410	230,052	25,173	53,166	205,036	557	991
Secondary:							
Ministry of Education	19,892	39,875	4,038	9,165	35,910	65	102

Holy Quran	n.a.	315	n.a.	49	91	n.a.	4
Al Amma Model School	430	525	93	141	685	1	1
Thaghr Model School	303	357	71	98	465	1	1
Adult (evening)	1,623	3,014	309	587	2,352	16	31
Secondary (girls)	7,616	17,571	1,347	4,417	16,529	18	50
Religious Institutes							
Imam Muhammad ibn Saud University	4,048	8,044	1,100	2,030	7,217	37	39
Islamic University	1,532	2,785	n.a.	534	1,953	3	3
Total Secondary[3]	35,444	72,486	6,958	17,021	65,202	141	231
Special Education	2,119	4,416	n.a.	n.a.	n.a.	15	28
Teacher Training Institutes:							
Boys' general	9,093	12,139	2,156	3,474	15,652	16	21
Boys' physical education	230	687	64	189	530	1	3
Boys' arts	262	500	96	147	522	1	3
Upgrading center	1,032	1,200	500	600	2,900	2	2
Teacher preparation course	511	n.a.	511	n.a.	600	n.a.	n.a.
Girls' general	4,561	12,961	1,220	3,504	11,090	26	31
Total Teacher Training Institutes[3]	15,689	27,487	4,547	7,914	31,294	46	60
Technical Institutes:							
Industrial	2,160	7,375	297	1,650	5,537	4	13
Commercial (day)	715	3,303	167	915	2,574	5	9
Commercial (evening)	260	1,268	161	231	682	3	6
Agricultural	n.a.	1,259	n.a.	131	226	n.a.	5
Technical (girls)	550	1,200	232	542	1,585	4	4
Total Technical Institutes[3]	3,685	14,405	857	3,469	10,604	16	37

Table 1. Saudi Arabia, Elementary, Intermediate, and Secondary Education, 1975 and 1980—Continued

Educational Program	Enrollment		Graduates			Schools	
	1975[1]	1980[2]	1975[1]	1980[2]	Plan Total	1975[1]	1980[2]
Adult Literacy Classes:							
Male	55,540	126,080	n.a.	10,688	34,620	1,015	2,015
Female	28,893	393,751	n.a.	43,477	89,078	99	1,312
Total Adult Literacy Classes	84,433	519,831	n.a.	54,165	123,698	1,114	3,327

n.a.—not available.
[1] Estimated.
[2] Projected.
[3] Totals exclude categories for which information is not available;

Source: Based on information from Saudi Arabia, *Development Plan 1395-1400 (1975-80)*, Springfield, Virginia, 1976, pp. 396-397.

Table 2. Saudi Arabia, Postsecondary Education, 1975 and 1980

Educational Program	Enrollment		Graduates		
	1975[1]	1980[2]	1975[1]	1980[2]	Plan Total
Teacher Training					
Postsecondary Level:					
Junior colleges (male) ...	n.a.	2,225	n.a.	959	1,674
Junior colleges (female) ..	n.a.	1,985	n.a.	692	1,038
Higher industrial center ..	105	375	42	106	285
Higher commercial center .	n.a.	741	n.a.	312	947
Science and mathematics center	100	4,929	n.a.	1,099	2,118
English language course ..	66	70	60	65	325
Total Teacher Training Postsecondary Level[3] .	271	10,325	102	3,233	6,387
University Level:					
University of Riyadh	5,638	10,496	581	1,803	6,859
(Graduate students)	n.a.	(276)	n.a.	n.a.	(231)
University of Petroleum and Minerals	1,497	2,651	155	459	1,727
(Graduate students)	(54)	(135)	n.a.	n.a.	(166)
King Abd al Aziz University	3,737	11,610	431	1,580	4,221
(Graduate students)	n.a.	(51)	n.a.	n.a.	(20)
Women's Teachers Colleges					
Riyadh	790	3,893	74	692	1,710
(Graduate students) ...	n.a.	n.a.	n.a.	n.a.	n.a.
Jiddah	219	2,895	n.a.	659	1,146
Women's College of Arts ...	n.a.	396	n.a.	n.a.	n.a.
Islamic University	890	3,987	128	506	1,521
(Graduate students)	n.a.	(176)	n.a.	n.a.	(92)
Imam Muhammad ibn Saud University	2,556	7,037	334	1,459	4,902
(Graduate students)	(96)	(1,541)	n.a.	n.a.	(1,444)
Total University Level[3]..	15,327	42,965	1,703	7,158	22,086

n.a.—not available.
[1] Estimated.
[2] Projected.
[3] Totals exclude categories for which information is not available.

Source: Based on information from Saudi Arabia, *Development Plan 1395-1400 (1975-80)*, Springfield, Virginia, 1976, pp. 396-397.

elementary grades, the enrollment base was much smaller. Nevertheless one observer estimates that less than one-third of those beginning first grade reach the sixth grade. Attrition at the higher levels was even greater; in 1975 there were eighteen elementary students for every secondary student.

The odds that an individual student, especially one from a modest background, would get very far in school were not great despite the government's desire to increase education. Authorities were divided on whether this resulted from lack of facilities or from lack of interest on the part of parents. It is far more likely that a boy will have a school to attend than that a girl will. In the early 1970s Saudi Arabia ranked among the lowest of all Arab countries in the ratio of girl to boy students at all levels. Girls were about 30 percent of elementary students, 20 percent of secondary students, and 8 percent of students in higher education. In 1975 about 500 of the approximately 3,000 towns, villages, and settlements of the country had a girls' school.

Saudi schools and universities at all levels include mandatory religious instruction; in elementary school about one-third of the time is devoted to religion. In the religious schools about two-thirds of the time is spent on religion. In the intermediate and secondary cycles of the nonreligious school the amount of time devoted to religion decreases but remains significant. A publication of the Ministry of Education states that the first requirement of a teacher is to "believe in God, be a guardian of Islam and be always anxious to transmit Islamic teaching to the Students, encourage them to hold to the Islamic faith, its intrinsic values, its propagation, and its defence." The second requirement is "to be completely aware of the damage of the degradation of moral values and family ties."

All students of the same sex follow a single undifferentiated curriculum in elementary school, but in intermediate school a number of curricular options begin to divide the students into career streams. Vocational curricula are available, but only the general academic course leads to academic secondary education and the possibility of university studies. This option is therefore the most keenly sought after. Vocational and agricultural training generally have been less successful in attracting students than planners had hoped; less than half of the goals of the Five Year Development Plan (1970-75) were met in this regard. Observers have ascribed the preference for academic training to the higher prestige of white-collar work and a general disdain for manual labor.

Commercial secondary education, begun in 1970-71, has had greater success, but students nonetheless prefer academic training at this level as well. After an introductory year for all general academic students the secondary academic curriculum offers two specializations, scientific and literary. The science track is considered most desirable because it leads to the greatest number of school and career options.

The impressive results of Saudi Arabia's educational expansion are probably most evident at the university level. From a single college with twenty-five students in 1957, the system had grown by 1975 to include teachers colleges for both men and women, specialized colleges, and five full-fledged universities: the modern-oriented University of Riyadh, the nation's oldest; the University of Petroleum and Minerals, a general technical university reputed to be one of the finest in the Middle East; King Abd al Aziz University, founded in 1967 as a small modern private school but during the 1970s rapidly expanding to a full university; and the religious-oriented Islamic University and Imam Muhammad ibn Saud University. In 1975 the government had plans for a sixth university, King Faisal University at Dammam-Hufuf. A new, modern campus for the University of Petroleum and Minerals came into complete use in the mid-1970s, including excellent computer and technical facilities and what is reportedly one of the best technical libraries in the Middle East. Several faculties of the University of Riyadh had already occupied the institution's new campus in 1976, and a complete move was scheduled to be finished by 1980.

Subjects taught in Saudi universities include science and engineering, pharmacy, medicine, commerce, economics, liberal arts, and a wide range of religious subjects. The five-year plan calls for the addition of a number of new secular subjects. Religion is scheduled to remain an important emphasis of Saudi higher education, however; one-quarter of university students in 1980 are to be enrolled in religious universities. The government sends students abroad to study subjects not available at home. In 1975 about 2,500 students were enrolled in foreign universities, about 63 percent pursuing the bachelor's, 14 percent the master's, and 23 percent the doctor's degree.

Women enroll exclusively in colleges or university departments for women or as external students at the University of Riyadh. At that university and at King Abd al Aziz University they view closed-circuit telecasts of university lectures by male professors and ask questions of the teacher by a remote hookup. The University of Riyadh is intended eventually to have a separate women's faculty and campus. Women students entered the medical faculty of the university for the first time in 1975, again as an exclusively female group. Some observers have suggested that clinical training for women students in an entirely female environment will present troubles in the later years of training. A more general problem in women's higher education is the provision of female university instructors in all required fields.

Despite marked progress in the development and provision of curricula, Saudi education generally has been criticized for the quality and style of instruction, which observers believe adversely influence the students. Instruction at all levels emphasizes rote learning and memmorization of lectures and assigned readings. Students reportedly show little curiosity, initiative, or critical ability; libraries, for example, are said to be little used. A study of Saudi education conducted by Saudi educators states:

> The curriculum at all levels is devoted to verbal ability first, and to writing ability second. Other skills are emphasized on a descending scale. Manipulation, perception, motor, and kinaesthetic skills are woefully underemphasized. All subjects are considered separate. We saw no interdisciplinary learning. Students are not encouraged or even able to exercise creativity either in motor-sensory skills or in literacy skills. Imagination seems to be valued lightly. As a result, teaching and learning in the average classroom tends to be stale, automatic, and fully prescribed.

At least three causes seem instrumental in this situation. First, traditional Islamic training was in this mold. Second, written examination prepared at the ministry were crucial to both the student's progress and the teacher's evaluation. Third, many teachers were inadequately trained. In the early 1970s only a minority of elementary teachers had a degree. More than 20 percent had no postsecondary education at all, and some, graduates of the former intermediate-level training schools for elementary teachers, lacked even secondary education.

* * * * * * * * * * * * * * *

Passing Brave by William Polk and William Mares vividly communicates the spirit of the great odes and the reverence in which they are still held. For a systematic survey of Islamic literature consult H.A.R. Gibb's *Arabic Literature*. A.L. Tibawi's *Islamic Education* provides a clear, concise introduction to the history and philosophy of education in Islamic lands. Saudi government educational statistics may be found in the *Development Plan 1395-1400 (1975-80)*. (For further information see Bibliography.)

CHAPTER 6
RELIGIOUS LIFE

Religion is the single most important factor in Saudi culture. Religious considerations dominate nearly all activities and policies of both the government and the people. Saudi Arabia owes its national identity to the fundamentalist version of Islam propounded in the late eighteenth century by Muhammad ibn Abd al Wahhab (also known as the Shaykh) and spread by armed forces of his early ally Muhammad ibn Saud (see ch. 2). The descendants of these two leaders, the Al ash Shaykh (House of the Shaykh) and the Al Saud (House of Saud), continue to share religious and political hegemony, the patrilineal descendants of the religious founder dominating the top religious posts and those of the political founder the top political posts. The present king and all his predecessors have been direct descendants of both Wahhab and the first Saud.

Saudi territory, furthermore, contains the holiest sites in Islam, which include the places where the Prophet Muhammad lived and preached and the sacred shrine to which Muslims from around the world have for centuries annually repaired during the pilgrimage season. Saudi Arabia thus serves as both the custodian of Islam's holiest places and the administrator of its most sacred rites. Islam itself arose from Arabian spiritual thought and social patterns. The country is thus more intimately bound to the faith than any other on earth.

Saudi authorities enforce the strictest and most traditional form of Islam practiced in the present day. Although some effects of modernization can be discerned in the twentieth century, the country has no indigenous elements that can be considered even remotely secular. All permanent residents are adherents of Islam. Religious proscription has the force of law. No public worship of any other religion is openly permitted. Although enclaves of Christian foreigners are tolerated, the country's small Jewish population emigrated to Israel in 1950, and no Jews have lived there since.

ISLAM

Tenets

In A.D. 610 Muhammad (later known as the Prophet), a merchant belonging to the Hashimite branch of the ruling Quraysh tribe in the

Arabian town of Mecca, began to preach the first of a series of revelations granted him by God through the angel Gabriel (see ch. 2). A fervent monotheist, Muhammad denounced the polytheistic paganism of his fellow Meccans. Because, however, the town's economy was based in large part on a thriving pilgrimage business to the shrine called the Kaabah and numerous pagan religious sites located there, his vigorous and continuing censure eventually earned him the bitter enmity of the town's leaders. In A.D. 622 he and a group of followers were accepted into the town of Yathrib, which came to be known as Medina (the city) because it became the center of Muhammad's activities. The move (hijra—see Glossary), known in the West as the Hegira, marks the beginning of the Islamic era and of Islam as a force on the stage of history; the Muslim calendar, based on the lunar year, thus begins in A.D. 622. In Medina Muhammad continued to preach, eventually defeated his detractors in battle, and consolidated both the temporal and the spiritual leadership of all Arabia in his person. He entered Mecca in triumph in 630 and returned there to make the pilgrimage shortly before his death in 632.

After Muhammad's death his followers compiled those of his words regarded as coming directly and literally from God into the Quran, the holy scripture of Islam; others of his sayings and teachings and the precedents of his personal behavior, recalled by those who had known him during his lifetime, became the hadith. Together they form the Sunna, a comprehensive guide to the spiritual, ethical, and social life of the orthodox Muslim.

The *shahada* (testimony, creed) succinctly states the central belief of Islam: "There is no god but God (Allah), and Muhammad is his Prophet." This simple profession of faith is repeated on many ritual occasions, and recital in full and unquestioning sincerity designates one a Muslim. The God preached by Muhammad was not previously unknown to his countrymen, for Allah is Arabic for God rather than a particular name. Rather than introducing a new deity, Muhammad denied the existence of the many minor tribal gods and spirits worshiped before his ministry and declared the omnipotence of the unique creator. God exists on a plane of power and sanctity above any other being; to associate anything with him, or to represent him in any visual symbol, is a sin. Events in the world flow ineluctably from his will; to resist it is both futile and sinful.

Islam means submission (to God); and he who submits is a Muslim. Muhammad is the "seal of the prophets"; his revelation is said to complete for all time the series of biblical revelations received by the Jews and the Christians. God is believed to have remained one and the same throughout time, but men had strayed from his true teachings until set aright by Muhammad. True monotheists who preceded Islam are known in Quranic tradition as hanifs; prophets and sages of the biblical tradition, such as Abraham, Moses, and Jesus (known in

Arabic as Ibrahim, Musa, and Isa), are recognized as inspired vehicles of God's will. Islam, however, reveres as sacred only the message, rejecting Christianity's deification of the messenger Jesus. It accepts the concepts of guardian angels, the Day of Judgment (last day), general resurrection, heaven and hell, and eternal life of the soul.

The duties of the Muslim form the five pillars of the faith. These are the recitation of the creed (*shahada*); daily prayer or salat; zakat, or almsgiving; fasting (sawm); and haj, or pilgrimage. The believer is to pray in a prescribed manner after purification through ritual ablutions each day at dawn, midday, midafternoon, sunset, and nightfall. Prescribed genuflections and prostrations accompany the prayers, which the worshiper recites facing toward Mecca. Whenever possible men pray in congregation at the mosque (from masjid, place of prostration) under a prayer leader and on Fridays are obliged to do so. The Friday noon prayers provide the occasion for weekly sermons by religious leaders. Women may also attend public worship at the mosque, where they are segregated from the men, although most frequently those who pray do so at home. A special functionary, the muadhdhin, intones a call to prayer to the entire community at the appropriate hour; those out of earshot determine the proper time from the sun. Public prayer is a conspicuous and widely practiced aspect of Islam in Saudi Arabia. Businesses close, and religious police enforce attendance (see Islam and Society, this ch.). Daily prayer consists of specified glorifications of God. Prayers seeking aid or guidance in personal difficulties must be offered separately.

In the early days of Islam the authorities imposed zakat as a tax on personal property proportionate to one's wealth; this was distributed to the mosques and to the needy. In addition free-will gifts (*sadaka*) were made. Although it has become a private matter in most Islamic lands, zakat remains a public duty of the believer in Saudi Arabia; the government collects zakat in the form of a tax. Furthermore many properties contributed by pious individuals to support religious and charitable activities or institutions have traditionally been administered as inalienable religious foundations (*awqaf*; sing, waqf). Such endowments support various charitable activities.

The ninth month of the Muslim calendar is Ramadan, a period of obligatory fasting in commemoration of Muhammad's receipt of God's revelation, the Quran. Throughout the month all but the sick, the weak, pregnant women, soldiers on duty, travelers on necessary journeys, and young children are enjoined from eating, drinking, smoking, and sexual intercourse during the daylight hours. Those excused are obliged to endure an equivalent fast at their earliest opportunity. A festive meal breaks the daily fast and inaugurates a night of feasting and celebration. The pious well-to-do usually do little or no work during this period, and some businesses close for all or part of the day. Since the months of the lunar calendar revolve through the solar year, Ramadan falls at various seasons in different years. Though a considerable test of discipline at any time of year, a fast that falls in summer imposes severe hardship on those who must do physical work or travel in the desert. Frayed tempers and poor work performance are annual concomitants of the fast.

Finally all Muslims at least once in their lifetime should, if possible, make the haj to the holy city of Mecca to participate in special rites held there during the twelfth month of the lunar calendar (see Islam and Society, this ch.). In Muslim countries generally, those who have completed the haj merit the honorific haji. In Saudi Arabia, however, performance of the haj is so common that the honorific is not used. The Prophet instituted the requirement, modifying pre-Islamic custom, to emphasize sites associated with Allah and Abraham, founder of monotheism and father of the Arabs through his son Ishmael (Ismail). In Islamic belief Abraham offered to sacrifice Ishmael, son of the servant woman Hagar, rather than Isaac, son of Sarah, as described in the Bible.

The permanent struggle for the triumph of the word of God on earth, the jihad, represents an additional general duty of all Muslims, construed by some as the sixth pillar. The Al Saud used this justification to rally warriors to its cause. In addition to specific duties Islam imposes a code of ethical conduct encouraging generosity, fairness, honesty, and respect and forbidding adultery, gambling, usury, and the consumption of carrion, blood, pork, and alcohol.

A Muslim stands in a personal relationship to God; there is neither intermediary nor clergy in orthodox Islam. Those who lead prayers, preach sermons, and interpret the law do so by virtue of their superior knowledge and scholarship rather than because of any special powers or prerogatives conferred by ordination.

Islam in Its Arabian Environment

Both in its broad outline and in many of its details, Islam reflects the social realities of Arabia in Muhammad's time. Authorities argue that the new religion served to provide an ideological basis for the evolution, already under way, of the area surrounding Mecca from a nomadic and tribal to a more urban and mercantile system of organization. Rather than rejecting entirely the religious heritage of his native region, Muhammad reintegrated elements of it to produce a new and greater whole.

Mecca had been a holy city for some years before the advent of Islam (see ch. 2). The *haram* (sacred area) surrounding Mecca was one of several such holy enclaves in which peace between otherwise hostile tribes was enforced by a holy lineage. Mecca was ruled by the Quraysh tribe; Muhammad belonged to one of the tribe's lesser clans.

Pilgrimage to Mecca was a long-established religious duty in Muhammad's time. Various tribes worshiped various gods represented at the Kaabah; the building only became decisively associated with Abraham and Ishmael through Muhammad's teaching. Each of these gods had the city under its protection, assuring the safety of its adherents within the *haram*. The presence of many shrines brought members of various groups to the city for commerce and other activities in addition to worship, secure in the knowledge that the gods and the Quraysh would punish breaches of the holy peace. Quraysh prosperity depended on the existence of numerous tribal deities whose adherents flocked to the city at set times of the year.

When Muhammad proclaimed the unique sanctity of Allah, therefore, he threatened both the commercial prosperity of Mecca and the basis of peace and social solidarity extant until that time. His insistence that the poor, regardless of family ties, had a legitimate claim on the community's resources also threatened established wealth; his own impoverished, orphaned youth made him sensitive to the needs of the poor and those lacking family connections. In substituting a single overarching god, he established the new religion as the basis for social organization and harmony in place of specific tribal ties and agreements. Loyalty to Islam replaced the ritual kinship ties that had worked to prevent violence between tribes. The blood feud was abolished as legitimate social control among Muslims. War became the sole prerogative of the state. Muhammad made this point most explicit in the revered sermon preached on his so-called farewell pilgrimage in A.D. 632; remembrance of this farewell sermon remains the central ritual of the haj. Although Muhammad brought these changes to reality in a relatively brief period, analysts believe that the evolution away from a wholly tribal to a unified state system had been going on for some time as the commercial dominance of Mecca grew.

Muhammad called on men of all tribes to accept Allah as their god and to accept Allah's messenger, himself, as their leader. When he seized Mecca, he destroyed 360 idols in the Kaabah and incorporated many of their names into the ninety-nine attributes of Allah. Before his death he firmly associated the Kaabah and its constituent black stone, an apparent relic of the ancient Arabian tradition of stone worship, with the cult of Allah and declared that only a Muslim may make the pilgrimage to Mecca or even enter the *haram*.

Muhammad had apparently hoped during his Meccan period that the Jews, with whose religion he was familar, would accept Islam as a fulfillment of their own monotheistic faith. After this hope was disappointed in Medina, he began to emphasize the strictly Arabian elements of his religion. He altered the qibla, or direction of prayer, from Jerusalem to Mecca; declared Ramadan, traditionally a sacred season, as a month of fasting; instituted Friday, the traditional market day, as the day of congregational prayer; and incorporated the kissing of the sacred black stone into the pilgrimage. Philip K. Hitti states, "In adopting the Kaabah and the pilgrimage he made his greatest concession to paganism and alienated his monotheism from its two sisters."

From the Jews and Christians, however, Islam adopted the concept of a holy scripture. Although the Arabian Peninsula had a rich and ancient tradition of oral poetry, the Quran was the first important work in written Arabic and, as such, has exerted a tremendous influence on the subsequent development of the language (see ch. 5). Muslims view the Arabic Quran as the literal word of God, the exact replica of an original in heaven. Rather than interpreting God's message or expressing it in his own words, Muhammad served as a stenographer, repeating verbatim the utterances of God.

Early Development

During his lifetime Muhammad held both spiritual and temporal leadership of the Muslim community; he established the concept of Islam as a total and all-encompassing way of life for man and society. Islam teaches that Allah revealed to Muhammad the immutable principles governing decent behavior, and it is therefore incumbent on the individual to live in the manner prescribed by revealed law and on the community to perfect human society on earth according to the holy injunctions. Islam traditionally recognized no distinction between religion and state. Religious and secular life merged, as did religious and secular law. The leader of the Al Saud was traditionally chief imam, or religious leader, and therefore head and defender of the Islamic community in his territory.

After Muhammad's death in A.D. 632, the leaders of the Muslim community consensually chose Abu Bakr, the Prophet's father-in-law and one of his earliest followers, to succeed him. At that time some persons favored Ali, the Prophet's cousin and husband of his favorite daughter Fatima, but Ali and his supporters (the so-called Shiat Ali, or party of Ali) eventually recognized the community's choice. The next two caliphs (khalifa, successor), Umar, who succeeded in 634, and Uthman, who took power in 646, enjoyed the recognition of the entire community. When Ali finally succeeded to the caliphate in 656, Muawiyah, governor of Syria, rebelled in the name of his murdered kinsman Uthman. After the ensuing civil war Ali moved his capital to Mesopotamia, where in a short time he was murdered.

Ali's death ended the last of the so-called four orthodox caliphates and the period in which the entire community of Islam recognized a single caliphate. Muawiyah then proclaimed himself caliph from Damascus. The Shiat Ali, however, refused to recognize Muawiyah or his line, the Umayyad caliphs; they withdrew in the first great schism and established a dissident branch, known as the Shia or

Shiites, in support of the claims of Ali's line to a presumptive right to the caliphate based on descent from the Prophet. The larger faction of Islam, the Sunni, claims to follow the orthodox teaching and example of the Prophet as embodied in the Sunna.

Originally political in nature, the differences between the Sunni and Shiite interpretations rapidly took on theological and metaphysical overtones. Ali's two sons, Hasan and Husayn, killed in the wars following the schism, became martyred heroes to the Shiites and thus repositories of the claim of Ali's line to mystical preeminence among Muslims. The Sunnis retained the doctrine of leadership by consensus, although Arabs and members of the Quraysh, Muhammad's tribe, predominated in the early years. Reputed descent from the Prophet still carries great social and religious prestige throughout the Muslim world. Meanwhile the Shiite doctrine of rule by divine right became more and more firmly established, and disagreements over which of several pretenders had the truer claim to the mystical power of Ali precipitated further schisms. Some Shiite groups developed doctrines of divine leadership far removed from the strict monotheism of early Islam, including beliefs in hidden but divinely chosen leaders and in spiritual powers that equaled or surpassed those of the Prophet himself.

The early political rivalry remained active as well. Shiism gained political dominance of Iraq, Persia (Iran), and Yemen; Shiites are also numerous in Syria and found in small numbers in most Muslim countries in the mid-1970s. Some Shiites live in Eastern Province of Saudi Arabia.

The early Islamic polity was intensely expansionist, fueled both by fervor for the new religion and by economic and social factors. Conquering armies and migrating tribes swept out of Arabia, spreading Islam with the sword as much as with suasion, and by the end of Islam's first century Islamic armies had reached far into North Africa and eastward and northward into Asia. The center of power soon passed from Arabia to more densely inhabited places.

Although Muhammad had enjoined the Muslim community to convert the infidel, he had also recognized the special status of the "people of the book," Jews and Christians, whose own revealed scriptures he considered perversions of God's true word but nevertheless in some sense contributory to Islam. These peoples, approaching but not yet having achieved the perfection of Islam, were spared the choice offered the pagan—conversion or death. Jews and Christians in Muslim territories could live according to their own religious law and in their own communities if they accepted the position of dhimmis, or tolerated subject peoples. This status entailed recognition of Muslim authority, special taxes, prohibition of proselytization among Muslims, and certain restrictions on political rights.

The first centuries of Islam saw the community grow from a small and despised cult to a powerful empire ruling vast domains. They also saw the evolution of the sharia, a comprehensive system of religious law to regulate life within the community. Derived from the Quran and hadith by various systems of reasoning, four schools of religious law, the Hanafi, Shafii, Maliki, and Hanbali, are generally recognized; each Muslim theoretically acknowledges the authority of one of them. Technical points of legal doctrines separate the schools. Of the four, by far the most conservative is the newest, the Hanbali school. Its founder, the jurist Ahmad ibn Muhammad ibn Hanbal (d. 855), rejected the principle of *ijma*, which is the consensus of the ulama (learned of the community; sing, alim, learned), some other legal theories as a basis for law. He also permitted the widely accepted principle os *qiyas*, or reasoning by analogy, to be used only in limited cases. His interpretation thus is derived strictly and almost literally from the Sunna, especially from the hadith. The Hanbalis also emphasize the uncreated nature of the Quran; that is, they do not believe it to have been in any sense made on earth. Hanbal suffered for his views, which were regarded as very conservative, and later followers continued the conservative trend. The school lost numbers and influence under the Ottomans and only resurged under the followers of Wahhab. It has no important concentrations of adherents outside Saudi Arabia.

With the passage of centuries Islam gradually absorbed influences from sources other than the prophetic revelation. Pre-Islamic practices reappeared; people in the Arabian Peninsula resumed venerating trees and stones while maintaining their identification with the Muslim community. Various holy men achieved reputations for exceptional spiritual or magical powers. Stories of miracles circulated, and people began visiting these individuals or their graves to seek cures, fulfillment of wishes, or other favors. Despite orthodox Islam's absolute rejection of sainthood, the ignorant believed in the efficacy of local saints, in charms, and in amulets.

Bands of mystics, or Sufis (from *suf*, wool, of their rough clothing), sprang up claiming to achieve communion with God through various ecstatic or irregular means. Sufi orders gradually arose among both Sunnis and Shiites with recognized leaders teaching particular mystic ways to God. Sufism gained acceptance in large parts of the Islamic world. In most regions, including Arabia, people fell away from the singularly austere cult preached by the Prophet Muhammad and adopted practices that softened it and made it more personal and emotional.

ISLAM AND SOCIETY

Followers of Wahhab called themselves Muwahhidun (Unitarians) and their movement *al dawah ila al tauhid* (call to the doctrine of the unity of God). Others call them Wahhabis and their movement Wahhabism. Often opprobrious in the Muslim world, this designation has been used to imply that followers of the Shaykh raised him to unseemly heights or followed his teachings rather than those of the Prophet. The term has come into common use in the West, however, generally without the implications of unorthodoxy and is used here in this manner in the interest of clarity and uniformity.

The Wahhabi Movement

Muhammad ibn Abd al Wahhab was born in 1703 into a branch of the Banu Sinan in the Arabian town of Uyaynah. A descendent of generations of Hanbali qadis (religious judges), he followed the family tradition of religious studies, traveling to Medina, Basra, and Damascus, among other places. Even as a young man he showed signs of unusually extreme orthodoxy. Having studied widely and reportedly dabbled in Sufism, he returned to his native town where his family was prominent. There he began to preach his own views based on the teachings of the controversial and extremely conservative Hanbali legal scholar Taki al Din Ahmad ibn Taimiya, whose ideas went far beyond the Hanbali norm in strictness and literalness of interpretaion. Like his spiritual mentor Wahhab attracted unfavorable reaction because of the unusual severity of his teachings. He eventually left Uyaynah with his considerable household and property and was received into the village of Dariyah, which was ruled by Muhammad ibn Saud.

Wahhab quickly put into effect Taimiya's teaching that the ulama should combine with the *umara* (power holders, sing, *amir*) to create a true Muslim society. In 1744 he and Saud concluded a pact stating the the Al Saud would adopt, fight for, and propagate the Wahhabi doctrines and that in all conquered territory the Al Saud would hold political power and the Al ash Shaykh would hold religious power. Thus came into being the partnership that harnessed Wahhabi religious fervor to Saud's dynastic expansionism and that resulted in an immediate kingdom in the Najd and the eventual development of the modern state of Saudi Arabia (see ch.2).

Wahhab took a literalist view of the Quran and, like Taimiya before him, believed that the absolute and imcomparable unity of God was the core of true Islam. Thus the worst sin was *shirk*, the association of anything with God or the worship of anything other than God, such practices and beliefs denied Allah's basic nature. An important cause of *shirk*, Wahhab believed, was the adoption of *bida* (innovations) or practices not sanctioned by the Prophet or his followers earlier than the third century of Islam. Some of these "innovations" in fact predated Islam, but Wahhab denounced them as ungodly later accretions. Prominent among them were the customs of visiting saints and tombs and the veneration of trees and rocks. Forbidden *bida* also included rendering improper honor to the Prophet Muhammad, including the custom of celebrating his birthday. Particularly forbidden was the invocation of the name of the Prophet or of saints in prayers in the hope that they would intercede with God. Although the Wahhabis believe that Muhammad can intercede with God, Muhammed does so not in answer to specific requests but only in the case of an exemplary believer.

All special relationships with God are absolutely rejected, whether they involve Sufis, saints, or Shiite imams, as are all ecstatic practices believed to foster such relationships. Only prayer and obedience to duty provide access to God, and that access is equal for all true believers. Wahhab accepted such Hanbali beliefs as the literal truth of the Quran, the ungodliness of knowledge not derived from it or the hadith, and the predestination of human events. He went beyond Hanbali teachings, however, in rejecting smoking, shaving, and strong language; requiring rather than merely encouraging attendance at public prayer; enforcing payment of zakat on so-called secret profits; demanding evidence of good character in addition to acceptance of beliefs for admission to the Muslim community; and forbidding minarets, embellishment of tombs, and aids to prayer, such as the rosary. He also insisted on strict enforcement of the sumptuary laws established by the Prophet and banned activities he deemed godless frivolity, such as music and dancing.

Unity for Wahhab implied not only the absolute oneness of God but the absolute singularity of the believer's devotion. The sole duty of human life is to serve and obey God with a resignation that accepts what comes as God's will. Service, furthermore, must be rendered strictly according to God's law. The believer's spiritual zeal thus combines with punctilious obedience to form total submission to God's unity. In the words of Henri Laoust, an authority on Hanbali law, Wahhabism implies "the most perfect sincerity placed at the service of the law."

For Wahhab any other approach to God constituted polytheism or *shirk*. Worse even than non-Muslims were Muslims of other sects or schools; by claiming to follow the true religion of Allah while practicing polytheism, Wahhab believed, they practiced hypocrisy. The duty of the good Muslim was to stamp out such mockeries of true religion. As they gained power, therefore, the Wahhabis proved total iconoclasts. They shocked much of the Muslim world, for example, by defacing the tomb of the martyr Husayn at Karbala, a particularly holy shrine to Shiites in what is present-day Iraq.

A Wahhabi does not practice his religion only as an individual. Like other Muslims Wahhab viewed the community as the ideal vehicle for enforcement of God's law. Law is the acting out of faith; Islam is the fulfillment of law. Wahhabis interpret the concept of jihad to include the obligation of the community to enforce the law and the reciprocal obligation of the believer to obey the constituted authority of the Wahhabi imam except when such obedience would lead to straying from the law. The leader therefore has the right and duty to enforce such ritual acts as fasting, attendance at prayer, and payment of zakat and to prevent sin, frivolity, and indecency. Officials known as *mutawwiun* (volunteers), also called religious police by Western writers, have traditionally worked under the authority of the Committee for Encouragement of Virtue and Discouragement of Vice to ensure at least outward conformity with Wahhabi standards.

Within their communities Wahhabis believe in the social equality of believers. The only permissible social distinction is between "true" Muslims and others (see ch. 7). The Wahhabi community ideally strives for the perfection of the example of the Prophet and his contemporaries, who are viewed as the noblest and most perfect humans. The followers of Wahhab regard his teachings so highly that they refer to the period preceding him as *jahaliyah* (ignorance), the term used within the broader Muslim community generally to refer to the period before Islam.

This should not be taken to imply that the Shaykh's followers in any way equate him with the Prophet. Rather than preaching anything new, he sought to return Muslims to the true religion of Allah and to the *al salaf al salih* (ways of the pious ancestors). No serious scholar of Islam has accused Wahhab of heresy. Like Muhammad, however, Wahhab provided religious justification for a political movement that sought to sweep away tribal distinctions and bind all Arabia into a unity based on religion.

After the initial successes of Saud and his immediate successors, the Wahhabi movement went into political decline until the early twentieth century and the rise of Saud's descendant, Abd al Aziz, sometimes cited as Ibn Saud (see ch. 2). A gifted leader, he once again harnessed religious fervor to political ambitions and forged the modern nation of Saudi Arabia under the banner of the Wahhabi cause. During the second and third decades of the twentieth century he tried a daring religiopolitical scheme to tame the beduin and ensure their loyalty. Arguing that proper religious devotion required a sedentary way of life and that warriors must always be in readiness to wage the jihad against unbelievers, he convinced many nomadic tribesmen to settle in the approximately 200 *hujar* (sing., hijra—see Glossary) he established. These communities—combined agricultural villages, military camps, and religious missions—permitted the intensive indoctrination of the beduin and the rapid mobilization of significant forces. Members of the *hujar* called themselves Ikhwan al Muslimin (Muslim Brethern) emphasizing, as had Muhammad, that the bonds of religion override those of tribalism.

The indoctrination of the Ikhwan succeeded possibly even too well for Abd al Aziz' purposes. The Ikhwan adopted the faith with a fervor bordering on fanaticism and often exceeded their leader's desires in raids against surrounding territories. Abd al Aziz finally crushed the Ikhwan forces with an army of townsmen and dispersed the *hujar*. Although many of the beduin warriors considered this a betrayal of their beliefs, it proved an important step in the founding of modern Saudi Arabia.

Religion in Modern Saudi Arabia

The pragmatism displayed in Abd al Aziz' dealings with the Ikhwan has remained a prominent feature of religion in Saudi Arabia. Although the country remains firmly committed to Wahhab's literal interpretation of Islam, it has permitted a tempering of some rigors of behavior. Nevertheless religion pervades all aspects of public and private life. The Quran is the nation's constitution, and the legal system ostensibly rests on the sharia (see ch. 8). Areas of legal dispute not treated in traditional Muslim law—for example, mineral leases, motor vehicle registration, and aviation—are covered in a body of *nizams* (administrative regulations).

Contact with the modern world and with non-Muslim civilizations first challenged Wahhabism in the 1930s. The worldwide depression and World War II cut into the Saudi economic mainstay, the pilgrim trade. The search for new resources uncovered the vast petroleum wealth that brought both unparalled opportunity and unprecedented problems. Adoption of modern technology appeared to many to contravene Wahhab's injunction against *bida*. Wahhabi theologians, however, distinguished between worldly and religious innovations; the former, such as telephones, coffee, and automobiles, were said to have no bearing on religion and were therefore permissible. Although conservative opinion disagreed, Abd al Aziz encouraged liberal interpretation; this dispute in fact contributed to his break with the Ikhwan.

The vast material wealth that flooded the country, and especially the exchequer of the royal family, appears to have weakened somewhat the religious impulse toward austerity so prominent in early Wahhabism. George Rentz, an authority on Wahhabism, has written, "High moral standards and religious devotion seem to be easier to attain in a harsh and poor environment than in a land of plenty." The trend toward opulence was most pronounced under King Saud, a son of Abd al Aziz; but his successor, King Faisal, disapproved of such lavish living (see ch. 2). Nonetheless, members of the royal family continue to buy luxuries on a large scale; social and economic distinctions between the royal family and the ordinary people contradict Wahhabi egalitarianism (see sh. 7). Although alcohol is officially forbidden, it is reportedly available within the kingdom, and cigarette smoking is increasingly tolerated as well. Minarets adorn some newer mosques, contrary to strict Wahhabi teachings. Although religious influence on education remains very strong, the development of a secular system alongside the traditional system represents an important ideological shift (see ch.5).

Despite these changes religious practice and opinion remain quite traditional both in Riyadh and in smaller and more isolated localities, and public frivolity is frowned upon throughout the kingdom. Businesses close for daily prayers. The public Friday sermon by members of the ulama keeps conservative views before the people. Religion dominates all mass communication media (see ch. 9). No public cinemas or places of amusement exist. Social and peer pressure encourages at least outward conformity with religious requirements. Observers report, however, that some individuals maintain a facade of piety to avoid trouble with the authorities rather than because of any personal religious convictions.

In addition to the Ministry of Pilgrimage Affairs and Awqaf other government instrumentalities active in the field of religion include the Committee for Public Morality, known literally in Arabic as the Committee for Encouragement of Virtue and Discouragement of Vice, and the Department of Religious Research, Ifta, Missionary Activities, and Guidance, which is responsible for authoritative decisions on questions of religious law and interpretation. William Rugh, an observer of Saudi Arabia, writes that the committees for public morality "have been a part of urban life since . . . the 18th century. . . . Even in the middle of the twentieth century in Riyad, although they no longer entered private homes to stop people from smoking or playing music, or to get them to go to mosques, the *mutawin [mutawwiun]* did enforce these and other habits in public places." They become especially influential during Ramadan but appear to be gradually losing importance, especially among the educated. Nonetheless they remain a conspicuous feature of Saudi life. Another government function is collection of zakat. The amount owed, either in cash or kind, depends on wealth; a beduin, for example, pays nothing if he holds five camels or fewer but pays one ewe (or equivalent cash) for each five camels owned above that.

Despite the official dominance of Wahhabism, followers of other legal schools, including some Shiites, live in the kingdom. The Hejaz, the region that contains the holy cities of Islam, has adherents of both the Shafii and Maliki schools of law, and some Malikite judges serve the Shiites in the Eastern Province.

The Haj

In 1975 approximately 1 million pilgrims converged on Mecca for the pilgrimage required of each Muslim possessing the means to accomplish it. To make a valid haj the pilgrim must join the huge crowds carrying out the prescribed rites between the eighth and thirteenth days of Dhu al Hijjah, the twelfth month of the Muslim year (see table A). Certain of the rites may be performed at any time but, although meritorious, such observance constitutes only the *umra* (lesser pilgrimage) rather than the haj, the culmination of a Muslim's religious life. For many pilgrims the performance of the haj represents the achievement of a lifelong ambition. Returning hajis report that a spirit of exaltation and high excitement infuses the entire congregation; the confluence of so many Muslims of all races, stations and nations in harmony and equality deeply moves many pilgrims.

To handle the enormous logistical and administrative problems generated by such a huge gathering, the Saudi government acts through the Ministry of Pilgrimage Affairs and Awqaf. The government issues special pilgrimage visas that permit a pilgrim to visit Mecca for the purpose of making the haj and also allow the customary side trip to Medina. No non-Muslim has knowingly been admitted to the *haram* of Mecca since the Prophet declared it forbidden to nonbelievers, although some Christian Europeans have penetrated it in disguise.

In fulfilling the commandment to perform the haj, the pilgrim not only obeys the Prophet's words but literally follows in his footsteps. The sacred sites along the pilgrimage route were well known and frequented by Muhammad; they formed the backdrop of the most important events of his life. It is believed, for example, that he received his first revelation at Jabal al Nur (Mountain of Light) near Mina (see fig. 9).

As it was in Muhammad's day, the *haram* of Mecca is a sanctuary in which violence to people, wild animals, and even plants is not permitted. The word *haram* carries the dual meanings of forbidden and sacred. Upon approaching its boundaries, clearly indicated by markers, the pilgrim dons an ihram if he has not already done so. For men this special garment consists of two seamless pieces of white cloth, one reaching from the waist to the ankles and the other going over the shoulder. Women wear a white gown and scarf and may make the pilgrimage unveiled (see ch. 7). Once dressed in the ihram, the pilgrim enters a state of purity in which he avoids bathing, hair cutting, nail paring, violence, arguing, and sexual relations. He also pronounces the *talbiyah*, a declaration of his desire to obey God by making the pilgrimage: "Doubly at your service, oh God." Many also frequently give the cry *labbayk* during their stay in the holy city. Used only at haj time, it is an archaic Arabic form meaning "I am here!"

Wearing the ihram the pilgrim is free to enter the *haram*, which Muslims believe was established by Abraham and confirmed by Muhammad. If they have sufficient time, they carry out the *umra* when they first arrive. These rites—circling the Kaabah, drinking from the sa-

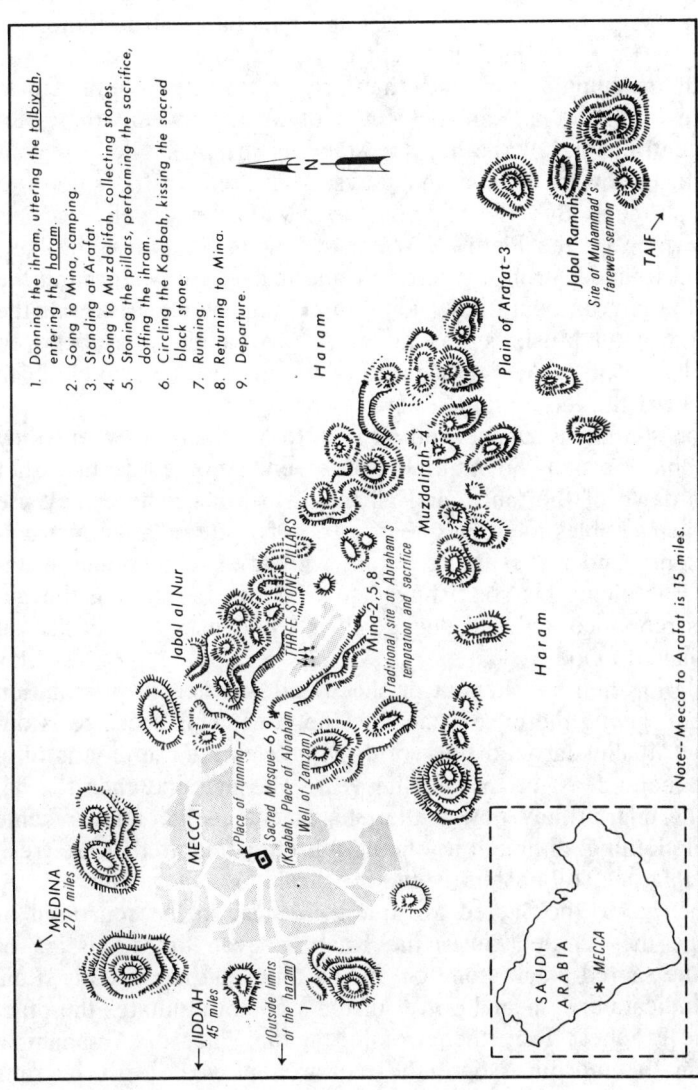

Figure 9. Saudi Arabia, Rites of the Hajj

Source: Based on information from Ismail Ibrahim Nawwab, "The Hajj: An Introduction," *Aramco World*, 25, No. 6, November-December 1974, pp. 4-5.

cred Well of Zamzam, and running between the hills Safa and Marwa—also constitute part of the haj. The pilgrim generally engages a guide (*mutawwif*) who instructs him in proper performance of the rituals and takes care of details of daily living.

On the afternoon or evening of the eighth the pilgrims go to Mina, where they spend the night in prayer and meditation in imitation of the Prophet. Many live in a vast tent city erected every year on the spot. On the morning of the ninth they proceed to the Plain of Arafat at the base of the Jabal Ramah (Mount of Mercy), where they perform the central ritual of the haj, the standing (*wuquf*). The vast congregation faces toward Mecca and prays. Many remain from noon to sundown, although this is not obligatory. Muhammad delivered his farewell sermon on the Plain of Arafat to a congregation at the base of the Jabal Ramah during his farewell pilgrimage. By performing the standing, the pilgrim figuratively joins that congregation to whom the brotherhood of all Muslims was movingly proclaimed. It is believed that the pilgrim leaves Arafat cleansed of his sins. Many also climb to a monument at the top of Jabal Ramah.

A cannon sounds at sunset, and all rush to Muzdalifah, where they collect pebbles, usually in multiples of seven. Another cannon shot announces dawn of the tenth, and all repair to Mina, where they use seven of their pebbles to stone one of a trio of white pillars constructed of masonry and representing Satan, who tried to dissuade Abraham from sacrificing his son Ishmael to God. In the stoning the pilgrims thus renounce evil and declare their willingness to sacrifice all that they have to God.

Each pilgrim then buys a goat or sheep and sacrifices it in imitation of Abraham, giving the excess meat to the poor. This sacrifice is duplicated by Muslims around the world, who celebrate the day as Id al Adha, the major feast of the Muslim year. The sacrifice ends the haj proper. The pilgrim may now bathe, shave, cut his hair, and resume his normal clothing, although he should put on garments that are fresh and new. Pilgrims still abstain from sexual relations, however.

They then go to the Sacred Mosque in Mecca. In the courtyard of the mosque they circle (*tawaf*) the Kaabah seven times, kissing or touching the sacred black stone or, failing this, saluting it. This ritual does not indicate any special power of the stone but imitates the practice of the Prophet. They then worship at the Place of Abraham, a spot within the mosque where the patriarch prayed. Most pilgrims also complete the running (*say*), moving as briskly as the crowds allow seven times between the hills Safa and Marwa; the route is now covered by a colonnade. This rite imitates the travail of Hagar, Ishmael's mother when, abandoned with her son in the desert, she desperately ran about seeking water. The angel Gabriel, however, opened the Well of Zamzam (now under the Sacred Mosque) with his foot, thus saving the future father of the Arabs. Most pilgrims drink the slightly brackish water before making the run. Many also bring home small bottles of Zamzam water, widely regarded as having curative powers. Most now return to Mina, where on successive days they again stone the pillars, and conclude their stay in Arabia with a visit to the Prophet's Mosque in Medina.

Maintenance of the holy pilgrimage sites is the responsibility of the Ministry of Pilgrimage Affairs and Awqaf. Under King Faisal the courtyard of the Sacred Mosque was enlarged so that is can hold 300,000 worshipers. The Kaabah, a fifty-foot hollow cube of stone blocks, is ritually cleaned for the pilgrimage by religious dignitaries. A reconstruction of an older structure, it is believed to stand near the graves of Hagar and Ishamel. In its southeast corner it holds the sacred black stone in a silver collar. Probably of meteoric origin, this stone has been worn smooth by the touch of countless lips and fingers. The ornate, gold-embroidered black damask cover (kiswah) of the Kaabah is replaced each year on the tenth of Dhu al Hijjah. A government factory produces the kiswah, which formerly came in a special litter at the head of the Egyptian caravan as the gift of the Egyptian people. Eighty artisans craft the covering by hand. The government also provides carpets and other decorations for the Sacred Mosque and the Prophet's Mosque.

* * * * * * * * * * * * * * *

Philip K. Hitti's *Islam: A Way of Life* offers an excellent general introduction to the religion. For concise discussions of the teachings of Wahhab see the first chapter of *Saudi Arabia in the Nineteenth Century* by Richard Bayly Winder and the article "Wahhabiya" in the *Shorter Encyclopedia of Islam* edited by H.A.R. Gibb and J.H. Kramers. Wahhabism's Hanbali background is amply described in *Essai sur les Doctrines Sociales et Politiques de Taki-D-Din Ahmad b. Taimiya* by Henri Laoust. Western readers will gain a vivid impression of the haj from the articles by Michael E. Jansen, Paul Lunde, and Ismail Nawwab in the special issue of *Aramco World* of November—December 1974 devoted entirely to the subject. (For further information see Bibliography.)

CHAPTER 7

SOCIAL SYSTEMS

Saudi Arabian society as it existed in the mid-1970s was almost an accident; after centuries of stagnation two unpredictable factors had galvanized scattered desert tribes and towns into unaccustomed unity and forced the new nation onto the center stage of world affairs. These factors were the brilliant charismatic leadership of Abd al Aziz ibn Abd ar Rahman Al Saud from 1902 until his death in 1953 and the discovery of the world's largest proven reserves of petroleum. Without these two elements the territory of Saudi Arabia might well have remained the home of fractious nomads and tradition-bound peasants and townsmen, one of the most backward regions of the Arab world. A shrewd and profound understanding of the mechanics and mentality of Arabian society along with a propitious genealogy permitted Abd al Aziz to weld the desert and the sown into a new nation loyal to himself. The fortuitous discovery of oil provided the resources to secure his new kingdom for his heirs and to begin its transformation into a society unlike any its founder had known.

Until the rise of Abd al Aziz in the early decades of the twentieth century, Arabian society had changed so little since the founding of Islam that one could accurately predict the mechanism Abd al Aziz would use to mobilize the beduin from reading the works of the fourteenth-century historian Ibn Khaldun. Through ingenious use of religious and tribal symbolism and organization, he was able to manipulate the traditional tribal structures of Arabia so that they supported not the independence of tribal units but loyalty to the House of Saud.

The social revolution accompanying the founding of the nation centered on symbols and institutions indigenous to Arabia. The social revolution accompanying the exploitation of oil brought to the peninsula ideas and influences totally foreign to its history. In place of the traditional importance of descent as the major criterion of social position, modern circumstance tends to favor modern secular education and technical knowledge. In place of the ethnic homogeneity that has long characterized most of the peninsula, the oil industry has attracted a large, polyglot population of foreign workers at both menial and professional levels.

The Saudi dynasty has nonetheless managed to preserve both its own social and political hegemony and the country's cultural heritage.

Government policy attempts, and to some extent succeeds, to circumscribe the influence both of the foreigners and of the cultural influences they represent. Although rapid social mobility is possible for perhaps the first time since the founding of Islam, social change has not thus far threatened the primacy of traditional values. Social change has taken place largely within the framework of traditional institutions; in 1976 some analysts considered it problematical, however, whether this situation could continue for long.

UNITS OF ORGANIZATION

Like other Middle Eastern countries, Saudi Arabia has long exhibited a tripartite cultural and ecological organization. Three distinct variants of Arabic culture developed to fill three major needs of the Middle Eastern environment. Nomadic and seminomadic pastoralists, whether the camel-keeping beduin or the lowlier sheep and goat herdsmen, exploit the marginally productive desert regions. Settled agriculturalists living in villages exploit oases and other regions that permit agriculture. Urban populations provide specialized commercial, religious, educational, and artisan services.

Because of the overwhelming predominance of the desert in the Arabian Peninsula, even as compared to most other Middle Eastern countries, the settled populations, or *hardhar*, have been relatively less important than elsewhere. In Arabian lore and tradition the life of the noble beduin tribes has long been the most valued of the three variants. Many see it as the quintessentially Arab way of life. In pre-Islamic times the word *a'rab* meant beduin; in modern desert colloquial useage it continues to refer to the tribe.

Within the tripartite division of Arab culture Saudi Arabia shows a high degree of cultural uniformity, a product of its long isolation. Except for inhabitants of the mountains of Asir, who are thought to have cultural ties to Yemen, and the fishermen along the Persian Gulf, the major elements showing cultural differentiation are the *ajnabi* or foreign residents of the Hejaz (see fig. 1). These people are not foreigners in the sense of recent arrivals employed in modern industry who are nationals of foreign countries. Rather they are the culturally assimilated descendants of foreign pilgrims to the holy cities of Mecca and Medina. Shiite Muslims of Eastern Province, who suffer social discrimination, are the only other important indigenous minority (see ch. 6).

The country's cultural homogeneity indicates a similar homogeneity of values. Founded on the triple foundation of Islam, family, and tradition, the Saudi value system has shown relatively little erosion. Observers note that modern administrative practice has had to accommodate traditional values rather than vice versa. Ibrahim Al-Awaji describes the Saudi society's central value succinctly: "The identity of the individual is identical with that of his group." He goes on to state, "Individual initiative is only encouraged when it serves and enhances the interests of the group." This belief finds expression in the general tendency to conform to and accept authority, to fulfill obligations rather than to achieve personal advancement, and to practice the favoritism and particularism that Al-Awaji calls "social duties."

These values indicate the importance of descent and family membership as determinants of social status in traditional Arabian society. Among all social groups, even including the *ajnabi*, familial or quasi-familial organizations have dominated and continue to dominate social life. For both historic and cultural reasons tribalism influenced settled populations to a greater degree than in many other Middle Eastern countries; tribalism is of course the mainstay of nomadic and seminomadic societies.

Although Abd al Aziz established the first social organization in modern times to integrate settled and nomadic populations of a wide area into a single centralized unit, the three variants of Arabian culture have long traditions of economic and social interaction; each carries out functions vital to the others. Previously relations had existed on a smaller scale and had occurred in the context of tribal sovereignty and independence. The ecological balance these relations represent had been absolutely basic to Arabian society, however.

The paucity of accurate demographic information seriously hampers discussion of Saudi Arabian social organization. As of early 1976 no census widely accepted as authoritative had been published (see ch. 3). Estimates of the proportions of the population living as nomads, seminomadic farmers, and townsmen vary widely. Because the total population is not accurately known, the proportion of foreigners cannot be judged; nor indeed is the number of foreigners accurately known. Estimates of the nomadic population range from 10 to 30 percent of the total population and even higher. Estimates of village population cover a somewhat narrower but still substantial range. Lack of clarity in typology further complicates the problem; various authors are far from uniform or precise in their definitions of beduin or in their distinctions between nomads and seminomads or migratory and settled tribesmen.

Available studies of Arabian societies largely reflect the tastes of researchers rather than the relative importance of the social units studied. The glamour of the beduin way of life has encouraged a large, colorful literature of travel and description; systematic studies of tribal life are more scarce. Settled life in Saudi Arabia has been almost totally slighted; most of the descriptions available are, from a social science standpoint, fragmentary. Much of the literature on social change is based on journalistic surmise rather than systematic study.

The Tribes

About 90 percent of the territory of Saudi Arabia is too arid for cultivation. The complex tribal organization of the desert permits use of this territory for raising domesticated herd animals through the techniques of pastoral nomadism. Because pasturage and water are insufficient in any given location to support a herd for the entire year, the herders move their animals from place to place according to seasonal availability. Pastoral migrations in Saudi Arabia are of the kind known technically as horizontal because they involve little change in altitude. Concentrated in the northern and central regions, beduin have culturally dominated these areas.

The true beduin tribe is a fully nomadic group based on camel herding. The tribes and animals exist in a symbiotic relationship; the animals supply most of the food and other needs of the beduin, and the tribesmen assure the animals' survival by locating, and guiding them to, adequate water and pasturage. This fine adaption to an extremely demanding ecological niche requires a versatile, portable technology that is, for its kind, extremely sophisticated. It also requires a high degree of very specialized knowledge and a flexible social structure that expands and contracts according to need.

Livelihood and social standing have traditionally depended in part on the nature of the animal herded. The highly mobile, highly warlike noble tribes long prided themselves on their herds of camels. Sheep and goat herdsmen, such as Hadidim, Mawaali, and Muntafiq, enjoyed lower but still generally respectable status, often as clients of the beduin. The true nobility of the camel-herding tribes rested not so much in the species of their flocks, however, as in their ability to enforce tribal claims to particular wells, waterholes, pastures, and oases. At the bottom of the social scale were groups of itinerants who earned their living not as herders but as servants and artisans to the herders; they, as well as lowborn groups who lived as herders, were treated as inferiors by the wellborn tribes, who would neither intermarry with them nor consider them equals in combat.

The low-status groups include the Sulubba of the region north of Al Jawf and Hail, who served the tribes as tinkers and guides and paid tribute to the beduins until the 1930s; the Hazim, who live as pastoralists among the Ruwala; and the Sherarat, who live as servants with the Ruwala, Huwaytat, and Shammar but are considered somewhat less base than the Sulubba because they will defend themselves. Certain tribes, such as the Awazim and Hutaym, live in the same manner as the beduins but are not accepted as equals because of lowly origins and a lack of tribal territory (see fig. 10).

Pastoral adaptation to the desert permits the exploitation of this territory and the entry of desert products into the economies of cities and towns. The tribes have traditionally supplied animals, both for

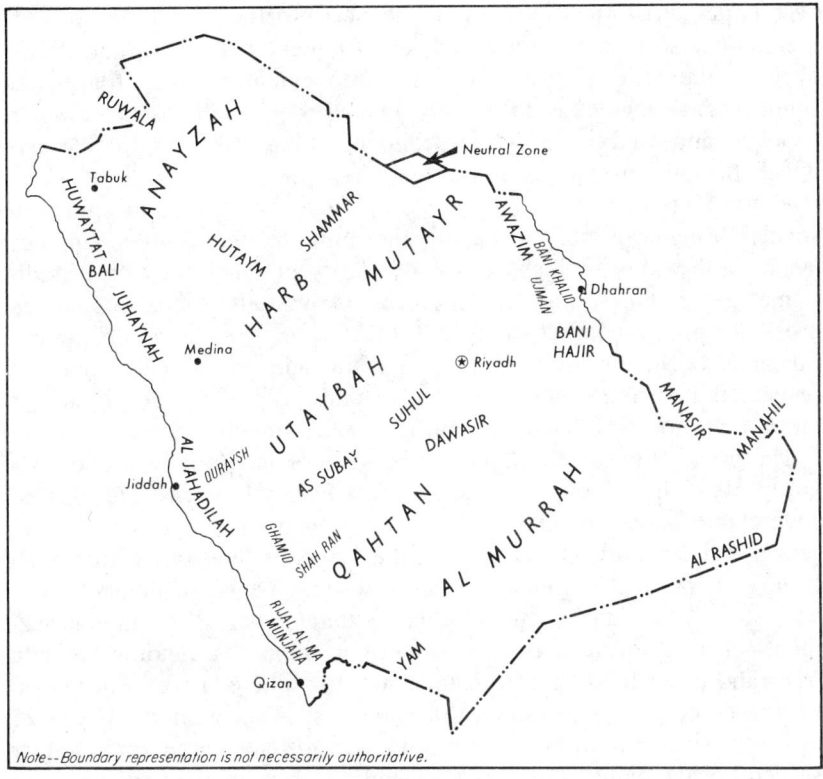

Figure 10. Saudi Arabia, Principal Tribes

meat and for draft, to the settled communities. The word *suq* (market) is related to the root *saqa* (to herd or drive) and originally indicated the place where the nomads herded their animals to allow prospective buyers to inspect them. The village, conversely, supplied agricultural products to the beduin. The town supplied artisanry and religious and governmental services. Long-standing special relationships exist between certain tribes and major towns in their territories. In Hail, for example, many residents number themselves among the descendants of the Shammar; the Al Rashid, shaykhs of the Shammar, ruled the town before the rise of the House of Saud. Khaybar in the Hejaz claims an old tie with the Anayzah tribe; sections of the town are named after major segments of the tribe. The Al Murrah have many ties both to their traditional center at the oasis of Najran and to their modern economic and political center of Hufuf.

Tribes herding camels have traditionally been larger and more powerful than those herding sheep and goats, although they have begun to adopt these less prestigious animals. In general, different households herd the various kinds of animals; often beduin hire members of lesser tribes to tend their sheep and goats. Beduin with camels can range over larger territories and venture deeper into the desert because of their animals' greater speed and less frequent need for water. The cycle of the pastoral year consists of movement between traditional summer camping areas at tribally owned wells with assured water supplies and traditional winter camping areas deep in the desert, which become usable as pasturage after the fall rains. The tribes tend to camp in relatively large groups in summer and to split into smaller, ranging groups to exploit the more scattered water supplies available in winter. Tribes exploit a territory to which they have traditional use rights, although the paths of various tribes sometimes cross, leading to conflict. In general the extremes of the annual migration may be hundreds of miles apart. Nomads traditionally have not respected international borders, and some tribes still cross one or more international boundaries on their yearly travels.

The noble tribes each claim a tribal *dira* or territory in which they enjoy use rights to pasturage and water. Formerly each tribe exerted sovereignty within its *dira;* this sovereignty or freedom was the essence of the nobility of the noble tribes. Specific lineages within each tribe own particular wells and oases where lineage members gather with their herds during the scorching summer heat. Substantial segments of most lineages live permanently in the oases, tending the date trees and other food-bearing plants that grow there. Livestock owned by these sedentary tribesmen are cared for along with the flocks of nomadic kinsmen; trees belonging to nomads are cared for by their settled lineage mates. Some tribal members spend part of the year living in houses in these oasis villages and part of the year migrating with their herds. The line between nomads and settled tribesmen is thus unclear in many cases.

Although the *dira* belongs to a particular group, any other group on friendly terms with the owners may, with permission, use pastures and wells. Except in cases of extreme scarcity, such requests are routinely granted. Even noble lineages or tribes sometimes find themselves forced upon the mercy of their neighbors by drought or other unusual conditions. Tribal sections therefore attempt to maintain as wide a circle of friendly relations as possible in order to have maximum available resources in time of need. In times of severe shortage the lower status groups, who lack their own territories and therefore live permanently at the pleasure of noble tribes, suffer the brunt of the scarcity because they are driven away first. Some students of beduin social structure have suggested that this mechanism allows the large landowning groups to adjust population to available resources.

In addition to its territorial structure a tribe is a complex social unit based upon the ramifications of patrilineal ties between men. A tribe is a group of related families claiming descent from a presumed founding ancestor. Within this overall loyalty, however, descent from intermediate ancestors defines several levels of smaller groups. In cases of conflict, groups of kinsmen mass at the appropriate level of opposition. For example, the grandsons of brothers form two groups in opposition to each other, but they form one unit in opposition to the descendants of the brother of their common great-grandfather.

In concrete terms tribal societies consist of larger and larger groups bound by weaker and weaker ties of loyalty. Donald P. Cole reported that in the late 1960s, for example, the Al Murrah tribe, one of the most famous camel-herding tribes, consisted of several units. The basic unit of organization, the household or tent (*bayt*), contained on the average about seven people (see The Individual, the Family, and the Sexes, this ch.). Approximately fifty households supposedly descended from an ancestor about five generations past form the lineage, the unit that owns the wells and surrounding oases and pastures used as summer camp. Four to six lineages combine into a clan, claiming descent from a yet more distant ancestor. The clan, although it lacks property, figures most prominently in tribal politics. The tribe, which consists of about seven clans, was formerly the military unit but in modern times has become the unit of interaction with the national government. During the summer whole lineages gather at the wells. During other seasons the tribesmen range in groups of one to several households.

Each of the fixed descent groups goes by the name of its presumed founder, preceded by the term *Al* (belonging to or people of) or *Bani* (sons of). The Al Murrah are the people of Murrah, the ancestor of the entire tribe. A member of the Al Murrah tribe, for example, may at various times also claim membership in the Al Athbah, the Al Buheh, or the Al Jaber, among other divisions.

In addition to these named groups, social scientists have identified the so-called sliding lineage, known in Arabic as the *khamsah* (from the number five) or as *al asif* (lineage). Composed of all patrilineal kinsmen within five generations of any particular individual, the *khamsah* takes responsibility for vengeance in case of murder. Because the *khamsah* of a given member of any single lineage may differ slightly from those of his fellows, this group becomes salient only in times of need. All members of a victim's *khamsah* are responsible for avenging his death and may take revenge on any member of the perpetrator's *khamsah*, which precipitates reciprocal revenge. Blood feuds, once under way, have a propensity for spreading rapidly and engulfing large numbers of people. One of Abd al Aziz' early steps in pacifying the desert people was to outlaw blood feuds, and they have been in abeyance since the 1930s. Blood money, however, remains the responsibility of the *khamsah*.

Beduin have traditionally exhibited to the highest degree the attitudes surrounding the concept of honor. Any slight or injury to a member of a tribal segment was an injury to all members of that group, and all members were responsible for the actions of their fellow tribesman. Honor inhered in the family or tribe and in the individual as the family's or tribe's representative. Slights could only be erased by appropriate revenge. Consequently, bloody and escalating feuds between tribes or subtribes often resulted from insults or slights to women. Although in intratribal conflicts individuals with blood ties in both groups often attempted mediation, conflicts between tribes were not usually amenable to negotiation.

It should be obvious that descent figures importantly not only in the ideology but in the politics of the tribes. Individuals possess detailed knowledge of their ancestry. Tribes even trace their descent to one or the other of two very ancient ancestors: Himyar, the son of Qahtan, whose descendants inhabit the south, or Adnan, son of Ishmael and grandson of the biblical prophet Abraham, whose descendants inhabit the north.

Rather than describing historical reality, beduin genealogy serves as a charter for the relations that exist among groups. Purported common descent, for example, provides a tie that permits one group to request aid from another. Examples even exist of tribes changing their ancestry in order to adapt to changed social conditions. The Bani Said of the Najd, for example, who inhabit a chain of villages, originally belonged to the Qahtan tribe. They currently claim to belong to the Atayba tribe, which controls the lands they inhabit; their original tribe, the Qahtan, lost control of the territory. The true social significance of ancestry lies in the realm of action; descent functions as a justification rather than a reason for group status. Emanuel Marx writes:

> The Bedouin genealogies are certainly inaccurate from a historical viewpoint. Even small groups usually have difficulty in tracing the kinship ties between all their members. It is therefore even harder to rely on details of ancestors who lived, according to Bedouin themselves, 7 or 8 generations ago. However, the genealogy does represent reality of a kind; it is the Bedouin's conceptualization of their distribution on the land and gives some indication of their political structure. It thus says very little about the past, but a great deal about the present.

Because of the ability of herding groups to expand and contract with climatic conditions and because of the tremendous distances and dangers involved in desert life, leadership was ordinarily consensual and kin based. The shaykh at each level of organization was the leader of its major lineage and could maintain control only through a judicious combination of suasion, prestige, and bravery. The beduin value of hospitality, owed to any traveler or stranger, permitted important shaykhs to use lavish entertainment in their guest tents to indebt men to them. The shaykh's majlis (audience or tribal meeting) provided the opportunity for tribesmen to present their views as equals.

The position of shaykh or amir, while the prerogative of a particular lineage, is not strictly speaking hereditary. The choice of the particular individual who will assume leadership is made consensually by the heads of families among those of the requisite descent position. The choice tends to go to a man known for his courage, leadership qualities and, in former days, for his luck in battle. Since the rise of the House of Saud the major function of the tribal amir or shaykh has not been to lead his kinsmen in war but to wield influence in their behalf with the government. Luck has therefore declined as a qualification, to be replaced by skill in dealing with the bureaucracy and the royal court.

The extreme hardship and precariousness of desert life do not permit great differences in material possessions, and the attitudinal system emphasizes equality and fraternity. Even the king, when greeted by tribesmen at his court, is called by his given name rather than by his royal title and is treated with the respect due to the first among equals rather than that due to a monarch. While camped in the desert the tribal amir occupies a tent similar to those of his fellow tribesmen. The scale of his hospitality rather than his material possessions distinguishes him from his fellows.

Settled Communities

In social terms Saudi Arabia's agricultural villages generally resemble its tribes, with the exception that the village replaces the tribe as the unit of loyalty. Descent from common ancestors provides the rationale for village organization as it does for tribesmen; many villagers in fact accurately claim descent from various sections of nomadic or seminomadic tribes. These ties of descent facilitate trade with herders and justify traditional relationships of dependence and protection.

Lineages are generally the functional units of village life. Some villages contain members of a single lineage, whereas others contain members of several related or unrelated lineages. Personal identity rests within the corporate identity of the kinship group. Social status depends on one's position within the lineage and the lineage's position within the village. Relations among lineages occur at the level of lineage headmen. Despite the strong pull of kinship, however, villages of some age that consist of more than one lineage nevertheless have developed feelings of unity based on long acquaintance, common economic interests and, in the past, the need for common defense.

Like their desert counterparts, village lineages find geographic expression; kin groups tend to cluster into residential units. Lineage mates occupy adjacent houses, sometimes hold nearby land in common, and often give their name to a quarter in the village. Any differences of religion, as between Sunnis and Shiites, or of occupation, as between peasants and artisans, reinforce social distinctions among lineages.

As is his tribal counterpart, the village headman is chosen by consensus from a leading family in which the position is traditional. His leadership takes the same consensual form; his majlis, like that of the tribal shaykhs, is open to all adult males, and he takes advice from the leaders of all important village groups. The headmen may also represent the village to the central government in the capacity of officially recognized shaykh. Government influence also exists in the form of townsmen settled in the village, such as schoolteachers or other civil servants. The influence of these individuals depends both on their own personalities and on the attitudes of the villagers toward social change.

Village social life depends almost entirely on kinship organization. In most villages no competing institutions exist. Private clubs, organizations other than athletic and cultural, and political groups are officially discouraged and in any case represent values foreign to village culture. A small café may serve as a male meetingplace, but most socializing appears to follow kinship lines.

Saudi towns and cities historically fall into two major categories, those outside and those within the Hejaz. The former have been described by Al-Awaji as "big villages" based on agriculture and the social relations among lineages. They are, in the words of Hermann Eilts, "more puritanical and xenophobic" than those along the western coast. Hejaz cities, however, long ranked as relatively cosmopolitan. Drawn over the centuries to the pilgrimage centers of Mecca and Medina, foreign Muslims remained in the holy cities to study, to work, or merely in the hope of dying on sacred ground. Their descendants constitute about one-half of the population of the cities of the Hejaz. In the early 1960s about one-fifth of the population of Mecca and one-third of the population of Medina were foreign nationals, and one-half of the remainder were of foreign origin. Authorities believe that the situation had not markedly changed in the 1970s.

The haj not only brought Muslims from around the world to the Hejaz but provided them with a livelihood after they had settled there. For many years people of foreign origin have worked in the haj trade, either as purveyors of goods or as *mutawwifun* (haj guides) (see ch. 6; ch. 13). Many *mutawwifun* have specialized in serving their former countrymen, thus taking advantage of their knowledge of foreign languages and customs. Mecca has had identifiable groups of East Asians, Indians, Turks, North Africans, and black Africans. In recent years the Saudi government has discouraged foreign pilgrims from settling in or near the holy cities, and the special haj visas permit only a relatively brief stay. Prospective pilgrims must demonstrate that they have the resources to return to their homes. The haji squatter settlements of former days have disappeared.

Because of their prominence in commerce and the heterogeneity of their populations, the Hejaz cities traditionally derived their social patterns from the relations of commercial and occupational groups rather than of lineages. Specialized trades and crafts were more highly developed in this area than anywhere else in the country, as were educational facilities. Various guilds, such as those in the haj services, figured importantly in the city's organization. In these groups, nonetheless, families rather than individuals are the basic unit.

Despite their relative sophistication, the Hejaz cities have experienced much less the effects of the discovery of oil than the more conservative cities of the central and eastern regions. The relative importance of the haj trade and the guilds controlling it has lessened, but the structure of the cities remains generally unchanged. The huge influx of wealth and people into old towns like Riyadh, Buraydah, and Unayzah, however, has transformed them from traditional, homogeneous, family-centered communities into congested melting pots of workers representing many cultures. The customary family-based life continues for many, but the distracting presence of foreigners and the wealth they represent have put serious strains on housing facilities, price levels, and public services in general.

THE NATIONAL SOCIETY

Abd al Aziz and the Saudi Revolution

The forging of the state of Saudi Arabia out of the various tribes, villages, and towns of northern and central Arabia took place during the early decades of the twentieth century under the leadership of Abd al Aziz, a scion of a leading lineage of the powerful Anayzah tribe and inheritor of the mantle of religious leadership of the puritanical Wahhabi (see Glossary) movement (see ch. 2; ch. 6). During the eighteenth century Abd al Aziz' ancestor, Muhammad ibn Saud, ruler of the town of Dariyah, had joined forces with the religious reformer Muhammad ibn Abd al Wahhab to found a politicoreligious movement that gained, then lost, an extensive tribal state in Arabia. Through intermarriage with the descendants of Wahhab, who are known as the Al ash Shaykh (House of the Shaykh), Muhammad ibn Saud had improved the already excellent ancestry of his descendants, who were of the princely Massalikh lineage. His descendant Abd al Aziz and all other royal members of the lineage that became known as the House of Saud or Al Saud are thus descendants of both Muhammad ibn Saud and Wahhab (see ch. 8; fig. 3).

The beduin reacted to Abd al Aziz' campaign to restore his lineage's and his sect's lost grandeur in a variety of ways; some ignored, some opposed, but many supported his cause. Despite their sometimes contradictory behavior, warrior tribesmen played a central role in the establishment of Saudi Arabia. In mobilizing them to his cause, Abd al Aziz exploited elements so basic to beduin social structure that they had been noted by the fourteenth-century scholar Ibn Khaldun, whom Donald P. Cole and others have called "the world's first sociologist." Cole writes: "According to Ibn Khaldun, the Beduin are proud and unwilling to acknowledge another's superiority. They are difficult to lead except when they follow a prophet or holy man for religion alone can diminish their haughtiness and restrain their jealousy and competition."

According to Ibn Khaldun's theory, relations between beduin and settled populations pass through four phases. At first religious enthusiasm permits a sedentary religious figure to lead beduin warriors to victory over a certain territory. Phase two sees the establishment of state institutions in an atmosphere of fervid puritanism. As the arts of civilization develop in phase three, the devotion to religion lessens. The beduin begin to become disillusioned and start to resume their former way of life. In phase four the state deteriorates, and the beduin return to the desert.

Although not all beduin joined his cause, Abd al Aziz was able to rally enough support to carry his movement through the first two stages. Many contemporaries of Abd al Aziz predicted the fate of stages three and four for the fledgling state. Recognizing the danger of tribalism, Abd al Aziz undertook a systematic program to weaken and even destroy the tribal structures that he considered threats to his leadership. After the discovery of oil he was able to consolidate his kingdom on an economic foundation undreamed of by Ibn Khaldun.

Abd al Aziz' first weapon against tribalism was religion. Arguing that true adherence to Islam required a sedentary way of life, he established a number of agricultural settlements known as *hujar* (sing., hijra—see Glossary) and convinced significant numbers of beduin to join them. These communities combined the features of religious revival center, military cantonment, and farming village. Residents, who came from a variety of tribes, called themselves Ikhwan al Muslimin (Muslim Brethren), a name that emphasized their rejection of tribal ties in place of religious ones. In addition to receiving training in the strict Wahhabi interpretation of Islam, the Ikhwan served as readily available standing armies for assaults on as yet unconquered areas. Abd al Aziz ultimately abolished the *hujar* and dispersed their residents for a number of reasons (see ch. 2). The religious zeal of the Ikhwan proved to exceed his own and became not only an embarrassment but an inconvenience as they engaged in unauthorized raids. Many Ikhwan eventually became disillusioned as Abd al Aziz opted for a limited, militarily defensible territory rather than continued holy war and as he permitted technological innovations that they considered ungodly. By this time, however, Abd al Aziz had firmly established his power among the sedentary population, and he eventually crushed the Ikhwan army with an army of townsmen.

After dissolution of the Ikhwan, Abd al Aziz continued to pursue policies that weakened the tribes as independent entities and strengthened their loyalty to him and his house. In the words of Taha el-Farra he "was able to control the Bedouin through detribalizing them"; that is, he stripped the tribes of their independence and sovereignty, integrating them into a larger political and social unit. He made them begin "to think of themselves as belonging to a national state in the person of their leader." Thus the House of Saud came to occupy a position in the nation similar to that of the leading lineages of a tribe. The king is seen as the shaykh of shaykhs in tribal terms, the leader of the lineage that leads all the tribes in the country. Beduin refer to the king not by his title but by his name and patronymic, just as they refer to tribal amirs. The several recent transfers of power underscored the tribal symbolism inherent in the Saudi kingship (see ch. 8). During the reign of King Faisal ibn Abd al Aziz Al Saud, for example, the Al Murrah beduin referred to themselves as the Al Murrah Al Faisal, the People of Murrah of the People of Faisal. This terminology did not indicate presumed descent but loyalty phrased in tribal terms.

Abd al Aziz and his successors also used the ancient tradition of political marriage to cement relations with many of the tribes. These marriages serve to form strong bonds of obligation and amity between the new in-laws, and Abd al Aziz judiciously exploited these possibilities in his many marriages (see ch. 8). He took advantage of the obligation of the killer of a family head to care for the new widows and orphans and married the widows of foes, such as those of the men of the powerful Al Rashid, thus cementing relationships with former enemies. He married women of the princely lineages of many important tribes. Thus, when members of the House of Saud took over rule of cities and towns from their former tribal rulers, the new officeholders were often in-laws or relatives of the important local tribes.

Abd al Aziz also drew the tribes under the control of the central government by manipulating their economic base. He claimed title to all land for the state but offered to deed it back to those who would reclaim it. He abolished tribal law or *urf* and declared sharia law as the only valid legal code. He outlawed intertribal warfare; the *ghazw*, or raid with the intention of stealing livestock; and the blood feud, declaring that the state rather than the tribe would enforce adherence to the code of honor.

Because fighting and raiding had occupied a major portion of the men's time, these changes stripped the tribal males of many of their important functions. Military service, however, offered an acceptable alternative. The Royal Saudi National Guard, for example, consists exclusively of beduin, and many tribes have substantial contingents enlisted (see ch. 14). Cole states: "In the absence of warfare, the only activity the reserve unit [of the Al Murrah] usually has to perform is monthly attendance at the headquarters to receive their salaries." The National Guard thus ties the beduin fighting men to the government and permits them to retain their dignity as warriors, and the monthly payments supplement their otherwise meager earnings. The shaykhs function as troubleshooters with the government rather than as military commanders, their former role. Cole continues: "Instead of attempting to destroy tribal unity, the national government . . . through the structure of the National Guard provides a mechanism for maintaining tribal unity at the same time that it incorporates the tribes into its own power structure." Thus it retains the illusion rather than the substance of tribal independence.

Under King Abd al Aziz social stratification developed along national lines. At the top stood the House of Saud, along with other members of the ruling class, such as important tribal leaders and members of the ulama, especially the Al ash Shaykh. The noble tribes, subsidized by the government as the exclusive source of the National Guard came next. Below them were lesser tribes, who were permitted to enlist in other military units. Finally came the ordinary townspeople and peasants. Within this system descent and birth were the major determinants of social position, and few avenues for social mobility existed outside of one's own group. Although this social structure functioned adequately while Saudi Arabia was a small, poor desert kingdom, it proved unequal to the demands of unparalleled wealth and world prominence.

Oil and Affluence

The social consequences of the exploitation of oil developed gradually at first, largely as a response to the almost total absence of modern technological and managerial skills in Saudi Arabia. The Western foreigners, primarily American, who arrived in the early years of the oil industry lived in encapsulated communities; avoidance of significant social influence on Saudis by foreigners within the country has been and remains a government policy. As the vast scale of the wealth became apparent, however, the government determined to achieve Saudi control of the nation's resources. This required the development of the first modern school system in Arabian history, the sending of Saudi students for training abroad, and the development of technical and professional colleges and universities (see ch. 5). The demand for services ranging from the highest degree of skill to menial labor generated by the country's newfound wealth brought large numbers of expatriates of many nationalities. The increased numbers of Saudi university graduates trained in technical subjects introduced a significant new element into the social structure.

In attempting to master the vast new wealth made available by oil, the government was forced to deal with problems far more complex and technical in nature than any in its previous experience. Throughout the 1950s nearly all government ministers had been either members of the House of Saud or closely tied to it through personal relations. The sole exception was a secularly educated member of a Jiddah mercantile family. In 1960, however, five ministerial posts, two of which formerly had been held by relatives of the king, went to secularly educated commoners. Four of these men, graduates of Cairo University, had good family connections; the fifth, a graduate of the University of Texas, was chosen for his technical knowledge of the petroleum industry.

These appointments were indicative of a significant trend that had been developing since the middle 1940s, when the first Saudi university graduates came home from abroad, and that gained strength during the 1960s when the graduates of the University of Riyadh, founded in 1957, began to enter the job market. This was the emergence of the modern-educated Saudi professionals, government officials, and entrepreneurs, called by many writers the new middle class. Although many members of this class came from prominent families, their most salient characteristic was that they were knowledgeable, even expert, in a variety of nontraditional fields and that they intended to build their careers primarily on their expertise. In the words of William Rugh, "They are the first group of people in their society who are not automatically members of a class because of their family ties." Rather they place "reliance on secular, non-traditional knowledge to attain their positions."

Until after World War II there was no middle class in Saudi Arabia except for one or two score commercial families concentrated in port towns. Many of these traders were of non-Saudi origin and maintained commercial ties with firms in their ancestral homes. They were Muslim, however, and were assimilated into local society. Other town occupations included religious specialties and small shopkeeping.

Oil, however, provided both the impetus and the opportunity for the development of a new middle class. Public employment grew during the 1950s from a base of a few hundred to 50,000 civilian and 35,000 military and paramilitary, and the number increased by another 50 percent in the following decade. Opportunities for educated young Saudi men were practically limitless and, unlike most countries in the Middle East, Saudi Arabia suffered essentially no brain drain.

Because of the small number of appropriately trained Saudis, many positions in the modern sector went to foreigners. By the late 1940s over 5,000 foreigners worked for the Arabian American Oil Company (Aramco), then American owned. The number of foreigners in the oil industry decreased in the 1960s and early 1970s as Saudis took over increasingly responsible positions (see ch. 12). As the general economy grows, however, the number of foreigners continues to increase. Above the elementary grades the schools and universities are staffed mainly by foreigners; employees of consulting firms and other interna-

145

tional businesses man the large amounts of sophisticated equipment the Saudis have imported for use in health care, communications, transportation, economic planning, and other endeavors. Foreign experts advise the government and private investors in all manner of undertakings. Foreigners dominate at the other extreme of the labor market as well; hundreds of thousands of Yemenis and Sudanese fill the menial jobs that the Saudis do not deign to take. In the middle ranges of white-collar occupations are large numbers of Palestinians, Lebanese, Jordanians, Syrians, Egyptians, and Pakistanis who work as teachers, clerks, and small merchants. No accurate census of foreigners existed in early 1976; some observers suggested that their numbers approach those of native Saudis, but the suggestion that foreigners make up about one-third of the total population seemed more probable.

In the face of this enormous influx of foreigners, many of them with modernist ideas, the government has steadfastly kept to its policies of social and religious conservatism (see ch. 6). King Faisal, for example, issued periodic proclamations to his people to maintain their traditions of dress, modesty, and decorum. Some observers suggest that the presence of foreigners has increased the use of the veil among women as a means of culturally differentiating Saudis from the "guest workers." There can be no doubt, however, that some desire for liberalization of mores exists among Saudis; the fact that the government regularly exhorts the people to cultural purity is an indication of this.

The emergence of many secularly educated Saudi commoners into positions of official if not personal power has to some extent altered the national stratification system. Another trend with the same effect has been the accumulation of vast private fortunes by commercial interests, especially government contractors and concessionaires of important foreign brands of manufactured goods. Observers note a simultaneous increase in both social stratification and social mobility, results of the new money flooding the country. Differences of wealth and poverty are increasing; opportunities for personal advancement are increasing as well.

At the top of the social structure the House of Saud still holds unchallenged economic and political power. The lineage descended from Abd al Aziz and his collateral relatives has grown to enormous size, consisting in the 1970s of several thousand members, and has intermarried with many of the most prominent tribal groups of the country (see ch. 8). Its members are active in all aspects of government, commerce, and industry and enjoy the perquisites of their privileged position.

Below the royal group is a lower upper class consisting of wealthy businessmen and landowners, high government officials, and the leading members of the ulama, especially the Al ash Shaykh. The middle class consists of the professionals and government workers and the small businessmen, both modern and traditional. Although the middle class is larger than the upper class, both are small in relation to the population as a whole. The masses of workers, farmers, and tribesmen compose the remainder of the society.

The emergence of the new social order has significantly affected many elements of the population. As modern secular knowledge has gained ground, traditional religious knowledge has lost exclusive authority; the main competitors of the new middle class for power and authority are not the upper class but the members of the traditional middle class, especially graduates of the religious-school system. Although family ties remain very important, the new demand for specialized knowledge and the new opportunities for amassing wealth have opened some careers to talent as well as connections.

The tribes and villages have also felt the effect of the oil economy. Movement to cities from rural areas has been and promises to remain a prominent trend. From the earliest days of the oil industry tribesmen and rural people have worked for Aramco, rising from laborers to skilled workers. Men seeking work in industry commonly leave their wives and children at home in the care of relatives, thus retaining their ties with their tribe or village. Many, however, have adopted a more modern way of life by settling their families in Aramco communities. Moving one's wife and children away from the ancestral home marks a definitive break with the traditional way of life. So many men have left their rural homes to seek work that at least one village has been reported to have an adult population 70-percent female.

The new economic opportunities have combined with long-term droughts and government inducements for settlement to undermine the nomadic way of life. The movement of the beduin to towns began in earnest with the collapse of the Ikhwan when former herders who had sold their animals and spent their capital were unable to return to their nomadic way of life. The beduin, however, have not reaped the richest advantages of economic development. They generally receive little education and have few skills valuable to modern industrial, commercial, or bureaucratic pursuits. Their own dignity, furthermore, prevents them from taking the unskilled menial jobs for which they are most qualified; they associate this kind of work with lowborn peasants rather than with members of noble tribes. The only modern line of work, apart from soldiering, that fits the skills and self-image of many beduin is chauffeuring or truck driving. Because of government subsidies to the tribes, many beduin are able to subsist without accepting jobs they consider demeaning.

As more and more nomads become wholly or partially sedentary, their egalitarianism has begun to break down. Economic success in the desert depends on factors largely beyond human control—rainfall and the health of the flocks—that affect all herders in a region equally. In the oases, however, houses, trees, and plots are held as private property rather than as tribal preserves. Some households therefore, especially those of notables, are able to afford solid brick houses while others live in shacks or tents. A rudimentary social stratification according to economic means is beginning to emerge in these situations. Roughly groups break down into an upper stratum of the well-to-do and the shaykhs, a middle stratum of tribesmen who have less substantial holdings in the oases and may spend more time in the desert, and the poorest tribesmen, who remain nomadic. Although all tribesmen are equals in terms of their tribal identity, the old ideology remains fully operative only in the desert.

Despite all the pressures against it, many beduin reportedly want to retain their nomadic way of life, although with modifications to suit modern circumstances. Significant numbers of herders have switched from camels to sheep and goats—less prestigious but more lucrative. The pickup truck has come into such common use as a transporter of people, animals, and supplies that one author reported extreme difficulty in securing a small number of riding camels and traditional camel saddles. Trucks have made it possible to carry sheep to desert pastures the animals could not formerly reach on foot and to carry water to the animals instead of bringing the animals to the water. Some observers have expressed fear of overgrazing by sheep and goats of desert pasturage formerly reserved for camels; sheep and goats graze an area much more thoroughly than camels.

Permanent settlements have also sprung up around the Trans Arabian Pipeline (Tapline) pumping stations deep in the desert. Each has permanent supplies of water, and many beduin have camped nearby on a semipermanent basis, some even building brick houses. Many haul water in trucks from the stations to their herds in the desert. A small town near each station has brought government officials and a small bazaar within easy reach of the nomads.

Although the tribes have lost many of their former functions, the government continues to deal with tribesmen through tribal leaders. The position of shaykh is very much coveted, providing as it does allowances, perquisites, and considerable social influence. Holders of the positions naturally resist all pressures toward assimilation of the tribes or even of tribal sections. It has been reported that some tribal sections even have multiple shaykhs, the better to advance their interests. The government, which must certify and deal with the shaykhs, had hopes of assigning them on a territorial rather than a strictly tribal basis, but as of 1976 this plan had not taken effect.

Despite his passing as the viable ruler of the desert, the beduin remains a highly important symbolic figure, representing the glorious and romantic image of a warrior past. In a society undergoing increasing modernization, however, the reality of the living tribesmen tends to be somewhat less glorious. Foreign observers have noted that people express pride in their beduin ancestry but show contempt of present-day beduin. The relative position of the beduin has deteriorated since the onset of economic development despite absolute improvement in the beduin's material circumstances. As the new middle class comes to prominence with the government, it is likely that the influence of the beduin will deteriorate even further. The older generation of officials can remember the beduin armies fighting for Abd al Aziz or at least have heard their fathers talk of those days. Many had grown up in close association with beduin.

The new generation, however, spent their youth attending schools in towns or abroad; they have little community of interest with the uneducated nomadic or seminomadic tribesmen. Cole states: "The king and the princes continue to receive them [the beduin] and to accord them favored status in recognition of the past, but bureaucratization of the governmental process is well advanced and continuing in Saudi Arabia, and I doubt that the younger generation of nomads can rely on these special connections with high officials who now must concern themselves more with international and high level policies."

Although Saudi society is being transformed, it is unclear whether basic values have changed or are changing anywhere near as markedly as Saudi Arabian society. Many observers emphasize that family connections still play an important role in career advancement and that the nonmodern educated still have many avenues open to them. Personalism and particularism still dominate the value system. In addition to the traditional emphasis on family relations, however, the phenomenon of social cliques within the bureaucracy has begun to gain attention. Often composed of co-workers or former schoolmates, these groups meet periodically for cards and socializing and appear to exert a not inconsiderable influence in bureaucratic decisions. Al-Awaji states: "Objective considerations are of a secondary importance in determining the selection of employees and in assuring the necessary cooperation within the organization. It is common to see many friends and relatives of top officials working in their ministries, departments, and divisions."

These values are, if anything, more prominent in the private sector. Personalism has not diminished; the boundaries of one's own group have merely been redrawn. Rugh observes: "A young Saudi with a Harvard business degree must still deal with a highly personalized and family oriented business environment in which personal trust is as important as efficient cost accounting." Although some resentment exists between the traditional and modern elements of the business community, the successful business houses combine the traditional manner with modern management practices.

THE INDIVIDUAL, THE FAMILY, AND THE SEXES

Social life in Saudi Arabia centers in the family; no other institution of even roughly comparable strength exists. Family loyalty and particularism pervade all aspects of life. The household is composed of kinsmen, and among the tribes family ties ramify into tribal structure. The individual's loyalty to his family overrides most other obligations. Ascribed status generally outweighs personal achievements in regulating social relationships. One's honor and dignity are tied to the good repute of his kin group and especially to that of the group's women. Family solidarity finds expression in part in the strict and closely guarded privacy surrounding family life.

Sexual segregation is absolutely basic to Saudi social life and is enforced by law. Women may not drive cars or attend classes with men. Saudi women veil outside their homes, and foreign women are expected to dress with extreme modesty. Mixed social gatherings occur only among foreigners and a few highly sophisticated Saudis. Sex is one of the most important determinants of social status. Men dominate women in most aspects of life. Because of the systematic, lifelong seclusion of women, men and women constitute largely separate subsocieties, each with its own values, attitudes, and perceptions of the other.

Family and Household

Saudis reckon kinship patrilineally, and the household is based on blood ties between men. Ideally it consists of a man, his wife or wives, his married sons with their wives and children, his unmarried sons and daughters, and possibly such other relatives as a widowed or divorced mother or sister. After the death of the father each married son ideally establishes his own household to begin the cycle again. Because of the centrality of family life, it is assumed that all persons will marry when they reach the appropriate age; many divorced and widowed persons remarry for the same reason. In most areas adult status is only bestowed on married men and often only on fathers.

The beduin tent household follows the same general pattern, although the establishment of new households may be somewhat more common among the nomads than among settled folk. Remarriage of parents sometimes precipitates the establishment of new households; no adult man will live in a tent in which his mother is not the senior wife nor in one of a second husband of his mother. A divorced or widowed mother may sometimes live in her own tent with no adult male, but a man tries never to live in a tent without a woman.

Although statistics on household forms were not available in early 1976, the extended family household was quite common, and social values decidedly favored it. Only among the new middle class does the nuclear family household have significant appeal. Even nuclear households often form parts of extended families living in adjacent houses rather than the same house.

Whatever combination of kinsmen composes it, a household may be viewed as a unit of consumption. The men contribute their earnings to the senior male, who spends them in the interests of the entire group. Because women may not transact business in public places, marketing is done by either male family members or male servants.

Traditionally the individual subordinated his personal interest to those of his family and considered himself a member of a group whose importance outweighed his own. It is still not common for persons to live apart from a family group. Men living apart from their family to work at jobs prefer to live with kinsmen or at least fellow tribes. Grown children ordinarily live with parents or relatives until marriage; for a girl of a respectable family to do otherwise would be unthinkable. Child-rearing practices train the young to be docile members of a family group rather than independent individualists.

Symbolic of the subservience of the individual to his family is the fact that the traditional Arabic system of names always associate the individual with specific others. Both men and women are known by their given names and that of their fathers until the birth of a first child, at which time they adopt a new name within their local community. For example, a man called Muhammad ibn Ali whose wife gives birth to a son named Husayn would become Abu Husayn (father of Husayn), and his wife would become Umm Husayn (mother of Husayn). If the firstborn child is a girl, parents may use her name until the birth of a son.

Marriage is a family rather than a personal affair. Because the sexes ordinarily do not mix socially, young men and women have few or no acquaintances among the opposite sex, although among beduin a limited courtship is permitted. Parents arrange marriages for their children, finding a mate through either their own social contacts or a professional matchmaker. Among both village and tribal populations the preferred marriage partner is a child of the father's brother, and such marriages are apparently fairly common. In most areas in fact a man has a right to forbid his father's brother's daughter from marrying an outsider if he wishes to exercise his right to her hand. If the ideal cousin marriage is not possible, marriage within the patrilineal kin group is the next choice; tribes practice close to total endogamy. The only common exception is a marriage with an outsider contracted for political reasons. Endogamous marriages offer several advantages for all parties: the bridewealth payments demanded of the bridegroom's kin tend to be smaller; the family resources are conserved; no danger exists of an unsuitable match; and the bride need not go as a stranger to her husband's house. For these and other reasons endogamous marriage is very common. Although some Saudi men educated abroad have married foreign women, in the early 1970s the government officially banned such matches for its officials.

In Islam marriage is a civil contract rather than a sacrament. Consequently representatives of the bride's interests negotiate a marriage agreement with those of the groom's. Although the future husband and wife must according to law give their consent, they usually take no part in the arrangements. At times a young man might suggest to his parents whom he would like to marry; girls usually have no such privilege. The marriage is registered by the bridegroom and the bride's male representative rather than by the girl herself. The contract establishes the terms of the union and, if they are broken, outlines appropriate recourse. Special provisions inserted into the standard contract become binding on both parties to the union.

Islam gives the husband far greater discretion and leeway than the wife. For example, he may take up to four wives at one time, provided he can treat them equally; a woman can have only one husband at a time. A man can divorce his wife by simply repeating "I divorce thee" three times before witnesses; a woman can instigate divorce only with extreme difficulty. Any children of the union belong to the husband's family and stay with him in case of divorce. Although economic factors discourage divorce, the one-sided nature of the law symbolizes the woman's subservient position. Men of course exercise authority in the home. They expect virginity of their brides, but no such expectation exists for bridegrooms.

Men and Women

The social milieu in which the family lives affects the circumstances of the wife to some extent. In towns and villages male social life goes on outside the home, usually in the shops, cafés, or majlis, where friends meet to chat, discuss politics, or transact business. In the desert, however, women fulfill important economic functions without which the family could not exist. As a result tribal women occupy a position of relative importance and enjoy relative freedom. They never veil, for example. Although casual social contact between the sexes of the sort common in the West is not known, segregation of the sexes is much less pronounced than in settled communities.

Artisan and merchant families earn their living from the skills of the men, and women make little contribution. Their responsibilities are often limited to the household. In such circumstances it is more likely that women are confined to the home and their social contacts and interests limited to an exclusively feminine sphere. The houses of financially comfortable settled families traditionally contain distinct men's and women's areas: the reception room where the man of the family entertains male guests and the women's quarters, from which adult males other than relatives and servants are excluded (see ch. 4).

Unlike their rural sisters, who move more freely in the fields, villages, and desert, urban women walk in the street veiled and chaperoned, discreetly avoiding coffeehouses, suqs, and other public gathering places as well as any social contact with men.

Saudis assume, often explicitly, that men and women are different kinds of creatures. Women are thought to be weaker than men in mind, body, and spirit, more sensual, less disciplined, and in need of protection both from their own impulses and from the excesses of strange men. In courts of law the testimony of one man equals that of two women. The honor of the men of a family, which is easily damaged and nearly irreparable, depends on the conduct of their women, particularly of sisters and daughters; consequently women are expected to be circumspect, modest, and decorous and their virtue to be above reproach. The slightest implication of unavenged impropriety, especially if publicly acknowledged, could irreparably destroy the family's honor. Although family honor resides in the person of a woman, it is actually the property of the men of the natal family. An unfaithful wife, for example, shames her father and brothers far more than her husband. Enforcement of honor, even at the cost of their sister's or daughter's life, is the obligation of the men of a family. Any social standing whatsoever, and even minimal respect, is impossible without it.

Arab societies generally value men more highly than women, and both sexes concur in this estimation. In the words of R. Z. Uzayzi and Joseph Chelhod, men view women as "a necessary evil. . . . What man expects of her is to perpetuate his line, and what he seeks in her is less the companion of his life than the mother of his children." Their upbringing quickly impresses upon girls that they are inferior to men and must cater to them and upon boys that they are entitled to demand the care and solicitude of women. The birth of a boy occasions great celebration, whereas that of a girl does not. Failure to produce sons can be grounds for divorcing a wife or taking a second. Women therefore are often desperately eager to bear sons.

Most women marry in their middle teens. The young bride goes to the household, village, or neighborhood of the bridegroom's family, where she may be a stranger and where she lives under the constant critical surveillance of her mother-in-law. A great deal of familial friction centers on the difficult relationship between mother-in-law and daughter-in-law.

A woman only begins to gain status, security, and approval in her husband's family when she produces boys. As a result mothers tend to favor their sons, ordinarily nursing them longer than their daughters. In later life the relationship between mother and son often remains very warm and intimate, whereas the father is a more distant figure. Observers suggest that women compensate for the emotional shortcomings in their often rather impersonal marriages and submerged adult lives through their relationships with their sons, who as adults often remain in or near the parental household. The wife who enters such a home finds herself in a distinctly secondary position. Furthermore a girl's own parents are by tradition eager for her to marry as soon as she reaches puberty to forestall any mishap to her virginity; she therefore is not encouraged to remain in the family home.

Although women's power is based largely on their relationships with male relatives, it is far from negligible. Respected women with wide social contacts in feminine society often act as important sources of information for their menfolk; women can gather a good deal of news about what is being thought and done in the homes they visit, whereas men are forbidden by etiquette from even discussing the female relatives of their friends. Women play crucial roles in marriage arrangements, which often carry important political overtones. Their support or opposition often determines which matches come about. Their visits to their natal households serve to strengthen ties between allied men. Their labor makes male hospitality possible. Within the privacy of the family circle, their opinions often carry weight in male decisions. It has been suggested by several authors, for example, that a wife of King Faisal exercised significant influence in royal deliberations as does the mother of the so-called Sudairi Seven (see ch. 8).

The development of the educational system has for the first time presented women with options other than traditional marriage and household life. Women of all ages have reportedly responded enthusiastically to those new opportunities, both because of a desire for self-improvement and because modern-educated men, who are considered highly desirable, often prefer an educated wife. It is not at all clear, however, whether education has changed or will change the basic nature of relations between the sexes in Saudi Arabia.

Female education was originally permitted with the understanding that traditional standards of segregation would remain in force. Education of women through the graduate level now takes place in totally segregated institutions. Saudi educators have made imaginative use of such technological innovations as closed-circuit television to facilitate segregation. The fewer than 2 percent of Saudi women who work outside the home generally do so in such entirely female environments as maternity clinics, girls' schools, wholly female offices, and social agencies serving women. Some women work as radio and television announcers but as yet have not been permitted to appear on the screen.

* * * * * * * * * * * * * * *

Louise Sweet's "The Arabian Peninsula" briefly but informatively reviews ethnographic knowledge of Arabia up to the late 1960s. Two works by Donald P. Cole, the first and as of early 1976 the only anthropologist to publish studies of Saudi Arabia based on modern ethnographic research, complement

Sweet; *Nomads of the Nomads* describes beduin social and ecological organization, and "The Enmeshment of Nomads in Saudi Arabian Society" discusses in detail the relations between a beduin group and Saudi society at large. "Emergence of a New Middle Class in Saudi Arabia" by William Rugh considers an important aspect of social change. Marianne Alireza presents a lively account of family life from a Western woman's viewpoint in *At the Drop of a Veil*. (For further information see Bibliography.)

SECTION II. POLITICAL

CHAPTER 8

GOVERNMENT AND POLITICS

The dynasty of the House of Saud (Al Saud) was in a stronger position in early 1976 than ever before in its history. King Khalid ibn Abd al Aziz Al Saud was adhering to the policies that his half brother, King Faisal ibn Abd al Aziz Al Saud, had formulated before his assassination in March 1975. The primary emphasis of those policies was to promote modernization of the country without losing the many traditions incorporated in its Islamic society.

The monarchy itself is not hereditary. It is limited by the dictates of the sharia (the sacred body of Islamic law) and designation to the throne is made by the royal family's choice, sanctioned by the ulama. This designation rests upon a consensus of support from a wide base of established Islamic traditions. Specific groups in the society must make up part of the consensus that offers legitimacy to the king: the royal family, the principal tribal leaders, the Council of Ministers, the Consultative Council, the ulama, and the armed forces. In early 1976 King Khalid appeared to be in full command of the loyalty of all these elements. Amir Fahd ibn Abd al Aziz Al Saud, half brother of King Khalid, formally received this consensus to perform the duties of crown prince and, as in the case of the selection of the king, this occurred within hours after the death of King Faisal. In the event of the king's demise, a consensus would again be sought to confirm Fahd's succession.

In the national society the integration of religion, state, and social forms continued to prevail, and the king's position continued to be the focus of all lines of power. Following traditional practices he is the head of state, the shaykh of shaykhs in the ancient pattern of Arabian social structure, the supreme religious leader, and the commander in chief of the armed forces. Assisted by the Council of Ministers, whose members are appointed by and responsible to him, and an extensive civil service, he exercises authority within the framework of Arab tradition and the sharia law as supplemented by decree law, particularly during the 1960s and early 1970s.

King Khalid, in addition to being head of state, continued in 1976 as prime minister and working executive head of the government. In the absence of a legislative body the Council of Ministers functioned as the instrument of royal authority in legislative as well as executive matters; there were twenty ministries in early 1976. In addition to the king as prime minister the Council of Ministers was composed of two deputy prime ministers and the twenty ministers. In a reorganization of the Council of Ministers in late 1975 Khalid appointed Crown Prince Fahd to the office of first deputy prime minister and designated Amir Abd Allah ibn Abd al Aziz Al Saud as the head of the Royal Saudi National Guard and as the second deputy prime minister (see ch. 14). Governmental decisionmaking functions remained highly centralized in the office of the king and the Council of Ministers.

Since the formal establishment of the Kingdom of Saudi Arabia in 1932, successive kings have developed a central government to assist them in running the country. Since 1953 a formal council of ministers has replaced the appointment of ministers to the king's office. In 1976 the Council of Ministers was responsible for advising him on the formulation of general policy and for directing the activities of the ministerial bureaucracies created to execute national policy. Legislation is by royal decree or on minor matters by ministerial regulation sanctioned by the king. Justice is administered according to sharia law—as defined by the Hanbali school of Islamic religious scholars—by a system of religious courts under the authority of the king through the Ministry of Justice, created in 1970 (see ch. 6). An extensive system of governmental bodies administers decree law or regulations within separate jurisdictions.

All political power rests ultimately with the king, who is responsible for protecting the institutions of Islam and the interests of the Islamic community, for defending the state, and for furthering the interests of the nation. Other sources of political influence are based on affiliation with the king's office and those around him. No substantial internal opposition had emerged in early 1976. Most of the population apparently continued to regard the government's policies as beneficial to them or were not affected by them and accepted Khalid's continuance of a policy of gradual, adaptive change. Some dissatisfaction existed with the pace of modernization and the conservatism of some of the ulama, but active dissent took the political form of disenchanted small groups rather than any widely based movement.

The use of the term *family* in this chapter follows the practice of much of the literature on Saudi Arabia. Mainly written by political and economic analysts, this literature has generally ignored the structural distinctions drawn by anthropologists and other students of tribal organization. The various families mentioned here, such as Saud, Sudairi, Jiluwi, and Al ash Shaykh, are by no means analogous in terms of tribal or internal structure. Some are clans or lineages, whereas others are subtribes: the Jiluwi, for example, are a branch of the Al Saud; the branch of the House of Saud that has thus far produced kings is the Al Faisal. For consistency's sake this chapter will follow the customary usage. A more technical discussion of tribal structure appears elsewhere (see ch. 7).

ROYAL FAMILY, RELIGION, AND POLITICS

House of Saud

The political development of Saudi Arabia has been centered in the position and growth of a tribal family that had built a dynasty comparable with few others in 1976. From the meager beginnings of the Saud family, many generations ago, have emerged a country named after them and a royal family with 5,000 or more living members. The descendants of a man who ruled only an Arabian city-state in the eighteenth century formed a nation-state of vast influence in the world—the Kingdom of Saudi Arabia.

It was not until the mid-nineteenth century, however, that events took place that produced the predominance of the lineage of the present members of the royal family. These events concerned the bitter internal dissension that followed the assassination of Turki ibn Abd Allah (ruled 1824-34) by a family member. The members of one branch of the family, the sons of Saud ibn Abd al Aziz (ruled 1803-14), pitted themselves against Turki's sons, Faisal and Jiluwi, in a battle to determine who would rule the family (see ch. 2). Eventually Faisal, assisted by his brother and Abd Allah ibn Thunayyan (from a third branch of the family), gained undisputed control as ruler and became the most successful leader of the family until the time of his grandson, Abd al Aziz ibn Abd ar Rahman Al Saud, in the early twentieth century.

Until that time the Saud dynasty had two well-defined links to the past—the lineages of its founder, Muhammad ibn Saud, and that of Muhammad ibn Abd al Wahhab, the religious leader responsible for the branch of Islam called Wahhabism (see Glossary) (see ch. 6). As the twentieth century began, there were three surviving branches—Al Abd Allah, Al Faisal, and Al Jiluwi—but only the Al Faisal could be noted as an important lineage, and this remained true in the mid-1970s.

Much confusion followed the death of Faisal in 1865, and his successor, Abd ar Rahman (ruled 1875, 1889-91), was forced into exile in Kuwait from 1891 through 1902. This period, however, produced an important link between the Saud dynasty and the ruling family of Kuwait, Al Sabah, which still existed in 1976. Abd ar Rahman's son, Abd al Aziz, who became the first king of Saudi Arabia, was only eleven years old when his father took him into exile.

At the age of twenty-one, Abd al Aziz returned the rule of the Saud family to Riyadh by defeating the ruler of the area, Abd al Aziz ibn Rashid (see ch. 2). Riyadh, the family's traditional capital, was located in the eastern part of the Arabian Peninsula known as the Najd (see fig. 1). The perpetuation of the dynasty and the events that led to the creation of a kingdom, however, depended on other actions of Abd al Aziz in addition to conquest.

Because there were many tribal families throughout the whole of the Arabian Peninsula, the young Abd al Aziz used political marriage to consolidate his power. He married approximately twenty women from such influential families as the descendants of Wahhab (whose direct male descendants are known as members of the Al ash Shaykh family), the Sudairi family, the Jiluwi family, and many others. The success of this method of extending the influence of the Saud family is witnessed in the present day in that almost every major tribal family has some connection with the royal family.

Another change in the nature of the Saud dynasty was in the notion of legitimacy that its rule was based on. Each head of the dynasty had held the title of imam (see Glossary), which had passed to the family after the death of Wahhab. Although Abd al Aziz was the paramount political leader after 1902, his father, Abd ar Rahman, remained head of the dynasty and retained the title of imam until his death in 1928. The formal use of the title of imam ended with his death. Abd al Aziz assumed the title of sultan in 1921 when he achieved complete victory over the Rashidis, and six years later he gave up this title to become king of the Najd and the Hejaz, forming the basis for a united kingdom under his rule within five years.

By 1932, when the kingdom was established, Abd al Aziz, assisted by his sons and numerous tribal leaders, had established his rule over most of the territory of present-day Saudi Arabia. He lived for twenty-one years after the creation of the kingdom and during this period personally managed most of the affairs of the country.

A prototype of a ministerial system did appear, however, as Abd al Aziz brought members of the royal family, leaders of the tribal families, and some non-Saudi Arabs into his Consultative Council as advisers, a body with an ancient tradition in Islamic history. This action was followed by the appointment of Amir Faisal as minister of foreign affairs in 1931, and this in turn led to the creation of Saudi Arabia's first council of ministers in 1931. The designation of his eldest son, Saud, as crown prince in 1933 seemed to complete his plan for political stability. As Abd al Aziz became gradually weakened by advanced age, however, he recognized the need for a more fully developed political administration and became concerned over Saud's leadership potential. The new country would have to spend ten troubled years, however, before Abd al Aziz' fears were allayed.

Succession to the Throne

Although Saud was personally chosen by his father to succeed him, many influential groups within and surrounding the royal family also had to take active roles. Precedents were set for a committee of senior amirs—from Abd al Aziz' brothers and sons—to sanction Saud's succession. He received formal support from many other members of the royal family, the senior ulama, and numerous tribal leaders. This affirmation of allegiance to a king was established as a prerequisite before he could begin his rule, as was a new king's pledge to defend the country, its religion, and its people. In effect these procedures have become a bilateral oath between the king and the ruled that if broken could bring about the deposition of the king.

If the king is deposed, the determination of his successor can be somewhat difficult. The process of succession is not based on primogeniture—the tradition in most monarchies of choosing the eldest son of the preceding ruler. Arabic traditions of succession generally dictate that the most able member of the family should be the successor, even if he is not the next oldest son.

Providing for effective succession has been limited to only three actual experiences for the royal family. The first two successions—Saud and Faisal—were determined by Abd al Aziz before his death; only the succession of the present king, Khalid, offers an example that could be seen as a test of the system. There are precedents to be considered in choosing a successor, and these begin with the choice of crown prince.

The country's first crown prince, Saud, was named not in the tradition of the most able but rather in an attempt by Abd al Aziz to create a formal process of succession, possibly based on the British system, with which he was familiar. He named his eldest surviving son crown prince and later, having second thoughts about the choice he had made, decided to establish formally a council of ministers of which Faisal, whom he considered his most able son, was designated prime minister in addition to being crown prince when Saud succeeded to the throne. In taking such a step Abd al Aziz probably intended Faisal to head the government and be responsible for all decisions during the period Saud reigned. Saud became king one month later when his father died suddenly.

The country's first approach to dealing with succession was not entirely effective. In fact it put into office a man who was obviously unable to cope with the assigned duties and was eventually deposed. The fact that the system was still flexible enough to include the tradition of replacing a ruler who had lost consensus in favor of a family member who had gained it may indicate the present method's potential for handling crises of legitimacy.

For many reasons Saud did not maintain his original consensus for very long. Before he began his reign, many had opposed him, feeling that Faisal was the obvious choice to succeed his father (see ch. 2). During Saud's eleven-year reign Faisal was idle until 1958 when, except for a brief period he was, as his father had intended, head of the government and ruled with an authority that formerly had been reserved to the king. In late March 1964 Faisal had the king accept a decision by the royal family and the ulama that reduced Saud's powers even further. The king's Royal Guard was removed from his personal command and placed under the Ministry of Defense and Aviation, the royal court was abolished, and the king's income was cut in half and that of the royal family reduced sharply. From then on Faisal was in complete control of the government, and seven months later the royal family deposed Saud and proclaimed Faisal king. After the consolidation of power and authority in the monarch the divisions in the royal family were healed. This ended the attempt to formulate a primogeniture system of succession; instead there was a return to the traditional process that determines a successor by his known ability to lead and receive consensus.

Muhammad, the next oldest son of Abd al Aziz after Faisal, was not named crown prince by Faisal; rather, after consulting many influential groups and the committee of senior amirs, Faisal chose Khalid as the most desirable. Muhammad, as a member of the amir group, disqualified himself, establishing yet another precedent in the process of succession.

Although many observers became skeptical over this return to a traditional way of doing things, the succession of Khalid to the throne abated their fears. Within hours of Faisal's assassination on March 25, 1975, a committee of senior amirs met and left intact Faisal's plan for succession, naming Khalid king and Fahd crown prince. Renewing the precedent set by Muhammad, Nasir and Saad, both older half brothers of Fahd, disqualified themselves. The decisions were made and announced very quickly, without the dissension among branches of the royal family that many people had feared.

The Next Generation

The successors of Abd al Aziz have thus far been chosen from his surviving sons (see fig. 11). It is probably safe to say that future kings will also be chosen from the descendants of Abd al Aziz, if not from his many sons then from his grandsons. There are many influential amirs, however, descendants of Abd al Aziz's brothers or cousins, who should not be completely discounted.

Abd Allah ibn Abd ar Rahman, Abd al Aziz' brother, was considered the senior member of the family in 1976. Abd Allah and his two living brothers—Ahmad and Musaid (minister of finance and national economy from 1962 to 1975)—were referred to as the "uncles." Along with their sons, they were influential in family decisionmaking. The branches of the royal family that were descended from the nineteenth-century rulers Faisal and Abd ar Rahman also had influential positions in the family and government.

The most obvious source of future leaders is the "nephews," grandsons of Abd al Aziz. Many of these amirs were among the first to receive an education in the United States or Western Europe, and they have returned to play important roles in the government. For the most part they include Faisal's sons and the sons of the so-called Sudairi Seven, one of whom is Crown Prince Fahd, and exclude numerous other grandsons who have failed to become educated or contribute to the family.

Because Abd al Aziz' mother was a Sudairi, all of his descendants have and will continue to have connections with that family. The strongest inroads into the royal family were made by another daughter of the Sudairi family, who gave birth to seven sons by Abd al Aziz, all of whom have gained prominent positions as the Sudairi Seven. In early 1976 four of them were ministers or vice ministers, one was a provincial governor, one a deputy governor, and the last was in charge of the family's vast financial affairs.

The mother of the two eldest surviving sons of Abd al Aziz also had Sudairi connections through her father. Her first son, Muhammad ibn Abd al Aziz, is a member of the committee of senior amirs, and her second son is King Khalid.

Examples of successful grandsons of Abd al Aziz are Faisal's third son, Saud ibn Faisal ibn Abd al Aziz Al Saud, who was appointed minister of foreign affairs in October 1975, and Crown Prince Fahd's son, Faisal ibn Fahd ibn Abd al Aziz Al Saud, who in early 1976 was director general of youth welfare in the Ministry of Labor and Social Affairs. They will probably continue to play important roles in the royal family as well as in the government; so will many of their brothers and cousins.

A phenomenon that has been a tradition in the Saud dynasty is the intermarriage of cousins, either cousins within the royal family or those already related by marriage to the royal family. A typical example of this is Saud ibn Faisal. He was born of Faisal's marriage to a woman of the Thunayyan family who was related to the royal family through Abd al Aziz' great uncle Abd Allah. Saud ibn Faisal married a daughter of King Saud, who had Sudairi connections through her father, the son of Abd al Aziz' first wife and a member of the Sudairi family. Therefore Saud ibn Faisal's children will have strong connections within both the Sudairi and Jiluwi families and, through their grandfather Faisal, with the Al ash Shaykh family.

The consolidation of influence and power by intermarriage, however, is only one method that the royal family of Khalid's generation has continued to use. Beginning with his generation, and certainly an important aspect in the next, are the younger amirs who have chosen to seek success in nongovernmental roles. In 1976 more than ever before royal amirs pursued careers in business, technological fields, and the professions.

Decisionmaking in Saudi Arabia

Although by the mid-1970s the political system in Saudi Arabia was becoming increasingly complex because of the country's attempt to develop rapidly, the procedures for making decisions remained much as they were during Abd al Aziz' reign. Policy was determined in the final analysis by one person, the king; its formulation depended on few other individuals. In 1976 many Saudis might be involved in formulating any single decision, but it was still the king who decided what that policy should be.

Since the legitimacy and therefore the authority of the office of the king was based on his ability to maintain a consensus among numerous factions within the country, his power was not truly absolute. This need for consensus has been a traditional feature in maintaining leadership in the Saud dynasty and is well documented.

Although there are no political parties in the kingdom, the position of the royal family in the decisionmaking process can best be described by using an analogy with a political party or political interest group. After being selected by his peers, a leader constantly consults his committee of senior advisers in the process of making decisions that concern the party (royal family) or conditions affecting the society (Saudi Arabia). The leader's ability to make decisions and maintain legitimacy, however, is determined through the support of party leaders and members. Party leaders (amirs, senior ulama, and others) who are close to the leader fill positions (such as governors, ministers, military officers, and others) that maintain influence over the party members (remaining members of the royal family, tribal leaders, and the general Saudi population).

This analogy presents a model of a single-party system, and the decisions that are made depend on the functioning of the party at all levels. The royal family is open to dissension from inside and outside its ranks, but no organized opposition is permitted (see ch. 14). This was the system that evolved under the rule of Abd al Aziz, and it remained a primary rule in 1976.

King Faisal's Era

Faisal, more than other member of the Saud dynasty, was well known throughout the world. The patterns of his rule were passed on to him not only by his father but also by his grandparents. Faisal was the only son of Abd al Aziz' second wife (of the Al ash Shaykh family), who died shortly after his birth. Born in 1905, he was the first of his generation to be born in the traditional Saud capital of Riyadh.

As an only child Faisal profited from his name (after the nineteenth-century family hero, Faisal), his position of birth (second oldest after the early death of the firstborn, Turki) and, most of all, the lineage of his mother's family from Wahhab. In the home of his grandparents, where he was raised while his father continued his conquests over Arabia, he received an excellent education in the sharia tradition and quickly outshone his older brother Saud. At the age of fourteen Faisal was chosen to represent his father and head a mission to the United Kingdom; this was the first of many diplomatic and government roles he occupied in preference to Saud.

Faisal's era began with the death of his father. Faisal's first goal was to continue his father's policies despite the obstacles his brother, the new king, laid in his path. Considering the level of development that the country had reached before Abd al Aziz, change in the economic and social sphere did occur during his reign, but the traditional political system remained almost untouched.

As long as Abd al Aziz ruled, the great prestige he enjoyed gave little room for opposition to his reign. King Saud, however, was forced to deal with the growing political and social awareness of his people without the unquestioned ability and authority of his father. Saud's efforts to preserve paternalistic political patterns and his failure to use the rapidly growing oil wealth effectively for the betterment of the society aroused growing resentment. During his reign he became more and more isolated; rejecting the traditional bases of support, he sought to install his sons and intimates in all positions of responsibility. Only Crown Prince Faisal had the position to challenge him to any significant extent. Saud's main obsession was to strengthen his personal Royal Guard in order to preserve his rule.

In early 1958 the senior amirs of the royal family compelled Saud to transfer full executive responsibility to Faisal, who had also been prime minister since 1953. Faisal immediately enacted a number of regulations in an attempt to put the government on a functioning level again. These actions in turn instilled discontent in those groups that had profited from Saud's patronage through royal subsidies to the Saud family members, government contractors, and important tribal leaders throughout Saudi Arabia.

By late 1960 Saud was able to gain back his executive authority by taking advantage of opposition to Faisal by a small group in the royal family, although it was Faisal's resignation that facilitated his return. This power struggle was continually complicated by the king's health, and in November 1961 he was forced to leave for the United States for further treatment. He had no choice but to delegate temporary executive powers to Faisal once again, and by March 1962 the king's poor health caused him to name Faisal deputy prime minister and acting head of the Council of Ministers. Thus barely fifteen months after he had resigned from government, Faisal regained effective if not formal executive power.

In October 1962, as a result of threats to the regime brought on by the situation in Yemen, Saud resigned his role as prime minister in favor of Faisal. During the next year Faisal took a number of steps to consolidate his position. He replaced Saud's sons in the Council of Ministers by three of his most loyal half brothers—Khalid, Fahd, and Sultan—and an uncle, Amir Musaid ibn Abd ar Rahman. He removed most of the Royal Guard from the palace for duty along the Yemen border and presented his proposal for a basic law of Saudi Arabia. These acts were facilitated by the king's absence from the country during much of 1962 and 1963.

During Faisal's reign, which formally began with the deposition of Saud in 1964, he instituted a number of social reforms, albeit cautiously. Education and welfare services were expanded, and slavery was abolished. It was his 1962 proposal for a basic law, however, that set the subsequent pattern for decisionmaking. In an official decree Faisal established the supreme role of the king in all governmental affairs by permanently uniting the office of prime minister with the king's many other responsibilities. Faisal felt that the king must be decisive in all his actions and that at the highest point of government no dissension should take place. He probably also remembered his advantage as prime minister from 1953 to 1960 and the power this position offered him although Saud was king.

Under Faisal's rule the only decisions not made directly by him were those of his ministers, and these ministerial policies, no matter how trivial, were always sanctioned directly by him. His choice of participants for the decisionmaking process was an effective method of controlling and reinforcing his authority and of avoiding possible splits in the government. His office was open to many people, but he remained above the complexity of the governmental process.

Faisal took a gradualist's approach to decisionmaking during his reign. When he was successful, it was not because the problems were less difficult or complex but because he responded to them by using the traditions of the Saud dynasty. Hence decisions affecting the basic structure of Saudi society were enacted gradually or not at all. This not only forced change to occur according to tradition but permitted Faisal to maintain the consensus of support throughout his reign. Furthermore his approach to leadership also met the challenge of the outside world when the position of Saudi Arabia began to have influence beyond its borders (see ch. 10).

For the most part Faisal adhered to the principles of the sharia. For example, it was not so much that the influence of the ulama declined during his era as that there was a return of the king's compliance with religious traditions in implementing policies, and this tended to quiet most of the protests of the religious authorities. His paternalistic rule, however, was not always as successful as many had hoped.

Faisal had probably intended that Saudi Arabia, with its Islamic system of government, would become a modern theocracy, but the world, and in particular his region of the world, offered many drawbacks. Until the middle and late 1960s Faisal had always listened and responded to his country's traditional form of egalitarianism, often called beduin democracy, and he continued the tradition of the majlis (see Glossary) even to the scenario of his assassination. Despite some efforts, economic development and change by the early 1970s had not been accompanied by changes of comparable magnitude in the basic political and social outlook.

Faisal's concern over the rising tide of Arab radical movements, the Arab-Israeli conflict, and other external pressures, including the opposition to him by Gamal Abdul Nasser of Egypt, replaced his former preoccupation with domestic programs to improve social and economic conditions (see ch. 10). Increased government expenditures were channeled into defense, and the country's infrastructure requirements were put at a lower priority (see ch. 11). It was only the fortune of changing situations in the oil industry that offered Faisal's regime new hope. It was the discovery of oil that facilitated his father's ability to rule, and it was the discovery and then the management of Saudi Arabia's oil resources, particularly after 1973, that would offer the country and Faisal renewed prestige and stability (see ch. 12).

The events of the first half of the 1970s, including the substantial increases in oil revenues, the October 1973 War between Israel and Egypt, Jordan, and Syria, and the renewed friendship between Egypt and Saudi Arabia after Nasser's death, produced a situation of lessening tension, externally and internally. Faisal found himself in a position of newfound strength, immense wealth, and unexpected alliances. Saudi Arabia's first Five Year Development Plan (1970-75) lived up to expectations, although it was not meant to lead to drastic changes. The end of Faisal's reign, however, was highlighted by a period of high expectations for change in the country, and pressures for development from every quarter were left for Saudi Arabia's next king.

King Khalid (1975-)

With the assassination of Faisal and the efficient succession of Khalid, the process of decisionmaking appeared to take on some new features. Khalid clearly remained the king, the chief of state, the head of government, and the commander in chief of all military forces, but he delegated to Crown Prince Fahd considerable authority to oversee most day-to-day affairs.

At the end of Khalid's first year as king, foreign observers were convinced that all prominent and influential members of the royal family were unreservedly committed to a continuation of the system of which Khalid as king was the public symbol, i.e., the dominance of the House of Saud. In the opinion of those observers the several discernible groups within the royal family not only posed no threat to the unity of the House of Saud but actually strengthened the family, and there was no public evidence of dissension within the family.

The most prominent group of senior family members was that headed by Crown Prince Fahd, whose full brothers Sultan, Turki, and Naif respectively held the positions of minister of defense and aviation, vice minister of defense and aviation, and minister of interior. Amir Abd Allah, the National Guard commander, was sometimes described as the focal point of another center of influence and as one of the more important links of the House of Saud to the noble beduin tribes (see ch. 7). According to many observers the reorganization and expansion of the Council of Ministers on October 13, 1975, displayed a balance between two major royal family groups as well as a regional balance in the distribution of portfolios.

Other Sources of Political Influence

The process of development and the rapid pace of world affairs have sharply increased the complexity of administering a government that continued to maintain a highly centralized structure. The new diversity of the Council of Ministers highlighted these changes and the council's role as a body of significant political influence in 1976. When Abd al Aziz was displeased with one of his personal ministers, he could dismiss him with little effect on the system, but this was more difficult to do in 1976.

In addition to the royal family members in the Council of Ministers, there were a number of very influential commoners who, because of their expertise or affiliation with the royal family, shared far more responsibility for decisionmaking than in the past. They commanded the loyalty of powerful bureaucracies in some cases and were to be contended with if the government hoped to implement its policies. The ministers served at the pleasure of the king, but the king and his brothers and nephews were increasingly dependent on these men to accomplish the goals of the future. Foreign analysts suggest that these commoners will maintain their position of influence and probably gain even greater shares of power.

Foreign observers generally agreed that these ministers—the more prominent of whom were Shaykh Ahmad Zaki Yamani, head of the Ministry of Petroleum and Mineral Resources; Ghazi Abd ar Rahman al Qusaibi, head of the Ministry of Industry and Electricity; and Hisham Muhi al Din Nazir, head of the Ministry of Planning—seem to hold the king and the leaders of the royal family in great esteem. They regard the Islamic state under Khalid as the natural way of political expression and basically accept his policy of gradual, adaptive modernization. Some dissatisfaction exists about the pace of modernization, but the government's policies tended to stay ahead of this complaint at least for the majority of the people. The phenomenon of political stability in Saudi Arabia seems to have two sources: the participants in the political system tend to form segmental elite groups and remain separated from each other—the military, the technocrats, the business community, and others—and those individuals who have gained positions of political influence have done so by their implementation of policy and decisions made by the traditional few at the top.

These segmental groups have been called the new middle class of Saudi Arabia. They seem content to participate in the development of the country and receive high compensation rather than disturb the organization of the system. The lack of education among the Saudi population and the drastic need for highly trained and capable people at all levels of government permit the unlimited absorption of as many Saudis as are achieving skills and expertise, and this situation will probably continue (see ch. 5).

The potential of political influence, however, was greater in some of these groups than in others. For example, in 1976 the National Guard continued to recruit from among the beduin tribes in the rural regions (see ch. 7). They are highly trained to offer internal security to the country but give total allegiance to the royal family, to whom they are perpetually tied. The armed forces, however, increasing in both numbers and sophistication during the 1960s and early 1970s, had developed resources for capable leadership in addition to the many members of the royal family in the officer corps (see ch. 14).

The ulama, as a group of religious scholars, perceive their role in relation to government as very active. They are the traditional guardians of the Islamic orthodoxy of political decisions. Approval or disapproval of political acts by this group is expressed through the issuance of a *fatwa*, or legal decision. In a substantial way the ulama were responsible for the transfer of executive powers from Saud to Faisal in 1962 and for the deposition of Saud in 1964. These powers of legitimizing authority continued to be important in 1976. Faisal's manipulation of this group, seen as a decline in their political influence, went as far as the establishment of the Ministry of Justice in 1970—an area traditionally under the jurisdiction of the Al ash Shaykh family. With the reorganization of the Council of Ministers under Khalid, however, the new minister of justice was a member of that family, indicating a return of this group's influence (see Legal System, this ch.).

The profound economic transformations at work in the country since the discovery of oil, particularly since 1965, have brought about corresponding changes in the social structure (see ch. 7). This has been generated not only by the phenomenal growth in the oil industry but by the consequent expansion of the central government, creating new wealth and new aspirations among young Saudis. Many Saudis seeking the skills necessary to participate in the country's prosperity sought education abroad and came in direct contact with other cultures—Western, for the most part. After returning to Saudi Arabia few seemed concerned with more rapid political change in the direction of any of the countries they had visited. Reinforced by the ability to gain wealth and status in their occupations, these young Saudis have been preoccupied with their own situation in society and have apparently not pressed for dramatic changes in the political realm.

The mechanics of managing a program of rapid development have increased the political influence of the many merchant firms and businessmen. Commercial and financial elites, however, have gained the affiliation with the government they deem necessary to carry on their business activities, and the form of political influence they have successfully achieved has only been in relation to this. Like the young upward bound Saudis, they are seen to be content in their position and hope to become the great industrialists of the country rather than gain high office.

GOVERNMENTAL SYSTEM

Legal Bases of Government

Experience with written constitutions and constitutionally based representative institutions has never been present in Saudi Arabia. Throughout the country's brief history as a state political control has been authoritarian and centralized in direct royal rule. Nevertheless it is possible to trace the development of the legal basis of the present Saudi government through the significant documents that are the foundation of the governmental system.

The central institution of political authority is sharia law, which determines the boundaries of every aspect of the political process. Consequently the regulation and organization of government at all levels has been a cumbersome chore. One of the principal effects of the sharia on government has been to compel official regard for piety and for prescribed forms but, since the Saudi kings have been of orthodox religious temperament, this has not unduly restricted their personal inclinations except for the need to exercise discretion in introducing modern methods or innovations.

In 1976 the likelihood that a formal constitution would appear in the near future was slim. Each of Saudi Arabia's four monarchs has pledged to formulate a constitution during his reign, but the attitude of the royal family, as well as other influential groups, tends to be that a constitution is not needed and that the present legal (or written) basis of government is sufficient.

Many significant political processes have been carried on in the absence of written political authority. Their meaning has been established by centuries of tradition and custom and cannot be abruptly altered either by enactment or by general consent, but the traditions can gradually be altered to fit new political realities. As the Saud family began to claim authority over almost 80 percent of the Arabian Peninsula in the early twentieth century, the present Kingdom of Saudi Arabia also began to take form, and modern precedents and written laws were added to the traditional bases for the establishment of a government.

Before Abd al Aziz united the country, he ruled entirely on a personal basis. Subordinate leaders were primarily his royal advisers and in 1925 became an organized body called the Consultative Council. The council still existed in 1976 but had almost no influence in the government's policymaking.

Government in the province of the Hejaz in the 1920s provided another modern precedent. When Abd al Aziz conquered the Hejaz in 1925, he found a more advanced state of government than that of Najd. This was because of the influence of the Ottoman Empire, which had long controlled the area, and because of exposure to the West through contacts with pilgrims to Mecca (see ch. 2). To accommodate and preserve the advanced institutions of the Hejaz, Abd al Aziz issued what is known as the Organic Instructions of 1926, or the Constitution of the Hejaz. For the most part this law described already existing institutions and practices and guaranteed their continuation—a precedent that has been followed by his successors to varying degrees.

The Najd was made a kingdom and united with the Hejaz in 1927 to make its status equal to that of the Hejaz. Although this can be seen as a precedent for the future, a more important one was established by a decree creating a council of ministers in 1931. Its first president was Amir Faisal, and its responsibilities were to manage the affairs of the Hejaz while Abd al Aziz held control over the rest of the kingdom. This decree was formulated by the Consultative Council under the direction of Abd al Aziz. After the formal union of the country in the Kingdom of Saudi Arabia in 1932, these documents remained as a general statement of government until the 1950s.

The recognition contained in the Constitution of the Hejaz that law created by man could supplement the revealed law of the sharia was crucial to the evolution of a modern state. The development of law continued and accelerated, particularly after World War II, but was subordinated to the sharia, with which no law may be in conflict. The traditional form of patriarchal rule by the king with the consent of a few ministers and the Consultative Council was adequate until the administrative and financial complexities brought on after World War II by the sudden flow of oil revenues necessitated a revision. The increased volume of governmental business, requiring a corresponding increase of administrative personnel and leadership, led to the gradual development of a ministerial system outside the royal cabinet.

The ministerial system was not formally institutionalized, however, until October 1953, when Abd al Aziz issued a decree creating the Council of Ministers under the leadership of a prime minister. The decree marked a significant step in the creation of modern institutions of government. For the first time the various ministries were brought together into a single body having competence over the affairs of the entire country, at home and abroad. Nevertheless the Council of Ministers still had no executive authority; ministers appointed by the king were to consider the affairs of the country and recommend decisions to the king, who approved all decisions before they became law.

The first meeting of the Council of Ministers was held on March 7, 1954, in Riyadh, three months after the death of Abd al Aziz and the succession of Saud. The results of the first sessions were two decrees issued on March 17: the Constitution of the Council of Ministers and the Constitution of the Divisions of the Council of Ministers. In the mid-1950s most government ministries were transferred from Jiddah to Riyadh, signifying a final move in the consolidation of governmental institutions in the Saudi dynasty's traditional homeland in the Najd.

The next significant step in the development of the legal bases of government, one providing the legal basis of the ministerial system, was the decree called Regulations of the Council of Ministers of May 1958. This document revised the council's statute and reorganized the council from a purely advisory body into a formal, policymaking body having both executive and legislative functions. The new law advanced the government another step toward a well-defined ministerial system.

The nature of the central authority and the extent of its powers, however, had still not been drawn together into a national constitution, and a need for such a general statement was felt by various elements of the influential groups close to the king. Several attempts to develop a formal constitution were made during the late 1950s and early 1960s, but none got beyond the stage of proposal. The first public demand for a constitution occurred in 1960 when Amir Talal ibn Abd al Aziz Al Saud led a group of liberal members of the royal family in proposing a draft document to Crown Prince Faisal, who was then serving as prime minister. This proposal was immediately refused, and no person or group publicly proposed a constitution thereafter.

In November 1962 Faisal responded to the obvious desires of these discontented leaders by announcing the preparations of a basic law, which promised to delineate the basic rights of a citizen, to set forth the fundamental principles of government, and to state the relationship between the government and the governed. A legislative authority was to be included, and preliminary steps toward the organization of local government under the authority of the central government were to be taken. At the same time a ministry of justice and a supreme judicial council were promised, and immunity of the judiciary from political pressures was to be guaranteed.

Although many of the social and economic reforms that were to be part of the proposed basic law had been promulgated, no unified constitutional law describing the nature and extent of royal power had been issued by early 1976; but the judicial organs had been established (see Legal System, this ch.). Crown Prince Faisal succeeded his half brother, King Saud, in 1964, and the reunion of power and authority in the monarch under King Faisal soon healed the divisions in the royal family that grew out of Saud's reign (see ch. 2). In the first year of his undisputed rule Faisal decreed two important changes; the first united the offices of king and prime minister, which reinforced his position over the royal cabinet and Council of Ministers, and the second gave the king the exclusive power to appoint, dismiss, and accept the resignations of ministers. The ministers were again made responsible directly to the king, and in 1976 the king's formal powers were as extensive as they had been under the reign of Abd al Aziz.

Central Government

Office of the King

Saudi Arabia has always been an absolute monarchy with few limits on the powers of the ruler. Those limitations include the Hanbali interpretation of the sharia and the necessity of providing political accommodation to members of the royal family, traditional leaders, and other influential participants in the governmental system and in the society. This position of the king has been reinforced through the reigns of three monarchs, from the creation of the country in 1932 that brought it formally into the world community until the assassination of Faisal in March 1975. The king, Khalid, shows no signs of changing to any substantial degree that position or the authority of the office of the king (see fig. 12).

The multifaceted role the king of Saudi Arabia played in 1976 had evolved over time. Abd al Aziz firmly established the traditional roles of shaykh of shaykhs of the beduin tribes and leader of the Islamic community. While initiating the modern roles of chief of state and chief of the armed forces, Abd al Aziz named Crown Prince Saud the country's first prime minister when he created the Council of Ministers in 1953. When Saud became king, the prime ministry was delegated to Crown Prince Faisal. The separation of the positions of head of

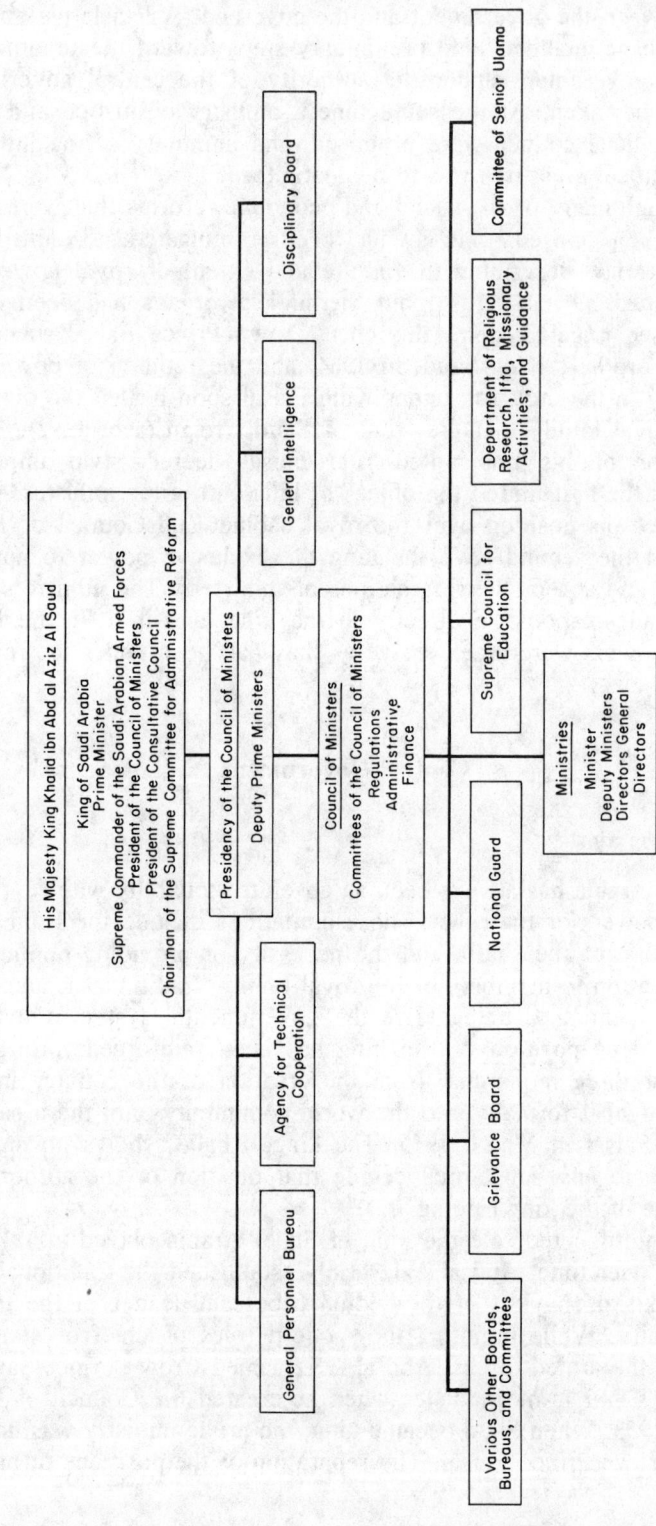

Figure 12. Saudi Arabia, Government Structure, 1976

state and head of government between 1953 and 1964 resulted in the rivalry between Saud and Faisal that returned the role of head of government to the king, where it remained in early 1976.

The office of the king, not defined by a constitution, has also changed somewhat during each reign, but it is remarkably similar in form to Abd al Aziz' first royal cabinet. Some of the organs that were influential in Abd al Aziz' time—the consultative council and public morality committees—hold lesser contemporary importance, whereas members of the newer organs—the national security council and the supreme committee for administrative reform—are very influential. Notably the office of the royal advisers has continually been an important section of the king's office. Outside the formal organization of government, the highly organized committee of senior princes performs essential functions, such as choosing successors to the throne and reacting to King Khalid's policies.

The king, assisted by the royal cabinet, is the center of all political activity. Executive and legislative functions ultimately derive their authority from the king, who also exercises judicial authority on occasion. It is to the king that all foreign representatives are accredited, and it is the king who appoints ambassadors and other envoys sent abroad. He names all ministers, other senior government officials, and governors of the provinces and selects all military officers above the rank of colonel. All legislation or decree law is either by royal decree or by ministerial decree sanctioned by him. The king is the highest court of appeal and has the power of pardon.

The investiture of the king takes place in a traditional ceremony that is a form of contract between the ruler and the ruled. The king promises to govern in accordance with the laws of Islam and the traditions of the country. The people express their support of the newly chosen king by personally paying allegiance. Technically either the king or the people may break the oath. Should a king not rule in accordance with the general precepts of the sharia, he would violate his mandate and could be legally deposed.

The nature of royal power has varied with the ability and personal style of the ruler and the circumstances of the time, probably because his powers are not defined. Abd al Aziz ruled almost singlehanded, in a way close to the ideal of absolute monarchy. His son Saud attempted to handle modern problems in a complex period of history in the same traditionalist, paternalistic fashion.

A change came in the reign of King Faisal, who revealed himself as capable of effectively carrying out the tasks of ruling a country emerging from traditional society. Faisal sought to adapt Islamic principles to the solution of problems introduced by modern industry and contacts with the outside world and to expand government services to satisfy the growing demands for improved living conditions and welfare. He was careful to present all changes in the context of Islamic orthodoxy. The gradualist approach he took in formulating his policies has been continued by Khalid during his first year as king.

Council of Ministers

The gradual development of the ministerial system is often cited as the major political accomplishment achieved by past kings of Saudi Arabia and by King Khalid, who expanded the Council of Ministers from fourteen to twenty ministries in October 1975. The existence of these ministries, however, should not be taken to imply that each is fully developed and efficiently organized. What had emerged by the mid-1970s was a diverse system of central government that attempted to respond to the needs of the country and its people, and this system had become more effective over time.

During the reign of Abd al Aziz the central government expanded its functions—built railroads and schools, took an interest in agriculture, established a postal and telephone service, and started the development of a defense system. Abd al Aziz soon found it necessary to establish ministries on what was at least an approach to the Western model. The first ministries established by him were foreign affairs, finance, and defense (see table 3). A fourth ministry, interior, was established in 1951. In 1953, when the Council of Ministers was formally established, it embodied nine ministries, and this number increased to twelve by the time of Faisal's reign.

In 1976 the Council of Ministers was made up of King Khalid as prime minister and president of the Council of Ministers; Crown Prince Fahd as first deputy prime minister and first vice president of the Council of Ministers; Amir Abd Allah ibn Abd al Aziz Al Saud as second deputy prime minister, second vice president of the Council of Ministers, and head of the National Guard; and twenty ministers appointed by the king. Ministers of state, ministers without portfolio, and royal advisers may also be appointed to the council. The king maintains his authority over the council through his extensive influence as head of both the Presidency of the Council of Ministers and the council itself. The Presidency of the Council of Ministers is an extensive body, both regulatory and executive in nature. Its responsibilities cover the final decision on all significant governmental policies and, after approving a specific action, supervision of its execution. It is an umbrellalike structure over the Council of Ministers and includes many subdivisions that are important to the functioning of the government as a whole, such as the general personnel bureau and the agency for technical cooperation. This extreme degree of centralization in government continues to delay the process of implementing changes and reacting to a need for action, sometimes over a very minor problem, because of differing opinions among the many groups having access to leadership.

Table 3. Saudi Arabia, Council of Ministers, 1975[1]

Ministry	Established	Significant Subdivisions or Areas of Jurisdiction
Agriculture and Water	1953	Desalinization Irrigation and land reclamation New water sources
Commerce (Originally part of the Ministry of Commerce and Industry, established in 1954)	1975	Foreign Capital Investment Commission Director General of Commerce Commercial disputes settlement committees Saudi Arabian Standards Organization[2]
Communications	1953	Deputy Minister for Roads and Ports Saudi Government Railroad Organization[2]
Defense and Aviation (Minister to the king created in 1944)	1953	Military inspection Meteorology Civil Aviation Saudi Arabian Airlines Corporation[2]
Education	1953	
Finance and National Economy (Minister to the king created in 1932)	1954	Director General of Budget Central Statistics Department Institute of Public Administration[2] Public Investment Fund[2] Saudi Arabian Monetary Agency (SAMA)[2] Saudi Credit Bank[2] Agricultural Bank[2]
Foreign Affairs (Minister to the king created in 1931)	1953	Diplomatic missions abroad Western Department Afro-Asian Department Islamic Affairs Department Petroleum Affairs Department Arab Affairs Department
Health	1954	Preventive medicine Curative medicine (hospitals) Director General of Inspection
Higher Education	1975	
Industry and Electricity (Originally part of the Ministry of Commerce and Industry, established in 1954)	1975	Director General for Industry Director General for Power Industrial Research and Development Center[2] General Organization for Silos and Flour Mills[2]
Information (Originally the General Directorate of Broadcasting, Printing, and Publishing)	1963	Director General for Broadcasting Director General for Television Director General for Publications Director General for Press and Public Relations Saudi News Agency

*See footnotes at end of table.

Table 3. Saudi Arabia, Council of Ministers, 1975[1] —Continued

Ministry	Established	Significant Subdivisions or Areas of Jurisdiction
Interior (Minister to the king created in 1951)	1953	Frontier Force and Coast Guard Passports and nationality Director General for Civil Defense Director General for Investigation Director General for Public Security Internal Security Forces College
Justice	1970	Supreme Judicial Council Sharia court system
Labor and Social Affairs	1961	Deputy Minister for Labor Affairs Deputy Minister for Social Affairs Supreme Committee for Settlement of Labor Disputes Director General for Social Security Director General for Youth Welfare General Social Insurance Organization[2] Saudi Red Crescent Society[2]
Municipal and Rural Affairs	1975	Deputy Minister for Municipalities, Provincial and Town Planning
Petroleum and Mineral Resources	1960	Deputy Minister for Companies and Technical Affairs Deputy Minister for Mineral Resources Comptroller General of Oil Accounts Organization of Petroleum Exporting Countries (OPEC) office Neutral Zone Office General Petroleum and Mineral Organization (Petromin)[2]
Pilgrimage Affairs and Awqaf	1962	Deputy Minister for Pilgrimage Affairs Deputy Minister for Awqaf Supreme Council of Awqaf
Planning (Originally the Central Planning Organization)	1975	Economic Experts Office Planning Office Follow-up Office
Posts, Telegraphs, and Telecommunications (Originally part of the Ministry of Communications)	1975	Deputy Minister of Communications Director General for Telecommunications Administration Director General for Posts
Public Works and Housing	1975	

[1] The first formal Council of Ministers was created in 1953.
[2] Autonomous agency or public corporation.

Although this system is time consuming and often inefficient, it is well suited to the many situations that come under the authority of the central government. Based on a continuing, overriding policy of moving gradually in all matters that may lead to substantial changes, the traditional principle of accessibility to leadership can scarcely be overemphasized. This process is based on the Quranic dictum that all people are equal, and most government officials, including the king, adhere strictly to it. Any official is available to the public almost every day; higher officials, however, are shielded. This custom fills much of the time of public officials down through the bureaucratic structure, especially in provincial and local government. In 1976 Khalid continued Faisal's practice of an open majlis at least once every week.

The four principal ministries—foreign affairs, defense and aviation, finance and national economy, and interior—were all established before the death of Abd al Aziz and almost always had royal family members as ministers; in the new Council of Ministers of October 1975 the new finance minister was a commoner, but the other three ministries continued to be headed by members of the House of Saud. They remained as important to the operation of the government in 1976 as they had been in 1950. The foreign affairs ministry was located in Jiddah, the others in Riyadh.

The ministries established in 1953 and those created during Saud's reign (1953-64) were all basically designed to implement development plans formulated by the king. Under Faisal's leadership, as crown prince and then king, a new trend in the expansion of the Council of Ministers was initiated. As crown prince, Faisal was responsible for the establishment of the Ministry of Information to coordinate the government's policies regarding the dissemination of information, publishing, and broadcasting (see ch. 9). This action represented the nature of a drastically changing internal environment in the 1960s, and it was in direct opposition to the policies of the rigidly conservative ulama, whose influence began to decline because of Faisal's ability to legitimate changes through traditional Islamic logic.

When the grand mufti of Saudi Arabia died in 1970, King Faisal, despite severe opposition, refused to appoint another grand mufti and instead took the opportunity to establish the Ministry of Justice he had promised in 1962. In a single action Faisal broke centuries of tradition that had given almost complete judicial authority to the senior religious leaders (see Legal System, this ch.). This ministry, however, received the necessary consensus of Faisal's advisers and in 1976 showed signs of the beginnings of a modern legal system.

It was the rapid change in the status and wealth of Saudi Arabia during the 1969-75 period that produced the most significant reorganization of the Council of Ministers. In early 1976 implications of the council of twenty ministers set up on October 13, 1975, were not clear, but some interesting changes had occurred.

The influential Central Planning Organization, formerly an organ of the Presidency of the Council of Ministers, became the Ministry of Planning, thus gaining formal recognition of its importance. The relationship of this new ministry to the ministries of finance and national economy and of petroleum and mineral resources will be of great importance, inasmuch as each of the three performs functions that influence the effectiveness of the others (see ch. 11).

The remaining six new ministries were formerly departments attached to other ministries. In a desire to build a national identity and organize government at the provincial and local levels, the Ministry of Municipal and Rural Affairs was drawn from the Ministry of Interior. The Ministry of Commerce and Industry was divided, creating the new Ministry of Industry and Electricity while maintaining the Ministry of Commerce as a separate organ. Further the new Ministry for Public Works and Housing was formed from a number of subdivisions of various ministries, and the functions of organizing higher education in the country were assigned to a new ministry, thus opening two posts on the Council of Ministers that emphasized education. Finally, the Ministry of Communications retained jurisdiction over transportation, including ports, but many of its previous functions were taken over by the new Ministry of Posts, Telegraphs, and Telecommunications.

Under the authority of the Council of Ministers are many autonomous agencies and public corporations. Formally organized in the structure of government, the more important are headed by executives who are sometimes more influential than the ministers to whom they are responsible. They do not have independent power, however, and derive their influence from affiliation with the king and his advisers. Noteworthy examples are the General Petroleum and Mining Organization (Petromin), under the authority of the minister of petroleum and mineral resources, and the Saudi Arabian Monetary Agency (SAMA) and the Institute of Public Administration, both under the minister of finance and national economy.

Civil Service

In the mid-1970s Saudi Arabia continued to suffer from a shortage of trained personnel. In the 1940s and 1950s the government relied heavily, even at the ministerial level, on nationals from other Arab countries, such as Syria and Lebanon, and on Palestinian Arabs. In 1958, however, Saudi Arabian citizenship was made a requirement for membership in the Council of Ministers and, with the increasing number of students returning from abroad, the trend by the early 1970s was to replace foreign nationals with qualified young Saudi officials. A parallel trend has been the increasing rise of commoners to high office, displacing certain members of the royal family. In 1976 there were only six ministers who were members of the royal family; the remaining fourteen ministries were headed by Saudi commoners.

The government is the principal employer in the country. Government employees, excluding the armed forces and National Guard, numbered approximately 150,000 in 1976. A major problem, however, has been to fill all the open positions in the civil service. The organization and employment of civil servants was under the authority of the General Personnel Bureau, an organ of the Presidency of the Council of Ministers. All non-Saudis employed, estimated at 15 to 20 percent of the total in the mid-1970s, were reviewed rigidly before being hired.

A fortunate consequence of Saudi society has been that the government attracts qualified professionals who may attain a good deal of status through government employment. The country has not felt the negative effects of a brain drain of the kind that has paralyzed many developing countries. Saudi Arabia is underpopulated, and educated Saudis are offered almost unlimited opportunities in government. This has been reinforced by the fact that there are no elected officials in the country and by the fact that Saudis who are educated abroad often receive financial support from the government and rarely remain abroad after completing their studies.

The Civil Service Code, established by a series of royal decrees in the early 1970s, governs the civil service and regulates the personnel bureau. Ironically, even with the country's shortage of manpower, the civil service has become overstaffed in many levels where little if any training is necessary, although in many cases there are severe shortages of skilled personnel.

Training, particularly in the more professional and highly technical areas, was increased in the 1970s. The personnel bureau identified the needs of the government, and under the direction of the Council of Ministers each ministry created a training section with assistance from the ministries of education and higher education and the Institute of Public Administration.

Local Government

Hegemony of the central government over the tribes, especially the nomadic beduin, remained indirect and in some cases nominal and was exercised through tribal shaykhs chosen by the heads of the most important families and lineages within the tribe. Before the unification of Saudi Arabia the people governed themselves through tribal councils—in some cases following their own customary law where it conflicted with the sharia—and exercised full autonomy within their area.

After the creation of a central government Abd al Aziz achieved a degree of cohesiveness between the tribes and the government by touring the countryside and holding royal majlis at which the tribal shaykhs made their positions and desires known to the king, by making numerous marriage contracts with important local families, and by subsidizing regional notables from the royal purse. A similar policy was followed by Saud, although by the 1950s the sedentation of the tribes and the increasingly direct application of the authority of the central government over the country made the use of such traditional means of government inappropriate.

At first Faisal continued to meet the tribal shaykhs almost daily through the institution of the majlis; later, however, he reduced this to once a week, on Thursdays. He made fewer visits to the tribal areas and sharply reduced the use of the royal treasury, making funds available to the royal family subject to the government's budget.

In 1963, as a result of Faisal's proposed basic law, a comprehensive statute was drawn up to standardize existing procedures of provincial government and in some cases to create new institutions. New posts were created, specific duties assigned, and old practices prohibited; the decree also linked the provinces closely to the central government. The regulations, consisting of forty articles, provided for the division of the kingdom into five provinces, which in turn were subdivided into districts and subdistricts. In carrying out the 1963 regulations, however, the minister of interior in conjunction with the Council of Ministers developed an alternative system of local government having six major and twelve minor provinces, each having districts and subdistricts.

In 1976 these eighteen provinces formed the major part of local government in the country. Since the enactment of the decree, however, a major impetus in developing local government has been the planned reorganization of the major cities—for example, the new general plan for Riyadh. None of the provinces has a formal capital—the governor is understood to reside within the boundaries of his province and not in a single municipality. This practice is derived from the traditional Islamic concept of territoriality, which gave tribal authority to a tribal leader over a bound territory for his jurisdiction. In fact the governor does reside in a specific town or city and administers the province from there, and it is his responsibility to ensure personal access by each of his citizens.

A governor is the central government's representative in the province. Appointed by royal decree, he takes an oath of allegiance to his religion, his country, and his king. Provincial governors administer their provinces according to the general policy of the country. Specifically the statute of provincial regulations requires the governor to implement the decisions of the courts, to preserve public order and security, to protect the rights and liberties of individuals within the limits of the sharia, to oversee and inspect the administration of the districts and subdistricts, to assist the national government in the collection of revenues, to supervise the affairs of the municipalities, and to oversee the work of all government employees in the province.

The tradition of a provincial council has been a central institution in Arabian history, but its formalization into written law only came to Saudi Arabia in 1963. Provincial councils assist the governor in an advisory capacity and are situated in the most important city of each province. A typical council—their standardization and regulation had not been set up by early 1976—had a term of two years and was composed of not more than thirty members, selected from the people of the province. Representatives have also been selected from the various ministries related to the affairs of the province.

Although the organization of the provincial council is vague in the 1963 regulations, its jurisdiction is clear. In municipal affairs the council is to cooperate with, and assist in, the performance of duties and the execution of projects. In educational affairs it is to propose and supervise the establishment of literacy campaigns, vocational training centers, and technical schools. In agriculture it is to propose the establishment of model farms, exhibits, and cooperative societies and to regulate local markets. These councils are responsible for the financial affairs of the provinces and the presentation of an annual budget for approval by the Council of Ministers.

The provincial councils are supplemented by a number of municipal councils located in the major cities. The provincial councils have no jurisdiction over matters within the jurisdiction of the municipal councils. The functions of the municipal councils are similar to those of the provincial council, and neither form of council is permitted to discuss military affairs or national policies, external or internal. The strict, formalized control over these councils by the central government is based on a concern for internal security (see ch. 14).

In 1976 most of the governors in office were either members of the royal family or leaders of the families related through marriage to the royal family. The governors of four of the six major provinces were royal family members; the post was traditionally seen as a step to eventual higher government position or as an honor bestowed on senior family members. The remaining two governors were important leaders of the Jiluwi family.

LEGAL SYSTEM

Background of the Legal System

In Islamic tradition God reveals not himself and his nature but rather his law, and it is usually accepted that law takes precedence over theology. Further there is no difference made between the sacred and the secular aspects of society. Saudi Arabia is one of the few countries that base their legal systems on the conservative unifying force of the sharia (Islamic jurisprudence), a body of law concerned with an individual's activities from the most private to the most public (see ch. 5).

Sharia law is not considered to be created by man but revealed by God. Because secular Western concepts have only begun to penetrate the country, the sharia remains the sole source of public and private law. It is a divine system of law in both its sources and its primary rules. In Saudi Arabia sharia law covers all fields of law—criminal, civil, and international.

In classical Islamic theory the four sources of sharia law are the Quran, the Sunna, *ijma* (consensus of ulama), and the qiyas. The Quran contains 200 verses of legal rules, compared with 6,000 religious verses. These verses of legal rules are moral and practical injunctions revealed to Muhammad by God and are the principal source of sharia law. The Quran is supplemented by the Sunna of the Prophet, or traditions regarding the examples set by the Prophet, and the hadith, or recorded statements and actions of the Prophet. The Sunna also includes many approvals of practice that were determined by the Prophet's silence about, or understood approval of, deeds occurring with his knowledge. The validity of various traditions as moral guides was decided in the early centuries of Islam by agreement among religious scholars.

The *ijma* set the precedent for another source of sharia law. In practice *ijma* is understood to be infallible; decisions of *ijma* may still be expressed in statements, actions, or silence. The final and much disputed source of sharia law is the qiyas, or analogy. When cases appear that find no precedent in the Quran, Sunna, or through *ijma*, a jurist must deduce a rule through the analogical method.

Four major schools of jurisprudence based on different interpretations of the sharia appeared in the second and third Islamic centuries (ninth and tenth centuries A.D.). The differences between the schools were not fundamental but were based on the degree of emphasis laid on the various sources of the sharia. These distinctions persist, although they have little significance in the daily lives of individual Muslims. Each tends to predominate for historical reasons in a given geographic area.

The Hanafi school, founded by Abu Hanifa in Iraq, was adopted by the Ottoman Empire and still predominates in regions where Ottoman domination had been strong, including the Hejaz and parts of the Eastern Province in Saudi Arabia. Malik Ibn Anas founded the Maliki school, based on the practice of judges at Medina; it predominates in North Africa, West Africa, Upper Egypt, and Kuwait. Ash Shafi, founder of the Shafii school of sharia law that is prevalent in Lower Egypt and in parts of the southwestern corner of the Arabian Peninsula, used qiyas less often than the preceding schools.

The fourth school of sharia law was founded at Baghdad by Ahmad ibn Muhammad ibn Hanbal (died A.D. 885). As the most conservative and rigid school it rejected all innovation, and its advocates, the Hanbali sect, use the Quran and the Sunna as sources of law and oppose the use of qiyas. The Hanbali school was strong for a time in Iraq and Syria but lost influence after the Ottoman conquest in the fifteenth century. It was not until the eighteenth century that it became a major school after being revived by Muhammad ibn Abd al Wahhab in the Najd and became the rallying point of the Sauds in their battles to unify peninsular Arabs. Because of its acceptance by the House of Saud, reinforced continually by the Wahhabi ulama, the Hanbali school still predominates in most of Saudi Arabia, although the other schools are recognized and respected.

The Hanbali school of sharia law forms the basis of the Saudi Arabian government as well as the legal system. It is the duty of the king as the principal religious leader to safeguard the practice of Islam throughout the country and to ensure full adherence to the prescriptions of the sharia. Beginning with the reign of Abd al Aziz sacred law has been supplemented from time to time by royal decrees issued to meet such new situations as those arising from industrial accidents.

Since the end of World War II, tax, corporation, and company law and labor, mining, and foreign capital investment regulations have also been codified. Although some integration of decree and sharia law is occurring, decree law for the most part is carried out separately from the sharia court procedures.

Royal decrees to all intents and purposes have the force of law. Legal scholars, however, note that these have the character of administrative regulations *(nizams)*, since the sharia does not give legislative power to the king or ruler. This situation derives its basis from the Hanbali opposition to, but not absolute rejection of, qiyas and support for *ijma* as opposed to the consensus of the total community. In Saudi Arabia this had afforded legislative functions to such bodies as the Consultative Council or the Council of Ministers with the sanction of the king.

Abd al Aziz incorporated an important concept into the 1926 Constitution of the Hejaz called *ijtihad* (personal reasoning), which permits a judge or ruler to make decisions concerning cases not explicitly covered by a provision of sharia law. This concept laid the foundation for expanding the legal system. It was at that time that Abd al Aziz chose the Hanbali school of law as the official basis of the judiciary.

In 1928 Abd al Aziz decreed the organization of the court system and the procedures to follow, setting precedents for the king to regulate these functions. These actions led to the Civil Procedure Rules of 1936 and 1952, a board of grievances in 1955, and finally to the creation of the Ministry of Justice in 1970.

After the 1962 budgetary provision was made, a ministry of justice was planned to administer the body of accumulating law and ministerial regulations necessitated by the new economic and technological situations and to coordinate this law with the sharia administration. This ministry was not immediately organized, however, but evolved gradually. In 1965 the Higher Juridical Institute was established to provide three extra years of study for selected graduates of the sharia college. This institute enables jurists to study intensively the religious-legal problems confronting the country because of modern development and to make recommendations for their solution.

Until 1970 the judicial system was under the authority of the office of the grand mufti and the committee of senior muftis. The grand mufti was a senior member of the Al ash Shaykh family, whose approach to the rigidly orthodox interpretation of sharia law he enforced. After the grand mufti's death in 1970 King Faisal established the Ministry of Justice by royal decree. The role of the grand mufti in the legal system was merged with that of the minister of justice, assisted by the simultaneous creation of the Supreme Judicial Council. The first minister of justice was Shaykh Muhammad ibn Ali al Harkan, ending the presence of an Al ash Shaykh family member as head of the judiciary. When the government was reorganized by King Khalid in October 1975 and probably in response to pressures from the ulama, Harkan was replaced by Shaykh Ibrahim ibn Muhammad ibn Ibrahim Al ash Shaykh.

Judicial Authority and Courts System

At the pinnacle of the judicial system is the king, who may act as a final court of appeal and as a source of pardon. Abd al Aziz was famed for personally dispensing justice in cases of every description, but he generally refrained from modifying legal interpretations of the ulama without first winning its members over to his view. Saud, Faisal, and Khalid have exercised judiciary power but to a lesser extent than Abd al Aziz.

Since 1953, and especially after the creation of the Ministry of Justice in 1970, the judicial system has expanded rapidly, and elements of the judicial authority are differentiated throughout the government (see fig. 13). The Ministry of Justice administers the sharia legal system throughout the country. The country's first development plan corresponded to the first five years of the existence of the ministry, and the number of courts increased from 207 to 241 and the number of judges from 321 to 464. Similarly the rise in population, economic and social development, and the increasing numbers of foreign workers resulted in an increase from 91,203 cases heard in 1969 to 99,632 in 1972.

The organization of the sharia law courts is basically uniform throughout the country, but administrative details may vary from province to province. Under the direction of the Ministry of Justice a major attempt has been made to expand the system and standardize procedures. The Supreme Judicial Council supervises the court system and may be appealed to in serious cases. The council cannot alter the verdict, but it may refer a case to the appeals courts for consideration.

At the lowest level the sharia law courts are called ordinary courts, or courts of first instance *(mahkamat al umur al mustajalah)*. These courts, found throughout the country, deal with minor misdemeanors and small claims and are generally presided over by an Islamic judge (qadi), who is appointed by the king on the recommendation of the judicial council. Trial by jury is unknown in sharia law. Since sharia is not case law, a judge does not have to follow precedent and is not bound by decisions of other judges or a higher court. The judges, however, have a reputation for incorruptibility and justice, and observers have often noted the essential fairness of sharia procedures. The competence of the courts at all levels is set according to the traditional divisions of sharia law: criminal law, family (domestic relations) law, and transactions between people (civil law). (Marriage is a civil contract, not a sacred bond.) Other branches of the ordinary courts deal exclusively with the affairs of the beduin with the same competence.

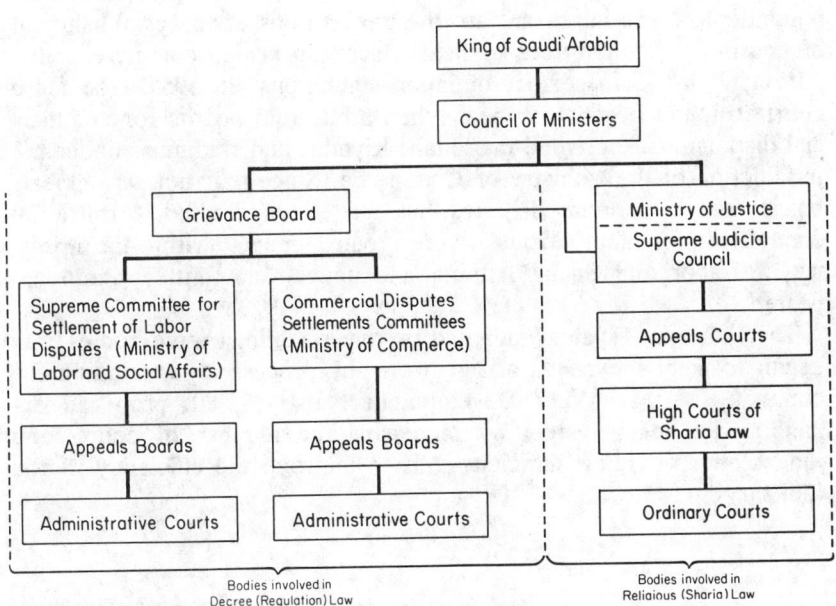

Figure 13. *Saudi Arabia, Organization of Judicial System, 1976*

The next higher courts, the high courts of sharia law (*mahkamat al sharia al kubra*), are located in larger towns and cities and have jurisdiction over all matters beyond the competence of the lower courts. Decisions from any of the sharia law courts may be appealed to the third and highest level of courts, the appeals courts. There are two appeals courts in the country: cases from the eastern provinces are appealed in Riyadh, and cases from the western provinces are appealed in Mecca.

For crimes not covered by sharia law, which are the results of the various regulations established by royal decree, the legal system has developed other mechanisms outside the sharia court system. A precedent was established by Abd al Aziz in 1926 when he set up a commercial court in Jiddah. This court was abolished in 1955, but in the same year the Board of Grievances was created under the authority of the Presidency of the Council of Ministers to function as the country's principal administrative tribunal. This office reviews complaints of injustice brought because of wrongful acts committed by Islamic judges and government officials; complaints are also brought by those who have no recourse in the sharia courts. The grievance board has assumed the role of final arbiter of justice, at least in cases of decree law, although decisions of an Islamic judge are known to be brought in the form of complaints to this body.

Finally the ministries of interior, commerce, and labor and social affairs perform important legal functions that are provided by the court system in most other countries. The Ministry of Interior, through the police under its jurisdiction, enforces the motor vehicle regulations. More important are the implications of the establishment of boards and committees to hear cases concerning commercial disputes and the enforcement of labor regulations. In 1965 a de facto court structure began to appear when arbitration boards for commercial disputes were created in Jiddah, Riyadh, and Dammam under the jurisdiction of the Ministry of Commerce. Since that time an appeals board for commercial disputes has also been created. Arbitration committees for labor disputes were created in 1969 within the Ministry of Labor and Social Affairs, and appeals committees soon appeared.

The sharia law system, adapted by these administrative bodies, has begun to meet the needs arising from the process of developing the country. The Five Year Development Plan (1975-80) proposed expanding the legal system by increasing the number of courts and judges and providing sufficient staff to improve the efficiency of the judiciary.

* * * * * * * * * * * * *

A standard work on the position of the king and the royal family in twentieth-century Saudi Arabia is Gerald De Gaury's *Faisal: King of Saudi Arabia*. Other recent publications on the royal family and politics are few, but Joseph J. Malone's *The Arab Lands of Western Asia* and Mordechai Abir's *Oil, Power and Politics* are useful sources. A 1970 dissertation describes the development of the country's governmental system: Soliman A. Solaim's "Constitutional and Judicial Organization in Saudi Arabia." This study is complemented by a 1973 dissertation by Hamad S. Al-Hamid, "The Legislative Process and the Development of Saudi Arabia," which also has an excellent analysis of the growth of Saudi Arabia's legal system. Finally, important sources for more background on the legal system are Noel J. Coulson's *A History of Islamic Law* and Herbert J. Liebesny's *The Law of the Near and Middle East*. (For further information see Bibliography.)

CHAPTER 9
MASS COMMUNICATIONS

In early 1976 mass communications in Saudi Arabia were closely scrutinized by government and religious leaders. The government had increased the capacities of the mass media system dramatically during the 1960s, but by the mid-1970s this system still lagged far behind other countries in the Middle East.

The Ministry of Information was the primary source of information policies and was in charge of promoting the image of Saudi Arabia both at home and abroad. Radio and television networks were government owned, and the country had a small but growing privately owned press. There is no constitution, so various royal decrees stipulate the guidelines to be followed by the media.

The development of mass communications in Saudi Arabia was primarily the result of King Faisal's reign (1964-75), making him the principal architect of the present-day system and responsible for its growth. His successor, King Khalid, has continued to promote progress in this area, which is viewed as essential both to broaden and intensify a sense of national identity among the Saudi people and to provide efficient means to carry out the country's foreign, economic, and political affairs.

GOVERNMENT, SOCIETY, AND MASS COMMUNICATIONS

The development of the mass communications system in Saudi Arabia has been done within the historical context of the country; religion and politics have determined the system's boundaries. The first major impetus behind the establishment of formal communication channels was King Abd al Aziz (reigned 1902-53). Until the late 1960s, however, the country remained extremely impoverished, and the traditional, informal channels of communication provided the primary means of transferring information within Saudi society.

Several factors have influenced and shaped the structure of the mass media, such as the size of the country, the diversity of domestic groups, the costs of printing and broadcasting, and the low literacy rate. Of far greater impact have been the religious and political traditions. The government and royal family have guided the press and broadcasting establishments from their creation and have promoted growth in this area only when expansion was necessary and in the government's, namely the family's, interests. The underlying stimulus for change was not through innovation or creativity but pragmatic planning.

Except for the publication of various government ministries, the press in Saudi Arabia has always been privately owned. It was founded in 1924 but remains poorly developed. Circulation has been uncertain and generally low, and the newspapers continue to depend largely on the government for financial support. The government, however, has not played a direct role in censoring the press; there has never been prepublication censorship. Rather, governmental influence is derived from its ability to suspend newspapers that publish materials offensive to it. These would include attacks on the institution of the royal family, mention of the term *Israel* (Saudis refer to the area as Arab Palestine), praise or condemnation of a foreign state in a manner not consonant with Saudi foreign policy, and infringement of the proscriptions imposed by the Islamic religious codes.

Because the population was almost totally illiterate in the early years of the kingdom, the government recognized the need to promote the introduction of the radio as a useful device to bring consensus among its people. Nevertheless it was not until 1949 that Abd al Aziz finally established the country's first local broadcasting station in Mecca in the face of strong initial disapproval on the part of the puritanical Wahhabi (see Glossary) ulama. He supported his act by ordering that parts of the Quran be broadcast and then asked, "Can anything be bad which transmits the word of God?"

Although the radio continues to be opposed by a few, its establishment has become the reference point when planning the introduction of other media, such as television and telecommunications. The approach adopted for innovations provided that any advance be done slowly and extensive efforts be taken to introduce any proposed change before it appeared. The increasing industrialization and use of Western technology have not seemed to affect this policy of moderation.

Ironically the minimal innovations that occurred have produced a number of contrasts within the Saudi population. In the mid-1970s many conservative factions continued to oppose the use of radios, and television was seen by them as a tool of the devil. Conversely many of the more affluent young Saudis derived great enjoyment from both radio and television and supported the few privately organized cinemas, which in 1976 were still not approved by the government. Furthermore the government supports the training of communication professionals and technicians while maintaining its influence over many of the informal communication channels.

Role of the Government

In 1953 King Saud (reigned 1953-64) by a royal decree established the first official regulatory agency to oversee the functions of the mass media in Saudi Arabia, the General Directorate of Broadcasting, Printing, and Publishing. Its function was to organize, coordinate, and supervise all channels of information throughout the country.

The agency expanded rapidly and gained influence by performing various important tasks: running propaganda campaigns; establishing offices in the capitals of other Islamic countries; disseminating "factual" news; and publishing its own newsletters, magazines, books, and pamphlets. Furthermore the government decided that all broadcasting activities would have to be under close government control. Another royal decree recognized this growth in information activities by establishing in 1963 a cabinet-level office to replace the agency —the Ministry of Information. The developments of mass communications since that time have been planned and directed by this organization. Interestingly the ministers of information have been from outside the royal family. Observers suggest that this reflects the king's reluctance to have the Saudi people identify this structure with him and the royal family.

The information ministry, with assistance from Faisal, changed drastically the nature of mass communications in Saudi Arabia. For example, in 1962 women's voices were introduced over the radio, and in 1971 women began appearing on television. Forty years after the creation of the first Saudi newspaper, a royal decree also changed the entire structure of the press institutions. In 1964 during his first year as ruler, Faisal decreed that, although publications would remain privately owned, each publisher must form a licensed organization according to the guidelines set by the law. These concerns were called press establishments, and all printing and publishing were placed in their hands.

Under the press law the government has practically taken over the control of the press, although the establishments themselves are in private hands. The state grants concessions to publish to a group of individuals (no less than fifteen), each of whom must be approved by the Ministry of Information. The group must have SR100,000 (for value of the riyal—see Glossary) in assets, and all members of the group must be Saudi Arabian citizens. Each press establishment is headed by a director general, who is nominated by the members of the group but approved by the ministry. The same condition must be met to establish an editor in chief, and a committee for the supervision of editing must be formed from the members of the group. The prime minister, who has always been a member of the royal family, has the right to revoke the concession of any press establishment.

Although this system of regulation seems to complete the government's control over mass communications, many observers have noted that since 1964 the organization and performance of the press have become much more efficient and the content of the newspapers much more sophisticated. Notably the policies maintained by both political and religious agencies of the government to control the selection of news were the same before the press law as they were after it. Compliance with the wishes of the royal family and the demands of religious leaders are the first considerations of a reporter.

The position of the country among the Islamic countries of the world, and especially in the Middle East, has stimulated the government to increase its capacities to disseminate information abroad. For example, when the Arab States Broadcasting Union was formed in 1969, Saudi Arabia refused to join for political reasons, but because of Saudi Arabia's new political status (stemming from the international energy crisis in the 1973-74 period) and vast wealth, Faisal joined the union in August 1974 to increase his influence and promote cooperation in the region.

In the autumn of 1975 a significant structural change in the government announced the country's concern to improve communication facilities. The Ministry of Posts, Telegraphs, and Telecommunications (formerly an agency within the Ministry of Communications) was created on October 13, 1975. This action illuminated a goal to improve the communication services, which have seriously hampered the country's economic and governmental activities. The new ministry was to implement the development of an ambitious five-year plan in this area. The desirability of upgrading communication services had been recognized many years earlier, but a lack of funds had postponed major improvements. Saudi Arabia's growing wealth since 1973 permitted and required development of a modern communication system, and in 1976 the government increased the subsidies to many publishing firms by 50 percent.

Domestic and Foreign Audiences

Less than 15 percent of the domestic audience is literate; therefore broadcasting has the greatest potential for reaching the largest number of people. The press accounts for a small audience within Saudi Arabia compared with the number of radio listeners. The press has its major impact on Saudi Arabia's growing elite, middle class, and educated working-class groups, the most influential people in the country.

The government has concentrated on improving the size and effectiveness of both radio and television. Unlike the press, broadcasting is for the most part government subsidized. Radio has the capacity to reach literally the entire population, but television still had not become very widespread in 1976.

Government information programs are mainly the responsibility of the information ministry, but other ministries (Ministry of Education and Ministry of Pilgrimage Affairs and Awqaf) conduct additional information activities of their own, employing various communications media to reach special target audiences. Aware of the importance given to word-of-mouth communication, the government also sends officials directly to the rural areas as a means of promoting interpersonal communication with local opinion leaders.

Printed information intended for foreign readers, including magazines and pamphlets published in several languages, was distributed through the Ministry of Information. In a move to improve the government's image and increase its influence abroad, the ministry began publishing an eight-page newsletter, *News from Saudi Arabia*. This publication outlines major events in the country and emphasizes the efforts of the government to modernize and develop the economy and society. Also, the government used advertising supplements publicizing Saudi developments. These have appeared in many of the world's major newspapers, such as the *New York Times* and the *Times* of London.

In the mid-1970s the Saudi Arabian Broadcasting Company operated an international service, broadcasting each day in Indonesian to Southeast Asia, in Urdu to Pakistan, in Persian to Iran, and in Swahili to East Africa. The Voice of Islam (Sawt al Islam) broadcast in Arabic to the Middle East daily. Another foreign service was beamed—in Arabic, English, and French—to Europe and North America.

The avowed purpose of these government-operated foreign broadcasting programs was to strengthen the position of Islam in those areas where it has taken root and to stress Saudi Arabia's role as the homeland of Islam. The increased need to be in contact with diverse areas of the world and to promote foreign investments in Saudi Arabia were added purposes of these efforts. In 1975 these programs totaled an estimated 900 hours a week.

Traditional Communication Channels

Informal channels of communication in Saudi Arabia assume special importance because of the low level of literacy, the importance of small-group meetingplaces, and the pervading influence of religious beliefs and institutions. Saudi Arabians continue to rely on informal word-of-mouth communications, which have played an important role throughout Saudi history. The urban coffeehouses provide a center where news is read aloud and broadcasts are interpreted and discussed. The nomads obtain news during visits to the villages and towns and transmit it as their caravans move from oasis to oasis.

The mosque remains one of the most important channels for communication. Saudi Arabian political leaders, and the king as the leader of the Islamic religion within the country, continue to use the mosque to explain their policies to the public. The importance of these informal channels of communication for mobilizing the people and directing and controlling public opinion increases the influence of the ulama as opinion leaders in the social system. The government seeks out these individuals, asking them to disseminate information among their congregations, in order to carry out information policies effectively.

The government hopes that through the increased distribution of radios and by decreasing illiteracy, formal communication channels will reduce the amount of distortion and exaggeration produced by the informal channels. In 1976 the government's efforts had been effective in promoting greater awareness among its people of events in the cities and abroad, and a nationwide public opinion seemed to be emerging.

SURVEY OF MASS COMMUNICATIONS SYSTEM

The Press

The press as an institution is a twentieth-century phenomenon in Saudi Arabia. In 1976 fewer than fifty newspapers and periodicals were published, primarily in Jiddah, Mecca, and Riyadh. The country had only six dailies, all of limited circulation. Circulation was particularly sparse in rural areas and provincial cities. Except for a few English-language newsletters and periodicals, all publications were printed in Arabic. It should be noted, however, that a single copy of a newspaper may be read by or to a large number of individuals, and circulation figures are poor indicators of audience size.

The combined circulation of the leading Arabic-language dailies in 1976 has been estimated at 70,000 at the most out of an estimated population of about 5.6 million (see ch. 3). Foreign-language dailies were of no significance.

Journalism has only recently attracted Saudis as a career. Until the 1960s and continuing in the mid-1970s reporters were trained principally in schools of literature and religion. The format of newspapers reflects the influence of Egyptian editors and technicians during the early years of development. The average Saudi daily has few pages, but the printing quality—poor in the past—has been substantially improved by new technological advancements. The front page carries important national news and a few highly selective international news items. Usually one page is devoted to women; by the mid-1970s special supplements, such as *New Eve* and *She* (published by the Yamamah Establishment), were edited by women.

The style, content, and language of news coverage and analysis have resulted in what an expert on the Saudi press, Abdulrahman Shobaili, has called "literary journalism." This depiction has changed somewhat since the development and expansion of education during the 1950s and 1960s, but the prevalence of reporters communicating in a literary style was still notable in the mid-1970s. The cartoon, which has been highly developed elsewhere in the Arab world (particularly in Egypt and Lebanon), only became established as a channel of communication in Saudi Arabia in the mid-1960s; cartoons were extremely popular among Saudi readers by the mid-1970s. Daily newspapers were circulated six days a week (Saturday through Thursday); no publications appeared on Friday, the Islamic sabbath.

Al Bilad is the leading newspaper in Saudi Arabia, becoming the country's first daily in 1952 (see table 4). *Al Medina al Munwara*, however, is probably the most authoritative because of its close associations with the royal family. Both are widely read among government workers, students, and professionals. A number of publications have been founded since the 1964 press reorganization decree; the major new publications are *Al Jazirah* and *Al Riyadh*, a new English-language publication, *Saudi Gazette*, was founded in 1975.

Three other forms of ownership were in existence in 1976. First, the government remained a major publisher, publishing the most widely read religious periodical, the *Hajj;* the government's official weekly gazette, *Umm al Qura;* and the English-language *News from Saudi Arabia*, which was widely circulated and played an important role in reaching audiences abroad. Next, the Arabian American Oil Company (Aramco) publications were important to both English-speaking and Arab audiences. The weekly publications, *Oil Caravan Weekly* (in Arabic) and *Arabian Sun* (in English) were the mainstay of the company's extensive information program for its employees and the general public, which also included the Arabic-language publication *Qafilat al Zaft*, the name of both a weekly and a monthly edition. Finally, certain professional journals or specialized reviews were unaffected by the 1964 press law. Included in this group were the *Saudi Economic Survey, Replica,* and *Al Manhal*.

Eight major publishing concerns, all approved after the press law was put into operation, account for most publishing in the country. Their facilities remained very limited in the mid-1970s, and book publishing had not advanced very far. The press establishments have improved both their quality and circulation, particularly in the more technical aspects of publication. As of early 1976 these establishments faced many obstacles and expected continued pressure from government and religious leaders. One of the major problems was the country's very high rate of illiteracy. In 1976 the Saudi press reported to a limited but enthusiastic audience, which will probably grow because of the country's new affluence and the advances in its educational system (see ch. 5).

Table 4. Saudi Arabia, Major Publications, 1975

Title	Circulation	Publishing House (Location)	Remarks*
Al Bilad	20,000	Al Bilad Publishing Organization (Jiddah)	Leading daily; founded in 1934; liberal
Hajj	5,000	Ministry of Pilgrimage Affairs and Awqaf	Religious monthly; founded in 1947
Al Jazirah	5,000	Al Jazirah for Press Printing and Publishing (Riyadh)	Weekly; founded in 1964
Al Manhal	3,000	Independent (Jiddah)	Literary monthly; founded in 1937
Al Medina al Munwara	20,000	Al Medina Publishing Organization (Jiddah)	Popular daily; founded in 1937; pro-government
Al Nadwah	10,000	Mecca Press and Information Organization (Mecca)	Daily; founded in 1958; conservative
News from Saudi Arabia	22,000	Press Department, Ministry of Information (Jiddah)	Weekly news bulletin; founded in 1961
Replica	n.a.	Government publication (Jiddah)	Daily newsletter in English; from Saudi newspapers and broadcasting service
Al Riyadh	10,000	Al Yamamah Press Establishment (Riyadh)	Daily; founded in 1965
Al Tijarah	1,300	Independent (Jiddah)	Monthly business review; founded in 1961
Al Ukadh	3,500	Al Ukadh Establishment for Press and Publishing (Jiddah)	Daily
Umm al Qura	5,000	Government publication (Mecca)	Weekly official government gazette; founded in 1924

See footnotes at end of table.

Table 4. Saudi Arabia, Major Publications, 1975—Continued

Title	Circulation	Publishing House (Location)	Remarks*
Al Yamamah	1,000	Al Yamamah Press Establishment (Riyadh)	Weekly; founded in 1952
Al Yaum	n.a.	Dar al Yaum Press and Publishing Establishment (Dammam)	Daily; founded as a weekly in 1965; became a daily in 1975

n. a.—not available.
*In Arabic unless otherwise specified.

Source: Based on information from *Middle East and North Africa, 1975-76*, London, 1975, pp. 611-612.

Broadcasting

Most of the advances in the area of broadcasting occurred during Faisal's reign, and in 1976 King Khâlid continued to support further development. The Saudi government controls all channels of broadcasting, and the Ministry of Information supervises broadcast activities. Efforts to establish a comprehensive radio system and later a television system were successful despite much opposition, particularly from religious leaders. Television is a vehicle intended for selected domestic audiences, but radio in Saudi Arabia is also important for international communication. The shortage of trained personnel and of the necessary technical equipment underlying every broadcast medium remained major problems for the government.

Radio services were introduced into Saudi Arabia in the 1930s, but the first indigenous program did not begun until 1949. In 1976 there were two major transmission stations, at Jiddah and Riyadh, and a third at Dammam that relayed programs from Riyadh. These services were maintained by the Saudi Arabian Broadcasting Company, an agency of the Ministry of Information. No commercial broadcasts were permitted. In 1974 it was estimated that there were about 120,000 radio receivers throughout the country.

Usually about eighteen hours of broadcasting were beamed from the Jiddah and Riyadh stations; during the religious seasons of Ramadan and the haj, schedules were subject to drastic change. The programs produced by these stations were exchanged immediately after being recorded. Except for news broadcasts, the texts of which were supplied by the ministry, the programs were always prerecorded. The only other radio service in Saudi Arabia was Aramco Radio, which broadcast in English for company employees.

All programs—domestic or imported—were censored by the program manager at each station. Religious standards included bans on programs containing references to such "offensive" matters as sex, drinking, or smoking. Although friendly countries may be promoted, there was avoidance of discussions on communism, socialism, racism, and Zionism that might disturb the "public peace." The Voice of Islam, which transmits only readings from the Quran, was the only additional radio service.

Television was introduced into the country by Aramco, which initiated the Aramco Television service for its employees in 1957. In 1962 the Saudi government, under the influence of Faisal (then crown prince and prime minister), called for the establishment of a Saudi Arabian television system. Jiddah and Riyadh were the sites of the inauguration of that system, opening in 1965. By 1969 there were five major stations—the first two and additional stations at Medina, Buraydah, and Dammam.

With the completion of these stations the entire country was within the reach of television, although receivers were available to less than 20 percent of the population. In 1974 the number of receivers was estimated to be 87,000. Saudi television is under the direction of the Saudi Arabian Television Service in the Ministry of Information. The antipathy of the conservative religious leaders to the introduction of television has forced the government to proceed cautiously with its program. Protests occurred continuously during the pretesting stage of development in the autumn of 1965, particularly in Jiddah. An unfortunate incident, the killing of Amir Khalid ibn Musaid by a minor policeman, highlighted these demonstrations. Almost ten years later his brother, Amir Faisal ibn Musaid assassinated King Faisal in March 1975 (both of the amirs were nephews of the king).

It is difficult to speculate about the eventual effects of television on a society that has never known theaters, nightclubs, or cinemas; this innovation is in total incongruence with the Saudi way of life. The religious content of both radio and television has been decreasing, and many of the imported programs, which are primarily from the United States, are said to be challenging the people's traditional values. Despite the strong opposition of religious leaders, television promises to be a very popular channel of communication.

The government continues to ban the public showing of films. It has permitted, without official sanction, private noncommercial showing of films, although the religious police have been known to enter private residences to confiscate films (see ch. 6). It is probable, however, that public cinemas will become legal because of the popularity of television and through the influence of urban elites who are the primary audience for the private showings.

Saudi News Agency

The control and dissemination of news in Saudi Arabia is almost exclusively through the Saudi News Agency, the only indigenous news service. As a semiofficial, government-owned enterprise under the jurisdiction of the Ministry of Information, its primary function is to centralize and bring regional and national news to the different channels of information inside and outside the country. Founded on January 23, 1971, Saudi News Agency furnished news to the domestic press and radio in attempts to formulate a national identity.

The English-language daily newsletter, *Replica,* summarizes important information from Saudi newspapers and broadcasts. For international news coverage the Saudi press in the mid-1970s relied on the services of Agence France Presse, Associated Press, Middle East News Agency (Egypt), Reuters, and United Press International. There were no news services from communist countries.

EXTERNAL SOURCES OF INFORMATION

The demand for mass communications in Saudi Arabia has increased even more rapidly among educated Saudis than its growth. As a result foreign books, periodicals, and films are being imported into the country, and foreign broadcasts are popular. All imported publications are subject to close scrutiny by Saudi government censors before being admitted.

The United States Information Agency (USIA) has had an established information program in the country for some time. Known as the United States Information Service (USIS) abroad, USIA distributed cultural and general-interest periodicals and pamphlets. In Jiddah the USIS library and information center served many visitors annually. There is a USIS film library in Jiddah. Some films are shown on Saudi television, and others may be loaned to the Saudi government; all films are responsive to Saudi Arabian religious and social values. An English-language center has been established, in cooperation with the Saudi Ministry of Education, in Riyadh. An important function of USIS has been the counseling of Saudi students interested in visiting the United States. The broadcasts of the Voice of America (VOA) program were beamed daily in Arabic to Saudi Arabia.

Broadcasts from other parts of the Arabian Peninsula, Egypt, and the other Arab nations can be heard in most parts of the country; Voice of the Arabs and Radio Cairo both beamed from Egypt were by far the most popular in the mid-1970s. Informational activities of the United Kingdom, France, and the Federal Republic of Germany (West Germany) were conducted by their diplomatic and cultural representatives, stationed in Jiddah. The Arabic program of the British Broadcasting Corporation (BBC) may be heard throughout the day, as can the Arabic-language program of the Voice of Israel. Both France and West Germany had Arabic broadcast services to Saudi Arabia in 1976.

The Soviet Union was reported to be very active in its information efforts, primarily through broadcasting, because diplomatic relations do not exist between the two countries (see ch. 10). The impact of communist information services was thought to be of very little significance among the Saudi people, however.

In 1976 various forms of information from African and other friendly states were disseminated. Many countries were banned from broadcasting into Saudi Arabia, although there was actually no way of preventing Saudis from hearing these broadcasts.

* * * * * * * * * * * * * * *

Those interested in a more comprehensive treatment of the development and present-day status of mass communications in Saudi Arabia should see "An Historical and Analytical Study of Broadcasting and Press in Saudi Arabia" by Abdulrahman S. Shobaili, "An Historical and Descriptive Analysis of the Evolution and Development of Saudi Arabian Television" by Douglas A. Boyd contains a great deal of information on broadcasts and remained the only other available source on this topic in early 1976. (For further information see Bibliography.)

CHAPTER 10

FOREIGN RELATIONS

In early 1976 Saudi Arabia's foreign policy continued to focus on the maintenance of its security and its military prominence on the Arabian Peninsula; defense of Arab unity and Arab interests; advocacy of shared goals and objectives by the world Islamic community; and expansion of commercial, industrial, and diplomatic relations with key industrialized oil-consuming, noncommunist nations, such as the West European countries, Japan, and the United States. These countries were the most important customers for the Saudi oil exports and were the sources for the economic and military goods and services that the Saudi government was purchasing on a seemingly ever-increasing scale (see ch. 13).

Saudi Arabia continued to perform a moderating role in intra-Arab politics. The government's greatest regional apprehensions were over the influence and politics of the radical or communist-oriented leaders of some Arab states. Moreover Saudi Arabia's concept of Arab unity differed from that of those Arab leaders who espoused alignments between or among states as a prelude to a permanent merger of states and governments. The Saudi view of Arab unity, rather, sought consensus and cooperation among independent Arab states. Saudi leaders defined this as the purpose of such multilateral organizations as the League of Arab States (Arab League) and the Islamic Conference (see International Setting, this ch.). A major theme promoted by Saudi foreign policy spokesmen was that of Islamic solidarity, which has a much broader potential base than Arab unity.

The major foreign policy decisions were made by King Khalid ibn Abd al Aziz Al Saud in consultation with his senior advisers. These advisers included, but were not necessarily limited to, Crown Prince Fahd ibn Abd al Aziz Al Saud and Amir Abd Allah ibn Abd al Aziz Al Saud, the first and second deputy prime ministers respectively; Amir Sultan ibn Abd al Aziz Al Saud and Amir Turki ibn Abd al Aziz Al Saud, minister and vice minister of defense and aviation respectively; Shaykh Ahmad Zaki Yamani, minister of petroleum and mineral resources; and Amir Saud ibn Faisal ibn Abd al Aziz Al Saud, minister of foreign affairs. Saud directed the day-to-day conduct of diplomacy and was a major foreign policy spokesman and negotiator. Because of the importance of oil production and export Yamani handled many of the more critical aspects of the government's foreign relations. Moreover the policy decisions of the king and his key advisers with respect to oil production and exports were made within the framework of the Organization of Petroleum Exporting Countries (OPEC) and in concert with the Organization of Arab Petroleum Exporting Countries (OAPEC). Saudi Arabia's active participation in those bodies constituted a vital part of its diplomatic effort (see ch. 12).

The founder of the kingdom, Abd al Aziz ibn Abd ar Rahman Al Saud, created the state by alternately using his armed forces and engaging in cautious personal diplomacy. By the mid-1970s the country had enjoyed over four decades of relatively stable rule, which in turn contributed to an avoidance of the experience of most of its neighbors—conquest or domination by an alien power. The country's rulers occasionally expressed concern about the nation's relatively weak military position, but as a result of internal stability, the nation's vast oil wealth, and the national tradition of independence, they conducted the nation's foreign affairs with considerable confidence and aplomb.

RELATIONS WITH MIDDLE EASTERN AND ISLAMIC STATES

Saudi Arabia, as the homeland of Islam, maintains a special significance to the Islamic world. More and more Muslims make the pilgrimage to Mecca each year—the lifetime goal of Muslims throughout the world (see ch. 4; ch. 6). Relations are closest, however, with the Arab states of the Middle East and North Africa. Saudi Arabia's bilateral relations with individual Arab states have always been integrated within a pattern of relations with all Arab states, although in the 1970s relations with the traditional Arab monarchies held the special interest of the Saudi government despite the fact that its relations with Egypt probably dominated all others.

Saudi Arabia's constantly increasing wealth has provided the government new leverage in its relations with Arab and Islamic countries. Through loans, grants, and investments Saudi Arabia has become a major contributor to those Arab governments with few resources for development and in the financial support of the military effort against Israel. The Saudi government's policy of providing aid and loans to promote the development and stabilization of Arab countries during the 1970s has been extended to include other Islamic and third world nations.

In the aftermath of the overwhelming defeat of Arab forces by the Israelis in the June 1967 War, King Faisal ibn Abd al Aziz Al Saud sought to restabilize Saudi Arabia's position among Arab states. At the Fourth Arab Summit Conference in Khartoum, Sudan, in August 1967 moderate Arab leaders agreed to provide financial subsidies to Egypt and Jordan. Saudi Arabia agreed to provide the largest amount if Gamal Abdul Nasser of Egypt would withdraw his armed forces completely from the Yemen Arab Republic [Yemen (Sana)] and cease his campaign against Arab monarchies. Nasser agreed.

From 1967 until his death in 1975 Faisal continued to practice a foreign policy that sought to neutralize at least some potential external adversaries through aid and assistance. This policy achieved for Faisal a position as an important Arab leader, particularly as the country's oil revenues escalated. He based his policy on the related desires of maintaining Saudi independence and establishing Arab unity. King Khalid has continued this effort. The country's relations with most of the Arab states have also been enhanced by its role as an intermediary between various Arab states concerning what has been called the Arab cold war.

The division among the radical Arab states and the moderate and conservative Arab states grew out of the events of the 1950s and 1960s during which time military coups in Egypt, Libya, and Iraq overthrew traditional monarchies, while such traditional states as Jordan faced conditions of internal instability. Beyond the political differences among the Arab states, the Arab-Israeli wars of 1948, 1956, and 1967 also produced frustrations and tensions among these states.

The death of Nasser in September 1970 began a new era in intra-Arab relations. President Anwar al Sadat's succession of Nasser resulted in a rapprochement between Egypt and Saudi Arabia. In the opinion of many observers it was Faisal's urging that prompted Sadat to expel the Soviet Union's advisers from Egypt in July 1972 as well as to rescind in April 1976 the Soviet Union's use of port facilities for its naval vessels at Alexandria. Saudi Arabia's emergence as an active leader in foreign relations within the Middle East is even more deeply rooted in the traditional style of personal diplomacy. In early 1976 King Khalid remarked that "We believe in the usefulness of direct contact among the leaders of the region, whether on a bilateral level or among a number of states."

Saudi Arabia's immense wealth has gained for the Saudi government this position of influence, even though the country remains far behind some states in the region in terms of military capabilities (see ch. 14). Saudi foreign policy within the region is based in part on its continued distrust of the radical Arab regimes and in part on its profound commitment to the Arab struggle with Israel. Despite the radical politics of the Palestinians, the Saudis generally endorse the goals and activities of the Palestine Liberation Organization. Saudi Arabia would prefer a final and rapid settlement of the Arab-Israeli conflict so that its plans for further internal development are not hampered. In 1976 the prospect of another Arab-Israeli war concerned Saudi leaders; they were generally committed to another oil embargo similar in nature to their use of what has been called the oil weapon during the October 1973 War. The use of the oil weapon in support of its

Arab allies, not only during the October 1973 War but also during the June 1967 War, resulted in the alignment of the foreign policies of some foreign powers behind the Arab efforts against Israel and the assumption by Saudi Arabia of a greater role within the Arab community.

Among the foreign policy successes of Saudi leaders has been their mediation of disputes between other Arab states. In 1975, for example, Saudi Arabia helped to mediate a dispute between Syria and Iraq about the Euphrates River waters. The Saudis have also sought to foster better relations between Egypt and Syria, whose governments sporadically cooperated and quarreled during the early and mid-1970s. Saudi efforts proved somewhat successful in 1973 by fostering a rapprochement between Egypt and Syria that probably contributed to the impressive Arab performance in the October 1973 War. After the second Egyptian-Israeli disengagement agreement in September 1975, relations between Egypt and Syria reached a low point. In early 1976 Saudi Arabia continued its efforts to bring the two countries together through a series of multilateral summit meetings—to include Jordanian and Palestinian leaders—scheduled for later that year.

Relations with other Arab states have improved in the 1970s, but these relations have not always been so friendly, as can be demonstrated by Saudi Arabia's relations with Iraq and Jordan. In the 1930s, when recognition among the Arab states was sought by King Abd al Aziz, the country made several treaties based on "Islamic friendship and Arab brotherhood." In the 1950s, however, shifting alliances in the Arab world made expedient a change in the former animosity between the ruling Saud family and the Hashimite dynasties of Iraq and Jordan. In May 1957 a growing suspicion of Egypt by Saudi leaders prompted King Saud to visit Iraq for the first time; at the conclusion of the visit the Saudi and Iraqi kings issued a joint statement condemning communism, imperialism, and Zionism.

The statement followed Saudi actions in 1956 that led to the deployment of Saudi troops in Jordan as a deterrent to the military threat during the crisis over the nationalization of the Suez Canal by Nasser and the further deployment of Saudi troops at the port of Aqaba, from which the British had withdrawn. It was during this same period that Saudi Arabia began financial aid to the Jordanian government as a replacement for British subsidies, and in April 1957, during a crackdown on antimonarchist elements in Jordan, Saudi troops again were posted in Jordan (see ch. 14).

The most significant change in Saudi relations with Iraq, however, came in 1958 with the overthrow of the Iraqi monarchy and the establishment of a radical, military regime. Although the Iraqi revolution produced tensions between the two countries throughout the 1960s and into the 1970s (escalated by support and assistance given Iraq by the Soviet Union), there were signs that relations between Iraq and

Saudi Arabia were improving in 1976. The agreement demarcating the joint boundary of the Iraqi-Saudi Neutral Zone was concluded in July 1975, and Iraqi leaders subsequently terminated their propaganda campaign against the Saudi government. Reciprocating these Iraqi actions Saudi Arabia has been instrumental as a mediator in helping to resolve the tensions between Iraq and its neighbors, Iran and Syria.

It was the threat of Nasser's actions in the Yemen (Sana) civil war that brought Jordan and Saudi Arabia into a closer alliance, and their relations for the most part have since been strong. A joint Saudi-Jordanian military command was brought into operation after Egypt's decision to support the republican coup in Yemen (Sana) and during the initial Egyptian-Saudi confrontation over the issue in November 1962. Jordan quickly proclaimed that an attack on Saudi Arabia would be regarded as an attack on Jordan. This commitment was not to be a unilateral measure, and during the June 1967 War Saudi Arabia sent an army brigade into Jordan marking the first time that Saudi Arabia took military action in the Arab-Israeli conflict. This Saudi brigade remained in early 1976 (see ch. 14). Furthermore the Saudi government was strongly committed to Jordan when King Hussein was severely threatened for a time both by Syrian and by Palestinian guerrilla aggression. Since the resolution of the Jordanian civil war in September 1970, which resulted in the continuation of the monarchy, Saudi Arabia has been an active mediator between Jordan and its Arab adversaries.

In 1976 a major concern of the Saudi government was the year-old civil war in Lebanon, and the Saudis were strongly committed to a position that opposed outside intervention or interference in Lebanese domestic affairs. The remaining Arab states all had cordial relations with Saudi Arabia. Even the radical regime in Libya had found common ground with Saudi Arabia; both countries continued to renounce communism, and Libya's leaders advocated Islamic conservatism.

At the regional level Saudi Arabia remains concerned with policies affecting the Red Sea, the Persian Gulf, and the whole of the Arabian Peninsula. The status of Saudi relations with the Persian Gulf states and the two Yemen governments has been vital to these interests. When Kuwait ended its client relationship with the United Kingdom in June 1961, the oil-rich country was immediately threatened by an Iraqi claim to its territory. Saudi Arabia supported Kuwaiti independence, however, by sending troops to defend it, and Saudi-Kuwaiti relations remained closely tied and broadly based into the 1970s.

In 1971 the century-old protective relationship between the United Kingdom and the states of the lower Persian Gulf—Bahrain, Qatar, and the United Arab Emirates—was replaced by full independence. As a result of the British decision in 1968 to withdraw from the Arabian Peninsula, Saudi Arabia began to increase its responsibility for collective security in the region, and a major goal of Saudi policy has been to find solutions to the many territorial disputes still unresolved concerning the gulf and its boundaries with these states.

Long-standing tensions on the Arabian Peninsula were reflected in Saudi-British relations over possession of the potentially oil-rich Buraymi Oasis on the undemarcated frontier between Saudi Arabia, Abu Dhabi (in 1976 a part of the United Arab Emirates), and the Sultanate of Muscat and Oman (in 1976 known as Oman). In December 1971, when Abu Dhabi gained independence and became part of the United Arab Emirates, the government began negotiations with Saudi Arabia; a final agreement on demarcation was concluded in April 1975. Other successful resolutions of conflicts in this area included the Saudi-Iranian agreement in 1969 that established a median line between their continental shelves in the Persian Gulf and the Iranian relinquishment in 1970 of its claim to Bahrain.

During April 1976 King Khalid made state visits to all the Persian Gulf states to promote even closer relations among them. The Saudi policies concerning the security of the Persian Gulf and the protection of the oil-producing states in particular have been in the direction of cooperation. As of early 1976 the government had reacted cooly to Iran's call for a formal collective security arrangement among these states, a reaction that is probably based on the reduction of Iraqi-Saudi tensions and on Saudi Arabia's consistent skepticism in its relations with Iran.

The most sensitive area of Saudi relations with states in the Arabian Peninsula in 1976 was its relationships with Yemen (Sana) and the People's Democratic Republic of Yemen [Yemen (Aden)]. Saudi relations with Yemen (Sana) have changed significantly since the end of the civil war in 1967, and observers estimate that Saudi Arabia provides Yemen (Sana) with the equivalent of US$200 million in aid yearly. Extremely poor and overpopulated, Yemen (Sana) not only depends on Saudi Arabia to provide a measure of security but because of Saudi-Yemen (Sana) ties, Yemen (Sana)'s major external threat, Yemen (Aden), was a potential threat to Saudi Arabia. In 1969 and as recently as 1973 Yemen (Aden) forces struck Saudi outposts along their common border. In 1975, however, Crown Prince Fahd held several meetings with the Yemen (Aden) foreign minister that resulted in an announcement on March 10, 1976, that the normalization of diplomatic relations between the two countries would soon follow.

Non-Arab Muslims throughout the world are accepted as Muslim brothers, but they are still regarded as foreigners within Saudi Arabia. Saudi Arabia has maintained strong relations with such non-Arab Islamic nations as Pakistan and Malaysia as a direct consequence of Saudi policy aimed at cooperation among Islamic states. The establishment of the Islamic Conference in 1971 was at the initiative of King Faisal and in 1976 included most of the Islamic governments of the world (see International Setting, this ch.). The Saudi abhorrence of communist nations has not prevented Muslim pilgrims from communist-controlled countries from traveling to Mecca.

INTERNATIONAL SETTING

United States and Western Europe

Saudi Arabian contacts with the Western world began only after World War II; before then the United Kingdom, intent upon controlling the route to India, was the major power in the Middle East (see ch. 2). In the mid-1940s the United States began to displace the British as the dominant Western influence, chiefly because of the expansion of oil exploration under the guidance of American-owned oil firms (see ch. 2; ch. 12). In this early period bilateral relations with Western governments were maintained primarily for economic reasons—those countries were the developers and consumers of the country's oil reserves. The growth of an adequate national defense system, however, became equally important to the Saudi government, and the country's relations with the United States were in part based on their shared defense concerns (see ch. 14).

During the 1970s and even more so after the sharp increases in government revenues after 1973, Saudi Arabia actively pursued a policy of expanding its relations with all Western industrialized nations. During the 1970s relations with Western countries become more formalized through establishing bilateral, high-level commissions formed to promote coordination in such areas of mutual interest as economic cooperation and military sales.

Although British officials were in fairly constant contact with Abd al Aziz before, during, and after World War I, full diplomatic relations with the United Kingdom date from 1937, when the British recognized the sovereignty of Abd al Aziz as ruler of the Hasa, the Najd, and the Hejaz (see ch. 8). In exchange Saudi Arabia recognized British paramountcy in Bahrain, the Trucial States, and other parts of the Arabian Peninsula. Saudi-British relations have since been determined by the encircling presence of political entities—vestiges of former empires—that lost their roles as British protectorates in the 1960s and 1970s. Few of the boundaries of the Saudi Arabian borderlands were precisely known in 1976, and a dispute over the Buraymi Oasis had complicated Saudi-British relations for many years (see ch. 3).

In November 1956 Saudi Arabia accused the British of aggression toward Egypt during the Suez Canal crisis and announced that it had broken diplomatic relations. Saudi-British relations were not resumed until January 1963. For the remainder of the 1960s relations continued to improve, and the United Kingdom played an important role in helping the Saudis modernize the Royal Saudi Air Force and the Royal Saudi National Guard.

The British decision in 1968 to end their military role east of the Suez Canal led to the rapid withdrawal of their influence by 1972, which improved their relations with Saudi Arabia. In 1976 the Saudi government expected the British government and British firms to take an active role in the Saudi second Five Year Development Plan (1975-80), and the first meeting of the Saudi Arabian-United Kingdom Joint Commission in London in March 1976 suggested considerable British participation.

Since its establishment in 1932 Saudi Arabia has been the most consistent Arab friend of the United States. With the exception of a few brief periods, the relations between Saudi Arabia and the United States have always been close, and many observers state that these ties have amounted to a special relationship. Saudi Arabia's leaders have had close relations with Americans since 1933 when King Abd al Aziz granted the Standard Oil Company of California an oil exploration concession (see ch. 12). Cordiality between the United States and Saudi Arabia has been based on the presence of vast deposits of oil in Saudi Arabia, the possession of advanced technological skills by American private industry, and the mutual benefits resulting from very broad government-to-government cooperation.

Formal diplomatic relations with the United States date from World War II when King Abd al Aziz was the only independent Middle Eastern leader friendly to the Allies. In 1943 the first official United States delegation arrived at Jiddah to negotiate the construction and lease of an air base at Dhahran, which was begun in 1944 and completed in 1946. In February 1945 King Abd al Aziz and President Franklin D. Roosevelt conferred briefly on a United States Navy vessel in Great Bitter Lake, Egypt, and in March 1945 Saudi Arabia declared war on Germany and Japan.

In June 1956, when the Dhahran air base agreement expired, the Saudis agreed to extend it only on a monthly basis. Early the next year the Saudi king paid a state visit to the United States and while there agreed to a five-year renewal of the lease in exchange for continued United States arms and aid. On April 2, 1962, the United States relinquished its rights to the Dhahran air base and turned it over, one of the world's larger airports, to the Saudi government.

When Faisal became king in 1964, he looked to the United States for cooperation in his many plans for the modernization of the country. The Saudi Arabian government entered into contracts with United States government agencies and American commercial and industrial enterprises for help of many specific projects (see ch. 11). Large numbers of young Saudis were trained by the United States government or attended American colleges. At first these students tended to take technical programs related primarily to the petroleum industry, but by 1976 Saudi students had branched out into such fields as the humanities and the social sciences (see ch. 5).

A new approach to Saudi-United States relations was initiated with the establishment of the United States-Saudi Arabia Joint Commission on June 8, 1974. This bilateral arrangement was designed to promote cooperation between cabinet-level members of both governments. The joint cooperation commission set up between Secretary of State Henry A. Kissinger and Crown Prince Fahd was composed of two major organs—the Joint Commission on Economic Cooperation and the Joint Commission on Security Cooperation—to work in areas of cooperation that were seen to be mutually beneficial (see fig. 14).

As Saudi Arabia's importance increased in the 1970s, problems in relations with the United States became more evident. The three primary conflicts recognized by both governments were the controversy within the United States over Saudi Arabian compliance with the Arab League boycott of Israel, the concern over possible transfer of arms bought by Saudi Arabia to other Arab states, and the strong ties between Israel and the United States.

Saudi relations with most Western states were cordial. Most of these were oil-consuming countries that also offered potential expertise and supplies of major value to the ambitious Saudi Arabian development plans in 1976. Saudi-French relations have improved since the resumption of diplomatic relations in September 1962; relations had been severed as a result of the Suez invasion and the Algerian crisis

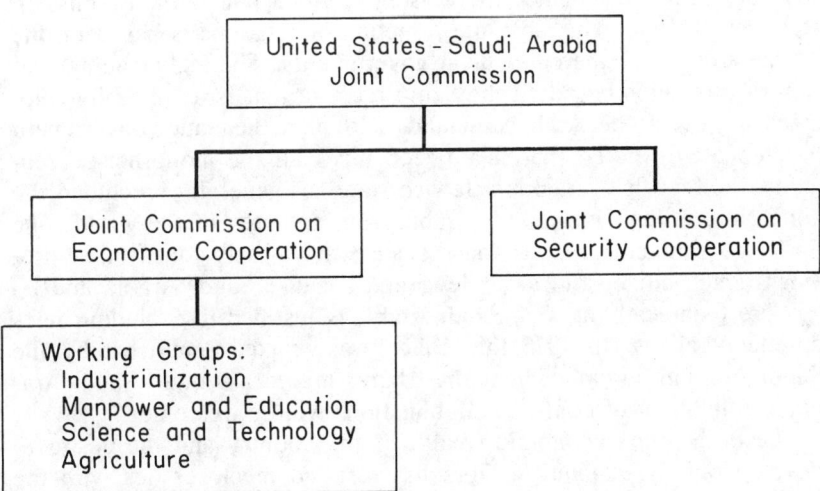

Source: Based on information from U.S. Congress, 93d, 2d Session, House of Representatives, Committee on Foreign Affairs, *The Persian Gulf, 1974: Money, Politics, Arms, and Power*, Washington, 1975, p. 258.

Figure 14. *Organization of the United States-Saudi Arabia Joint Commission, 1974.*

in 1956. In particular the Saudi government has increasingly looked to France as an alternate source of arms and equipment to continue the modernzation of the Saudi armed forces (see ch. 14).

Relations with the Federal Republic of Germany (West Germany) have been principally concerned with private companies engaged in business and government contracts in Saudi Arabia. In 1965 Saudi Arabia severed diplomatic relations with West Germany over its recognition of Israel, but relations were soon reestablished, and cordial relations existed between the two countries in the mid-1970s. Saudi Arabia has sought to buy arms from West Germany, and in early 1976 the West German government was apparently reconsidering its long-standing embargo on arms sales to Middle Eastern states.

Relations with Various Other Countries

Saudi Arabia maintains diplomatic relations with most of the oil-producing and oil-consuming countries and was among one of the first countries to promote the idea of interdependence of oil producer and oil consumer. Bilateral relations with other non-Muslim countries were determined by economic affairs, whether Saudi initiatives were designed to gain support from other countries to accomplish the goals of the country's current five-year plan or to assist African and other developing countries severely affected by rapid increases in the price of oil.

The Saudi government has not maintained diplomatic relations with any communist state since the closing of the Soviet Union's mission at Jiddah in 1938. This absolute rejection of relations is based on the official atheism of the communist governments. The technical state of war with Israel is based on the Saudi premise that Israel illegally colonized a part of the Arab homeland. Although the Saudi government has repeatedly noted that Islam recognizes all the monotheistic religions, the fact that Israel is a Jewish state has generally precluded the admission of Jews into Saudi Arabia from any area of the world. The Saudi government reasons that because the Israeli constitution provides Israeli citizenship to all Jews and because Saudi Arabia and Israel are technically at war, Saudi Arabia is justified in excluding Jews as enemy aliens. In 1975 this policy was relaxed somewhat by the Saudi Arabian announcement that "any foreigner sent to Saudi Arabia in fulfillment of contractual obligations will be welcome."

The burgeoning economic wealth of the country and the desire to develop rapidly in many sectors has resulted in closer ties with the more industrialized countries of Asia, especially Japan and the Republic of Korea (South Korea), in the interest of acquiring manufactured goods, technical expertise, and manpower needed to achieve modernization (see ch. 11). Although the Saudi government relied primarily on the United States to support their plans for modernization, Saudi Arabia has begun to move in many other directions in a desire to be as independent as possible in achieving its goals.

The country established diplomatic relations with the Republic of China (Nationalist China) in 1957; it maintains that relationship and has shown no inclination to establish relations with the People's Republic of China (PRC). Saudi Arabia has also vigorously opposed the policy of apartheid and has no relations with the Republic of South Africa or Southern Rhodesia.

United Nations and World Organizations

As World War II entered its final phase, Saudi Arabia abandoned its earlier neutrality and declared war on Germany and Japan in March 1945. This action established Saudi Arabia's eligibility to participate in the Conference on International Organization that convened in San Francisco in April 1945, and six months later—on October 24, 1945—Saudi Arabia became a founding member of the United Nations (UN). In subsequent years the country joined most of the specialized agencies attached to the UN and in 1976 was a member of fourteen of those organs.

Until the 1970s Saudi Arabia had not taken a very active role in UN affairs, except in its numerous complaints to the Security Council against Israel. Its reliance on and continued support of the UN, however, was demonstrated during the Yemen (Sana) civil war when, in conjunction with Egypt, Saudi Arabia financed most of the costs of the UN Observation Mission. In the General Assembly Saudi Arabia has usually aligned itself with fellow Arab states in promoting the interests of the developing nations and in opposing the dominant position of the industrialized countries in the specialized agencies. As an aggressive opponent of communism Saudi Arabia voted against the seating of the PRC in October 1972. Although it gave only limited support to the drive to expel Israel from the UN in the fall of 1975, it did vote in favor of the resolution adopted by the General Assembly on November 11, 1975, that classified Zionism as a form of racism.

Saudi Arabia has taken an active role in OPEC and OAPEC. Saudi Arabia was also a founding member in 1945 of the Arab League, a voluntary association of all Arab sovereign states designed to promote the mutual interests and coordinate the policies and activities of its members. The country has been represented at all seven summit conferences called by the Arab League.

King Faisal was also responsible for convening a summit meeting of Islamic heads of state in Rabat, Morocco, in September 1969, which led to the First Islamic Conference of Foreign Ministers in Jiddah in March 1970. These two high-level meetings resulted in a resolution to create a world organization called the Islamic Conference, which was then formally established at the Second Islamic Conference of Foreign Ministers, held in Karachi, Pakistan, in December

1970 to promote Islamic solidarity in economic, social, cultural, scientific, and other fields. In 1976 there was a total of thirty-eight member states, most of which have been represented at the organization's five Islamic Conference meetings. The conference in Kuala Lumpur, Malaysia, in June 1974 resulted in the formation of the Islamic Development Bank by twenty-four of its members to promote development that will be financed by the oil-producing countries. The bank officially began operation in Jiddah in August 1974.

MECHANICS OF FOREIGN RELATIONS

In 1931 King Abd al Aziz appointed his son Faisal minister of foreign affairs, the first ministerial office created under Abd al Aziz' rule. In fact Faisal had been an active diplomat for some time, and his appointment was primarily a matter of formality. Despite Faisal's position as foreign minister until Abd al Aziz' death in 1953, the king usually had the deciding voice in foreign policy formulation. This trend was also apparent during the reign of King Saud, except during those periods when then Crown Prince Faisal held executive powers. During Faisal's reign (1964-75) he served as his own foreign minister, and important foreign policy decisions came directly from his office.

In October 1975 King Khalid appointed Saud ibn Faisal as foreign minister—beginning again the separation of the positions of prime minister and foreign minister (see ch. 8). Saud has been an active foreign minister, continuing the practice of personal diplomacy by making frequent visits to foreign capitals.

Many other Saudi Arabian government officials also traveled extensively abroad; foremost among these officials in 1976 was Crown Prince Fahd. Kamal Adham, one of Faisal's close advisers and in early 1976 head of foreign intelligence, has been another frequent traveler to other countries to explain his country's positions to foreign leaders. In addition a number of the members of the Council of Ministers have been active in foreign diplomacy, notably the minister of defense and aviation and the minister of petroleum and mineral resources.

By 1976 the Ministry of Foreign Affairs had grown tremendously since the reign of Abd al Aziz. The minister was assisted by a permanent undersecretary and a staff of deputy ministers that included Saudi Arabia's ambassadors. The permanent undersecretary was directly responsible for administration and organization of the ministry, including international conferences and UN affairs, legal affairs, and economic affairs. In addition the permanent undersecretary was responsible for the performance of the deputy and assistant deputy ministers who headed the six major departments: Diplomatic Missions Abroad, Western Department, Afro-Asian Department, Islamic Affairs Department, Petroleum Affairs Department, and Arab Affairs Department. Supporting these departments were the offices of protocol, consular affairs, administration, cables and wireless, and public relations and press.

In early 1976 the only ministry with headquarters in Jiddah was the Ministry of Foreign Affairs; all of the other ministries had their headquarters in Riyadh, where the foreign office expected to move by 1980. The foreign diplomatic missions (there were fifty-nine in 1976) were also located in Jiddah. Therefore, when a foreign diplomat in Saudi Arabia needed to deal directly with a senior government official outside the foreign ministry, the diplomat had to travel to Riyadh, a distance of over 500 miles. Many ambassadors accredited to Saudi Arabia use the Jiddah embassies to carry out diplomatic relations with other countries, especially those on the Arabian Peninsula. In 1976 Saudi Arabia had established diplomatic relations with sixty-nine countries and maintained diplomatic missions in most of them.

The foreign ministry and the diplomatic missions were staffed by career diplomats—many of whom had been trained abroad—and members of the royal family or other important families. The dominant role of the king was still evident under the reign of Khalid. In his role as head of state and prime minister the king appoints and receives all ambassadors and, in conjunction with the Council of Ministers, directs the negotiation and ratification of all treaties.

* * * * * * * * * * * * * * *

Interesting aspects of the diplomatic history of Saudi Arabia are presented in Gerald De Gaury's *Faisal: King of Saudi Arabia*. The present-day foreign relations of Saudi Arabia are analyzed in Mordechai Abir's *Oil, Power and Politics*, Hanns Maull's "Oil and Influence: The Oil Weapon Examined," and *The Persian Gulf, 1975*, a series of hearings before the Special Subcommittee on Investigations of the Committee on International Relations, U.S. House of Representatives. United States-Saudi Arabian relations are discussed in Emile A. Nakhleh's *The United States and Saudi Arabia: A Policy Analysis* and William R. Polk's *The United States and the Arab World*. (For further information see Bibliography.)

SECTION III. ECONOMIC

CHAPTER 11

CHARACTER AND STRUCTURE OF THE ECONOMY

Saudi Arabia is extremely rare among countries in the dependency of the economy on government expenditures. Except for payments by the oil companies to employees, contractors, and suppliers—minor parts of the economy—the large oil revenues accrue to the government, whose spending circulates the oil money through the economy. In the mid 1970s probably no country in the world had a more direct and immediate control of the income flow and the major decisions affecting the economic life of its citizens.

Saudi Arabia also is rare among developing countries in its dedication to private initiative. In spite of the immense economic power inherent in the government's control over the distribution of oil revenues, the government has avoided as much as possible the development of a large public sector. The government's spending pattern focuses instead on improving the living conditions of the population, developing the human resources of the kingdom largely by expanding education, and building up the infrastructure on which a modern economy could develop. By 1976, however, the building and business boom under way since 1973 had overtaxed the economy. The flood of imports exceeded port facilities, and labor and material shortages were extensive. The increase of the money supply meant too much money chasing too few goods. The expanding economic activity involving ever increasing numbers of foreign workers posed a very real threat to the society's values. A growing number of Saudis wondered if the country were buying too many problems and too little development.

STRUCTURE OF THE ECONOMY

Only since World War II has Saudi Arabia begun to emerge from the economic isolation imposed by the hot climate and desert terrain of the Arabian Peninsula. For thousands of years the economy consisted basically of autonomous clusters of people around wells and oases. Most of the population were engaged in agriculture, including nomads who raised livestock on the limited forage produced by the localized and· infrequent rains. Local craftsmen produced the few items required by the people concentrated around the scattered sources of water. Trade was limited largely to camel caravans and the annual influx of pilgrims visiting the holy places in the Hejaz (see ch. 4; ch. 6; ch. 13). Production was on a small scale for small markets and nearly subsistence in nature.

The discovery of oil in 1938 by an American company started a transformation of this primitive economy. An indirect contribution was the modern equipment and techniques that accompanied the American oilmen's entrance into the kingdom. Development of the oil fields required ancillary construction of roads, ports, housing, electric generating plants, and water systems. Saudi workers had to be trained in many new skills. In addition the concentration of oil field employees and the range of services the company and the employees needed opened totally new economic opportunities for innovation and large-scale operations by Saudi merchants and contractors. In short the discovery of oil ended the kingdom's isolation.

The discovery of oil also contributed directly to a high rate of growth for the kingdom's economy. The oil deposits proved to be extensive, providing the basis for nearly continuous expansion of production and export of petroleum products (see ch. 12). By 1976 the country had the largest crude oil reserves and was the world's largest petroleum exporter. Saudi Arabia ranked third among crude oil producers in 1975, after the Soviet Union and the United States, and had the capacity to be first if world markets required it. The Saudi petroleum industry was enormous even by international standards, and it completely dominated the rest of the economy. The oil sector's share of gross domestic product (GDP) amounted to about 87 percent in fiscal year (FY) 1975 (see table A). Largely because of the exploitation of the country's petroleum resources, GDP per capita in 1975 amounted to the equivalent of approximately US$6,000 based on the official population estimate of a little over 7 million (US$7,500 if the population was about 5.6 million as most observers reported) (see ch. 3).

The growth and transformation of the Saudi economy is easier to describe than to measure. Few statistics were recorded before the 1960s, and the second Five Year Development Plan (1975-80) admitted inadequacies in many statistics maintained in the mid 1970s. Moreover definitions of some statistical categories were altered, making it difficult to develop consistent time series. A high degree of precision should not be attributed to many Saudi statistics; they are, like the statistics of many developing countries, in the process of refinement as the statisticians work to improve them.

Even without adequate statistics it is apparent that the petroleum industry paced the economy in the 1940s and 1950s. During the 1960s, when national account data became available, growth of the non-oil sector nearly matched that of the petroleum industry. GDP increased at an annual average rate of 10.5 percent between FY 1963 and FY 1970 in current prices (the growth rate probably was about 8.5 percent a year in constant prices). The annual growth rate during this period was 10.7 percent for the petroleum sector and 10.0 percent for the non-oil sector. Because of the similarity of growth rates for the oil and non-oil sectors, there was little change in the oil sector's share of GDP; it went from 53.5 to 54.5 percent between FY 1963 and FY 1970.

The rate of growth of the Saudi economy became astronomical in the 1970s as a result of the tremendously higher returns the government received for each barrel of oil produced (see ch. 12). GDP (in current prices) increased an average of nearly 55 percent a year between 1970 and FY 1975, and the oil sector averaged nearly 70 percent a year. The economist's usual practice of using constant prices to avoid the variations caused by price changes would be inappropriate in this instance because the higher prices the kingdom received represented real purchasing power in world markets. The Saudi second development plan instead measured the economy's growth between FY 1970 and FY 1975 by calculating real national income, which included adjustments for the effects of changes in the terms of trade; real national income increased at an annual rate of 44.8 percent. In the opinion of most observers the abnormally large increases in world crude oil prices during the early 1970s were not likely to be repeated, and the growth rate of the Saudi economy during the last half of the 1970s should be closer to the historic pattern of the 1960s.

Although the sharply increased prices for petroleum products greatly diminished the importance of the non-oil sector during the early 1970s, the economy continued to diversify. The non-oil sector grew at an impressive 11.6 percent a year (value added in constant prices) between FY 1970 and FY 1975. The economy was still primitive, but considerable progress has been made since the 1930s, particularly in transportation, health, education, and living conditions (see ch. 3; ch. 4; ch. 5).

The sectors of the non-oil economy in which the greatest development occurred were construction, trade and services, transportation and communications, and government services (see table 5). Construction increased sharply during the early 1970s as part of the government's increased oil revenues was channeled into development projects. Between 1970 and 1975, for example, about 3,000 miles of paved roads were built; seventeen berths for ships were completed; and fifteen airports, eight sewage projects, fifteen public hospitals, five new industrial buildings, 75,000 new housing units, and 12,000 classrooms were completed or under construction. Employment in the construction industry rose from 140,000 in FY 1970 to 314,000 in 1975, making it the second largest source of employment after agriculture. The demand for construction had to be met by recruitment of a substantial number of foreign workers. Even with foreign recruitment construction labor was in short supply, and labor costs doubled between 1972 and 1974. Costs of construction materials also had nearly

Table 5. Saudi Arabia, Gross Domestic Product by Sector, Fiscal Years 1963, 1970, and 1975[1]

(in millions of riyals at current prices)[2]

Sector	1963	1970	1975[3]
Agriculture	866	984	1,409
Crude oil and refining	4,578	9,347	128,727
Other mining and quarrying	16	47	175
Manufacturing (excluding oil refining)	157	431	902
Utilities	101	273	333
Construction	311	934	4,362
Transportation and communications	537	1,243	3,638
Trade and services		1,555	3,934
Ownership of dwellings	1,110	661	1,637
Total Private Sector	7,676	15,475	145,117
Government services	886	1,675	3,600
Total Gross Domestic Product	8,562	17,150	148,717
Oil sector (in percent)	(53.5)	(54.5)	(86.6)
Non-oil sector (in percent)	(46.5)	(45.5)	(13.4)

[1] For dates of fiscal years see table A.
[2] For value of the riyal—see Glossary.
[3] Preliminary estimate.

Source: Based on information from Ramon Knauerhase, *The Saudi Arabian Economy*, New York, 1975, Table 4.1, p. 58; and Saudi Arabia, *Development Plan 1395-1400 (1975-80)*, Springfield, Virginia, 1976, Table II-2, pp. 15-16.

doubled by 1974 because of the high rate of construction in the 1970s. The number of Saudi contractors and their abilities continued to increase, but only large international contractors were able to handle many of the large projects.

The rapid expansion of the trade and services sector in the 1970s was primarily the result of the increase in wholesale and retail trade associated with the high and growing volume of imported goods (see ch. 12). Domestic trade more than doubled in value between FY 1970 and FY 1975 (in current prices at the wholesale level), and distribution and sale of imported goods accounted for between 70 and 75 percent of domestic trade during the period. The increased consumer purchasing power combined with the larger volume of goods to be sold created opportunities for economies of scale in merchandising operations. In the mid-1970s retail chains, full line department stores, and modern shopping centers began to emerge in major cities. The larger number of foreign businessmen as well as the increased business activity expanded the demand for hotel rooms, restaurants, and financial, insurance, legal, and real estate services. Although hotels and restaurants had been constructed, the demand for such facilities in 1976 far exceeded their availability. Foreign businessmen could not count on individual rooms or confirmed reservation. Real estate values around major cities had appreciated considerably by 1976, and rental of a villa suitable for an executive might be as high as the equivalent of US$70,000 per year.

The transportation and communications sector had grown considerably since the camel caravan era, but facilities still lagged behind demand. A transport survey, encompassing future requirements for ports, airports, roads, and pipelines and examining ways to improve the efficiency of the system, was completed in 1974 with the assistance of the International Bank for Reconstruction and Development (IBRD, commonly known as the World Bank). Because the inadequacies of the system imposed a major constraint on the kingdom's development plans in early 1976, the survey presumably would guide the government in its organizational and investment effort to improve transportation. For example, ships waited months to unload; part of the problem was berthing space, part was port clearance, and part was the internal distribution from the ports.

Domestic commercial transport doubled between FY 1970 and FY 1975. The primary mode of transport was by truck. The number of commercial vehicles increased from 35,000 in FY 1968 to 91,000 in FY 1973. More than 20,000 trucks were being imported annually in the mid 1970s, but truck transport was largely based on individual owner operators. The more efficient fleet operations had developed primarily in petroleum and cement transport. Observers suggested that encouragement be given to fleet operations and to construction of modern truck terminals and storage areas as a means of speeding cargo movement. Intracity and intercity passenger transport was falling behind the requirements of the greater urbanization the kingdom was experiencing (see ch. 3).

Government services expanded relatively slowly until the 1960s, largely reflecting the greater number of government workers and gradual salary increases. When the emphasis on economic development began in the 1960s, the government accelerated expenditures for health and education in order to develop the country's human resources (see ch. 5). By FY 1975 government services constituted 18 percent of the non-oil economy.

Manufacturing (excluding oil refining), utilities, and mining have had high rates of growth, but they started from an extremely small base and in the mid 1970s remained minor parts of the economy. Development of these sectors was largely based on private investment, and investors had been somewhat hesitant until the 1970s. The wider distribution and rising incomes of the general population spurred private investments in these sectors in the mid 1970s.

Agriculture has been a major disappointment to Saudi planners. Despite substantial investments by the government, such as irrigation and drainage projects, subsidies, and agricultural settlements, the value added by agriculture increased by only 1.6 percent a year (in constant prices) between FY 1963 and FY 1972 (see ch. 13). Incomes were low in the agricultural sector, causing farmers and nomads to seek employment in better paying jobs in urban centers. The importance of the agricultural sector had been declining steadily from its preeminent position in the economy in the 1940s.

MONEY

The political instability and lack of banking facilities until almost the mid twentieth century caused the people of Arabia to put their trust in coins having a metallic content equal to their value. A number of gold and silver coins, such as the Maria Theresa dollar, the British gold sovereign, the Indian rupee, Turkish coins, and the silver riyal of the Hashimite government of the Hejaz, circulated in Arabia in the 1920s, but the British sovereign was more or less the standard of value in the area.

The first Saudi money was a minor coin issued in 1925. In 1928 the Saudi government issued the silver riyal which initially had a fixed relationship of ten riyals to one British gold sovereign (then worth about US$4.87). This relationship placed the kingdom on a bimetallic standard. Variations in world gold and silver prices required adjustment of the exchange rate and the silver content of the riyal to bring its value into line with world prices. International factors affecting the British sovereign also complicated Saudi efforts to achieve currency stability; in 1952 a Saudi gold sovereign of the same size, weight, and fineness as the British sovereign was introduced. Good counterfeits of lower gold content soon appeared, however, and the Saudi sovereign was withdrawn in 1954.

The annual flow of pilgrims to Mecca was a major source of foreign exchange for many years after the establishment of the kingdom in 1932. After the Saudi silver riyal was issued, the pilgrimage created a large seasonal demand for riyals. In 1953 "pilgrims' receipts" were introduced as a form of paper currency printed in the various languages of the pilgrims. As the name implies, the receipts were for the pilgrims' foreign currencies. Although not legal tender, the pilgrims' receipts circulated relatively freely in the kingdom because they initially had full foreign exchange backing and were more convenient for everyday use. The receipts familiarized the Saudi people with paper money and provided flexibility to the money system—seasonally at first and as a substitute currency when riyals left left the country as the world price of silver rose late in the 1950s. Not everybody learned to trust paper money, however; in 1976 some Saudis continued to convert notes immediately into coins.

The official value of the Saudi riyal (SR) was established at SR3.75 to US$1 in 1954, the international value of the silver content of the riyal at the time. The rise in international gold and silver prices, which led to an outflow of these coins from the kingdom, had caused the government to stop minting the riyal by 1955 and the gold sovereign even earlier. Most of the currency in circulation during the remainder of the 1950s was in pilgrims' receipts, which no longer had full foreign exchange backing. A leveling off of oil revenues after 1956, combined with a high level of government spending, created budget deficits and led to heavy borrowing by the government. The resulting inflation and demand for imports caused the free market value of the riyal to fall. Exchange controls and import restrictions, introduced in July 1957, proved ineffective in maintaining the value of the riyal. By early l958 the free market exchange rate for the riyal had fallen to SR6.25 to US$1.

A stabilization plan was drafted with the help of experts from the International Monetary Fund (IMF) and implemented in June 1958. By late 1959 budgetary surpluses had provided funds to repay about one half of the government's indebtedness, wholesale prices had fallen about 15 to 20 percent, and the value of the riyal on the free market had appreciated to SR4.5 to US$1. The success of the stabilization plan resulted in further financial measures affecting the budget process, banking, and the currency in 1960. Effective in January 1960 the official value of the riyal became SR4.5 to US$1, equivalent to 0.197482 gram of fine gold per riyal. The riyal was divided into twenty qurshes, instead of the twenty-two previously, and each qursh consisted of five halalas. Saudi monetary authorities were empowered to issue paper riyal notes with 100 percent gold or foreign currency backing and to sell and buy in the foreign exchange market to stabilize the national currency. The pilgrims' receipts were withdrawn in exchange for the new paper riyal. The exchange controls and the dual exchange rates instituted in the late 1950s were abolished.

During the international currency realignments of December 1971 and February 1973, the par value of the riyal was maintained. Because the United States dollar had depreciated, the riyal appreciated in terms of the dollar; in December 1971 SR4.14 equaled US$1, and in February 1973 the rate became SR3.73 to US$1. In March 1973 the par value of the riyal was appreciated about 5 percent, with IMF concurrence, to SR4.28255 to one SDR (special drawing rights—an accounting unit of the IMF), equivalent to 0.20751 gram of fine gold per riyal. The change in March 1973 appreciated the riyal to SR3.55 to US$1. In September the riyal was permitted a wider fluctuation around its SDR peg, which in fact linked it to the United States dollar.

The 1960 currency measures abolished restrictions on foreign exchange transactions for current or capital purposes by residents and nonresidents. Foreign exchange can be freely bought and sold, although transactions involving the currencies of Israel, Southern Rhodesia, and South Africa are prohibited. The riyal became a strong, stable currency during the 1960s as a result of the fiscal reforms. The rapid increase of oil revenues by 1976 only increased its strength.

BANKING

Commercial Banking

Commercial banking is a modern addition to the economy of Saudi Arabia. Before oil revenues became significant, banking was inhibited by the relatively small use of money and the Quranic injunction against interest on loans. A few banking functions existed, such as moneychangers (largely for the pilgrims visiting Mecca), who had informal connections to international currency markets, and noninstitutionalized suppliers of credit, particularly relatives.

The first commercial bank, the Netherlands Trading Society, was established in 1926. Additional commercial banks, Saudi and foreign owned, were formed after World War II as oil revenues accelerated. Their business was mostly short term financing of imports and some financing of enterprises catering to pilgrims. The number of banks continued to increase until the 1960s, when the government halted entrance of additional banks.

In late 1975 twelve commercial banks with seventy-seven branch offices operated in the kingdom. Two of the banks, the National Commercial Bank and the Riyadh Bank, were Saudi owned; three were owned by non-Saudi Arabs; and seven were owned by other foreign interests. The two Saudi banks had the greatest number of branch offices (fifty-four) and by far the broadest deposit base. Some of the foreign banks had been the most active lenders, however. There were three clearinghouses for checks, in Jiddah, Riyadh, and Dammam.

The head offices of all but one of the commercial banks were in Jiddah, long the commercial center of the kingdom. The center has been shifting to Riyadh, however, as government disbursements of oil revenues have increased. Only the two Saudi banks and three of the foreign owned banks had branch offices in Riyadh in 1975; the government deliberately limited the number of banks in the capital. Some observers attributed the leading position of the First National City Bank (of New York) among the foreign owned banks to its offices in Riyadh. Several of the other foreign owned banks had pressed to obtain approval for Riyadh branches, but government approval had not been granted by 1975.

Commercial banking expanded at about the same rate as the economy during the decade of the 1960s. Bank deposits increased at an average annual rate of about 10 percent. Time deposits grew a little faster than demand deposits, reflecting growing acceptance of savings accounts by some of the population although many still distrusted banks. Government officials encouraged the commercial banks, through subsidies when necessary, to increase the number of branch offices to improve accessibility. By 1970 branches were operating in virtually every town of 10,000 or more people and in some towns having as few as 5,000. In lieu of interest commercial banks used fee schedules that rewarded depositors and entailed costs for borrowers.

Bank credit to the private sector expanded at an average rate of about 11 percent a year during the 1960s, another sign of growing acceptance of commercial banking. The more rapid increase of loans compared with deposits reflected the limited use of credit at the beginning of the decade. Bank liquidity still remained unusually high in 1970 by usual banking standards. In fact banks were increasing investments abroad because of insufficient domestic lending opportunities. Credit was cheaper in the kingdom than in most areas of the world. About one-half of the total commercial bank loans to the private domestic sector went to finance imports, about one-fifth as advances to contractors, and the remainder to finance industrial and other ventures. During the 1960s the commercial banking system became an effective agent for mobilizing savings to finance economic development.

The pace of banking became hectic in the 1970s as oil revenues and government spending accelerated. The money supply expanded at about 40 percent each year in FY 1974 and FY 1975 compared with an annual average rate of 10 percent during the 1960s (demand deposits made up roughly 45 percent of the money supply). Commercial bank deposits increased at an annual rate of about 32 percent between FY 1971 and FY 1973. In FY 1974 deposits increased by 44 percent, and by the end of the fiscal year in July 1975 deposits had increased by another 55 percent. Time deposits were increasing faster than demand deposits. Clearinghouse activity also reflected the hectic pace. The number of checks cleared increased by 29 percent, and their value increased by 95 percent in FY 1974 (the latest data available in early 1976).

The flood of deposits was at first not matched by a corresponding increase in lending during the early 1970s. Bank credit increased by less than 4 percent a year between FY 1971 and FY 1973. Some banks refused new deposits, and some increased their investments abroad because of a surplus of funds. The demand for credit jumped sharply in 1973 as the building boom gained momentum from the rapid rise of oil revenues. Bank credit expanded 77 percent in FY 1974 and over 90 percent in FY 1975. Much of the credit went to finance construction and imports, but there was a surge of borrowing to finance real estate speculation, new business, and existing firms that found their cash flow and capital insufficient to finance expansion.

By late 1975 the commercial banks were strained. The increased lending since 1973 had reduced liquidity, but this posed no immediate constraint because deposits continued to grow and the banks' liquidity had previously been extremely high. The strains were on staff and space, both of which were still geared to the level of business of several years earlier. Most of the banks were undercapitalized and were trying to increase their capital because the conservative Saudi banking regulations imposed penalties when an individual bank's business exceeded specified ratios to capitalization. The banks were also finding it difficult to adjust to the medium and long term financing borrowers were seeking in the mid 1970s. This was a form of business the banks were neither used to nor prepared for.

Government Banking Institutions

Government financial institutions emerged slowly as a need developed or as oil revenues made new services possible. During the latter stages of unification of the country a small agency conducted such limited treasury and central bank functions as collecting and channeling public revenues, minting coins, and handling government purchases. A newly formed office under the king's finance minister took over these functions in 1932.

A major step toward modernization of the monetary and financial system was taken in 1951 when the Saudi finance minister requested technical assistance from the United States government. By then oil revenues had become substantial, and a number of banks had been established. The governmental machinery was inadquate to cope with the problems that had evolved.

The American financial advisers prepared a plan for a modified central bank. After Saudi officials made sure the bank would not contravene Islamic law, the plan was adopted. The new bank, called the Saudi Arabian Monetary Agency (SAMA), began operations in October 1952. Subsequently several branch offices were opened in major urban centers.

The monetary functions of SAMA included stabilization of the value of the currency through reserve funds kept separate for monetary purposes and buying and selling of precious metals for the government account. SAMA was also to regulate commercial banks, exchange dealers, and money changers. SAMA was not authorized to issue paper currency until 1960 but did issue the pilgrims' receipts (see Money, this ch.). SAMA acted as depository for all government funds and paid out these funds for purposes approved by the minister of finance and national economy. SAMA's charter stipulated that it would conform to Islamic law. It was not to be a profitmaking institution and could not pay or receive interest. There were several additional prohibitions, including one against extending credit to the government. This was dropped in 1955, and SAMA financed about one half of the government's debt that built up in the late 1950s. SAMA also abandoned full foreign exchange cover for pilgrims' receipts as the government became increasingly pressed for funds.

In 1960 several decrees carried through a currency reform. The riyal was designated as the currency unit and legal tender, and SAMA was authorized to issue paper currency with 100 percent cover and to buy and sell gold and foreign exchange to stabilize the national currency. SAMA was to publish an annual report on its operations; the report became a valuable source of information and statistics on the Saudi economy.

A major banking control law—issued in November 1966—clarified and strengthened SAMA's role in controlling the banking system. Applications for a license to operate a bank were submitted to SAMA, which submitted the application along with its recommendation to the Ministry of Finance and National Economy. The Council of Ministers set the conditions for granting licenses to foreign banks, however. The law stipulated that, when a bank's deposit liabilities exceeded fifteen times its reserves and paid up capital, 50 percent of the excess must be deposited with SAMA. The law also stipulated a narrow range for the ratio of liquid assets commercial banks must maintain against deposit liabilities and the ratio of reserves to deposits commercial banks must maintain on deposit with SAMA. In 1975 reserves of commercial banks to be deposited with SAMA were set at 10 percent of demand deposits and 5 percent of time and savings deposits. The liquidity ratio commercial banks were required to maintain against deposit liabilities was 20 percent. SAMA has closely supervised the commercial banks to ensure sound and usually conservative banking practices.

Several restrictions inhibit SAMA's implementation of monetary policy. It cannot extend credit to banks nor use a discount rate because that is a form of interest. SAMA has little flexibility in setting reserve and liquidity requirements for commercial banks, although the requirements can be extended after government approval. SAMA's primary tool for expanding the credit base is placing deposits in commercial banks. SAMA followed a neutral monetary policy at least through 1975 because the demand for credit was less than the banking system had available. It remained to be seen in early 1976 whether SAMA would take actions to cool the overheated Saudi economy and how effective it would be in such endeavors.

Of the other government financial institutions, the Agricultural Bank is the oldest. Establish in 1963, it has steadily expanded its lending to farmers. It provided medium- to long-term, interest-free agricultural loans, but the bulk of lending has been medium term for machinery and similar assets. In 1975 it operated branches in ten cities supervising forty-three local offices. Its capital amounted to SR103 million in FY 1975, sufficient to satisfy the credit needs of 6 percent of the farmers. The bank was also the vehicle for payment of subsidies to farmers.

The Saudi Industrial Development Fund was established in March 1974 to provide interest free, medium to long term financing for the private sector subject to an administrative charge of 1 to 2 percent. Only Saudi firms were eligible to obtain loans, which could amount to 50 percent of the total financing required. Loans could not be used for working capital. Initial capital was SR500 million. The fund is managed by Chase Manhattan Bank, which provided a staff of project analysts.

The Saudi Credit Bank was established in 1971 to provide interest free loans for low-income Saudis who could not obtain credit from commercial banks. Initial capitalization was SR5 million to be supplemented by interest free loans from the government and SAMA. The bank's loan regulations, which required cosigners, various forms of security, or approval to deduct monthly payments from the borrower's salary, appeared as restrictive as American consumer commercial credit terms. The first office opened in Riyadh in December 1973, and other branches were planned for Jiddah and Dammam.

The Real Estate Development Fund was established to finance the purchase of homes by Saudi citizens. The fund lent up to 70 percent of the cost of land and construction free of interest. Requirements to qualify for a loan appeared minimal. The fund apparently was established in 1975 with an announced capital of SR250 million, although more than SR1.5 billion in loans reportedly had been committed in 1975. Because of the tight housing situation in 1975 finding a house to buy probably was more difficult than financing its purchase.

The General Investment Fund was the organization by which the Saudi government financed investments in large scale, publicly owned industries. The fund held shares in several large ventures, such as the Saudi Arabian Fertilizer Company, but could sell the shares to the public when the ventures became profitable. The fund was under the direction of the Ministry of Finance and National Economy, and its capital in 1975 was SR3 billion.

PUBLIC FINANCE

Saudi budgets were primarily an accounting device to maintain control of government expenditures of oil revenues in the general interest. The intricacies of the budget and the authority of the finance officers have grown as oil revenues increased. In the early days of the kingdom public funds and the king's purse were largely indistinguishable. The great importance that the Islamic religion attaches to charity and generosity influenced the spending pattern. Expenditures for religious endowments, hospitality, and royal patronage reached unprecedented heights before budget reform in the late 1950s altered allocations toward social and economic development.

The first formal budget was published in FY 1948, and three additional budgets were published in the next decade. These early budgets were no more than rough estimates of revenues and expenditures and were not closely followed. Data on actual revenues and expenditures were not published.

Efforts were made to strengthen the budgetary process. SAMA assisted the Ministry of Finance, which was formally established in 1953, in centralizing receipts and disbursements authorized by the budgets. In 1954 the Ministry of Finance was expanded to the Ministry of Finance and National Economy with greater power to supervise and audit the accounts of other ministries. Budget deficits, government borrowing, inflation, and the declining external value of the riyal between 1956 and 1958 proved that these measures were insufficient.

A stabilization program was instituted in June 1958, incorporating IMF advice. The program restricted government spending, imposed new taxes and higher import duties on nonessential imports, applied exchange controls and a dual exchange rate for the riyal, and provided for a budget surplus by which past government indebtedness was to be repaid. This debt amounted to about SR1.8 billion in June 1958, slightly more than one-half of which was owed to internal lenders—primarily SAMA—and the rest to foreign creditors. The stabilization program was effectively implemented, causing the external value of the riyal to appreciate, internal prices to fall, and budget surpluses, from which debt repayments were made, to form. The debt to SAMA was virtually repaid by early 1960, and by the end of 1961 practically all of the internal debt was liquidated and a start made on repayment of the external debt.

Budgetary improvements were part of the stabilization program and financial reforms of the 1958-60 period. After these reforms the Council of Ministers, which included the prime minister, became the primary policymaking body (see ch. 8). The Council of Ministers had to approve the budget before it was submitted to the king for final approval as well as approve transfers of funds from one budget category to another, expenditures not included in the budget, and changes in the revenue base.

The Ministry of Finance and National Economy has overall responsibility for preparation of the budget. The budgetary process began with a request to all ministries for detailed budget estimates for expenditures by major categories: personnel, supplies and services, other current expenditures such as subsidies, and capital expenditures.

The replies were to be returned by the fifth month of the fiscal year for review by the Ministry of Finance and National Economy and other organizations as required. In 1965 the Central Planning Organization (CPO) was established; its representatives reviewed capital expenditures, and presumably defense and other ministries sat in on parts of the budget review. The budget was submitted to the Council of Ministers at least one month before the beginning of a new fiscal year, which began on the first day of the seventh month, Rajab, of the lunar year (see table A). The budgeting process was believed to have remained essentially unchanged after the ministerial reorganization in October 1975 (see ch. 8).

The budgetary reforms also greatly increased the publication of information. Annual estimates of revenues and expenditures, usually indicating principal revenue sources and expenditure allocations by ministries, have been published at the beginning of fiscal years since FY 1962. Clarifying information about current and capital expenditures was published separately by the finance ministry and SAMA. SAMA published information about total actual receipts and expenditures but without details for subordinate parts of the budget.

By law a budget in deficit cannot be submitted to the Council of Ministers and the king for approval. The legal requirement has been met by including funds from sources other than current revenues and at times handling some expenditures outside the budget. One source of financing was an economic development fund built up from one time payments by oil companies in settlement of an issue under negotiation over a period of time. This fund was depleted in 1969. Another source of financing was a general reserve, which held funds from earlier budget surpluses. Saudi assistance to Egypt and Jordan in the years after the 1967 Arab-Israeli war was excluded from the budget. Another device used to balance the budget was to carry an entry for "expected savings" (the term was not explained), which was deducted from total expenditures.

The overall fiscal performance has been good since the budgetary reforms at the beginning of the 1960s. Estimates of revenues were reasonably close until the 1970s, when oil revenues increased much faster than estimated (see table 6). Actual expenditures were generally below estimates except between 1968 and 1970, when Saudi assistance to Egypt and Jordan was the primary cause of the deficits. The internal and external debt incurred in the late 1950s was repaid in the early 1960s, and the kingdom has since avoided indebtedness. In fact the trend in the 1970s has been toward budget surpluses and building or reserve funds caused by the unusually rapid increase in oil revenues and a shortfall in development expenditures. Capital expenditures usually have long lead times, making it difficult to estimate with precision how much will be spent in a given year.

Table 6. Saudi Arabia, Summary of Accounts, Selected Fiscal Years, 1964-76[1]
(in millions of riyals)[2]

	1964[3]	1970[3]	1972[3]	1973[4]	1974[4]	1975[4]	1976[4]
Budget Allocations							
Revenues							
Oil revenues	2,284	4,848	9,956	12,203	21,266	94,432	86,969
Customs duties	136	242	313	315	330	400	n.a.
Other revenues	206	876	513	682	1,214	3,415	n.a.
Total	2,626	5,966	10,782	13,200	22,810	98,247	95,847
Expenditures							
Current	2,136	3,284	5,146	6,400	8,547	19,346	36,556
Development	550	2,682	5,036	6,718	14,263	78,901[5]	74,379
Total	2,686	5,966	10,182	13,118	22,810	98,247	110,935
Estimates of Actual Revenues and Expenditures							
Revenues	2,583	5,668	11,120	15,790	n.a.	n.a.	n.a.
Expenditures							
Current	2,139	3,254	4,263	5,068	6,284	15,250	n.a.
Development	263	2,163	3,378	4,178	10,253	15,000	n.a.
Aid and miscellaneous	n.a.	662	662	902	2,935	11,955	n.a.
Total	2,402	6,079	8,303	10,148	19,472	42,205	n.a.
Surplus or deficit (-)	181	-411	2,817	5,642	n.a.	n.a.	n.a.

n.a.—not available.
[1] For dates of fiscal years see table A.
[2] For value of the riyal—see Glossary.
[3] Compilations and estimates by International Monetary Fund.
[4] Provisional data subject to revision.
[5] Includes SR52,504 million available for allocation to projects but not allocated.

Source: Based on information from Said H. Hitti and George T. Abd, "The Economy and Finances of Saudi Arabia," *International Monetary Fund Staff Papers*, XXI, No. 2, July 1974, Table 16, p. 282; Saudi Arabian Monetary Agency, *Statistical Summary*, No. 2, Dammam, 1975, Table 9A, p. 59; and "Saudis Will Cut Spending to Cool Economy," *Middle East Economic Digest*, London, 20, No. 10, March 5, 1976, p. 29.

Revenue Sources

Budget receipts were dominated by oil revenues, which accounted for more than 90 percent of total revenue in the 1970s. The higher return per barrel of oil produced since 1970 increased the importance of oil revenues, but even in the 1960s they accounted for 85 to 90 percent of revenues. Royalties had been the primary source of oil revenues until 1950, when an income tax was levied on the oil companies (see ch. 12). Since then the income tax has become the more important source of oil revenues, accounting for about 65 percent of oil revenues in 1961 and about 80 percent in 1973. When the government completes purchase of the Arabian American Oil Company (Aramco), probably in 1976, royalties and the income tax presumably will become small revenue sources because earnings from oil exports probably will be entered under another budget heading.

Customs duties are the most important among the other sources of revenue. Import tariffs have been kept low for basic items and usually modest for most other imports, although during times of budgetary and balance-of-payments problems duties on nonessential imports have been increased to generate additional revenue or to restrict the level of imports. Some other indirect taxes produced minor amounts of revenue.

Different income taxes were applied to Saudis and foreigners. The main tax on Saudis, zakat, was based on the Quranic injunction to all Muslims to aid the poor. The zakat, although not truly an income tax because it was based on net worth, was levied on Saudi nationals and businessess at a rate of 2.5 percent. The government attempted to collect one-half, and the other one-half was to be paid as a moral obligation. Collections from the zakat increased slowly, and the government experimented with various ways to collect the tax to increase receipts but without much success. Many observers believed collections were lower than they should have been because of the voluntary reporting of income and assets. A roads tax, levied on payrolls at 2 percent for persons earning SR400 or more, was another revenue source resembling an income tax. It yielded substantially more than the zakat, but the tax was repealed by 1975. In 1971 a jihad (see Glossary) tax was levied on Saudis to increase revenues, but it was discontinued the next year when oil revenues increased.

An income tax was levied on non-Saudi individuals and businesses at progressive rates. The rates were lower for non-oil businesses and recorded separately from taxes on oil companies. The income tax on foreign non-oil businesses and individuals was a growing source of revenue and yielded much higher revenues than direct taxes on Saudis.

There were a number of other minor sources of government revenues, such as port fees, license fees, fees on papers of value, excise taxes, and earnings from government companies and investments. Most foreign experts saw many ways tax revenues could be increased and collection improved but foresaw little change; oil revenues after 1973 provided more funds than the government could spend.

Budget Expenditures

Budget expenditures are the means by which most of the income from the oil sector is spread among the population. Allocations for current expenditures were deliberately kept low in the early 1960s in order to generate budget surpluses to repay the government's indebtedness. Current expenditures were again held down for several years before FY 1972 as the government struggled to set aside funds to assist Egypt and Jordan. Between FY 1960 and FY 1970 budget allocations for current expenditures increased slowly, at an average rate of 2.3 percent each year. They increased very rapidly after FY 1971 as oil revenues increased, averaging 45 percent a year between FY 1970 and FY 1975.

Allocations for development expenditures increased more rapidly than current expenditures after the effort to develop the economy began in the early 1960s. The capital budget averaged an annual increase of nearly 9.4 percent between FY 1960 and FY 1970. The increases in the 1970s became astronomical, particularly in FY 1975, when they increased five and one-half times over the level of the previous year. The large allocations were in part to create reserve funds in the full realization by budget officials that such large increases could not be spent that rapidly. The budget information concerning capital projects presented two difficulties: a large part of the budget allocations for projects was in an unidentified, "other" category (about 50 percent in 1970s), and actual development expenditures were not available in detail. It was not possible to determine the actual spending by individual ministries. After FY 1970 development allocation followed the goals of the first Five Year Development Plan (1970-75).

Administration has consistently been a major element of expenditure allocations (see table 7). This reflected the increasing size of the government. Current and capital expenditures on defense increased rapidly in the 1970s, and separate, more accurate, data for FY 1972 and FY 1973 indicated that defense received 31 and 38 percent of total capital outlays. Expenditures to develop transportation and education also made up major categories of government spending. Agriculture and industry received only a small part of government funds. Funds for the royal family peaked at SR248 million in FY 1960 and were reduced in FY 1963. Since FY 1965 the yearly budget allocation for the royal family has remained constant at SR173 million.

Table 7. *Saudi Arabia, Budget Allocations by Function, Selected Fiscal Years, 1966-74*[1, 2]
(in millions of riyals)[3]

Function	1966	1968	1970	1972	1973	1974
Agriculture and industry	406	537	468	706	856	1,297
Infrastructure	841	1,054	1,059	2,049	2,299	4,299
Education, health, and social affairs	960	944	1,045	1,823	2,465	3,284
National defense	572	743	851	2,695	3,951	5,716
Administration[4]	1,441	1,659	2,543	2,909	3,547	5,210
TOTAL	4,220	4,937	5,966	10,182	13,118	19,806

[1] For dates of fiscal years see table A.
[2] Includes allocations for current and capital expenditures.
[3] For value of the riyal—see Glossary.
[4] Includes some defense expenditures through 1970, as well as expenditures unallocable under other items.

Source: Based on information from Said H. Hitti and George T. Abd, "The Economy and Finances of Saudi Arabia," *International Monetary Fund Staff Papers*, XXI, No. 2, July 1974, Table 17, p. 284.

LABOR

Data on the work force are suspect because of the uncertainty concerning the size of the population (see ch. 3). The problem is compounded by the large number of non-Saudis in the work force. The second Five Year Development Plan (1975-80) indicated that there were 314,000 foreign workers in 1975, although many observers believed that the actual number was between 1 and 1.5 million. Part of this discrepancy probably arose because workers from other countries of the Arabian Peninsula did not need work permits, and there were many Yemenis, for example, working in the kingdom. The second five-year plan admits inadequacies in employment statistics and shows separate tables for the total work force in 1975, in which the figures differ by about 7 percent.

In spite of difficulties with data there was general agreement on certain broad trends. Only a small part of the Saudi population worked. This was in part because of the very small number of women in the work force—1 percent of the female population in 1975, according to the second five year plan. Most observers agreed that there had been a decline in the number of workers engaged in settled farming and nomadic herding. The rural inhabitants had moved to urban areas, taking jobs in construction, trade, transportation, and government, the fastest growing economic sectors. Employment with the government, for which probably reliable statistics were available, increased an average of 8.4 percent a year between FY 1970 and FY 1975, compared with 6.4 percent for the rest of the economy (see table 8).

Observers agreed with the planners that the Saudi economy was heavily dependent on foreign workers in a broad range of occupations. Foreign workers were employed as teachers, accountants, equipment operators, scientists, and managers, for example. The Saudi work force lacked skilled and highly trained personnel. Nearly every foreign business was required to institute training programs; these plus the government's vocational and educational programs were raising the skills of the labor force slowly but perceptibly. Saudis avoided menial labor, and many observers described stevedores, construction laborers, hotel employees, and workers in other unskilled jobs as non-Saudis and often Yemenis.

The planners expected the accelerated growth of the second five-year plan to increase the economy's dependence on foreign workers. Total employment was expected to increase by a little more than 800,000 between FY 1975 and FY 1980, about 500,000 of which would

Table 8. *Saudi Arabia, Employment by Sector, Fiscal Years 1967, 1970, and 1975*[1,2]
(in thousands)

Sector	1967	1970	1975
Agriculture	464.8	445.8	426.1
Crude oil and refining	14.0	13.4	21.3
Other mining and quarrying	11.2	13.7	26.4
Manufacturing (excluding oil refining)	41.1	34.7	44.4
Utilities	8.3	12.2	18.3
Construction	104.0	141.5	314.2
Commerce	95.8	130.2	211.0
Transportation and communications	44.0	62.1	103.2
Private services	223.4	137.5	188.4
Government employees[3]	n.a.	112.7	168.8
TOTAL	1,006.6	1,103.8	1,522.1

n.a.—not available.
[1] For dates of fiscal years see table A.
[2] Includes non-Saudi workers.
[3] Includes civilian defense employees.

Source: Based on information from Saudi Arabia, *Development Plan 1395-1400 (1975-80)*, Springfield, Virginia, 1976, Table II-1, p. 11; and U.N. Industrial Development Organization, *Summaries of Industrial Development Plans*, III, Vienna, 1973, p. 259.

be foreign workers. The number of Saudis in the work force was expected to increase 3.1 percent a year compared with 21 percent a year for foreign workers. Many of the foreign workers presumably would be employed in construction, transportation, and manufacturing because employment in these sectors would expand the most (approximately 120,000 new jobs). The plan also anticipated an increase of approximately 112,000 professional and technical jobs that would require a substantial number of foreign workers because Saudis were not being trained that rapidly. The government, recognizing the need for additional workers, eased procedures to obtain work permits and entry documents in 1975. Many economists expected that the low availability of labor, particularly highly skilled labor, would be a major constraint on development between 1975 and 1980.

PLANNING

The kingdom's first organization devoted to planning economic development was established in 1958 as a result of suggestions by an IMF team of advisers that was helping devise a stabilization program to remedy the country's fiscal and monetary problems. Membership in the first planning committee was broadened in 1959, but it remained essentially a group of high officials too busy to give much attention to planning. Their activities were largely limited to tariff problems of the business community. A further reorganization of planning occurred in 1961, but this group concerned itself more with budgetary review than with planning. The CPO was established in 1965 and elevated to the Ministry of Planning in October 1975.

Planning was limited in the 1960s partly because of financial constraints and the decision to rely primarily on the private sector for much of economic development. The premise was that private investment would take place when the prerequisites were developed. The government effort focused on developing human resources and the transportation system and other aspects of the physical infrastructure. Shortages of trained economists also plagued the planning process. In addition the acceleration of planning after the appointment of a new president of the CPO in 1968 indicates that planning may earlier have lacked strong leadership.

The CPO had developed a four-step process for drawing up plans, and the Ministry of Planning will presumably continue essentially the same procedures; its staff and leadership were drawn largely from the CPO. The first step involved analysis and reports on the status of the economy. Then the CPO and the concerned ministries worked out broad recommendations for submission to the Council of Ministers to correct problems and to stimulate economic growth. On approval the broad strategy was transformed into specific recommendations and targets with the assistance of the ministries concerned and then submitted to the king for final approval. The CPO then assisted the Ministry of Finance and National Economy in monitoring the plan and events affecting it.

The CPO's power was circumscribed by the other ministries. The Ministry of Finance and National Economy controlled funding and may have been the primary authority on plan follow-up. The CPO charter referred to cooperation and assistance by the CPO in working with planning sections in other ministries, suggesting CPO had little formal authority over a ministry's adherence to the plan. It was not clear by early 1976 what effect the elevation of CPO to a ministry in late 1975 has had on its relations with other ministries.

Although the planning process improved, economists noted a lag in implementing plan recommendations. An example was the grain storage flour mill complexes that in the 1960s were being discussed with foreign firms. Even though the first development plan allocated funds to the project, it was not certain by 1976 that the project had been finally approved. Foreign observers were not sure why implementation lagged. Even such prerequisites for development as basic surveys and feasibility studies for some proposals had to be repeated in the second plan because of failure to carry out similar recommendations in the first plan. Some observers believed that the plans gave insufficient attention to timing sequences and priorities by which implementation could be judged. Others went further and suggested that the ministries were too independent, lacking understanding and commitment to mesh their individual activities into an overall plan.

The slowness in implementation partially negated the planning process by disrupting the phasing and linkages between and among sectors and adding to the economic costs. Some of the problems and constraints readily apparent in 1976 would have been mitigated had the recommendations of the first plan been implemented as quickly as funds became available.

The First Five Year Development Plan (1970-75)

The first Five Year Development Plan (1970-75) was submitted to the king on August 16, 1970, and became effective for the fiscal year that started on September 2, 1970. The plan contained numerous general economic and social goals along with policies, programs, and projects to achieve them. GDP was planned to increase an average of 9.8 percent a year and the oil sector 9.1 percent a year. The non oil economy was expected to increase more rapidly that the petroleum industry and thus make a start on reducing the dependence on oil. The agricultural sector was planned to grow by 4.6 percent a year, a substantial increase over the growth rate during the 1960s. Manufacturing was expected to grow at 14 percent annually, a little faster than in the

1960s. Education, mining, transportation, and trade were anticipated to have relatively high growth rates.

Planned budget allocations totaled the equivalent of nearly US$9.2 billion, 45 percent of which was to be allocated to capital projects (see table 9). Allocations to government were by far the largest, reflecting the fact that this was in essence the budget for five years in an economy that relied primarily on private investors for development; defense had 23 percent of total allocations and public administration 19 percent. Transportation and education also received large allocations.

The unanticipated large expansion of crude oil production and particularly the huge increase in revenue per barrel between 1971 and 1975 contributed to an exceptionally high rate of economic growth, one far beyond the planners' expectations. The plan was drawn in a period of fiscal constraint that was expected to persist. As oil revenues increased, budget allocations were increased, and activity throughout the economy was stimulated. Total actual spending kept to the plan in the first three years, but data were not available in early 1976 to assess total actual spending over the plan period or actual spending by sectors.

The results for other plan goals were mixed. The huge increase in oil revenues diminished the importance of the non-oil economy,

Table 9. *Saudi Arabia, Summary of Planned Financial Allocations by Sector, Five Year Development Plan (1970-75)*

(in millions of United States dollars)

Sector	Recurrent[1]	Projects	Total	Percent
Administration	1,510	205	1,715	18.7
Defense	884	1,239	2,123	23.1
Education and cultural affairs	1,367	273	1,640	17.9
Health and social affairs	358	69	427	4.7
Utilities and urban development	277	739	1,016	11.1
Transportation and communications	393	1,269	1,662	18.1
Industry	71	173	244	2.7
Agriculture	216	110	326	3.6
Trade and services	18	10	28	0.3
TOTAL	5,094	4,087	9,181	100.0[2]

[1] Covers personnel costs and other current expenditures including miscellaneous special expenses of the state budget.
[2] Figures do not add to 100.0 because of rounding.

Source: Based on information from U.N. Industrial Development Organization, *Summaries of Industrial Development Plans*, III, Vienna, 1973, p. 297.

but the latter registered a significantly higher growth rate during the plan than during the 1960s. Petroleum refining increased at only 4.0 percent a year instead of the planned 9.1 percent a year, and growth in other manufacturing was also less than planned because the planned investments in hydrocarbon based industries were not implemented. The roadbuilding plans proved far too ambitious. The planners had to estimate the growth of the agricultural sector without actual date, and it remained to be seen if agricultural output improved as substantially in the 1970s as estimated. Despite some failings valuable experience was gained for future plans, and the kingdom was fortunate to have had a plan to guide the government during the period when huge investment funds became available.

The Second Five Year Development Plan (1975-80)

The second plan was submitted to the king on April 27, 1975, and became effective for the fiscal year that started on July 9, 1975. The plan contained numerous general social goals similar to the first plan but with some specifics, reflecting the large funds available to the government. Some of these social goals included, for example, a start on free medical service, interest-free loans and subsidies for family purchases of houses, free education and vocational training, subsidized prices for essential commodities if required for a minimum standard of living, interest free credit to those with limited incomes, and extended social security benefits and support for the needy (see ch. 4; ch. 5).

Besides social, welfare, and educational goals, often left out of the plans of developing countries, the plan outlined several economic goals with policies, programs, and projects to achieve them. GDP was to grow at an annual average rate of 10 percent over the plan period increasing from the equivalent of US$42 billion in 1975 to US$68.6 billion in 1980 (in 1975 prices). Production of crude oil was assumed to grow at 10 percent a year and refining at 5 percent a year with the qualification that these figures were notional and actual expansion of the oil sector (the plan figure was 9.7 percent a year) would reflect numerous variables, many of which depended on developments in the world economy. The non oil sector was anticipated to increase at an annual rate of 13.3 percent, thus increasing its importance in the economy. The planners thought that 1975 might have marked the peak of oil's importance in the economy.

The targets for economic growth appeared reasonable and may well turn out to have been quite modest. Much depended on the demand for petroleum as the industrialized countries of the world recovered from the recession of the mid-1970s. The growth targets for nearly all portions of the non-oil economy were about the same as or less than during the 1970-75 plan period. The two major exceptions were government administration and defense, which were to increase appreciably; because the government controlled oil revenues, it was unlikely that these two sectors would fail to grow as the government planned. Growth of the agricultural sector was planned at 4 percent a year, up from an estimate of 3.6 percent a year between FY 1970 and FY 1975. It remained to be seen if agricultural production was even appreciably higher in the 1970s than during the 1960s.

The sheer size of the investments of the plan intrigued businessmen all over the world. The government's planned financial allocations totaled approximately US$142 billion, and an additional amount of private investment was planned (see table 10). The financial size of the plan was increased several times as the magnitude of oil revenues became clear during its preparation, the final investment figure being more than double the figure with which the planners began. The planners acknowledged that investments of this magnitude would create bottlenecks and other problems and anticipated shortfalls in actual spending. The financial side of the plan apparently was not closely integrated with growth estimates for the economy.

The largest share of planned government financial allocations, amounting to 23 percent of the total, was to continue development of the economy's infrastructure. The next largest share, 19 percent, was for economic resource development. The total of these two categories represented the planned investments for economic development. An

Table 10. Saudi Arabia, Summary of Planned Financial Allocations by Function, Five Year Development Plan (1975-80)

(in billions of United States dollars at 1974-75 prices)

Function	Amount	Percent of Total
Economic resource development	26.2	19
Human resource development	22.8	16
Social development	9.4	7
Development of the physical infrastructure	32.1	23
Total Private Sector	90.5	64*
Administration	10.8	8
Defense	22.2	16
Miscellaneous	18.0	13
TOTAL	141.5	100*

*Figures do not add to total because of rounding.

Source: Based on information from Saudi Arabia, *Development Plan 1395-1400 (1975-80)*, Springfield, Virginia, 1976, p. 85.

effort was made to balance growth in the various regions of the country by spreading investments, but the possibilities were limited. The long-term goal is to reduce the economy's dependence on oil, but the plan might temporarily increase the dependence because of investments totaling US$15.1 billion in refineries, a gas-collection system, and manufacturing plants based on hydrocarbons.

The second five-year plan was very ambitious. It reflected freedom from any financial constraint. Almost any project that had ever been proposed appears to have been included. The planners acknowledged that Saudi Arabia's development did not face the financial problems of most developing countries, but they anticipated other formidable constraints that would hamper the kingdom's economic growth.

Constraints on Development

A major constraint on growth in early 1976 was the transportation system. The ever-increasing flood of imports since 1973 became too much for the system to handle. Ports constituted the primary bottleneck. Long lines of ships waited at every port, some for as long as four to five months before unloading. Many experiments were tried to speed up the unloading, but they were unable to keep pace with the increasing imports. The latest reported experiment was to use helicopters to carry nets of cargo ashore. Some observers suggested that, even if the ships could be unloaded, the rest of the transport system would not be able to distribute the goods. Because storage facilities were very limited, imports would be left exposed to the weather.

Inflation was perhaps the biggest threat to the economic plan. The economy showed signs of overheating by 1974. Government spending after that put more and more money in circulation. By early 1976 the clogged ports, an acute housing shortage, zooming construction costs, and a growing manpower shortage were forcing prices up at an accelerating rate that some observers estimated at as high as 50 percent in 1975. The government's first reactions were to reduce taxes, increase salaries of government employees, reduce some prices, and import additional goods to ease prices. These measures added to the problems. Because of the structure of the banking system standard monetary policies could not be applied (see Banking, this ch.). The primary measure available, and a most effective one under the circumstances, was for the government to reduce spending. By early 1976 many observers expressed the view that the government would soon move in that direction.

The boom conditions and possibilities for large contracts contributed to a potential for corruption. Western firms paid large sums to Saudi agents with unspecified duties to aid in obtaining contracts. Foreign businessmen reported having to pay fees to get papers forwarded, goods shipped, and other ordinarily routine matters executed.

The objectionable and disruptive aspects of the boom period leading up to 1976 reinforced and added to the number of conservative Saudis who wanted development to go slowly. The conservatives had feared that importing an additional 500,000 workers to accomplish the development spelled out in the second five year plan would prove too disruptive to Saudi society. Long before the planned number of foreign workers had arrived, other factors of the development plan were disrupting the society. Some of the young, foreign trained Saudi planners were reportedly among those urging a slowdown in development expenditures.

The visible signs in early 1976 pointed to a cutback in the Saudi development effort. There was no indication of the degree, however; that apparently would depend on the relative strengths of those arguing moderation and those urging rapid development at the highest levels of the government. The issue could become important to oil consuming countries because the argument for slowing development was often coupled with a reduction of crude oil production.

* * * * * * * * * * * * * * *

Ramon Knauerhase's *The Saudi Arabian Economy* provides basic and extensive information on the Saudi economy. Saudi Arabia's *Development plan 1395-1400 (1975-80)* contains considerable statistical data and information on changes in the economy and those planned for the future. An article by Said H. Hitti and George T. Abd in the *International Monetary Fund Staff Papers*, July 1974, contains a brief but comprehensive survey of the Saudi economy with supporting statistical data. The *Annual Report* published by the Saudi Arabian Monetary Agency provides yearly summaries of economic developments in addition to considerable statistical data. (For further information see Bibliography.)

CHAPTER 12

THE PETROLEUM INDUSTRY AND FOREIGN TRADE

The oil sector completely dominates the economy of Saudi Arabia. In the mid-1970s petroleum contributed more than 80 percent of gross domestic product (GDP), more than 90 percent of government revenue, and 99 percent of foreign exchange earnings. Only in the number of jobs was the oil sector relatively unimportant; the capital-intensive nature of the oil industry required few workers, but the skills learned by former oil company employees were put to use and brought significant modernization to other parts of the economy.

Saudi Arabia's oil was also important outside the kingdom. The country was the world's third largest producer of crude oil (after the Soviet Union and the United States) in 1974 and possessed the productive capacity to be the largest. Saudi petroleum reserves were the world's largest, providing such wealth that the kingdom had the second largest foreign exchange reserves in the world. Oil had lifted Saudi Arabia from relative obscurity to a position of international as well as regional importance.

Several factors contributed to the kingdom's growing importance. Its proven petroleum deposits were huge, accounting for more than one-quarter of the world's known reserves. The country consumed little oil domestically, allowing the bulk of its high production to be exported; no other country could match Saudi Arabia's petroleum exports. Industrialized areas of Western Europe and Japan were heavily dependent on Saudi oil. Saudi support was critical to the Organization of Petroleum Exporting Countries (OPEC) in revolutionizing petroleum prices and ending the era of cheap energy in 1973. Continuing Saudi support was necessary for OPEC to sustain the high price for oil, and reduced Saudi production was essential to make the oil embargo weapon of 1973 credible (see ch. 10). Saudi monetary reserves posed a destabilizing threat to world money markets should the Saudi government decide to be disruptive.

Government officials stressed their moderate policies and their dependency on world prosperity and stability. Their argument that they had acquired such large monetary reserves only because they continued to export the oil the world needed was incontestable. Some asserted that they would prefer a lower rate of production, one that matched the economy's import needs, to the accumulation of more money than they could profitably invest; in their phrase—why give up good oil for bad paper subject to all sorts of risks?

Saudi officials have attempted to put their sudden and enormous wealth to good use. Imports increased more than threefold between 1972 and 1974. Part of the gain was in food imports to improve the diet of the country (see ch. 4). Substantially larger imports of materials and equipment for economic development contributed to the growth of imports. A huge development program was launched in 1975 that was to increase imports for several years (see ch. 11; ch. 13). Financial grants of about US$850 million were given in 1974 to other countries, largely other Arab countries. International Bank for Reconstruction and Development (IBRD, commonly known as the World Bank) bonds worth US$750 million were purchased in 1974 to help provide funds for developing countries. Nearly US$3.8 billion of direct investments were made in economies of other countries during 1974. Nevertheless these expenditures were small compared to the kingdom's earnings.

Probably no country in history experienced the rags-to-riches transformation of Saudi Arabia in 1974. Average earnings per barrel of oil produced went from US$1.56 in 1973 to more than US$10 in 1974. Total oil earnings jumped from US$4.3 billion in 1973 to US$22.6 billion in 1974. Even with more imports and increased aid to foreign countries amounting to more than 10 percent of GDP, Saudi Arabia still had almost US$11 billion that it could not profitably use and that went into foreign exchange reserves. The country truly was exporting oil far beyond its own financial needs. Stability and prosperity in many industrialized countries depended on Saudi Arabia's continuing that policy.

OIL: THE INTERNATIONAL SETTING

The era of cheap energy ended for the world in 1973 after OPEC took control of pricing from the international oil companies. The change shocked most of the world. For Saudi Arabia, however, the wealth and influence of the country suddenly took a quantum jump.

One factor contributing to the sharp change in the price of energy was the steeply rising world demand caused by the mechanization of so many activities during the previous 100 years. One estimate indicated that the fuel and power consumed by an average modern American amounted to the energy equivalent of 200 full-time servants. Between 1962 and 1971 the estimated world demand for energy increased at an annual rate of 4.8 percent, a rate that would result in a doubling in fifteen years. Energy requirements were accelerating so rapidly that observers predicted critical energy shortages in the next century and the exhaustion of known oil deposits long before that. The primary energy sources—coal, oil, and natural gas—were being depleted at an astonishing rate.

Accompanying the growth in energy demand was a radical shift in the source of energy. In 1859, when the world's first oil well began producing in Titusville, Pennsylvania, men and animals supplied much of the world's power needs, supplemented by waterwheels, windmills, and steam generated by burning coal and wood. Coal powered an early part of the industrial revolution; in 1910, for example, coal supplied 90 percent of the American commercial energy requirement. Coal still made up over half of the world's commercial sources of energy in 1960, but oil was rapidly displacing coal as the world's primary fuel.

Petroleum had been used long before the Christian Era; Noah reportedly waterproofed his ark with bitumen. Petroleum was added to Middle Eastern mud bricks for waterproofing and was employed in mortar. Early man also used oil for medicinal purposes and to fuel lamps. Until modern times, however, petroleum was collected from natural seepage. Not until 1859 when a drilling rig was set up on Oil Creek near Titusville was oil sought commercially.

The oil industry grew rapidly after the first well came in. Within a decade Russia, Romania, Canada, Italy, and the United States were producing oil. Several more countries began producing soon afterward, and oil was discovered in Iran in 1908.

The primary use for petroleum was as a lubricant and as lamp fuel for the industrialization and urbanization during the late nineteenth century. In 1900 about 58 percent of petroleum consumption in the United States, the largest producer and consumer of oil, was in the form of kerosine for heaters and lamps; most of the rest was as fuel oil for heating and power plants.

Development of the internal combustion engine vastly expanded the demand for petroleum products. World War I and World War II greatly accelerated engine development. Improvements in petroleum refining accompanied diversification and refinement of engines. Research added to the uses for petroleum products; a whole new field of petrochemicals emerged, producing dyes, fertilizers, and other products and increasing the demand for crude oil.

Petroleum was cleaner, more convenient, and cheaper than other fuels. In addition it was the unique fuel for internal combustion engines, feedstock for petrochemicals, and base for lubricants. As a result the market for oil grew much more rapidly than the total demand for energy. World consumption (excluding communist countries) went from 1 million barrels per day (see Glossary) in 1915 to more than 5 million barrels per day in 1940 and 35 million barrels per day in 1971. Between 1962 and 1971 world consumption of petroleum increased at an annual rate of 7 percent, a doubling in ten years. Of the energy consumed in 1970 by noncommunist countries, a little more

247

than one half came from oil. Coal accounted for nearly one-quarter, natural gas supplied about one-fifth, and nuclear power provided less than 0.5 percent; hydropower contributed the remainder.

Another factor contributing to the sharp rise in the price of energy was the growing international trade in petroleum products. The Soviet Union passed the United States as the largest producer of crude oil in 1974 as a result of the declining output of American fields that set in at the end of the 1960s. Both of these main producers, however, consumed most of their own production. The Soviet Union had exported relatively small amounts of petroleum since the 1950s, and the United States had begun importing increasing quantities of oil to meet consumption needs some years before. The main stimulus for the international petroleum trade came from the rapid economic growth and increased oil consumption in Western Europe and Japan after World War II. These countries lacked significant crude oil deposits, necessitating large and increasing imports to satisfy growing consumption needs. Between 1962 and 1971 the petroleum imports of Western Europe more than doubled, and Japan's increased more than fourfold. Petroleum became the most important commodity in value in international trade, and by the mid 1970s petroleum products accounted for more than one-half of all seaborne commerce.

Geologists have determined the outlines of a large basin extending from the Taurus Mountains in southeast Turkey to the Arabian Sea in the south and underlying western Iran, eastern Saudi Arabia and Iraq, and most of the Persian Gulf. In 1974 this basin held 62 percent of the world's proven reserves. The development of these Middle Eastern fields, particulary after World War II, made them the world's most important crude oil source, supplying 39 percent of world production in 1974 (see fig. 15). Crude oil production costs have been low because pressure in these prolific fields is generally high, and transportation costs have been low because the fields are relatively close to water routes. The countries owning these reserves have relatively small populations, little domestic oil consumption, and an interest in exporting oil. As a result Persian Gulf states became the most important exporters of petroleum products, supplying 63 percent of the oil in international trade in 1974.

Structure of the International Oil Industry

Another factor contributing to the sharp rise in the price of energy was the changing structure of the international oil industry. The industry consists of separate phases—exploration, crude oil production, refining into usable products, transportation, and marketing —and each phase requires costly investments. Even with modern techniques, for example, only 10 percent of the wells drilled in new fields produce oil or gas, and only 2 percent of the wells are signifi-

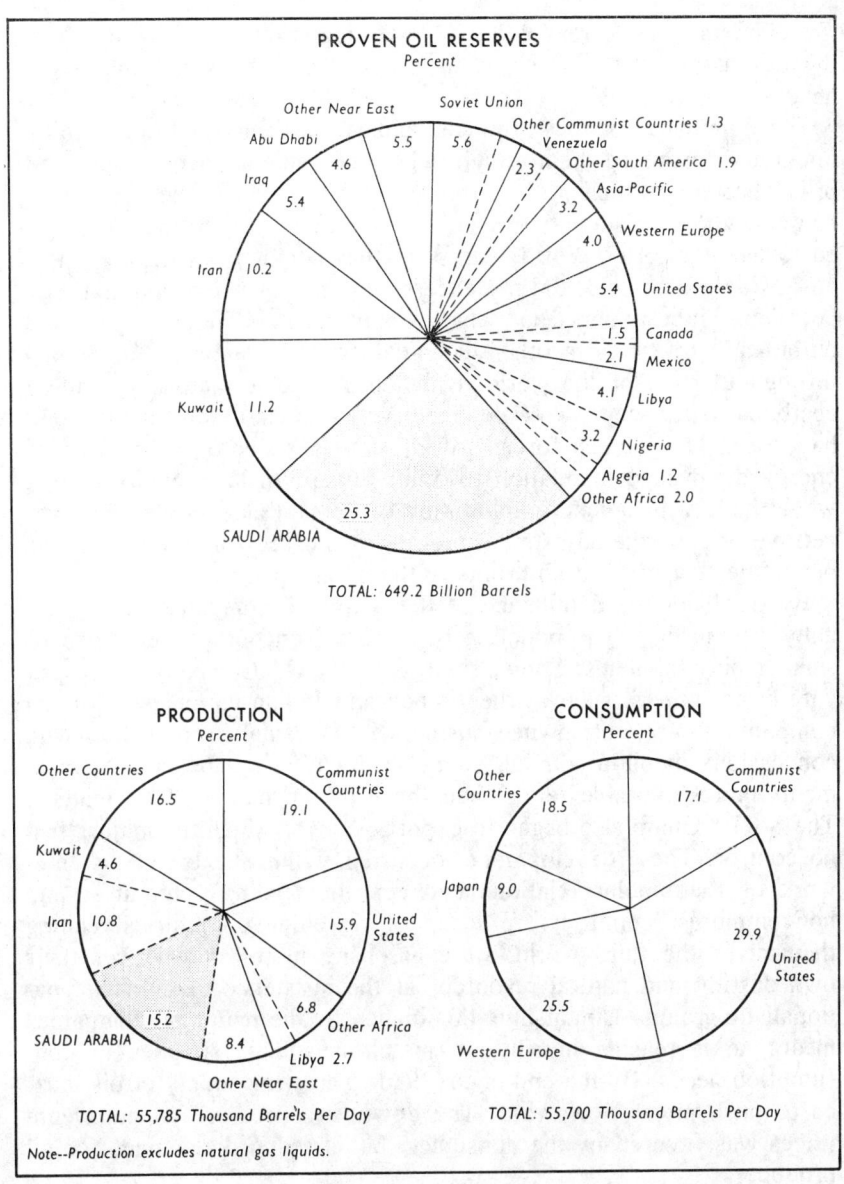

Figure 15. World Oil, 1974

cant producers. The industry as first developed consisted of a few very large companies vertically integrating all phases from exploration to marketing.

The petroleum industry before World War II was dominated by seven or eight major oil companies. Five of these were American, the others European. These major companies held most of the foreign concession agreements for exploration and development. This gave the companies a degree of horizontal integration; they could adjust the output of crude from various areas to match overall marketing needs.

The dominance of these few companies, vertically and horizontally integrated, provided them a high degree of influence over supply and price through mutuality of interests if not collusion. The companies had an interest in stability of petroleum markets, which they attempted to maintain after World War II so that output from the rich, low cost Middle East fields did not excessively disrupt petroleum markets, petroleum investments, and employment in the United States and output and revenues in other high-cost crude oil areas. Coal mining throughout most of the world, which had become increasingly more costly as richer seams were depleted, was less disrupted than it might have been had it been forced to adjust to cheaper oil. The price of energy diminished in relation to other prices but less rapidly than it would have with quicker exploitation of Persian Gulf crude and competitive pricing; the adjustment process was eased for many countries but at the cost of windfall profits to the oil companies.

By the 1950s the dominance of the major oil companies was gradually diminishing. The booming oil business encouraged entrance of smaller oil companies. Some, such as Getty Oil Company, were private firms; others, such as the French and Italian national petroleum companies, were state owned businesses. The smaller companies won concessions in oil producing countries by offering the host governments more favorable terms than those of the major oil companies. The Soviet Union also began to export oil, over which the majors had no control. These developments occurred within the broader framework of the bipolar relations between the leading communist and noncommunist countries. A group of developing countries, calling themselves the third world, were asserting more control over their own destiny and natural resources at the insistence of domestic nationalistic groups. Diminishing dominance by the major oil companies meant an increasing inability to match petroleum supplies to consumption needs. By the end of the 1950s a growing supply of oil started to push prices downward. The downward pressure on petroleum prices was favored by the consumer, but it reduced revenues for oil producers.

Oil Pricing

Oil pricing is a vast and controversial subject complicated by the vertical integration of much of the industry and the secretiveness of the companies involved. Price can simply match supply and demand, or it can incorporate political decisions to achieve some possible noneconomic goal. The United States, although an avowed advocate of free enterprise and free trade, had long interfered in the pricing of some commodities, as in the former support prices for major agricultural crops, and has regulated phases of the domestic oil and gas industry for particular goals that to a degree affected international prices of petroleum. Other oil-producing countries have also sought to exert various controls over their petroleum resources with the result that oil pricing and trade have reflected forces other than just supply and demand.

The major international oil companies are largely housed in the United States and have domestic fields, refineries, and outlets to be concerned about. There have been many United States congressional investigations of the oil companies, and their operations in foreign countries have been watched, threatened, and in some instances taken over by the host government. The oil companies have not been the free agent, concerned only with maximizing profits, that has often been their popular image. That is not to say, however, that they did not wield considerable domestic as well as international power, do unsavory things, or secure huge profits.

Early in the 1900s the United States was the major exporter, and international crude oil pricing by the major oil companies was based on the United States price plus transportation costs. This was a base point pricing system in which the price was that of the Gulf of Mexico plus transportation costs to the buyer regardless of from where the oil was actually shipped. There were other oil-exporting countries at the time, but the oil companies' price was the same to India, for example, even if the oil was shipped from Iran, with transportation costs substantially less than from the Gulf of Mexico. This system worked where there were a few oil companies with mutual interests, and it protected their investments in the United States and other areas as well as providing a high return for developing fields, such as those in the Middle East. How much the oil company kept and how much the government owning the field received depended on the concession agreement, but there was not a downward pressure on the price of crude oil produced in the new foreign fields in the Caribbean and Middle East.

Between 1945 and 1950 the increased supply of crude from foreign fields, the entrance of some independent oil companies, and United States pressure applied through its help in rebuilding postwar Europe brought about major modification of the single base-point price system. The major oil companies set crude oil prices in conjunction with transportation costs from actual point of shipment to establish a series of equalization points—points where the landed price of Middle East oil was the same as crude from the Gulf of Mexico and Venezuela. The equalization point was first southern Europe, then London, and eventually New York. The shifting of the equalization point northward and westward increased transportation costs, thereby requiring lower quotations for Middle East crude and providing it with a competitive advantage in European markets formerly held by United States, Mexican, and Venezuelan crude.

The oil companies were caught in conflicting squeezes. The cost of production of Middle East oil was a fraction of that in Venezuela, which in turn was substantially less than that in the United States. If prices were based on cost of production, Middle East crude would have forced other countries out of the market. The oil companies, American politicians, and American businesses did not want this. In fact Morris A. Adelman in his authoritative study The World Petroleum Market concluded that an effective coalition in the United States limited imports of foreign oil for the large United States market for at least ten years before official import quotas were established in 1959. The oil companies would have profited by more imports. The Venezuelans also did not want to be forced out of crude production. The Middle Ease oil-producing countries, however, would have been happy, at least for a while, if the companies had taken more oil, because their revenues would have gone up. The oil companies faced a no-win situation. Each producing country wanted to remain in the oil business and earn more money but neither suffer competition from cheap suppliers nor have the price of their oil go down. The dominance of the major companies over the industry reduced for all producers the pain of adjustment to the large supply of low cost Middle East crude entering the market.

From about 1950 to the early 1970s there was a system of posted prices for each country—prices at which oil companies would sell crude oil to anybody. Transportation costs were not included. "Anybody" generally meant independent oil companies that the major oil companies did not want to encourage; so posted prices were higher than the actual price at which the bulk of crude oil sales took place. Moreover a short-term oversupply of crude also developed in the late 1950s as newly discovered fields began to produce, causing a downward pressure on crude oil prices. By the 1960s if not earlier, the posted price became only a reference point for calculating the taxes and royalty payments due oil-producing states under the concession agreements.

Moreover economists have had difficulty in analyzing the pricing system because of inadequate data to establish what actual market prices were; perhaps four fifths of crude oil sales were bookkeeping transactions within integrated companies. There is widespread agreement, however, that actual market prices of crude oil had a substantial downward trend between 1950 and 1970 although posted prices remained fixed for prolonged periods.

The posted price per barrel of Saudi Arabian light (34 degree) marker crude oil was US$2.05 in June 1948, US$1.70 in November 1950, US$2.08 in June 1957, US$1.80, in August 1960, and US$2.18 in February 1971. The marker price is the basic price for a typical regional crude—in this case Arabian light used for the Persian Gulf—from which regional prices are derived.

Although the major oil companies exerted considerable influence on crude oil prices, the oil industry was not a closed system, and market forces had an impact. Before 1973 crude oil was priced largely in the context of supply and demand; after 1973 crude oil pricing took into consideration the costs of other energy sources and the long-term supply of petroleum. The frame of reference for pricing decisions was vastly broader and less favorable to consumers than the one that had previously prevailed.

Organization of Petroleum Exporting Countries

The sheer size and the integrated nature of the major international oil companies afforded them considerable advantages when negotiating concession agreements with countries having known or probable oil deposits. Moreover many of the concession agreements were arranged with developing countries generally lacking in sophistication and usually hard pressed for funds. The governments of these countries often failed to appreciate the value of their resources and frequently were so desperate for funds that they lacked bargaining power even if they understood the value of their oil. Saudi Arabia was certainly in this position in 1933 and 1939 when the original concession agreements were let.

Efforts by oil-producing countries to exercise control over their resources without causing excessive domestic economic and financial disruption were difficult because of the pressures the oil companies brought to bear. Mexico nationalized its oil industry in 1938, but it was a costly and prolonged experience. When Iran nationalized its oil industry in 1951, the oil companies refused to buy or transport its oil, causing a severe financial and political crisis in the country for some years.

The Organization of Petroleum Exporting Countries (OPEC) was formed in September 1960 by Saudi Arabia, Venezuela, Iran, Iraq, and Kuwait to develop some bargaining power among oil-exporting countries vis-à-vis the international oil companies. Other countries subsequently joined. By late 1975 Algeria, Ecuador, Gabon, Indonesia, Libya, Nigeria, Qatar, and the United Arab Emirates were members; applications for membership by other oil-producing countries were under consideration.

The foundation document of the organization noted the dependence of its member on revenue from oil exports, the wasting nature of their petroleum resources, and the interdependence of all countries. The first objective of OPEC was restoration of crude oil prices to the 1958 level and stabilization of prices through mutual cooperation with the oil companies. The resolution acknowledged the need for oil prices to balance the interests of producing and consuming nations as well as provide a fair return on investments of the oil companies. The founding members agreed to stick together against efforts by the oil companies to woo or apply sanctions against any member country that was following a unanimous decision of OPEC.

OPEC authority consists almost entirely of its semiannual (or more frequent) conferences of high-level representatives from each member government. Unanimously adopted resolutions of these conferences became oil policy for the member governments. In 1974 OPEC countries controlled about 70 percent of the world's crude oil reserves, 65 percent of world oil production, and 90 percent of petroleum exports; OPEC resolutions therefore had considerable impact.

Conferences are supported by a full-time staff, including a secretariat, an extensive petroleum library, a legal department versed in petroleum matters, and a technical department that follows technical developments in the oil industry. OPEC selected Vienna as its headquarters site. An economic commission was established in 1964 with liaison to the top levels of the oil departments of the member governments. The economic commission collects data, including apparently some very good petroleum statistics, and prepares studies. In early 1976 the studies were not available to the public but appeared to have been the basis for many of OPEC's resolutions since 1970.

OPEC was more that a decade in gestation. Part of the initial impetus came from Venezuela, which in 1943 began to press the international oil companies for more control over and a better return on its oil resources. Conscious of Mexico's difficult experience, Venezuela established contacts with Middle East oil states in an attempt to develop coordinated efforts among oil exporters. Some analysts have interpreted the rapid development of the Persian Gulf oil fields after World War II both as a threat by the major oil companies against Venezuela to temper its demands and as the expansion of an alternative source of oil should the Venezuelan government demand too much. Other observers stressed the low cost and other advantages inherent in Persian Gulf oil as a natural cause for development of Midddle East fields.

The Middle East countries recognized the usefulness of concerted action to protect their interests. Many of these countries, however, were desperately in need of revenues and pushed the oil companies to take more of their oil to increase their income. Not until the oil companies unilaterally cut the posted price in the spring of 1959 to reflect the glut of oil on the market and the growing discounts that they had been giving on posted prices did a movement begin toward joint action. In response to the price cuts the League of Arab States (popularly known as the Arab League) sponsored the first Arab oil conference in the summer of 1959; Venezuela and Iran attended as observers.

As a result of the contacts developed during the 1959 conference, Saudi Arabia and Venezuela issued a joint statement in May 1960 urging all oil-producing countries to adopt common policies to safeguard their economic interests. In August 1960 the oil companies further cut the posted price of Middle East crude oil. The price reduction lopped US$30 million from Saudi Arabia's estimated income for the year and thus severely hampered the efforts to balance the budget and execute development programs. When the Saudi Arabian minister of petroleum and mineral resources attended an emergency meeting of authorities from oil-exporting states in Baghdad after the price reductions, he argued vigorously and successfully for the founding of OPEC.

OPEC was unsuccessful during the 1960s in restoring crude oil prices to the level preceding the cuts of 1959 and 1960, but it won half the battle in that the oil companies did not make further cuts. OPEC also fostered negotiations with the oil companies to increase the revenues of the oil-exporting states. The negotiations concerned the methods of calculating—and increasing—royalty payments and taxes due the host government, which raised the costs of producing crude oil. The added costs at least partly explained the absence of further price cuts in a situation tending toward oversupply in the international crude oil markets.

The payments due the host governments were spelled out in the concession agreements granted the oil companies. The more important concessions had been granted before World War II, when the host governments had little bargaining power. As a result the financial return to the host governments was usually quite low. Venezuela started major adjustments in concession agreements in 1943 by legislating a 50 percent tax on the net income earned by the oil companies in Venezuela. The so-called fifty-fifty profit-sharing arrangement, in reality a tax imposed on each barrel of oil produced, was negotiated by Saudi Arabia with the Arabian American Oil Company (Aramco) in 1950, raising the Saudi per barrel revenues very substantially. Fifty-fifty profit sharing became standard in the Persian Gulf by 1952. OPEC helped refine the calculations of taxes and royalties to the advantage of the host governments during the 1960s. OPEC also helped the oil-exporting governments negotiate substantially better terms in concession agreements granted after its founding.

The June 1967 War between Israel and several Arab states started a chain of events that led to a transformation in the world energy market. The war closed the Suez Canal, and several Arab oil states embargoed oil exports briefly. The canal remained closed until June 1975. The transportation problems of the much longer haul around Africa to Europe were partly offset by use of new supertankers and by increasing oil production in Africa, particularly in Algeria and Libya, which were close to southern Europe. The dependence on North Africa became even greater in 1970 as a result of civil war in Nigeria and disruption of operations of the pipeline from Saudi Arabia to the Mediterranean coast in Lebanon (see Saudi Arabian Oil, this ch.). The new military regime in Libya seized the opportunity of its enhanced position to cut back crude oil production and to secure higher posted prices and tax rates from the oil companies under the threat of cessation of exports if the regime's demands were not met. An independent oil company, Occidental, agreed to the much more favorable terms for Libya, and other oil companies acceded to Libyan demands in September 1970.

Meanwhile the Algerian representative to OPEC in a July 1970 speech requested that other members seize control of the pricing of their internationally traded crude oil. OPEC followed with a unanimous resolution in December 1970 calling for substantial revisions and increases in crude oil pricing. Negotiations were held in Tehran in February 1971 for the Persian Gulf region. The posted price of Persian Gulf oil was raised by more than one-third, provision was made for yearly increases for inflation of about 5 percent a year until 1975, and the tax rate was raised to 55 percent. Libya negotiated an agreement in April 1971 whereby it won a substantially larger increase in the posted price plus an increase of the tax rate to 55 percent. Algeria pressed for an increase in crude oil prices above that won by the Persian Gulf but less than that won by Libya. Venezuela legislated rather than negotiated price and tax increases in March 1971.

These assorted actions effectively transferred control over crude oil prices from the oil companies to the producing states. When the United States dollar was devalued in 1971, a clause in the Persian Gulf and Libyan agreements was invoked for new negotiations. An 8.5-percent increase in posted prices was arrived at in Geneva in January 1972 to compensate for the devaluation. Further negotiations took place in Geneva after the United States devaluation in 1973.

OPEC members had long discussed taking over control of crude oil production in their countries, and it was evident that they would eventually act. Algeria and Libya seized properties of some concessionaires in 1971, and Iraq nationalized some of its fields in 1972. Meanwhile some OPEC members, largely from the Persian Gulf, began negotiations with the oil companies in January 1972 for a gradual takeover of company operations. The Saudi minister of petroleum and mineral resources, Shaykh Ahmad Zaki Yamani, led the OPEC negotiators during several months of hard bargaining. The main result was 25-percent participation in ownership by the oil states plus 5-percent annual increases from 1979 to reach 51 percent by 1983. Compensation to the oil companies for the equity they yielded was arranged, and phasing the oil states into actual sales was scheduled so that the companies could continue to meet their sales contracts.

The device of participation was far less drastic than nationalization and in particular retained the services, technical skills, and marketing chains of the oil companies during the takeover. The takeover schedule was tremendously accelerated by events in 1973 and 1974. By 1975 most oil states already had 60-percent participation, and Saudi Arabia was reportedly negotiating for 100 percent equity with retention of Aramco skills and services under contract.

The October 1973 War between Israel and Arab states created further disarray in the oil market. A selective embargo and phased cutback in crude production was imposed by several Arab countries. No oil-consuming country was seriously hurt by these actions, because the oil companies juggled supplies to keep oil flowing to all countries, but all consumers felt the threat and a supply pinch. Bidding for oil reportedly reached US$17 a barrel.

OPEC took the opportunity to raise the price of crude oil by more than 100 percent during 1974. The posted price was US$5.12 a barrel in October 1973, and the price became US$11.25 effective January 1, 1974. The posted price remained a reference price for assessing taxes and royalty payments. The actual selling price of crude was 93 percent of the posted price, or US$10.46 per barrel. A 10-percent increase decreed by OPEC in September 1975 raised Arabian marker crude to US$12.38 posted price and US$11.51 actual price per barrel. OPEC justified the more than fourfold increase in prices of crude between 1971 and 1975 as necessary to approximate the true cost of energy, compensate the oil producers adequately for depletion of their limited resources, and make up for the long period when oil prices were kept low while prices for manufactured goods continuously increased.

The impact of the changes on government revenues was tremendous. Saudi Arabia's revenues per barrel, averaged from total production and revenue receipts, increased from US$0.22 in 1948 to US$0.89 in 1970. By 1973 they had reached US$1.56. The higher posted price, the increase of the tax rate to 85 percent, the increase of the royalty rate to 20 percent, and the increase in participation to 60 percent raised average revenues per barrel to above US$10.10 in 1974 and US$11.15 after the September 1975 price increase.

By early 1976 OPEC members had control of crude oil pricing and a large degree of control over production. The members had not given OPEC authority to allocate production among producers, however, and OPEC had no formal means of matching supply to demand. The need arose immediately; world oil consumption declined in 1974 and declined further in the first half of 1975 because of a recession in the industrialized countries and conservation measures by all oil consuming nations. Strains were apparent among OPEC members in 1975.

In early 1976 OPEC remained a loose confederation of diverse nations that had united to combat the power of the international oil companies. Its diversity may be its salvation in the difficult task of controlling supply to maintain price. There are two main groups within OPEC. The first is made up of oil exporters with large reserves and small populations, such as Saudi Arabia and Kuwait. This group might be called the low price group, because they were earning more oil revenues in 1975 than they could profitably invest. Immediate higher prices were not very attractive because they probably would intensify development by industrialized countries of new technology and energy sources. Their interest was in a moderate price and a slow rate of exploitation so that their reserves would continue to finance their economic development long into the future.

The second group might be called the high-price group. It was made up of countries, such as Iran and Indonesia, that had relatively small reserves, large populations, and economic potentials other than oil. Because their reserves would not last long, they wanted to maximize current earnings on their limited reserves through high prices, which they would invest primarily in their own country to develop other resources and industries for self-sustaining growth. Some of these countries pushed for substantially higher oil prices in 1974 and 1975. Iran, for one, wanted OPEC to raise crude oil prices in September 1975 by 20 percent or more.

In 1974 and 1975 OPEC members maintained their united front and even increased export prices in the face of reduced demand for crude oil by importing countries. A few countries cut back crude production to avoid an oversupply that might lead to price cutting by members pressed for funds. Saudi Arabia and Kuwait shouldered much of the burden of lower crude production and revenues to avoid pressure on OPEC prices in 1975. The Saudi minister of petroleum and mineral resources had said that his country would accept quite low production to support OPEC's prices and a united front but would not lower production so that another oil-exporting country could increase its share of the market.

Saudi Arabia's huge reserves and production potential make it pivotal to OPEC decisions and probably provided veto power in most OPEC discussions, although support from another major exporter probably would be needed to push through Saudi proposals against strong opposition. Saudi officials finally agreed to the September 1975, OPEC price increase of 10 percent although originally advocating a maximum of 5 percent. The Saudi position was supportive of OPEC during 1975, helping to overcome strains in the organization, but Saudis appeared unwilling to accept higher prices in the immediate future.

Another source of tension within OPEC appeared in late 1975 as a result of the September price increase. It was left to regional groups of OPEC members to determine the actual application of the price increase to the premiums and discounts on each country's crude oil, which varies because of sulfur content, gravity, shipping costs, and other factors. Kuwait tried to arrange a regional meeting, but it fell through, and the country posted its own adjustments to the overall price increase. Iraq took a strong stand against the Kuwait prices, implying that they were undercutting Iraq's prices. The issue had not been resolved by early 1976 and posed a destructive force within OPEC. Even minor price-cutting could destroy the unity of the organization, leaving some oil producers worse off than they were before. The low production costs in Middle East countries gave them a distinct advantage over producers with high costs. Price competition could be ruinous for some countries and costly for all.

Organization of Arab Petroleum Exporting Countries

The Organization of Arab Petroleum Exporting Countries (OAPEC) was formed in 1968, largely on the initiative of Saudi Arabia, to provide a supplemental organization for the major Arab oil exporters. Saudi Arabia, Kuwait, and Libya were the founding members. Membership was originally limited to Arab states whose "principal and basic source of national income" was oil. The OAPEC constitution was subsequently amended to permit Egypt and Algeria to join. By 1976 Bahrain, Iraq, Qatar, Syria, and the United Arab Emirates had joined, bringing the membership to ten countries.

OAPEC has two functions. One is to develop cooperation and promote Arab interests, such as the fund of US$80 million established in 1975 for Arab oil-importing states experiencing foreign exchange difficulties. The second function is to promote joint ventures among interested members in various phases of the oil business. The organization was a juridical entity that could participate in commercial ventures. By early 1976 OAPEC had formed the Arab Maritime Petroleum Transport Company; the Arab Shipbuilding and Repair Company, its first project to be a dry dock in Bahrain; and the Arab Petroleum Investments Company to finance petrochemical plants in the Arab world. OAPEC representatives decided in 1975 to set up an Arab energy institute to study alternative energy sources and the best use of oil and to establish a petroleum services company in Libya to study downstream (see Glossary) investments. OAPEC was also working on the question of a single Arab currency.

SAUDI ARABIAN OIL

The petroleum industry contributed about 70 percent of the value added to GDP in fiscal year (FY—see table A) 1973. The higher oil prices of 1974 increased the importance of the oil sector, to more than 80 percent of GDP in FY 1975, but precise figures were not available in early 1976. The industry was capital intensive, and employment in it was relatively small. Total employment of Saudis in the oil sector probably was less than 20,000.

The government owns all petroleum deposits as well as all other subsoil resources. The exact size of proven reserves (the crude oil that could be recovered from known fields with existing technology) was subject to interpretation. A Jiddah newspaper, in an article on the oil industry that reflected government data, reported proven reserves in 1974 as 137 billion barrels. The authoritative Oil and Gas Journal (Tulsa, Oklahoma) listed reserves as 132 billion barrels in 1974. A United States government publication showed reserves as 165 billion barrels in 1974. Yet in 1975 Aramco reported the kingdom's proven reserves as 108 billion barrels. Natural gas was also found—reserves in 1974 amounted to about 51 trillion cubic feet—but that associated with crude oil production was largely flared (see Glossary).

Saudi Arabia had the largest proven reserves of any country, and the reserves amounted to more than 25 percent of the world's total. Saudi reserves would last nearly forty-five years at the 1974 rate of exploitation. Estimates of the reserves have frequently been revised upward as new fields were discovered or as the contents of a field were revalued. Exploration was continuing, and three new fields were discovered and three others confirmed in 1975. Further discoveries were expected by Saudi officials.

All of the oil found by early 1975 had been in Eastern Province, although exploration was being conducted in the Red Sea off Saudi Arabia's west coast. Exploratory wells in the Rub al Khali (Empty Quarter) brought oil to the surface in 1974, and in 1975 two fields had been discovered there. The Ghawar field was the world's largest, stretching about 150 miles in length and measuring up to twenty-two miles in width (see fig. 16). The field was so large that names were given to separate parts. The Safaniya field was the world's largest offshore field. These two fields plus the Abqaiq field accounted for about four-fifths of all crude lifted in 1972. Several fields, those more distant from Ras Tanura, were relatively undeveloped.

The quality of crude oil is based on the density (measured by gravity standards established by the American Petroleum Institute) and the amount of sulfur and wax it contains. Light crude oil is generally more desirable because it yields more of such high-value products as gasoline. Seven of the Saudi Arabian fields in 1973 produced a crude of a kind designated Arabian light, four produced Arabian medium, and one produced Arabian heavy. In 1972 over 75 percent of the crude lifted was Arabian light. The field in the partitioned Kuwait Neutral Zone produced Arabian heavy (see ch. 3). Sulfur compounds are an undesirable ingredient often contaminating crude oils. Saudi Arabian crudes had relatively high sulfur content, averaging about 1.77 percent. Several sulfur-removing plants were located near the fields to clean the crude before it was sent to refineries or shipping terminals.

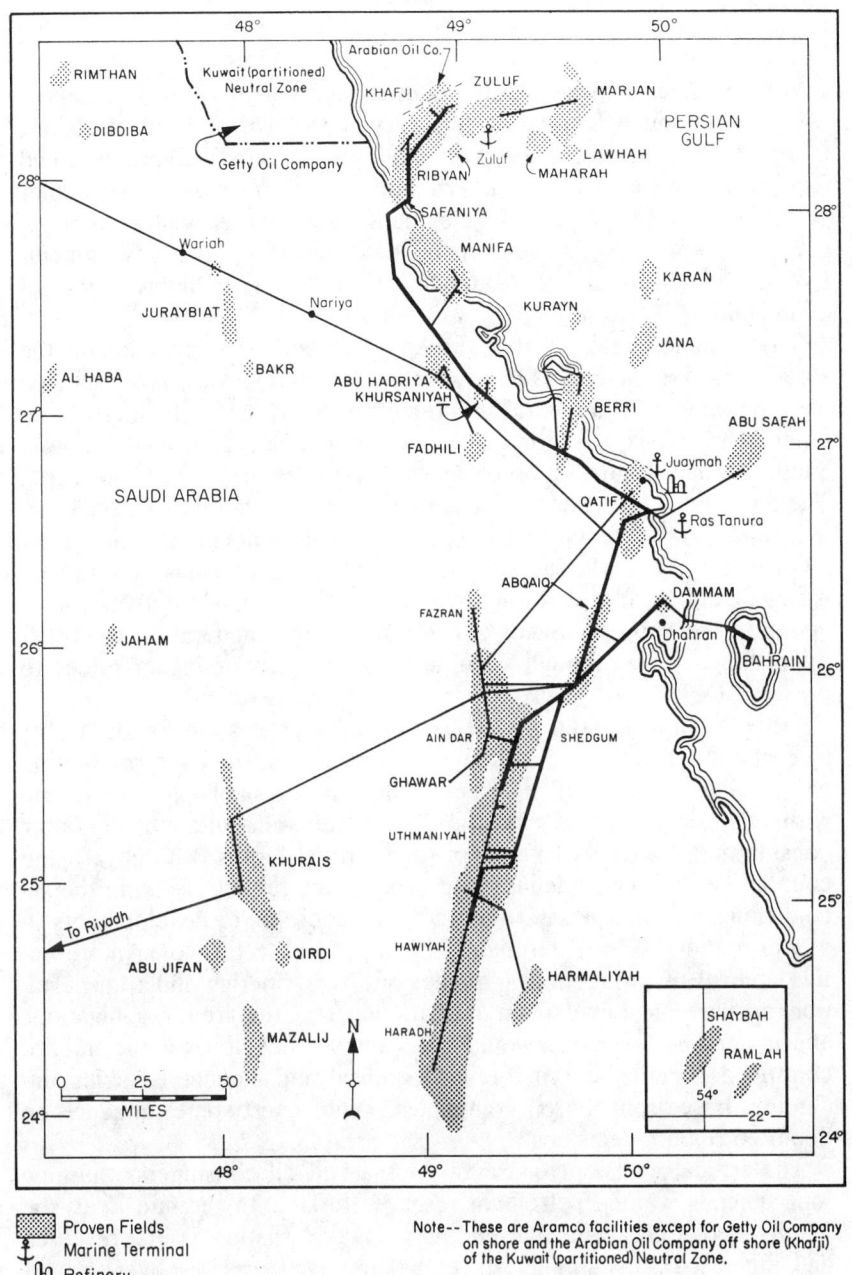

Source: Based on information from *Aramco: A Review of Operations, 1975*, Dammam, 1976, map p. 20.

Figure 16. Saudi Arabia, Oil Fields and Facilities, 1975

Saudi Oil Policies

What policies Saudi officials adopted relative to Saudi oil reserves were tremendously significant for most of the world. Many decisions that by 1975 had become the prerogative of the Saudi government had formerly been made by the international oil companies. In particular petroleum investment and development decisions as well as production and export levels were to be determined by the government. Events had so changed the situation that past Saudi policies might not be indicative of future policy.

Saudi officials claimed that the kingdom was as dependent on the stability and prosperity of the consuming nations as those nations were on Saudi oil; the world was interdependent, and self interest and other reasons would promote moderate policies for Saudi Arabia. Saudi officials argued that past Saudi policies had been moderate. Their position was that the oil embargo and production cutbacks in 1973 and 1974 were not crippling, only strong enough to make their point (see ch. 10). The kingdom had avoided drastic measures such as nationalization and opted for a gradual takeover of oil company operations in the country. Saudi officials had urged moderation in OPEC price discussions although yielding to proponents of higher prices to preserve OPEC unity.

Little is known about the decisionmaking process in Saudi Arabia (see ch. 8). After the government assumed control over production and pricing of oil, Saudi petroleum officials, probably in conjunction with other key members of the government and undoubtedly after consultation with those members of the royal family who govern the country, set broad guidelines and production ceilings, leaving the oil companies to manage day-to-day affairs according to developments in world markets. The government objective was to take over more active control of production and sales and of refineries and transportation as part of downstream operations. The required organizations and expertise, however, would take time to develop. In the interim continued dependence on foreign technical and managerial skills, including those from the oil companies, might exert some influence on Saudi petroleum decisions.

The critical decision for Saudi Arabia and oil consumers was how long officials wanted petroleum reserves to last. In the mid 1970s the Saudis were well aware that oil and gas were wasting assets; reserves had increased substantially since the first well was discovered, and Aramco claimed that it had discovered more reserves each year than it had produced. Nevertheless the primary concern of some senior Saudi officials continued to be the estimated life of reserves (reserves divided by yearly production), and they concluded that the trend was decidedly downward. The kingdom's resources other than oil were meager, and economic development and prosperity were difficult to imagine without the petroleum industry as their base (see ch. 11). The long-term view of the government appeared to be that reserves must be made to last for many years; government officials argued against too high a current price on crude oil because it would encourage development of alternative energy sources as well as conservation by industrialized countries, diminishing the relative value of oil in the distant future, when Saudi Arabia would be in greater need of funds to finance economic development. Perhaps implied in this view was a fear that too high a price might tempt rapid exploitation of reserves.

Saudi oil policy in the situation existing after 1975 would reflect the balance achieved between Saudis desiring relatively rapid modernization and development of the economy and the country and Saudis wanting slow change to preserve old values. The production potential existed to more than double crude oil output very quickly after 1975 if economic recovery and demand by industrialized oil consumers warranted it. Authorization for expanded production would depend partly on how much money was required for economic development. Saudi officials committed themselves to continuing oil exports, but some officials argued that their oil was more valuable to them in the ground than it was converted into foreign balances that were subject to price inflation, exchange rate risks, and sequestration.

Saudi officials had pledged to keep oil flowing to consumer nations, and in 1975 they authorized production of 8.5 million barrels per day, significantly more than was lifted and more than the world markets could absorb that year. The commitment to a continuing flow was the result of Saudi Arabia's dependence on a stable and prosperous world. Saudi and United States government officials agreed that the Saudi development program could be financed by crude oil production and sales markedly lower than even the reduced levels of 1975 and 1976 (see ch. 1). The import requirements of consuming nations under high economic growth conditions were not known, however; economic recession had hidden their potential demand since the new, high price levels were established. At some point consumer demand might become higher than Saudi officials were willing to exploit their oil reserves to meet. Serious tensions between producers and consumers could emerge if consumer demand exceeded what Saudi officials considered reasonable and passed into what they considered exploitation.

The potential effectiveness of the oil weapon will be enhanced and its selectivity refined as Saudi Arabia and other oil producers get more involved in marketing and petroleum transport. Saudi Arabia's large foreign financial reserves allow shifting the balances to create monetary instability as a corollary to the oil weapon or as a separate measure in support of foreign policy objectives. The increased dependence of Saudi Arabia and the other oil producers on much larger imports from the oil consuming nations might restrict their use of the oil weapon, but for the oil consumers to limit their exports to oil producers would require a degree of policing greater and more effective than the industrialized countries have achieved in previous attempts to pressure or embargo exports to particular countries. In any event the oil weapon is probably more effective as a threat than in its actual implementation as a means to change policies in consumer nations.

By early 1976 Saudi petroleum policies had not changed. In fact there was considerable effort to indicate policy continuity with the past, particularly after King Faisal's assassination in March 1975. Nonetheless the petroleum industry had changed drastically, and the country was being rapidly transformed; in such an atmosphere petroleum policies could also change.

Production

The first oil drilling started in April 1935, but it took the seventh well, in March 1938, to find oil in commercial quantities. Production from the first field, Dammam, was piped to the coast and barged to the Bahrain refinery; the first barge in September 1938 marked the beginning of Saudi Arabia's petroleum exports. By the spring of 1939 a pipeline, storage and tanker facilities, and a small refinery were completed at Ras Tanura. The king turned the valve to load the first tanker on May 1, 1939. World War II hampered development, and production remained at about 4 to 5 million barrels a year between 1939 and 1943.

During the war three additional fields were discovered. The United States government, concerned over the war's drain on its petroleum reserves, allocated priorities for materials to enable Aramco to finance and construct larger facilities at Ras Tanura; the work was completed about the war's end. The stage was set for a rapid expansion of production, which climbed from 21 million barrels in 1944 to 143 million barrels in 1948. The high rate of growth of output continued through 1952, the rate of increase averaging more than 46 percent a year between 1945 and 1952. The need for oil by Japan and West European countries as recovery progressed in the late 1940s and early 1950s spurred production.

Saudi crude production grew slowly between 1952 and 1960, averaging an annual rate of growth of only 6 percent; supplies were entering the world market from fields developed throughout the world after World War II. The Getty Oil Company, owned by American investors, began producing crude from the partitioned Kuwait Neutral Zone in 1954, but production was never very large. Saudi Arabia's share amounted to less than 35 million barrels in the peak year of 1964, after which production was usually considerably less.

World demand caused crude production to increase at a faster rate in the 1960s, particularly after the June 1967 War. The rate of growth averaged a little over 11 percent a year during the decade. The Arabian Oil Company, owned by Japanese, Kuwaiti, and Saudi interests, began producing crude from its offshore fields in the partitioned Kuwait Neutral Zone in 1961. Production climbed steadily, but Saudi Arabia's share amounted to only 63 million barrels by 1970.

Production of crude continued its rapid growth in the 1970s (see table 11). Output increased more than 2 1/2 times in the 1970-74 period (an annual rate of 22 percent) in spite of the slackening of demand in 1974. Aramco still dominated production, lifting almost 3 billion barrels (averaging 8.2 million barrels per day) and accounting for 97 percent of total production in 1974. Aramco production was about 2.5 billion barrels in 1975, a daily average of 6.8 million barrels. Getty Oil Company produced 30 million barrels and Arabian Oil Company 69 million barrels in 1974.

Aramco projections anticipated a crude oil production capacity of 11 to 12 million barrels per day by the end of 1975. Whether capacity had reached that level was uncertain because of the problems with reser-

Table 11. *Saudi Arabia, Oil Production, Revenues, and Exports, Selected Years, 1938-74*

Year	Crude Oil Production (in millions of barrels)	Government Oil Revenues (in millions of United States dollars)	Oil Exports (in millions of barrels)	Oil Exports (in millions of United States dollars)[1]
1938	1	3	n.a.	n.a.
1946	60	10	n.a.	n.a.
1950	200	57	n.a.	n.a.
1955	357	341	280	n.a.
1960	481	334	n.a.	n.a.
1965	805	663[2]	727	1,335
1970	1,387	1,214	1,382	2,296
1971	1,741	1,885	1,722	3,651
1972	2,202	2,745	2,221[3]	5,235
1973	2,773	4,340	2,861[3]	8,761
1974	3,095	22,574	3,242[3]	34,607

n.a.—not available.
[1] Value is for Aramco exports, which were valued at posted prices, not actual prices. Moreover this value figure does not represent incoming foreign exchange as exports usually do because foreign sales were handled by international oil companies where most sales were intracompany bookkeeping transactions.
[2] Includes a special payment of US$46 million resulting from negotiations concerning methods of calculating taxes and royalties; it was actually earned in earlier years.
[3] Exports exceeded production in the government statistics for unknown reasons.

Source: Based on information from *Aramco Handbook*, Dhahran, 1968, p. 135; Saudi Arabian Monetary Agency, *Statistical Summary*, No. 2, Dammam, 1975, pp. 62-65; and Saudi Arabian Monetary Agency, *Statistical Summary*, December 1969-January 1970, pp. 40-42.

voir pressure that had developed in major producing areas. Aramco's longer range projections had anticipated increases of production capacity of between 1 and 2 million barrels per day each year during the remainder of the 1970s and a production capacity of 20 million barrels per day by 1980 or 1983. Saudi officials indicated in 1975 that production capacity probably would not expand as rapidly as Aramco had planned earlier because of the reduced demand for petroleum on world markets.

During the oil embargo and production cutback associated with the October 1973 War, Saudi Arabia's cutback of production amounted to about 15 percent between October 1973 and March 1974 (measured against production in the third quarter of 1973). The reduction was greater in the fourth quarter of 1973 than later. Production eased upward in the early months of 1974 until the restrictions were removed in the spring, but monthly production throughout 1974 generally remained below the level immediately preceding the embargo. Production in 1975 was 17 percent below the level of 1974 because of the conservation measures and economic recession in many oil-consuming countries.

Almost all petroleum production was for export. Domestic consumption of petroleum products had always been small, totaling a little more than 6 million barrels in 1964. By 1973 domestic consumption had increased fourfold, but it still amounted to only 25 million barrels, less than 1 percent of crude production. Industrial fuels made up just over half of the products consumed. Gasoline consumption amounted to 5.9 million barrels in 1973.

Natural gas was not produced intentionally. Gasfields were capped because more than enough gas was produced along with oil. Aramco had more than twenty-six separator plants to remove gas from crude oil. Some gas was pumped back into particular fields to increase pressure and thus to enhance recovery of crude. A little industrial use of gas was made in the fields, and a few other industries were using gas as energy or feedstock. These uses consumed less than 20 percent of the gas produced, however. The rest was flared—a tremendous waste of energy.

Refining and Transportation

Saudi Arabia's primitive transportation system required immediate development by Aramco of means of transporting the oil after it was first discovered. From the very first the company relied on pipelines, and its pioneering work advanced pipeline technology for other parts of the world. The early lines were small, six and ten inches in diameter; later lines were much larger, reaching fifty-six inches in diameter, some of the largest in use when they were constructed. Aramco's pipeline network exceeded 1,500 miles in 1971.

The pipeline network collects the crude from producing areas including those offshore and leads it generally toward the refining and shipping terminal at Ras Tanura. A spur line (capacity about 185,000 barrels per day) runs from the Dammam field to the refinery in Bahrain. A main line runs from Qatif junction to the northwest, where it joins the Trans Arabian Pipeline (Tapline), which carries crude to a Mediterranean outlet near Sidon, Lebanon. Continued operation of Tapline had become problematical by 1975 because of declining costs of sea transport by large tankers and disruptions to pipeline operations by sabotage and governmental interference in the countries Tapline crossed.

The shipping terminal at Ras Tanura has been under nearly continuous expansion since it was first built in 1939 and is one of the world's largest oil ports. The early installation consisted of piers at which small tankers could tie up. This inshore wharfing was expanded and by 1974 could handle at least ten small tankers simultaneously. A sea island was also constructed about a mile offshore to handle the larger tankers whose draft was too great for the shallow shores of the Persian Gulf; by 1973 this terminal could handle eight supertankers simultaneously. In 1973 the Ras Tanura terminal had the capacity to load more than 439,000 barrels per hour.

Another large sea terminal for crude oil and bunker fuel, located at Juaymah about twenty miles northwest of Ras Tanura, began operations in late 1974 with a loading capacity of 1 million barrels per day. A fifty-six-inch submarine pipeline led about seven miles offshore to a control platform where smaller lines ran to the mooring buoys at which tankers loaded. Construction was under way in 1975 to double the capacity of Juaymah. Another small offshore loading terminal was located at Zuluf.

Of the crude produced in 1974 by Aramco 89 percent was loaded on tankers at the three Persian Gulf sea terminals, 6 percent piped to the Ras Tanura refinery, 3 percent sent to the Mediterranean via Tapline, and 2 percent delivered to the Bahrain refinery via pipeline. Less than 0.5 percent was used locally. A total of 4,470 tankers loaded nearly 2.9 billion barrels of crude and products at Aramco's Persian Gulf terminals in 1974.

The Aramco refinery at Ras Tanura was the largest by far in Saudi Arabia. The small "teakettle" refinery first built in 1939 had been replaced by a much larger one. Its rated capacity in early 1976 was not readily known, but refinery runs of crude averaged about 518,000 barrels daily in 1973. Only a small part of Aramco's crude oil was refined, and Aramco's exports included only 7 percent of refined products in 1974.

A small refinery was constructed in Jiddah in 1968 to refine products for the western part of the country. Capacity had been expanded by 1975 to a throughput of 45,000 barrels of crude per day. The General

Petroleum and Mineral Organization (Petromin), a government corporation, held majority interest in this refinery. Crude was supplied by tanker from Eastern Province. A separate Petromin plant to produce lubricants (50,000 barrels a year) was built in Jiddah to take advantage of the refineries output.

Petromin had another small refinery in Riyadh with a capacity of 15,000 barrels per day of crude. This refinery supplied products for the central part of the country. Crude was brought in by railroad from fields along its route in Eastern Province until 1974, when a twelve-inch pipeline from the Khurais field to Riyadh was completed.

Getty Oil Company and Arabian Oil Company had refineries in the Kuwait partitioned Neutral Zone that processed some of Saudi Arabia's share of the crude produced in the zone. In 1974 Getty's exports of refined products belonging to Saudi Arabia amounted to 11 million barrels, and Arabian Oil Company's exports of refined products belonging to Saudi Arabia were 6 million barrels.

The Saudi government was greatly interested in the downstream operations of refining and ocean tanker service. More than 160 proposals for export refineries had been considered by the authorities in the 1973-75 period, but none of the projects appeared definite by early 1976, although the refinery at Yanbu on the Red Sea appeared to have a good chance of materializing. As a joint venture with Mobil Oil Company it would produce largely for export. If approved, a pipeline would be constructed across the northern part of the country and down the western side to supply crude to Yanbu and also the Jiddah refinery. This was a long-term, expensive project.

The government was also interested in entering the tanker business in order to have the facilities to move its own oil in support of sales and to diminish its dependence on the oil companies. Several joint venture shipping companies, including some with major oil companies, had been formed by early 1976, but there was no information available about the number of ships or the extent of operations. Saudi Arabia's maritime laws had not been framed with international shipping in mind, and in 1976 most or all of the Saudi ships continued to sail under other flags, such as Liberian.

Concession Agreements

Abd al Aziz, who was soon to become the first king of Saudi Arabia, had not gained control of the western part of the country when he granted the first oil concession in 1923 (see ch. 2). A British investment group called the Eastern and General Syndicate was the recipient. The syndicate, which was not in the oil business, gambled on the possibility that they could sell the concession, but British petroleum companies showed no interest. The concession lapsed and was declared void in 1928.

Arabian American Oil Company

Discovery of oil in several places around the Persian Gulf suggested that Saudi Arabia probably contained petroleum deposits, but several major oil companies were precluded from attempting to obtain concessions in the kingdom by the Red Line Agreement, which kept companies having part ownership of the operating company in Iraq from acting independently in a proscribed area of the Middle East. Standard Oil Company of California (Socal), which was not excluded by the Red Line Agreement from the Persian Gulf, gained a concession and found oil in Bahrain in 1932. Socal then decided to seek a concession in Saudi Arabia and began negotiations in February 1933. The concession agreement was signed in May and became effective in July 1933. The concession was assigned to the California Arabian Standard Oil Company (Casoc), formed and owned by Socal. The name of the operating company in Saudi Arabia was changed to Arabian American Oil Company (Aramco) in January 1944.

In 1936 Socal sold part interest in Casoc to Texaco to gain marketing facilities for the crude being discovered in its worldwide holdings. Additional partners, Standard Oil Company of New Jersey (Exxon) and Socony-Vacuum (now the Mobil Oil Company), were added to Aramco in 1946 to gain investment capital and marketing outlets for the large reserves being discovered. The participation agreement of 1972 gave the Saudi government 25-percent ownership in Aramco. The government's equity increased to 60 percent in 1974, and negotiations were under way in 1976 for total government ownership of Aramco. It was fairly certain that complete Saudi ownership would come in 1976 or shortly thereafter.

The original concession called for an annual rental fee of 5,000 British pounds in gold or its equivalent until oil was discovered, a 50,000-pound loan in gold to the Saudi government, a royalty payment of four shillings gold per net ton of crude produced after the discovery of oil, and the supply free of charge to the government of specific quantities of products from the refinery Aramco was to build after oil was discovered. (In 1933 the British pound was worth about US$4.87, and the United States dollar was many times more valuable than it was in 1975; there were twenty shillings to the British pound.) The company received exclusive rights to explore, produce, and export oil from most of the eastern part of Saudi Arabia for a period of sixty years free of all Saudi taxes and duties. The terms granted by the government were liberal, reflecting the king's need for funds, his low estimation of future oil production, and his weak bargaining position. He had only the year before gained control of the whole country.

The original concession agreement was modified many times. The first modification was in 1939 after the discovery of oil in 1938. This added to Aramco's concession area and extended the period to 1999 in return for payments substantially higher than the first agreement and for larger quantities of free gasoline and kerosine to be supplied by Aramco. In 1950 the fifty-fifty profit-sharing agreement was signed, whereby a tax, called an income tax but actually a tax on each barrel of oil produced, was levied by the government. This agreement considerably increased the government's revenue. Further modifications increased the government take—slowly until the 1970s and rapidly thereafter (see Oil: The International Setting, this ch.). At the beginning of 1975 Aramco's concession amounted to about 85,000 square miles (73,000 onshore and 12,000 offshore) after the company had relinquished more than 80 percent of the original 496,000 square miles.

Once the existence of oil in quantity was ascertained, the advantages of a pipeline to the Mediterranean Sea seemed obvious in that about 2,000 miles of sea travel and the transit fees of the Suez Canal could be saved. The Trans Arabian Pipeline Company, a wholly owned Aramco subsidiary, was formed in 1945, and the pipeline was completed in 1950. Many innovations were required to keep costs down and make operations competitive with tankers. The Tapline links Sidon in Lebanon to Qaysumah in Saudi Arabia (754 miles), where it connects with the pipelines (315 miles) gathering the oil from Aramco's fields. Initial capacity was 320,000 barrels per day, but capacity was expanded and amounted to 480,000 barrels per day in 1975. It transported 3 percent of the country's crude output in 1974, much less than full-capacity operation.

Tapline created serious problems. Saudi Arabia demanded 50 percent of the profits from the start, and a settlement, although applied retroactively, was not reached until 1963. It also took years to settle the payments to Jordan, Iraq, and Lebanon for transit. The fees were subsequently increased by the countries involved. The line was sabotaged and out of operation for varying periods in the early 1970s. While operating costs of Tapline were going up, the supertankers were reducing seaborne costs. In February 1975 Tapline stopped pumping for export because the price of crude at Sidon was not competitive with the Ras Tanura price. In late 1975 and in early 1976 a limited amount of crude was pumped to refineries in Jordan and in Sidon.

From the very start Aramco had to concern itself with more than just oil. The primitiveness of the kingdom required construction of almost every facility needed. A port to bring in equipment had to be built; water had to be found and delivered to work areas; and housing, hospitals, and offices had to be constructed just to get development going. Almost no Saudi was familiar with machinery, local construction firms hardly existed, and the unavailability of most materials locally necessitated very long supply lines.

Perhaps because of the country's primitiveness and the need to get involved in many activities, perhaps because of the signs of large petroleum reserves, or perhaps because of a new philosophy in oil company operations, Aramco placed great emphasis on understanding the customs, needs, and aspiration of the people of the country and developed close relationships with its hosts. Working for Aramco was intended to be a career, which meant for the Americans who made up its top management that they were in the country not for a short tour, as in many oil company operations, but for practically all of their professional lives (see ch. 7).

Aramco adopted the long-range policy of having Saudis take over whenever possible. Training programs of many kinds, including sixty annual scholarships in foreign universities, were established. Among other occuptations, Saudis were trained as doctors, supply experts, machinists, ship pilots, truckdrivers, oil drillers, and cooks. Many of these Saudis fanned out into the local economy to establish businesses, introducing modernity in numerous ways. Others remained with Aramco and advanced in responsibility. By the beginning of 1976 there were 19,012 Aramco employees, of whom nearly 14,500 were Saudis. Saudis held 46 percent of the 968 supervisory positions in 1975. Most of the non-Saudis were also non-Americans, such as Pakistanis and Egyptians. Americans numbered about 1,600 by the beginning of 1976.

Saudis also had developed many businesses with Aramco assistance, with which Aramco contracted for work in order to divest itself of supply and service sidelines. For example, some 400 major contracts were let in 1975 totaling about US$250 million. The contracts included such projects as off-road hauling of oil drilling rigs, rental of light vehicles, and local warehousing and sales by merchants. Aramco and its expatriate employees of all nationalities spent nearly US$1.2 billion in Saudi Arabia in 1975 for services, welfare, and taxes (excluding company taxes).

Aramco undertook various projects outside the oil industry to help the country. At the request of King Abd al Aziz, Aramco teams helped find water and develop agricultural projects. The Saudi government paid the company to build a modern port at Dammam and to construct a railroad from Riyadh to the port. Aramco built and paid for the operation of schools for its Saudi employees, although the schools became part of the government's educational system. The company's costs for this program had amounted to US$79 million and by 1976 included fifty-four schools. The company financed and subsidized home ownership in local communities for more than 8,600 Saudi employees since 1951. Aramco helped finance medical programs, such as trachoma research (see ch. 4). Aramco generators supplemented local supply, and the company guaranteed loans for local power suppliers to buy additional generators.

Most foreign observers and many Saudis agree that Aramco contributed much toward development of the country and created a good image of American business. Efforts to determine the company's profits encountered severe difficulties because of the secretiveness of the oil industry, but one study concluded that the owners' rate of return between 1934 and 1964 probably was between 21 and 28 percent. Even if the profitability had been far less, Saudi nationalism still would have required that the government gain control over the country's major resource. That control was close to realization in early 1976, but Saudi officials said they would need Aramco's services for some years in the future. The negotiations under way in early 1976 for the government to achieve 100-percent equity in Aramco presumably included contractual relationships for future services by the company's staff.

Other Foreign Oil Company Concessions

Subsequent concessions granted by Saudi Arabia contained progressively better terms for the kingdom as a result of the actions of the oil-producing states generally and the increasing sophistication of Saudi petroleum officials specifically. The Saudis requested more in exchange for concessions, including opportunities for active participation in subsidiaries that might be set up. The major oil companies were less interested in such terms, and Saudi officials began dealing with smaller and newly formed companies that were anxious to gain crude oil supplies. The concessions went to smaller companies and for the most part were areas relinquished by Aramco.

The next concession was granted to Getty Oil Company (formerly Pacific Western Oil Corporation) in 1949 to explore and exploit hydrocarbon resources in the Saudi share of the partitioned Kuwait Neutral Zone for a period of sixty years (see ch. 3). Aramco had relinquished this area in 1948 partly because the ruler of Kuwait had won very favorable terms for a concession in his share of the partitioned neutral zone, and Aramco did not want to match it.

In return for the concession Getty agreed to pay US$9.5 million in a onetime payment; to pay US$0.55 royalty for each barrel of crude and a 12.5 percent royalty from sale of natural gas; to pay 25 percent of net profits of sales refined outside the zone; to pay 20 percent of profits from refining operations in the zone; to pay 25 percent for the net capital gain if the concession were transferred; to sell 25 percent of the stock to Saudi Arabia if a subsidiary were established for the zone; to deliver free specified petroleum products to Jiddah and Riyadh; to build a refinery in the zone; and to establish certain employee benefits. The terms gave the kingdom a much better return and a chance for part ownership.

In December 1957 a concession was signed with the Arabian Oil Company, then owned by Japanese interests, granting exploration rights offshore the partitioned Kuwait Neutral Zone for a period of two years, subject to extension. If oil were discovered in commercial quantities, an exploitation lease was to be granted for forty years.

Subsequently Saudi Arabia and Kuwait each became 10-percent owners of Arabian Oil Company.

Arabian Oil agreed in return to pay US$1.5 million a year during exploration and an additional US$1 million a year applied retroactively to the whole exploration period should oil in commercial quantities be found; to pay a 20-percent royalty—with a guaranteed minimum—for crude, natural asphalt, and natural gas produced; to establish an integrated company that would pay taxes on all phases of operations inside and outside Saudi Arabia; and to pay additional sums to bring Saudi Arabia's take up to 56 percent of the company's new annual income from all operations if royalties and taxes were below 56 percent. The government had the right to buy between 10 and 20 percent of the shares, depending on specific conditions, of any newly formed company once oil in commercial quantities was discovered. The company agreed to build a refinery when production reached 30,000 barrels per day and to relinquish unexploited areas on a specified schedule. The concession added to government income and was an advance in other ways over the Getty concession.

In 1965 a concession agreement was signed with Auxirap (also known as Auxerap), a subsidiary of a French state-owned petroleum company, for exploration in specific onshore and offshore areas along the Red Sea. In 1968 an American oil company, Tenneco, bought one-third interest in the concession. An exploration license was granted for a two-year period subject to renewal under specific conditions. On discovery of oil in commercial quantities an exploitation license would be granted for thirty years. A Saudi company was to be established in which the government would be offered 40-percent equity after the granting of an exploitation license. The agreement spelled out arrangements for French and Saudi voting rights on the board of directors and management of the company.

The agreement provided for a sliding scale of royalties going up to 20 percent, taxes to be paid according to Saudi laws, a sliding scale of rentals for concession areas through the life of the agreement, and favorable definition for Saudi Arabia of how various calculations would be made. Limitations were set on refinery capacity, ensuring Saudi Arabian agencies participation in marketing, and there were backup provisions for sales to the company if Saudi agencies could not complete their own sales. Company-owned or Saudi tankers would haul the crude to destinations.

The agreement with Auxirap differed markedly from the earlier concessions. One difference, reflecting changing economic conditions in the kingdom, was the shift away from immediate funds to long-range returns should oil be discovered. The concession also reflected the ideas expressed in OPEC. Finally the concession expressed the government's intent to participate in near equality in ownership and management of the petroleum industry and not just in the production of crude oil. There were provisions, however, that government marketing of crude would not disturb marketing for the concessionaire.

The next concessions were granted to Petromin, which assigned its rights but not its concessions to joint ventures with foreign oil companies. Petromin's first joint venture was with Agip Mineraria (Agip), an Italian state company, to explore in specific parts of the Rub al Khali area. Agip sold half of its interest to a subsidiary of Phillips Petroleum Company, an American firm. A large part if not all of this concession was relinquished in 1973 after exploration failed to discover oil.

The significant aspects of the Agip agreement concerned exploitation if oil were found. Petromin reserved the right to but up to 40 percent of the equity, under certain conditions, of the Saudi company that had to be set up for exploitation and marketing, although Petromin could market its own share of crude. If production reached 200,000 barrels per day, an integrated petroleum company with a refinery and marketing organizations was to be established and was to employ a specified proportion of Saudis; the integrated company would be in part a training mechanism.

In 1967 Petromin assigned its rights in certain areas on the Red Sea coast to a group consisting of the Natomas International Corporation, the Sinclair Arabian Oil Company, and petroleum agencies of the Pakistan government. Additional foreign companies subsequently joined the group. The agreement was similar to the Agip agreement except that Petromin could retain 50 percent of the exploitation rights, once oil was found, by paying 50 percent of the exploitation costs. Oil in commercial quantities had not been discovered by early 1976.

Petromin

The General Petroleum and Mineral Organization (Petromin) was established as a public corporation wholly owned by the Saudi government in 1962. It was to develop industries based on petroleum, natural gas, and minerals by itself or in conjunction with other investors, foreign or domestic. Its activities included development of mining and steel mills (see ch. 13). Only its activities related to hydrocarbons are discussed here.

In some respects Petromin was a national petroleum company, but it was more than that. The intention was not to bring petroleum activities under government control but to establish an organization that would act as a catalyst in industrial development. Private investment, foreign and domestic, was encouraged, but Petromin would enter joint ventures with private investors or undertake its own investments in needed industrial development when private capital was not available on the scale required.

Petromin became the distributor of petroleum products in the kingdom partly by purchasing Aramco's local marketing facilities. It became part owner with private Saudi investors of refineries located in Jiddah and Riyadh and 51-percent owner of a urea plant using natural gas for feedstock. Sulfur recovery from natural gas was also part of its operations. Operating affiliates for petroleum exploration and drilling were established with foreign oil firms. Petromin marketed some crude abroad on its own account. The organization was also granted exploration concessions in 1967.

At the low cost of energy before the 1970s the oil companies had found it uneconomical to invest in the pipelines and facilities necessary to use other than a small proportion of the gas realized from crude oil production. By the mid-1970s the higher cost of energy and the effort to build industries in the country afforded possibilities to use natural gas. The Five Year Development Plan (1975-80) included a nearly US$5 billion gas-gathering and treatment system, to be constructed and operated by Aramco. Major sections were to be completed by 1979 and would provide feedstock for petrochemical plants to be established by Petromin.

As a result of the ministerial reorganization of October 1975, Petromin was stripped of some of its activities. In early 1976 full details were unavailable, but it appeared that Petromin's responsibilities were largely confined to those directly related to exploration, production, refining, distribution, and marketing of crude oil and products. The businesses, such as the fertilizer plant and steel mill, in which Petromin held part interest, as well as responsibility for petrochemical plants planned for the 1975-80 period, were transferred to the new Ministry of Industry and Electricity.

FOREIGN TRADE

Saudi Arabia has participated in international trade for thousands of years but largely as a transit route for goods from somewhere else (see ch. 2). Until its oil fields were developed, the area that is present-day Saudi Arabia had little to offer the world and was largely self-sufficient, engaging only in localized, cross-border trading.

The original oil concession allowed Aramco to import and export on its own and for its own needs as long as the required payments were made to the king. It took some years before the export of oil affected the government or the economy. Governmental organizations developed slowly, and their formation was partly molded after the American model. Foreign trade and most other business was left to private entrepreneurs.

Saudi Arabia developed few controls over foreign trade, at least in part because initially there was little organization to administer controls. In addition foreign trade other than that conducted by the oil companies was small, and much of the early importing was for members of the royal family and a few others who had foreign exchange from oil revenues with which to pay for imports.

By 1976 there were still few controls on foreign trade. The tariff structure was scaled primarily to produce revenues, not prohibit imports. Tariffs were adjusted to protect budding industries, and at times imports of luxury goods were discouraged by high import taxes, but for the most part customs duties were moderate. Import licenses were required and provided the government some measure of control over imports. Foreign exchange was not controlled, and an importer who had the financing and a license could import freely. Saudi Arabia was a rare exception to most developing countries, which tend to control imports very closely. The difference was not just oil revenues, for Saudi Arabia has had lean years when foreign exchange was tight. There was a different philosophy and governmental approach to controls in the kingdom.

Exports

Saudi Arabia exported little besides oil. A few products, such as agricultural produce, were sold to some of the nearby states and shaykhdoms. These local products amounted to about US$20 million in 1973, but they were so dwarfed by oil exports that available statistics did not indicate their nature or destination.

Saudi exports took a tremendous jump between 1973 and 1974, increasing from US$8.7 billion to US$39.2 billion, because of the price increases for crude oil. There are two points to note about Saudi exports. In most economies, exports are produced by a number of domestic suppliers who receive payment for their work. The export proceeds, in either foreign or local currency, are distributed among producers. In Saudi Arabia, however, the oil companies were the petroleum exporters; the government alone received payments, in the form of taxes and royalties, and except for the local salaries paid by the oil companies the government alone possessed the option of how and in what form the money would be used and who would receive some of it.

The second point was that Saudi export statistics published by the Saudi Arabian Monetary Agency (SAMA) and those published by the International Monetary Fund (IMF) in its monthly International Financial Statistics were essentially the quantity of oil exports reported by the oil companies, which were valued at posted prices. Posted prices usually exceeded the actual price paid for shipments of petroleum (see Oil: The International Setting, this ch.) In addition foreign exchange did not accrue to the Saudi banking system in amounts approximating the value of exports at posted prices as would be the case for the usual kind of export; the foreign exchange available to Saudis to pay for imports was primarily the amount received from the oil companied in the form of royalties and taxes, an amount considerably less than petroleum exports valued at posted prices. Thus the value of exports in published statistics was an approximate valuation of exports but not of foreign exchange earnings.

Since petroleum exports became important, West European countries have been the primary buyer of Saudi exports. These countries received 42 percent of Saudi exports in 1968 and 53 percent in 1973. Italy was an important buyer, accounting for 10 percent of Saudi exports in 1968 and 1973; exports to the Netherlands increased from 6 percent of all exports in 1968 to 9 percent in 1973. Both of these countries imported crude for refining and distribution of products to other parts of Europe. France also increased its imports of Saudi petroleum, taking 5 percent of Saudi Arabia's total exports in l968 and 9 percent in 1973.

East, Southeast, and South Asian countries were the other large buyers of Saudi exports, accounting for 28 percent in 1968 and 24 percent in 1973. Japan was the single most important buyer of Saudi oil, accounting for 21 percent in 1968 and 15 percent in 1973. Exports to other countries were relatively small and were spread throughout the area.

The Near East (West Asia) had accounted for 7 percent of exports in 1968 but only 4 percent in 1973, partly because of limits on the amounts of crude that could be pumped to Bahrain for refining. United States imports from Saudi Arabia increased significantly, rising from 2.5 percent of total exports in 1968 to 5.3 percent in 1973. Latin America, Africa, and Oceania bought most of the remaining Saudi exports. Between 1967 and 1973 there was a shift away from exports to Africa and Oceania and toward Latin America.

Imports

Saudi imports reflect growing prosperity and economic development. The total value of imports grew almost continuously in the 1960s and 1970s, averaging an annual growth of more than 15 percent between 1958 and 1973. Provisional estimates of imports were about SR13 billion (for value of the riyal—see Glossary) in 1974, nearly double the amount in the previous year. Preliminary evidence for 1975 indicated an additional and substantial increase in imports.

The value of imported foodstuffs grew from about SR315 million in 1958 to SR1.9 billion in 1973, reflecting the prosperity that led away from the traditional diet of rice and lamb to more varied, imported foods (see table 12). The change has been remarkable as wealth has spread among the population, marketing services have improved, and regularized shipping, including refrigerated ships, have become available. United States Department of Agriculture experts estimated that by the mid-1970s Saudi Arabia was importing about two-thirds of its food. One change was the increased popularity of bread and other bakery products requiring growing imports of wheat and flour (see ch.

4). Wheat and flour imports in 1974 were projected at about double the 1973 level and nearly triple the 1972 level. Rice imports increased in quantity after 1972, but there was also a shift to higher grades from Pakistan, India, and Thailand, adding to the value of rice imports. Meat continued to be imported mostly in the form of live animals, but frozen meats, particularly chicken, had increased substantially.

Imports of building materials were strongly related to economic development. The country's almost completed lack of wood required

Table 12. *Saudi Arabia, Imports by Commodity Group, Selected Years, 1968-73*

(in millions of riyals)*

Commodity	1968	1970	1971	1972	1973
Food and Beverages					
Animals and meat	197	142	147	196	270
Milk and milk products	71	91	107	120	245
Fruits and vegetables (fresh and canned)	106	130	149	152	304
Cereal grains	202	288	239	238	257
Other	220	360	455	516	799
Total Food and Beverages	796	1,011	1,097	1,222	1,875
Building Materials					
Timber and wood	48	62	78	75	131
Cement	43	48	58	35	47
Iron bars and sheets	70	107	82	131	186
Pipes and parts	75	83	149	155	122
Other	67	84	96	84	48
Total Building Materials	303	384	463	480	534
Textiles and Clothing	153	142	203	344	657
Machinery					
Cars, trucks, and tractors	217	273	255	382	544
Machinery (general)	181	231	304	500	576
Machinery (agricultural)	42	59	53	89	48
Machinery (electrical)	8	3	3	8	10
Household appliances	45	31	33	79	117
Other	353	421	451	628	1,228
Total Machinery	846	1,018	1,099	1,686	2,523
Chemical Products	137	180	240	244	397
Miscellaneous	343	462	565	732	1,366
TOTAL	2,578	3,197	3,667	4,708	7,352

*For value of the riyal—see Glossary.

Source: Based on information from Saudi Arabian Monetary Agency, *Statistical Summary*, No. 2, Dammam, 1975, pp. 72-73.

most of it to be imported, and the higher the rate of construction, the more was imported. Completion of cement mills and a steel mill reduced the need to import these construction materials, but in 1974 and 1975 demand had outrun production capacity, requiring substantially higher imports for the construction boom under way.

Machinery had become the most important category of imports by 1973, an importance destined to grow with the many projects planned during the 1975-80 plan period. Imports of vehicles and general machinery dominated the category, a pattern that would probably continue during the five-year plan. An interesting side note was the growth of imports of electrical appliances while imports of electrical machinery remained low and nearly constant. This trend would exacerbate the inadequacy of the electric power supply.

The distribution of imports by group shifted a little between the late 1950s and mid-1970s. By 1973 imports for economic development had gained a little at the expense of consumption goods. The trend probably accelerated in 1974 and 1975, and it was expected to continue as the country attempted to implement its heavy investment program.

The major industrialized countries supplied most of Saudi Arabia's imports. The United States was the most important, accounting for 19 percent of all imports in 1973; this was a decline, however, from the 24 percent of imports in 1968. Japan supplied 15 percent of imports in 1973 compared with 8 percent in 1968. West European countries supplied 28 percent of imports in 1973; the Federal Republic of Germany (West Germany) and Great Britain each accounted for 7 percent of the kingdom's imports. Imports from Western Europe were 33 percent in 1968, West Germany and Great Britain being the most important. Middle East countries supplied 21 percent of imports in 1973 compared with 19 percent in 1968. Lebanon alone furnished 11 percent of imports in 1973 (9 percent in 1968). Small amounts of imports came from many other countries throughout the world.

Imports and Exports of Services

Before the discovery of oil Saudi Arabia's receipt of foreign exchange was almost exclusively from Muslims making the pilgrimage to Mecca (see ch. 6). Pilgrims still provided some foreign exchange earnings in the 1970s. Saudi monetary authorities estimated earnings from pilgrims at about US$40 million in 1963, rising to about US$250 million in 1973. Considering the growing expenses necessary to handle the pilgrims, including such investments as the Jiddah airport for pilgrims, roads, buses, sanitation, water services, and housing, it was questionable whether receipts from pilgrims covered costs in the present day (see ch. 13).

Pilgrimage receipts were one of Saudi Arabia's exports of services (see table 13). Another important export service was the sale of bunker oil, largely to tankers transporting petroleum exports. Bunkering alone yielded nearly US$200 million in 1974. The rise in exports of services in the 1970s, however, was mainly because of the earnings, largely interest but including some profits, from Saudi investments abroad. These earnings exceeded US$1 billion in 1974.

Imports of services were essentially an offset entry to the petroleum exports valued at posted prices that reduced the value of petroleum exports to the sum that the government had received in royalties and taxes from the oil companies. Since petroleum exports were overvalued by the use of posted prices, imports of services were also

Table 13. *Saudi Arabia, Balance of Payments, Selected Years, 1968-74*[1]

(in millions of United States dollars)

	1968	1970	1971	1972	1973	1974
Exports (FOB)[2]	1,725	2,089	3,505	5,110	8,719	39,230
Imports (FOB)[2]	-786	-829	-866	-1,275	-2,116	-3,892
Trade Balance	939	1,260	2,639	3,835	6,603	35,338
Exports of services	212	283	341	464	758	2,101
Imports of services	-1,026	-1,208	-1,795	-2,543	-4,263	-13,721
Private unrequited transfers (net)	-132	-183	-208	-267	-390	-518
Government unrequited transfers (net)	-85	-81	-68	-56	-374	-847
Balance of Goods and Services	-92	71	910[3]	1,433	2,334	22,352[3]
Capital Movements						
Short term (net)	23	-11	43	-179	141	-319
Long term (direct investment)	-14	20	-111	75	-625	-3,735
Long term (other)	130	77	-23	31	-3	-38
Foreign exchange reserves	106	-87	-796	-1,187	-1,622	-17,204
Other	-50	0	0	0	0	-750[4]
Errors and Omissions	-103	-70	-23	-173	-225	-306

[1] A minus sign indicates a debit—an outflow of foreign exchange or a buildup of Saudi external investments.
[2] Free on board.
[3] Figures do not add to total because of rounding.
[4] Purchase of US$750 million of bonds issued by the International Bank for Reconstruction and Development, the largest single subscription.

Source: Based on information from International Monetary Fund, *International Financial Statistics*, XXVIII, 11, November 1975, p. 355.

probably overvalued. The overvaluation of oil exports and imports of services created no accounting problems because the net value was zero, but it probably contributed to political problems.

The category private unrequited transfers consisted almost entirely of remittances sent home by foreign nationals working in Saudi Arabia. This figure exceeded US$500 million in 1974 and was expected to increase substantially during the next few years as Saudi Arabia brought in additional foreign workers to implement the five-year plan.

Government transfers were essentially Saudi aid grants, provided largely to other Arab countries. IMF experts estimated these grants at nearly US$850 million in 1974, but there was no assurance that all grants-in-aid had been included. Military help provided to Egypt and Syria, for example, may not have been included in that data provided IMF by the Saudi authorities. Government transfers nearly doubled between 1966 and 1967 and had doubled again by 1968, reflecting Saudi help to Arabs after the June 1967 War.

Balance of Goods and Services

The balance of goods and services has usually been favorable since the early 1960s. The exceptions were 1968 and 1969, when negative balances required the monetary authorities to draw on reserves built up in earlier years. Increases in aid to other Arab countries, increased imports, and higher transportation costs for imports resulting from the closing of the Suez Canal in 1967 caused the negative balances. Foreign observers noted the Saudi frustrations created by their huge oil resources in contrast with their limited income, which would not permit them to help other Arabs and undertake modest development at the same time.

The negative balance of goods and services in 1968 and 1969 added to the smoldering resentment of some years over other aspects of the balance of payments. The overvaluation of the import of services assigned to the oil companies in order to offset the overvalued exports of petroleum was included in the computation of national accounts. As a result the cost of services of the oil companies worked out to about 25 percent of GDP during the 1960s. The fact that the cost probably was overvalued or that the cost was not compared with oil company investments went largely unnoticed. The important point for many Saudis was that government data showed that about one-fourth of their economic effort went to the oil companies. This concern, fueled by the problems in 1968 and 1969, contributed to government actions in conjunction with OPEC in the early 1970s to take control of pricing and production of the Saudi oil industry. The effect of the increased oil prices on the balance of goods and services was remarkable. In 1974 the balance went up by about US$20 billion.

Saudi Use of Its New Wealth

Saudi officials and institutions were unprepared for the sudden increase of wealth. It takes staff, expertise, and hard work to invest money wisely. Up to about 1973 the Saudi experience had been largely that of stretching limited funds to cover domestic projects considered most essential. Saudi Arabia may have had somewhat less pressure on foreign exchange than many developing countries, but it did not have an abundance of funds. In 1974 the situation reversed; suddenly the problem became what to do with all the money flowing in, with long term consequences for the kingdom and the international money markets.

In the mid 1970s the focus of Saudi investment continued to be the domestic economy. Investment in and development of the human and material resources of the country were fundamental concerns behind Saudi Arabia's nearly three decades of efforts to change the pricing of, and return on, its petroleum exports. As money became available to the government, imports, investments, and development were expanded, but the increments were small. The economy lacked sufficient skilled personnel, developed institutions, and adequate ports and transportation to absorb the huge and sudden inflow of funds in 1974, and it appeared in early 1976 that many bottlenecks would keep the economy's absorbency low for years.

The government was keenly aware that the petroleum reserves were a wasting asset in a country with few other resources. Many officials realized that, once a barrel of oil had been lifted, it had to be turned into an asset that would provide financing for further economic growth when the petroleum deposits were exhausted. Care had to be exercised not to waste funds in poor investments.

Saudi monetary officials were conservative by experience and as a function of their elite position in a conservative society (see ch. 7). A royal decree of 1959 required 100-percent backing for all currency in circulation by gold or by foreign exchange convertible into gold. The decree was followed, making the Saudi currency one of the strongest in the world, but it also developed a tendency to keep reserves in liquid, short-term assets. Foreign exchange reserves stood at US$662 million on December 31, 1970, US$3.9 billion on December 31, 1973, and US$14.3 billion on December 31, 1974. By the end of September 1975 foreign exchange reserves had reached US$21.1 billion.

These large, short-term funds created concern in world monetary markets. They were concentrated in a few banks, reportedly expanded from about a dozen to more than thirty by early 1975. Banks generally lend money on longer term than that of the Saudi deposits, and the shifting of Saudi funds could place banks in very shaky positions. The sheer size of Saudi reserves by 1975, moreover, second largest in the world, could cause disruptions and instability in most money markets if they were suddenly moved about.

Saudi officials recognized the disruptions they could create in money markets and stressed their interest in monetary stability. They backed up their words in 1974 and 1975 by keeping deposits static despite numerous opportunities to switch funds in order to obtain a better return. By late 1975 the international financial community was less articulate about its fears, but the banking community and government officials around the world were still worried that Saudi monetary authorities might, because of another Arab Israeli war or some other reason, exercise their power to create serious financial instability with their huge reserves.

The Saudi government had tried to place its oil revenues in places other than short-term deposits in major money markets. Reported grants-in-aid increased tremendously in 1973 and 1974, and these may not have been all the grants provided, particularly in the area of military equipment. The focus of grants was primarily but not exclusively other Arab countries. Direct investments increased nearly sixfold between 1973 and 1974 and amounted to about US$3.7 billion in 1974.

The announcements of Saudi financial involvement in various foreign investments projects in 1974 and 1975 were overwhelming. The range of investments was wide, from the sophisticated to the mundane. Even the mundane, such as a sugar project in Sudan, involved modern technology; and the more sophisticated the technology, the more difficult to evaluate the investment potential. Perhaps this was why many of Saudi Arabia's foreign investments went to financial institutions that in turn made investments in specific projects. The information available in early 1976 would not permit a breakdown of Saudi investments in enterprises with a capability for project evaluation, but the impression was that financial institutions had received a considerable amount of the funds.

It made sense for Saudi Arabia to put investments in institutions with an expertise in investments. The Saudis have gone further by hiring investment professionals, requesting World Bank aid in project evaluation, and contracting for consultants in investment operations. They are trying to develop an expertise in long-term financial investments to remove the need to keep large sums in short-term deposits and foreign government securities.

Announcements of the flow of Saudi funds showed a concentration in the "confrontation states" of Syria and Egypt, particularly the latter. One compilation of such announcements reported that Saudi pledges of aid to confrontation states, that is, those states that have militarily confronted Israel, amounted to about US$2 billion between October 1973 and early 1975. The pledges of Saudi aid to Egypt have been extensive, ranging from rebuilding parts of the war-damaged Suez Canal cities to specific small investments in conjunction with the World Bank.

Saudi Arabia was trying to find sound investments for its sudden wealth, but the difficulties were immense for both domestic and foreign projects. Most observers expected them to succeed as Saudi institutions developed to handle the new wealth. Nobody was certain how long the process might take, however; and until they succeeded, many people would have a financial stake in Middle East developments.

* * * * * * * * * * * * * * *

There are numerous books and articles concerned with aspects of the international petroleum industry, and many more are being published. Morris A. Adelman's *The World Petroleum Market* is a basic, detailed investigation that provides background for more recent developments. The *Aramco Handbook*, 1968 and 1976 editions, and Ramon Knauerhase's *The Saudi Arabian Economy* provide basic detailed information concerning the Saudi petroleum industry and its relationship to other parts of the economy. An article by Mariano Gurfinkel in the *International Monetary Fund Survey* ((October 13, 1975) provides a useful guide for understanding posted prices and deriving governmental revenues from them. During the early and mid-1970s there were numerous reports of alarming drops in reservoir pressure in some of the major Saudi oil fields. For information on this controversial and technical issue, readers should consult the U.S. Congress 93d, 2d Session, Senate, Committee on Foreign Relations, Subcommittee on Multinational Corporations, *Multinational Corporations and United States Foreign Policy* and Christopher T. Rand's *Making Democracy Safe for Oil.* (For further information see Bibliography.)

CHAPTER 13

AGRICULTURE, INDUSTRY, AND DOMESTIC TRADE

Agriculture, industry, and trade evolved many centuries ago in forms that reflected the harsh, arid conditions of the Arabian Peninsula. There was little reason or way for the economy to change until oil was discovered in the 1930s (see ch. 12). With oil came money that bought trucks and transportation equipment (see ch. 3). A transport system, even only partially developed, provided a basis for a different form of economic organization. No longer were communities isolated from one another. Surplus products in one area could be economically transported and sold in another. Production and trade no longer had to be organized to supply an isolated community.

Communities in ancient Arabia were not completely isolated, however. Animals provided a means of transport for man and cargo, but only the camel was capable of making the most difficult passages. Consequently raising camels and driving camel caravans became important means of earning a living. The widespread introduction of trucks beginning in the 1950s rapidly made these occupations obsolete. Yet in the mid-1970s many beduin continued raising camels, for which there was not much of a market. These beduin subsisted with the help of the government and were slow to change their way of life.

Other parts of the agricultural economy were also slow to change because some basic conditions remained nearly constant. Only a small area of the kingdom, mainly in the southwest, had sufficient rainfall to support cropping. Farming in the rest of the country was scattered, clustered around wells and oases. Traditional techniques persisted, and farm incomes were low. Agricultural production had increased slowly, and many farmers had left their fields for better paying jobs in the other rapidly expanding sectors of the economy.

By the mid-1970s, however, there were signs of change in agriculture. More farmers were shifting from subsistence agriculture to commercial farming. The change was most noticeable in the truck farms growing vegetables for nearby urban areas. The change in consumer tastes as urban incomes increased diminished the demand for dates and the cultivation of date palms. Some beduin had shifted to raising sheep and goats, providing very marketable products although restricting their nomadic way of life.

Industry changed more quickly. When oil was discovered, industry consisted almost entirely of local craftsmen, such as makers of camel saddles and smiths who made jewelry, brassware, and cooking utensils. As urbanization increased, transportation improved, and incomes increased, it was relatively easy to build a plant to produce for a large market. For example, bakeries and other food-processing plants, a detergent factory, cement mills, and even a steel rolling mill were constructed with foreign technical help. The value added by manufacturing rose accordingly, averaging an annual increase of over 11 percent (in constant prices) between fiscal year (FY—see table A) 1962 and FY 1974, although industry remained a very small sector of the economy.

Trade, the link between producer and consumer, was strongly affected by the rise of incomes resulting from increasing oil revenues. Domestic output of agricultural and industrial goods failed to keep pace with consumer demand. The gap was filled by imports. In the 1950s a few merchants obtained franchises from international companies for the local sale of the companies' products, making the merchants wealthy by the 1970s. Most merchants, however, continued operating small shops or stalls serving a very limited market and involving a small inventory and turnover.

The haj trade, the annual flow of Muslim pilgrims to Mecca and Medina, has always dominated the economy of the area surrounding these holy places (see ch. 6). It still does partly because modern transportation had increased the number of pilgrims to above 1 million annually in the mid-1970s. It took a highly organized combination of government and private services to supply the needs of the visitors and enable them to make a successful pilgrimage (see ch. 4). The government's participation has lessened the exploitation of pilgrims that persisted well into the twentieth century.

Discovery of oil injected a new and powerful element into an economy that had been isolated for centuries from developments occurring in most of the world. Saudi people and economic organizations took time to adjust. The years between 1945 and 1975 were a period of transition accompanied by tremendous improvement in transportation. The large investments in agriculture, industry, and transportation planned for the 1975-80 period should accelerate the transition. Most observers anticipate the greatest change in manufacturing and the least in agriculture but substantial progress throughout the economy toward modernity.

AGRICULTURE

Poor soils and very little water were the facts of life for the people of the Arabian Peninsula throughout their long history. They evolved intricate social and economic techniques to earn a living from the harsh environment. The delicate balance was upset when a central government was established in the 1930s and further disrupted by high oil revenues and widespread use of trucks.

The transition from the ancient to the modern world was particularly difficult for the agricultural sector. Revenues from the oil sector stimulated most economic activities, but they had the least effect on agriculture. In little more than a generation agriculture declined from the most important sector of the economy to one of the least important. As the other sectors grew rapidly, the importance of agriculture in the total output of goods and services steadily declined. By FY 1975 agriculture's share was only 1 percent of gross domestic product (GDP) and only 9 percent of the non-oil economy.

From another point of view, however, agriculture remained the most important sector of the economy. In FY 1975 it was still the largest source of employment for the population, employing 27 percent of the work force. The second Five Year Development Plan (1975-80) estimated that there were about 311,000 settled farmers and 115,000 nomadic herdsmen in a total work force of nearly 1.6 million; these figures, however, as well as all data concerning agriculture, were little better than educated guesses.

The number of workers dependent on agriculture has steadily declined since the 1930s, but even in the 1960s more than half of the work force had been employed in agriculture. There were a number of factors causing the slow growth of agricultural output and the steady loss of workers but, most important, many problems were created. The kingdom went from self-sufficiency in food in the 1930s to a dependency on imports for perhaps two-thirds of the food consumed in 1975. Rapid urbanization overtaxed government services and created shantytowns (see ch. 4). An important segment of the population, the beduin, was largely bypassed in the economic improvements that followed the discovery of oil. In 1976 the government remained acutely aware of the problems and continued to help the agricultural sector.

The Agricultural Setting

The lack of water is the major constraint on agriculture. Rainfall is slight and irregular over most of the country (see ch. 3). There are no rivers, streams, or lakes in the kingdom. Agriculture is widely scattered, and actual cropping is limited to a fraction of 1 percent of the total area—to the places where water is available.

Where water was available, nearly independent economic units emerged long ago, consisting of mutually supporting agriculture, arts and crafts, and some degree of urbanization. Long distances of rough, arid terrain separated these scattered centers. The camel alone of all the animals was suitable to serve man in such conditions. It could go several days without water (depending on the season and the moisture content of its forage), eat very coarse vegetation, traverse rock and sand, and carry substantial loads over long distances. Camel raising and transportation by camel caravans were additional parts of the early economy.

The limited arable land, the near total absence of grasslands, and the special characteristics of the camel forced camel raising, and to a lesser degree other stockraising, into a nomadic pattern to take advantage of what forage was available. The beduin developed special skills to know where rain had fallen, where forage was available to feed their animals, and where they could find water en route to the various forage areas.

The beduin were not self-sufficient. They needed some foods and materials from the agricultural settlements. The near constant movement required to feed their animals limited their other activities, such as weaving. The settled farmer and the trader needed the nomad's camels. Separate beduin groups also contracted to provide protection to the agricultural and market areas they frequented in return for such provisions as dates, cloth, and necessary equipment. The beduin with their camels and horses provided what security the separate communities had. The beduin additionally supplemented their income by taxing caravans for passage and protection through their territory.

Beduin themselves needed protection. Operating in small independent groups of a few households, they were vulnerable to raids by other nomads. The tribe had the responsibility to avenge attacks on any of its members. Over the course of Arabian development the relationships among tribes, tribal members, and tribal components, both settled and nomadic, became fairly fixed and important to the economy.

The tribes established territories that they vigorously defended from any unauthorized intrusion. Within the tribal area parts of a tribe would find and develop springs and wells. Where water was sufficient, some parts of a nomadic tribe might shift from camel raising, with its extended range, to goats and sheep, which had to remain very close to water, or to settled agriculture, particularly the cultivation of date groves. The nomads would also graze and breed animals belonging to sedentary farmers in return for portions of the farmers' produce. By the early twentieth century landownership, water rights, and intertribal and intratribal relationships were delicately intertwined and had a long history.

Land Uses

Vegetation on which animals can forage grows over most of the country. The number of livestock it can support varies by area and by the amount and frequency of rain, but nearly all of the kingdom has a potential use as grazing land. According to the second five-year plan only about 1.3 million acres of land were cultivated in 1970. The government estimated that the cultivated area could be doubled with sufficient investment in irrigation and soil conditioning. Whether it was economically feasible to expand the cultivated acreage greatly was not clear by 1976.

According to the second five-year plan the acreage cultivated in the mid-1970s was substantially higher than the 700,000 acres reported in statistics published in the 1960s. It was thought that the more recent figure of 1.3 million acres cultivated represented a new estimate rather than a rapid expansion of the cultivated area; the second development plan mentions farmers abandoning their land and farmers leaving the virgin land that had been given to them largely uncultivated. There was some multiple cropping, and the cropped area was a little higher than the number of acres cultivated.

The main agricultural area was in the southwest corner of the kingdom in the Asir-Qizan area. The second plan reports that more than 75 percent of the cultivated acreage is in this area, in contrast with only about 40 percent reported in statistics of the mid-1960s. The Asir mountains are almost the only place in the country where rainfall is regular and sufficient to support cultivation. Because the bulk of the cultivated land is in this rain belt, only about 25 percent of the cropped area of the whole country is irrigated, according to the second plan. This contradicts statistics and investigations in the 1960s that indicated that about 80 percent of the cultivated land was irrigated.

The remainder of the cultivated land is widely scattered. Cultivation exists in the wadis draining eastward and westward from the mountains of the Red Sea coast and particularly in the vicinity of important western towns, such as Mecca, Medina, and Jiddah. In the central part of the country scattered areas with water, such as the environs of Riyadh and Buraydah, support cultivation. Cultivation in the Eastern Province centers on oases, such as Hasa and Qatif.

Forested areas are almost nonexistent. The soil and climate are not favorable for trees, and the trees that exist under the harsh conditions tend to be dwarfed and the wood porous and soft. The only forested area in the usual sense is on the upper slopes of the mountains of Asir and the southern Hejaz where rainfall is sufficient to support tree growth. Some trees are cultivated in other parts of the kingdom for windbreaks and to stop encroachment of sand dunes, while others, primarily the date palm, are cultivated for fruit. The wood from all trees is used for construction and firewood, but the kingdom does not have enough trees to have a forestry industry.

Landholdings

Inheritance under Muslim law is shared among all heirs, leading to fragmentation of agricultural land into small plots. Various kinds of ownership were devised to avoid fragmentation. One practice allows joint ownership by an extended family with the sharing of the cultivation and the produce among family members. Another practice places title to the land in a trust, often an endowment to a religious or charitable institution (waqf), while the original owner or his designees cultivate the land and keep the produce. An estimate made in the mid-1960s indicated that less than one-third of the arable land was subject to the Muslim inheritance law and hence to the fragmentation process.

The government owns the bulk of land. Only arable land and urban property is owned by individuals, extended families, village communities, and various kinds of institutions. Although the government requires all land titles to be registered, accurate information on holdings was limited in early 1976.

Saudi farms were small as a consequence of the inheritance and water rights. About 47 percent of the farmland was in plots of 1.25 acres or fewer in the mid-1960s (the latest available data in early 1976) and 67 percent in plots of 2.5 acres or fewer. Observers considered that in most parts of the country 2.5 acres were necessary to sustain a single family. Farms in the central part of the country tended to be substantially larger than elsewhere, partly because of extended family ownership and partly because of rewards granted earlier to loyal army leaders for their help in unifying the country. These larger farms used more machinery and hired more laborers.

From the data available foreign economists derived opposing opinions regarding tenant farming. Some estimates indicated that tenant farming occupied more than 67 percent of the cultivated land, whereas other estimates indicated that it occupied no more than 10 percent. The actual situation was probably somewhere in between, but the various kinds of ownership made it unclear whether tenant farmers were a minority or a majority.

Most landownership is valueless in Saudi Arabia unless it includes access to water. Most water rights can be sold, rented, and inherited independently of the land. In Asir and the coastal plain of the Red Sea, where precipitation is relatively plentiful, water rights are bound to the land, not to the individual. In general the developer of a water source such as a well has the rights to it unless he abandons it. This has created problems for nomads because many years may intervene between visits to a well they dug. If others just used the well, the nomadic tribe could frequently establish that the well was in territory where they had primary rights; but if another tribe improved the well, primary rights became difficult to establish. In more concentrated agricultural areas of settled farmers, rights, rules, and regulations concerning water are highly developed and complex. Additions to the original cultivated area may be left with secondary or no water rights, for example; they receive only surplus water after those areas with primary rights have been fully irrigated.

Most surveys suggest that in the mid-1970s farming was still largely at subsistence level with small surpluses bartered or sold to obtain the other essentials the family needed. The lack of adequate transportation until the 1960s restrained many farmers from considering commercial farming. Farmers used little fertilizer, insecticide, or machinery in cultivation. Most of the machinery used consisted of pumps to raise water from deep modern wells. There were few farm cooperatives.

Cropping Patterns and Production

It is difficult to measure growth of agricultural production because of the inadequacy of statistics. Perhaps the best measure is the annual average rate of growth for the agricultural sector's contribution to GDP as estimated by Saudi planners; they estimated that agricultural output (value added in constant prices) increased by 1.6 percent a year between FY 1963 and FY 1972.

The cropping pattern has changed since the 1950s, although statistics were lacking to measure the change. The cropping pattern used in most publications allotted 75 to 80 percent of the cultivated area to cereal grains, around 2 to 4 percent to vegetables, about 16 to 20 percent to dates, and the remaining 2 percent or so to other fruits, based on surveys made during the 1960s. This allocation was for a cultivated area only half the size described by the second five-year plan, however.

Most observers have noted a gradual decline in cultivation of date palms since World War II. Date trees grow almost everywhere in the kingdom and formerly provided an important staple in the diet of many people, particularly the beduin, as well as furnishing wood and fronds for building materials. The beduin cultivated and harvested dates at isolated oases. The best of the dates came from such large oases as Medina in the west and Hufuf in the Eastern Province. The decline in date cultivation has been partly attributed to fewer nomads, irrigation and drainage problems in the east, and the rising incomes of much of the population, which makes possible the purchase of rice and cereals in place of dates.

Wheat used to occupy the most acreage of any crop, and any surplus was easily marketed. Wheat cultivation was concentrated in the central part of the country, the Najd, and in the southwest corner, Asir. A preference for rice plus government price and subsidy policies appeared to have caused a sharp decline in wheat acreage and production by 1971 (see table 14). Some of the former wheat and barley acreage was probably shifted to millet, sorghum, and corn in the late 1960s.

Table 14. *Saudi Arabia, Production, Imports, and Consumption of Major Crops, Fiscal Years 1960-63 Average and Fiscal Year 1971*[1]

(in thousands of metric tons)

Crop	Fiscal Years 1960-63 Production[2]	Fiscal Year 1971 Production	Fiscal Year 1971 Imports[3]	Fiscal Year 1971 Consumption[3]
Wheat	129	74	237[4]	311
Barley	48	7	37	44
Millet	35	162	1	163
Sorghum and corn	16	147	18	165
Total	228	390	293	683
Dates	258	224	0	218
Other fruits	86	13	79	75
Total	344	237	79	293
Melons	171	470	0	451
Other vegetables	174	176	30	201
Total	345	646	30	652
Alfalfa	2,012	n.a.	n.a.	n.a.

n.a.—not available
[1] The cropped acreage was given as an average of 668,000 acres for fiscal years 1960 to 1963 and 1.3 million acres in fiscal year 1971.
[2] The annual average production for the fiscal years between 1960 and 1963.
[3] Imports plus production may not equal consumption because of exports. Imports and consumption data were not available for the 1960-63 period.
[4] Includes flour.

Source: Based on information from Edmond Y. Asfour, et al, *Saudi Arabia: Long-Term Projections of Supply and Demand for Agricultural Products*, Beirut, 1965, Table IV-1, p. 60; and Saudi Arabia, *Development Plan 1395-1400 (1975-80)*, Springfield, Virginia, 1976, Table IV-3, p. 115.

Many agronomists have noted the rapid growth of vegetable cultivation since World War II and have suggested that Saudi statistics do not adequately reflect this shift. Truck farming, particularly of melons and tomatoes, expanded substantially around most urban centers. The growth of towns, the higher urban incomes, and the improved transportation and marketing facilities all contributed to the increased cultivation of vegetables, but government policy affecting import duties and domestic prices was also very important.

Several cash crops were important to specific areas. As much as 4,000 tons of rice was grown in the Eastern Province during the 1960s, but production was negligible in FY 1971. Sesame was grown on the Tihamah coastal plain of the Red Sea. Small amounts of coffee, henna, and *qat*, a mildly narcotic plant, were grown in Asir.

Data on crop rotation and crop yields were too limited to be useful, although crop rotation was practiced in most areas. Three-tier cultivation was practiced on some irrigated areas in the Eastern Province and the Najd. Date palms were the primary crop and fruit trees and shrubs the second tier. Alfalfa and leeks were grown at ground level. Alfalfa was a major and high-yielding crop in the rotation cycle. It was too expensive for use by beduin, however, and was used primarily by farmers to feed their draft animals.

Stockraising

Stockraising, about three-fourths of it done by the beduin, contributed greatly to the economic, social, and cultural development of Arabia. The beduin adapted their life and learned the skills necessary to convert marginal, unused forage areas into a productive resource. The most skilled and most nomadic concentrated on camel raising. Their knowledge of their animals, the desert, and geography became legendary. When grazing conditions required, the most nomadic of the beduin ranged from the southeast corner of the kingdom to northern Iraq. The beduin way of life and its economic contribution were doomed when the country began to modernize, however.

Widespread use of trucks—rendering camels obsolete—was only one factor dooming the traditional nomadic economy. Unification of the country in 1932 placed police power in the central government, thus depriving the beduin tribes of the protection money they previously had earned or extracted from the settled population. The beduin were militantly independent, good warriors, and nearly always armed and therefore posed a threat to any government.

The pressure on the beduin has been to settle. Most observers indicated that the number of nomads had diminished over the years, but some beduin did not agree. The first Five Year Development Plan (1970-75) estimated that there were 151,000 nomads in the work force in 1966; the second plan estimated 115,000 in 1975. Estimates of the livestock population in the late 1960s amounted to 250,000 camels, 3.6 million sheep, 1.9 million goats, 22,000 donkeys, and 4,000 horses. These figures differed little from estimates made in the 1950s and 1960s. Most experts have expressed little confidence in livestock estimates. The skepticism appeared justified: the official estimates of the camel population barely decreased between 1951 and 1970, but William R. Polk and William J. Mares, informed and sympathetic observers of the Saudi society, report that in the late 1960s they had difficulty finding six camels, guides, and equipment for an expedition, even with government assistance.

There probably has been an increase in the sheep and goat population. A number of beduin, reluctant to give up their nomadic existence, shifted to raising sheep and goats for the urban, commercial markets. Sheep and goats require water almost daily and cannot travel the long distances between grazing areas and water sources that camels can. The government added many wells to facilitate the raising of sheep and goats. Also the government helped beduin obtain trucks to move water to their animals or to move animals to new grazing areas and wells. The limited range of sheep and goats from their water source has contributed to overgrazing of rangelands adjacent to wells, however. This was a serious concern to the planners of the second five-year plan.

A factor contributing to the overgrazing was the abolition in 1925 of tribal rights to grazing land. The intent of the measure was to reduce intertribal friction, but it also removed a tribe's interest in keeping the livestock population matched to specific grazing areas and its ability to do so. Most nomads had a keen sense of ecological balance and recognized that their continued existence depended on maintaining grazing land for long-term use. The government has sought but not found a means of regulating grazing as effective as the former tribal territories but less militant.

Sheep provide the bulk of the domestically raised meat. The indigenous sheep has hair rather than wool, which is used for making blankets and clothing. It has a broad, fatty tail from which an oil for cooking is obtained. The milk is used fresh or made into yogurt. Goats supplement the meat and milk supply and furnish the black hair from which beduin tents and rugs are woven. Production and slaughter of sheep and goats have been insufficient to meet the country's need for meat in the 1970s, and large imports have been required.

The beduin's usual disdain for settled farming, as well as his preference for the freedom of nomadic life, has frustrated the government's efforts to settle him. The government's inattention to the kinship orientation of most beduin contributed to the failure or very limited success of the formal agricultural settlement projects. The King Faisal Settlement Project at Haradh near the railroad between Riyadh and Dammam is an example. The project was a well-planned, expensively constructed, well-watered oasis of about 10,000 acres with housing for about 1,000 families in eight villages. It was started in the early 1960s when the sheep and goats of northern-based beduin had been decimated by a prolonged drought. Most of the construction was completed by 1970, and the fields were a lush green, but few nomad families moved in. The project was being developed in the mid-1970s as a feedlot to fatten the nomads' sheep and goats before their slaughter and marketing in the cities.

One close study of the beduin indicated that they were not antagonistic toward change and were settling down on their own initiative. Their attitude was essentially pragmatic, but they sought ways to retain small kinship groupings with a minimun of nontribal people in any settlement area (see ch. 7). In the long transition period since unification of the country they have managed to survive by government subsidies in various forms, earnings from jobs—usually as temporary laborers or semiskilled workers—and their livestock raising.

The government discouraged horse raising by the beduin because the horses had been used largely by raiding parties. By the mid-1970s horses had lost their economic significance, and most were part of the royal stables.

Cattle do not thrive in the kingdom. Most were in the southwest corner of the country, particularly on the Tihamah plain, and were used as draft animals. There were major dairies at Jiddah and Riyadh and smaller ones elsewhere. In the early 1970s cattle were imported from various places under experimental programs to improve breeds for dairy use and to develop beef cattle suited to local conditions.

Most farmers also raised poultry. Several poultry farms were established in the 1960s and early 1970s in an effort to increase meat production. Donkeys were raised primarily by settled farmers for farmwork and use in mountainous areas unsuited to camels.

Role of Government

Government policy is for private owners to develop agriculture. It has avoided much of the interference common in many other countries. Nevertheless government has played an important role in agriculture and plans to continue to do so for some years.

Since water is the major constraint on agricultural development, the government's interest in making the best use of water resources and the large costs of water development make the government the primary agent in expanding the amount of water for agriculture. Large pools of groundwater underlie parts of the country. The government has drilled numerous wells and put in pumps for both the livestock of nomads and irrigation by farmers. Part of the groundwater has existed for many thousands of years, and part is the drainoff of rains as the water flows underground from the mountains in the west toward the Persian Gulf in the east. As of early 1976 hydrological studies had not established adequately how much recharging occurs. The government intends to slow down exploitation of the groundwater, of which agriculture is the biggest user, until further studies are completed during the second plan period and an extraction policy is developed.

Since the early 1960s the government has built fifteen dams for water storage and flash flood control. The largest and most important was completed in the Qizan area in the mid-1970s to irrigate about 18,000 acres. Most of the other dams were also in the main agricultural area in the southwest corner of the country.

Another example of agricultural projects beyond the scope of private enterprise was the modification and expansion of the Hasa Oasis around Hufuf in the Eastern Province. This oasis, the country's largest, was home to about 160,000 people on about 20,000 acres when productivity began to fall sharply in the 1950s because of poor drainage, increasing salinity, and encroachment by sand dunes. In the early 1960s plans were drawn and construction begun with the help of West European firms to restructure the irrigation and drainage system. Some 900 miles of irrigation, 900 miles of drainage canals, and nearly 1,000 miles of new agricultural roads were constructed. The irrigated land was increased to about 50,000 acres. Meanwhile techniques developed by oil companies were used to halt the movement of sand dunes. The government helped farmers during the period of disruption. The improvements and additions made at Hasa were expected to increase the productivity and incomes of its farmers during the 1975-80 period.

The government has taken an active role in influencing prices. Saudi agriculture is generally high cost, particularly for wheat and other cereal grains. Fruits and vegetables were relatively more profitable and earned an actual profit at prevailing prices during the 1960s. When the Saudi currency was devalued in 1959, the government granted subsidies to importers of many basic foods to keep the prices low for the population. In addition a 10-percent tariff was levied on imports of fresh vegetables in 1962. The combined effect of these two measures was to accelerate an existing trend among farmers to plant vegetables and to diminish acreage planted in wheat and barley.

The government shifted the form of subsidies in the early 1970s to affect farmers' incomes more directly. In 1975 subsidies were paid to encourage production of wheat, sorghum, rice, camels, and sheep. Subsidies of about one-half the cost were also paid for farm machinery, fertilizers, and animal feed concentrates to encourage use of improved techniques. Direct financial help was also provided to farmers to establish or upgrade poultry and dairy farms.

By 1975 the government maintained model farms and experimental farms along with an embryo extension service to provide information and guidance to farmers. Certified seed farms were producing high-yield varieties of wheat seeds for distribution. An agricultural credit bank was established in 1963 and had forty-three local offices by the mid-1970s. Its capital had been increased more than tenfold and its lending activities expanded steadily over the little more than a decade of its existence. Still it satisfied the credit needs of only a small part of the agricultural sector.

The second five-year plan calls for improvement of techniques and expansion of productivity, and therefore individual incomes, in both settled agricultural and nomadic livestock production, but it admits to formidable problems. The plan even expressed fear that permanent damage might have been done by overgrazing on some rangelands and too rapid exploitation of some groundwater sources. The water table had fallen so low in some wells that the farms had been abandoned.

Overuse of water in some areas had produced salinity that reduced productivity and in extreme cases halted cultivation. Few foreign observers were optimistic about the future of Saudi agriculture; growth would be slow, and the economic gap between rural and urban dwellers was expected to grow. The problem could become particularly acute for the beduin, who already had been largely bypassed in the economic development of the mid-1970s.

Fishing

Fishing along with pearling was a historical occupation in the Persian Gulf and Red Sea but not particularly attractive to Saudis. There are a variety of seafoods suitable for commercial fishing in the country's offshore waters, such as sardines, mackerel, barracuda, tuna, and shrimp. In recent years the government has encouraged development of marine resources by private groups, but progress has been slow. Even though refrigeration facilities existed at Dammam and Jiddah, most fish was consumed fresh in coastal communities. There was little interest in or demand for fish among the Saudi population. Some shrimp was caught in the Persian Gulf and quick-frozen for shipment to Japan and the United States.

INDUSTRY

Industry has been slow to develop. Manufacturing, like agriculture, was largely self-sufficient before formal unification of the country in 1932; craftsmen produced a few items, which they often sold themselves in the local market (see ch. 2). It took time after unification for transportation to connect areas and for the oil wealth to filter down to the general population. It also took time after new techniques were introduced for entrepreneurs to manage the factors of production to produce and sell under the new market conditions.

The pace of industrialization began to accelerate in the 1960s. The average rate of growth of manufacturing (excluding oil refining and construction) was over 11 percent annually from the early 1960s to the mid-1970s. Employment in manufacturing outside the oil sector also increased, from about 34,700 workers in FY 1970 to about 44,400 workers in FY 1975, but the capital-intensive nature of many of the additions to industry during that period meant that employment grew at a slower rate than the value of manufacturing output. Nonetheless the industrial sector was still very small. Its contribution to GDP was 0.6 percent in FY 1975—less than 6 percent of the non-oil economy.

The government's primary approach to development has been to rely on private enterprise, but the General Petroleum and Mineral Organization (Petromin) was established in 1962 as a government-owned company to undertake development projects when private capital was insufficient or reluctant to invest. By 1975 Petromin's activities outside the petroleum sector included ownership of the kingdom's only steel mill, 51-percent equity (49-percent private Saudi capital) in the fertilizer plant at Dammam, and a sulfuric acid plant also located at Dammam. Besides using foreign expertise during construction of these plants, Petromin employed foreign companies to help in management.

The ministerial reorganization in October 1975 narrowed Petromin's responsibilities. Presumably these plants and others to be built after 1975 will become the responsibility of the Ministry of Industry and Electricity, and a company patterned after Petromin will take charge of the government's equity and management responsibilities. As of early 1976 such a company had not been identified, nor had formal transfer of Petromin's ownership been announced.

The government's reliance on private capital to develop industry may have avoided some costly, uneconomical state-owned investments of the kind that were all too common in many developing countries. It meant, however, that development would be slow until private Saudi investors accumulated the wealth and knowledge to invest their money in manufacturing businesses. Investments in trade, and more recently in real estate, were more attractive and less risky than in industry. Moreover the lack of a mechanism such as a stock market made it difficult for an investor to turn his equity into cash when he needed it. The government's tariff policies also had given investors concern; more protection for local manufactures was assured in the government's policy statement in 1974. The open import policy of the 1950s and 1960s had caused many Saudi investors to restrict their ventures to products that had little competition from imports.

By the mid-1970s Saudi private investors had become more active, applying for an increasing number of licenses for industrial businesses. Government policies and inducements were partly responsible. The greatly improved transportation system and the rising incomes of the population also contributed. The increasing numbers of applications included solely Saudi investments and joint ventures with foreign firms to produce a wide range of products.

Natural Resources for Industrial Use

One reason for the lack of industry in the kingdom was that natural resources that were known to exist before the discovery of oil were meager. More was known by 1975 about natural resources that might be commercially exploited, but geological mapping and survey work remained major tasks for the second plan period. Mining and quarrying were very small, amounting to 1 percent of non-oil GDP in FY 1975.

Water, a fundamental natural resource, was very scarce. Only along the southern Red Sea coast was rainfall sufficient for impoundment by dams for local urban, industrial, and some agricultural use. Most other areas relied on groundwater. The scarcity of water caused the Saudis to be the foremost practitioners of desalinization of seawater. Six desalinization plants were in or near operation by 1976 but supplying only a small part of the total water supply. Only two of the plants were large, those at Jiddah and Khubar. Substantial expansion of desalinization of seawater is called for in the second plan. Large additions to capacity at Jiddah and Khubar and major new plants at Yanbu and Jubayl were intended to supply the population and industrial growth planned for these areas.

Commercial mining was confined to nonmetallic minerals in 1975. Limestone, marble, gypsum, and salt were produced (see ch. 3). Limestone production supported three cement plants.

Nine known mineral belts had been identified in the western part of the country. Prospects for nonferrous minerals (copper, zinc, gold, and nickel) appeared promising enough that by 1975 four exploration licenses had been granted to international mining companies. A deposit of about 1.5 billion tons of low-grade (30 to 40 percent) iron ore near Jiddah had been discovered many years earlier and was to have been the basis for an iron and steel mill in Jiddah to supply the raw materials for the Jiddah rolling mill constructed in the late 1960s. Mining of this deposit had not started by 1976. The second plan anticipated that few if any of the metallic mineral deposits would be in production by 1985.

In 1974 about 3.6 trillion cubic feet of natural gas per day, associated with crude oil production, were flared (see ch. 12). Plans had been drawn and work started by the government in conjunction with the Arabian American Oil Company (Aramco) to gather and treat the natural gas for use as a heat source and feedstock for the future development of industry in Eastern Province. Industries that were expected to be developed based on the natural gas were electric power generation, desalinization of seawater, petrochemical processing, and steel and aluminum refining. A major industrial complex was to be located at Jubayl on the Persian Gulf as a prime consumer of the natural gas.

Electric Power System

Saudi Arabia's electric power system, or rather its lack of one, illustrated the early stage of the country's industrial development in the mid-1970s. It was 1950 before the first city had electricity. By the mid-1970s there were about fifteen private power companies supplying electricity largely to urban areas. Voltages and cycles differed between towns and even within some towns, preventing standardization of equipment and appliances by consumers. Service was marred by power failures, voltage fluctuations, and poor repair service for consumers. Hospitals and large industries often had their own generating facilities to maintain supply. There was almost no integration between any of the various power sources.

Generating capacity has expanded rapidly since the early 1960s. The installed capacity increased at an annual rate of over 17 percent between 1966 and 1972. Electricity generated and sold showed a similar growth. Nearly all of the increased consumption was by households. Electric consumption by industry remained less than 10 percent of total power generated between 1966 and 1972. The failure of industrial consumption of electricity to increase presumably reflected reliance of many plants on their own generators. There were 261 power stations with 1,256 megawatts of capacity in early 1974 (but it was not clear if generators at plants were included), and electric generation in major cities amounted to 1.47 billion kilowatt-hours in FY 1974. There were about 800 miles of transmission lines in early 1974. Aramco had more than 100 additional megawatts of generating capacity in its own network.

The government took measures to improve the electrical systems during the first Five Year Development Plan. New generators must be sixty hertz and distribution voltages 127 to 220 volts. Older systems will be gradually brought to these standards. Electric rates were reduced about 60 percent in 1974 by government order to lessen costs to consumers, causing an immediate large increase in demand. The electric companies ordered additional equipment with government financial assistance, but installation had not been completed by the end of 1975.

The second five-year plan anticipated the equivalent of nearly US$2 billion of investments in electric power facilities. The number of people with electricity was planned to increase from 2.2 million in 1974 to 3.8 million in 1980. Generating capacity was to expand by 3,282 megawatts and transmission lines by about 2,000 miles. The plan recommended tying together major towns and generators in selected areas in a grid system. The grid in the east would connect major towns and oases in the Eastern Province and the Najd. In the west the grid would extend from Jiddah through Mecca and Taif to Bishah and back to the coast at Qizan. A transmission line would also run from Yanbu to Medina and east into the mountains of the Hejaz, presumably to be the start of a transpeninsular link. Some of the new generating facilities were part of seawater desalinization plants to be installed on the east and west coasts. Completion of the planned projects would substantially upgrade the country's electrical power base.

Small-Scale Industry

The bulk of manufacturing activity is small scale. A survey of 9,638 manufacturing establishments in sixty-one urban regions in 1971 showed that nearly 95 percent employed fewer than five people; these were essentially handicraft shops. This kind of shop accounted for nearly half of the employment in all of the manufacturing sector. The survey did not indicate what these small manufacturers produced, but presumably they were largely shops of smiths (working with gold, silver, brass, and iron), carpenters (making carved screens, panels, and doors), and handloom weavers (weaving products like the famous wool cloaks from Hufuf). Some food processing probably was included in this manufacturing sector.

A second group of small-scale manufacturing establishments, numbering 746, employed between five and nine workers. These shops probably used a little more, but still simple, equipment. The range of activities probably included bookbinding and perhaps some printing; producing bricks and other building materials; repairing by small machine shops; food processing; and wood and metal forming.

More than one-half of the small-scale industry was located in the Hejaz and northern Asir, long the population and commercial center of the kingdom. A little over one-quarter of the manufacturing was in the central area, reflecting the growing urbanization around Riyadh and some of the oases of the Najd. The Eastern Province contained less than one-fifth of the establishments and the northern and southern areas the remainder.

Large-Scale Industry

The most recent data on large-scale industry publicly available in early 1976 were developed from a survey in 1970. The survey covered 294 manufacturing establishments from the largest, such as Aramco's refinery, to most of those hiring only ten people. The data available did not make it possible to isolate the oil refineries (see ch. 12).

The number of establishments producing various categories of products included seventy-seven food and beverage firms, sixty-six nonmetallic minerals, sixty-two metals and machinery, thirty-three paper and printing, twenty-two wood and wood products, fifteen chemicals and petroleum refining, and the remainder unspecified. These firms employed 12,600 workers. The bulk of the larger industries was in either the Eastern Province, particularly in the area of Dammam and Hufuf, or the western area, primarily Jiddah. The large Aramco refinery weighted the distribution of investments; the Eastern Province had nearly 70 percent of the capital but employed only 34 percent of the workers. The western area employed nearly 24 percent of the capital and 45 percent of the workers. The central region employed 7 percent of the capital and 20 percent of the workers. Other areas had almost no large industry even when the category required only ten workers in a plant to qualify. Although a substantial number of new manufacturing concerns had been established since the 1970 survey, the pattern probably had not changed much by 1975. Some notable products produced by the new plants were textiles and clothing, carpets, plastics and chemicals, and sanitary wares.

The 1970 survey found that most of the plants operated substantially below capacity. Underutilization averaged 64 percent for the plants surveyed. The reason the plants failed to operate near full capacity was not given but presumably included shortages of skilled manpower and materials, competition from imports, and limited domestic markets. The underutilization of capacity continued into the mid-1970s for some of the important industries.

Cement Industry

The three cement plants at Hufuf, Riyadh, and Jiddah form the country's second largest industry after petroleum refining. Capacity of the three plants was approximately 1.5 million tons annually. Production approximately doubled between FY 1970 and FY 1974, increasing from about 600,000 to 1.2 million tons. Domestic production supplied about 50 and 55 percent of cement consumption in 1970 and 1974 respectively. The building boom already in progress rapidly increased the price of cement, and the government had to import cement to ease the price in 1974 and 1975 (see ch. 11). It was not clear why cement production remained below capacity or why importers were slow in importing cement. There were a number of small factories using cement to produce pipes and blocks.

A sevenfold increase in cement capacity was planned for the 1975-80 period. The capacity of the existing plants was to be expanded about threefold, and six additional plants were to be built. The new plants were to be located in various parts of the country as part of the goal of balanced regional development. If the plan is implemented, capacity in 1980 will be over 10 million tons of cement a year.

Steel Industry

An integrated steel mill has been discussed for many years. The first phase was the construction of a rolling mill at Jiddah with a capacity of 45,000 tons of iron products a year based on three-shift operations. The mill began producing in 1967 using imported billets. Production rose slowly, amounting to 8,500 tons of reinforcing bars in FY 1970, about 13,000 tons in FY 1973, and 22,000 tons in FY 1974. Two-shift operations were not begun until 1974. The rolling mill was another example of underutilization of capacity.

The rolling mill was located in Jiddah in the expectation of eventually using iron ore located nearby (see ch. 3). After more than ten years mining of the low-grade ore in Wadi Fatima had not begun nor even been proved feasible, leaving the status of an integrated operation unclear.

The second development plan calls for feasibility studies to expand the Jiddah rolling mill to an annual capacity of 120,000 tons and to build another rolling mill along the Red Sea coast. The plan also calls for building a steel plant with an annual capacity of 3.5 million tons at the Jubayl industrial complex. Imported ore, possibly in slurry form carried in returning tankers, would be used to produce iron pellets by direct reduction with natural gas. Integrated operations would include a rolling mill for bars, shapes, and plates. Some of the production at various stages might be exported. In early 1976 negotiations appeared far advanced and involved 50-percent ownership by the government and 50 percent by a group of international companies, some of which were American.

Petrochemicals

Construction of a fertilizer plant was begun at Dammam in 1967 with a capacity of 300,000 tons of urea a year using natural gas as the feedstock. Production began in 1970 and by 1973 had reached 150,000 tons, most of which was exported because Saudi farmers used little fertilizers. In 1974 production reportedly approached capacity.

Although not the usual petrochemical plant, a sulfuric acid plant was constructed to process the sulfur recovered from crude oil production. The plant began operations in 1971 with a capacity of about 17,000 tons a year. Production reached 5,700 tons in 1972.

Construction of four separate ethylene-based petrochemical complexes was planned to begin during the second development plan period and to be completed in the 1980s; three will be in the Eastern Province and one on the west coast. Development was related to progress on the gas collection system and construction of pipelines to the western region.

Investment Policy

As in other parts of the economy, government policy is to encourage industrial development by private investors. The government undertakes projects reluctantly and primarily where project costs are too large to entice private entrepreneurs. Even in government projects join ventures with private companies, foreign or domestic, are encouraged.

A liberal foreign investment code was introduced in 1964. Full foreign ownership is possible, but at least 25-percent Saudi equity was required to qualify for some incentives. Industrial projects required a license, and license applications involving foreign capital were reviewed by a special committee consisting of representatives of most government agencies concerned with economic development. The Ministry of Industry and Electricity decided on the issuing of a license, usually on the basis of the committee's recommendation. An office in the ministry was established to provide all information and handle the paperwork associated with license applications involving foreign capital.

A government policy statement was issued in 1974 setting forth inducements to promote industrialization, particularly by private investors. The incentives applied to all Saudi enterprises and to those with foreign capital after specific approval. The major points included: provision of loans and equity participation; extension of assistance in preparation and evaluation of feasibility studies and other help in selecting and establishing industrial enterprises; exemption of imported equipment and raw materials from tariff duties; extension of preferential treatment of locally produced goods in government purchases and protection from competing imports; assistance in exporting products; provision of sites in industrial parks at nominal rents and granting of subsidies for training Saudi employees; and tax incentives. A major tax incentive was a five-year tax holiday for any new Saudi investment or new investment in which foreign capital was 75 percent ot less. The industrial parks at Riyadh, Jiddah, and Dammam were to be expanded and new ones developed at Jubayl and Yanbu to accommodate new investors.

The Saudi government's experience with American business had been generally favorable, and it anticipated making large purchases of equipment in the United States for the second development plan. The Joint Commission on Economic Cooperation, which was announced in June 1974, had the broad goal of expanding economic relations and the specific purpose of administering a technical assistance program for which the Saudis paid the costs. The commission produced, and both countries signed in February 1975, an investment guarantee agreement and a technical cooperation agreement, the latter to provide United States technical advisers for a variety of projects. United States-Saudi relations were close although the Saudi adherence to the League of Arab States (Arab League) boycott of some firms doing business with Israel created an irritant in the relations between the two countries in early 1976 (see ch. 10).

Planned Industrial Development

The sharp increase in oil revenue in the mid-1970s removed the financial constraints on industrial development. Money was available to finance any project thought desirable. The second development plan was prepared in this setting. Planned industrial investments amounted to the equivalent of nearly US$15 billion over the five years, excluding projects in electricity and transportation. Private investment would add substantial sums to the development of industry.

Although the government's long-term objective was to diminish dependency on the petroleum sectors, the focus of most investments between 1975 and 1980 was related to hydrocarbons. In the Eastern Province two export refineries and a lubrication oil refinery were planned to obtain the higher earnings from the export of petroleum products instead of crude oil. Construction of the gas-gathering system was to continue in order to supply three petrochemical complexes, two fertilizer plants, an aluminum smelter to produce 140,000 tons of ingots a year from imported alumina, and a steel plant to produce 3.5 million tons a year from imported iron ore by a direct reduction process with natural gas. Hydrocarbon development in the western region to the extent it proved feasible was to include an export refinery and a petrochemical complex as well as crude oil and gas pipelines to supply them. Discussions, negotiations, and some construction were under way by 1976. Many projects would not be completed until after the end of the second development plan in 1980.

The major industrial projects outside the petroleum sector were expansion of the cement industry and construction of three grain complexes in Dammam, Riyadh, and Jiddah. The grain complexes included unloading equipment, silos, flour mills, and mills to produce various livestock and poultry feed concentrates. The grain complexes eventually would store a six month's supply of grain. Some infrastructure projects, such as water desalinization and associated electricity generation, development of the industrial park at Jubayl, and expansion of the industrial parks at Riyadh and Jiddah, would facilitate private investments in manufacturing projects. License applications from private investors increased rapidly in 1974 and 1975.

Saudi officials admitted that the plan was extremely ambitious. Various constraints would hold up or delay implementation of some investments (see ch. 11). Detailed feasibility studies would probably cancel or reduce the size of some projects. Nonetheless most economists anticipated considerable expansion of the industrial sector during and after the second development plan period. Dependence on imports might not fall, but products made in Saudi Arabia would increase in local and world markets.

DOMESTIC TRADE

The Suq Tradition

The suq is the age-old Middle Eastern marketplace. In its historical development in Saudi Arabia most local markets were small because of long, arid distances separating communities. Craftsman, farmer, and nomad met at small weekly markets to exchange products. Few merchants participated in the weekly rural market. Barter was the usual method of exchange, and conversation was an integral part of the bargaining process.

Specialization by sellers was inherent in the ancient marketplace. The producer sold what he had produced. In larger markets or as time progressed, merchants emerged but usually confined themselves to a single product or a limited range of products. Specialty markets, such as the Hufuf Thursday morning camel and sheep market, were established, or general markets were subdivided into sections by commodity groups. Specialization in selling wares has persisted, even though urbanization has greatly enlarged the marketplace.

Conditions changed, but the suq tradition changed more slowly. Nevertheless by 1976 barter had given way to the use of money in most parts of the country. The merchant had replaced the producer as the seller of goods in most markets, and fixed prices rather than bargaining were becoming more common. Imported goods exceeded domestic products in many areas. Yet most trade was carried on by small shopkeepers relying primarily on family members if additional help was needed. A survey of commercial establishments in 1971 found that 72 percent were one-man businesses and that 97 percent consisted of four workers or fewer. Domestic trade was still largely organized in terms of small-scale producers, small markets, and small-scale merchants. Local products were usually poorly graded, sorted, and packaged. A network of wholesalers, retailers, and distribution centers was barely started.

Larger Merchants

There were exceptions to the preponderance of small-scale merchants. Several Saudi merchant houses developed, creating some of the wealthiest individuals in the kingdom. A few were merchant families of several generations, such as the Ali Reza family, probably the oldest Saudi merchant house, but most were newcomers to commerce. Two of the very wealthy merchants came to Saudi Arabia as houseboys from Oman. The growth of the businesses and the increased wealth of the merchants were primarily related to franchises for sales of the ever-increasing volume of imported goods.

The large-scale merchants tended to focus on a particular area. Aramco's purchases in the Eastern Province built up several wealthy merchant families who confined their operations largely to that province. The Ali Reza family had long been Hejaz merchants and have continued to concentrate on that locale. By 1976 there were not many merchants operating sales offices throughout the country. Smaller merchants handled sales in other regions.

The commercial firms usually did not specialize in particular lines of products, seeking instead the franchises they thought would prove profitable. Exceptions were three major firms that specialized in importing most of the kingdom's bulk foods. Nearly all of the merchants confined their activities to Saudi Arabia. Very few developed an overseas organization to conduct business in foreign countries. The leader of the organization frequently kept track of operations in his head and relied little on bookkeepers. Foreign observers noted that a large commercial firm with an accounting staff was the exception.

The company known as E.A. Juffali and Brothers is a classic example of the transition from rags to riches. The eldest brother raised the two younger brothers on a farm near Mecca. They opened a small shop to sell hides in the 1930s and subsequently stocked automobile tires in addition to their farming activities. They gained the first franchise for a city electric company in 1946 and the concession to supply electric power to Mecca in 1948. The brothers' association with the General Electric Company in establishing the power plants won them the franchise for General Electric products throughout the country, and during the 1950s they became sales representative for a number of other international corporations. Meanwhile they had established their head office in Jiddah and subsequently opened offices in at least six other major cities, breaking the pattern of local concentration followed by most of the other larger merchants. By early 1976 the brothers operated twenty-four industrial and commercial subsidiaries or affiliates in the country, including electric power companies and a cement plant at Dammam. The E.A. Juffali and Brothers conglomerate has been labeled the biggest, richest, and best managed of the Saudi merchant houses.

The Juffalis illustrated the merging of activities by most commercial families. Many obtained their wealth and influence from commerce but branched out into industrial and construction activities. In addition some of the families placed members in the government.

During 1975 allegations were made of large payments to a few of the major Saudi commercial firms by international companies seeking contracts with the government. Critics called the payments bribes and payoffs. Recipients defended the payments as legitimate commissions for services performed by their commercial organizations. In late 1975 the Saudi government outlawed payments to commercial agents for contracts between the government and international companies.

The Haj Trade

For many centuries the Muslim pilgrims visiting Mecca and Medina represented a source of income to be exploited by the people of the Hejaz, by the beduin tribes through whose territory the pilgrims passed, and by the government that claimed control over the holy area (see ch. 6). Even in the early years of the Saudi kingdom the taxes levied on pilgrims were a major revenue source for the central government and the primary source of foreign currencies (see ch. 2). Oil revenues eliminated the need to tax pilgrims, and the taxes were abolished between 1944 and 1952 (information from the Saudi government indicated differing dates). Haj-related revenue accruing to the government in the mid-1970s came only from charges for specific services, such as lodging on arrival at the port or airport and the transportation between Jiddah and Mecca. In the mid-1970s the government spent the equivalent of approximately US$50 million per pilgrimage and received only a fraction of that in return revenues.

One reason given by Abd al Aziz for his conquest of the Hejaz was to abolish the banditry, profiteering, and excessive taxation that made the pilgrimage so difficult for Muslims. The government has since improved conditions for pilgrims (see ch. 4). Substantial investments have been made in the mosques and sacred places near them and in the roads and facilities by which pilgrims arrive and depart. Nearly every department of government has tasks related to the pilgrimage. During the actual pilgrimage medical teams and field hospitals are set up, and thousands of policemen, national guardsmen, and boy scouts are deployed. Closed circuit television, helicopters, and two-way radios are used to help the pilgrims complete their pilgrimage. The Saudi government has become directly involved in supplying part of the services required by the pilgrims.

Supplying the food, water, and services required by pilgrims has long dominated the economy of the Hejaz. Each year as the haj season approached, economic activity increased and the general price level rose, a phenomenon common throughout any part of the world where a short tourist season supports many of the local inhabitants through most of the year. Prices charged the pilgrims used to be what the traffic would bear.

The government has made strenuous efforts to halt exploitation of pilgrims. In the mid-1970s the government set a number of prices, such as transportation charges to and from Mecca, rents for housing in Mecca, and the fees for guide services. Before the haj began, the price information was disseminated to the countries where the pilgrims originated. Some of the charges the government collected from pilgrims, such as those for transportation and guides, were paid by the government to the provider of the service, reducing the opportunity to overcharge. Not all abuses had been eliminated, but they had been substantially reduced. The government maintained facilities to follow up pilgrims's complaints of excessive prices or other problems.

The people of the Hejaz evolved a system long ago to care for the pilgrims, and the system remained essentially unchanged in the mid-1970s. At the center of the system was a master guide who took charge of a group of pilgrims whose language he could speak. The guide, supported by a staff, met and stayed with his pilgrims through the haj. The guide had contacts for housing and other supplies his pilgrims would need. This guide system numbered between 15,000 and 20,000 people in the early 1970s according to one estimate.

There were various organizations according to the kind of service rendered, but the master guides were organized into about eighty firms. The firms varied in size of staffs and standards, and their rates varied from the equivalent of less than US$100 to many thousands of dollars, depending on the services and accommodations to be furnished. In theory no one was ever denied a guide because of inability to pay. The guides had created the image that they were necessary for a pilgrimage, and they could not take the position that following the instructions of the Quran required money. The ease of travel has greatly increased the haj trade. The number of pilgrims increased sixfold in the 1950s and 1960s and doubled in the early 1970s. Nearly 1.25 million people made the pilgrimage in 1974. Caring for that many people under the circumstance of the haj is a logistical marvel. The visit extends little more than a week for many pilgrims, and in portions of the pilgrimage everyone moves en masse and must arrive at specific places at designated times. In 1974, for example, more than 66,000 vehicles carrying probably well over 1 million people were concentrated in less than a fifteen-mile stretch of road. The traffic problems so well known at large sporting events throughout the world are minimal in comparison.

By the mid-1970s supplying the materials and services for successful pilgrimages was primarily the responsibility of the merchants and people of the Hejaz under supervision and coordination by the government. Private firms imported and operated the vehicles necessary to transport the pilgrims. Merchants imported and purchased locally the perhaps 500,000 goats, sheep, and camels sacrificed during each haj. Merchants also stocked the food, trinkets, and other items they sought to sell to pilgrims. Some of the facilities, such as the haj airport built by the government at Jiddah, the haj housing at Mina, and reportedly the vehicles to carry the pilgrims, were used for only about one week each year (see fig. 9 on the rites of the haj, ch. 6). The transformation of the haj in less than fifty years from an arduous journey involving banditry and exploitation occurred primarily because of the policy and effort of the government.

****

Ramon Knauerhase in *The Saudi Arabian Economy* provides basic information on the various sectors of the economy. The Saudi *Development Plan 1395-1400 (1975-80)* contains considerable statistical data and discussion of economic strengths and weaknesses as well as plans for the future. Donald P. Cole's *Nomads of the Nomads* provides in very readable form his conclusions and insights on the beduin economic and social system. Michael Field in *A Hundred Million Dollars a Day* discusses the growth of financial institutions and wealthy families through the Persian Gulf. The article "The Hajj: A Special Issue" in *Aramco World* (November-December 1974) contains useful information concerning various aspects of the haj. (For further information see Bibliography.)

SECTION IV. NATIONAL DEFENSE

CHAPTER 14

NATIONAL DEFENSE AND INTERNAL SECURITY

In 1976 Saudi Arabia was one of the few nations to retain an absolute monarchy. The systems of national defense and internal security that were initiated by the country's first king, Abd al Aziz ibn Abd ar Rahman Al Saud, form the foundation on which the Saud dynasty rests. But the crystallization of effective organization and controls over Saudi Arabia's modern defense and security forces resulted from the policies of the country's third king, Faisal ibn Abd al Aziz Al Saud. Three organs of particular significance constitute the extremely centralized and comprehensive security system: the autonomous Royal Saudi National Guard, a paramilitary unit whose commander reports directly to the king; the Ministry of Defense and Aviation, responsible for the armed forces and civil aviation; and the Ministry of Interior, responsible for the remainder of the internal security forces, including the Public Security Police.

With the mission of ensuring Saudi Arabia's national defense, the armed forces in 1976 numbered nearly 50,000 men, including the Royal Saudi Army (the country's supreme armed force), the Royal Saudi Air Force, and the small Royal Saudi Navy. In the event of internal disorder the armed forces have the added mission of assisting in maintaining the internal security of the kingdom. In addition the National Guard, which numbered over 16,000 regulars in 1976, has the mission of supporting and assisting those forces responsible for national defense, although its primary mission is the maintenance of public order.

The armed forces and the National Guard were organized to counterbalance as well as to complement each other. A member of the Royal Saudi Army served as chief of staff of the armed forces under the authority of the minister of defense and aviation, who was directly subordinate to the king (see ch. 8). The king holds the traditional position of commander in chief of the armed forces. The National Guard was under the authority of a commander (head) appointed by and responsible only to the king. The remainder of the country's extensive security forces were directed by the minister of interior, who was also responsible to the king.

The kingdom has a clearly defined judicial system, based on sharia law but being modernized through decree law (see ch. 8). The House of Saud has rarely been threatened from within. An officer's rebellion in 1969 posed a brief threat to the government, but in 1976 there was no evidence of significant internal opposition or subversion. The assassination of King Faisal by one of his nephews in March 1975 was not viewed as a threat to the stability of the House of Saud (see ch. 8). As a monarchy surrounded by many nations who have overthrown monarchies, Saudi Arabia has been a target of propaganda campaigns attempting to undermine the Saudi government. During the early 1970s such activities decreased, however, probably because of Saudi initiatives to promote friendly relations with its neighbors and massive economic assistance to many of the country's former detractors.

Saudi Arabia's increasing wealth provided the government with the financial resources to modernize the military and public security forces, a project that has had a high priority since 1964, when Saudi Arabia faced its greatest external threat—its involvement in a civil war in Yemen—in 1976 the Yemen Arab Republic [Yemen (Sana)]. By early 1976 the capabilities of Saudi Arabia in national defense and internal security had been substantially improved, through more than a decade of foreign assistance for training, construction, and purchases of arms and equipment. Egypt, France, Pakistan, the United Kingdom, and others have provided differing levels of assistance, but Saudi Arabia has depended most on its close relationship with the United States in the area of security affairs.

ARMED FORCES, SOCIETY, AND POLITICS

In 1944 King Abd al Aziz created the office of the minister of defense and attached this first formal organization covering the development of the armed forces in Saudi Arabia to his own royal cabinet. It was not until 1953, however, that the present Ministry of Defense and Aviation was established as part of the country's first council of Ministers (see ch. 8). In 1951 a minister of interior was added to the royal cabinet, and in 1953 his office was established as the Ministry of Interior. These two important bodies plan, implement, and regulate the government's policies in the area of national defense.

The development of the military in Saudi Arabia started some time before the creation of these modern institutions, however. The years between 1902, when Abd al Aziz launched his campaign to regain power over most of the Arabian Peninsula for the House of Saud, and the appointment of the first defense minister were filled with turmoil and conflict that influenced the development of the kingdom's military and paramilitary forces.

Military Development in Saudi Arabia

Saudi Arabia was created in 1932 after the successful conquests of King Abd al Aziz. The first step in this process was the recapture of the country's present capital, Riyadh, in 1902; the surrounding province had been held by the Al Rashid lineage, the Saud dynasty's greatest rival. Victory depended not only on the size of Abd al Aziz' force or his strategy but on his charismatic personality and the support of the beduin tribes for the militant puritanism of the orthodox Islamic sect based on Wahhabism (see Glossary), and these factors established an important trend in the development of the military organization.

The loyalty of the beduin tribes in the Najd permitted the young Abd al Aziz to go from victory to victory, and by 1906 the loosely organized Saudi forces had regained control of the central Najd region. Abd al Aziz quickly realized that his future conquests would depend on a better organized force loyal to the House of Saud. He systematically sent Wahhabi missionaries to convince tribal leaders that their support and loyalty would be rewarded. Specifically Abd al Aziz requested that these tribes establish Ikhwan al Muslimin (Muslim Brethren) communities (*hujar*—see Glossary), based on the concept of religious brotherhood (see ch. 6). On the establishment of a community Abd al Aziz agreed to supply seed, farm tools, and money, as well as arms and ammunition; mosques, schools, and homes were also built in each settled community. In return for these supplies and services the tribal leaders agreed to supply Abd al Aziz with fighting men to support his campaign to unite the peninsula.

By 1913 Abd al Aziz' plan was so successful that he defeated a revolt of the Mutayr tribe and forced the remaining Turks out of eastern Arabia, for the first time using the Ikhwan forces to support his conquests. These victories gave Abd al Aziz access to the Persian Gulf coast between Kuwait and Qatar (see fig. 1). The Ikhwan communities were highly organized throughout the area and could be completely mobilized within ninety-six hours, with 25,000 men under arms, although usually no more than 5,000 men took part in a single action.

In October 1914 Abd al Aziz found himself on the side of the British, who declared war on Turkey on October 31, 1914. The Rashidis allied themselves with the Ottomans and with Ottoman assistance attacked deep within the Saudi territory. In January 1915 a battle was fought northeast of Buraydah with indecisive results; both sides withdrew and claimed victory. Negotiations with the British resulted in a treaty, signed in December 1915, by which the British recognized Saudi independence and the territorial integrity of the Najd and gave Abd al Aziz 1,000 rifles, a supply of ammunition, and 20,000 British pounds. A later agreement in late 1916 gave him a monthly subsidy of 5,000 pounds and a gift of 3,000 rifles with ammunition in exchange for his promise to keep 4,000 men in the field in his war with the Al Rashid.

The greatest success of the Ikhwan came with the conquest of the Hejaz. After World War I, when Hussein, the Hashimite king of the Hejaz, undertook defense negotiations with the Rashidi leaders, Abd al Aziz' reaction was swift and harsh. He sent Ikhwan raiding parties against Hail, which was captured in 1921. Emboldened by their successes, the Ikhwan disregarded Abd al Aziz' orders not to cross into Transjordanian territory. They raided and plundered several important oases in Transjordan, arousing the British allies of the Hashimite king of Transjordan to counterattack with aerial support and to decimate the Ikhwan raiders (see ch. 2).

During the early 1920s Abd al Aziz began the formation of an armed force separate from the Ikhwan forces and, when the undisciplined Ikhwan forces repeatedly moved on their own—as when they pillaged Taif and massacred several hundred of its inhabitants—Abd al Aziz used this new force to reassert his control over the Ikhwan. Under his command these forces occupied Mecca and laid siege to Jiddah and Medina, which he finally brought under his control in December 1925. This armed force, known in the present day as the National Guard, was often called the White Army.

For the next two years Abd al Aziz was primarily occupied with the development of a governmental organization to rule the vast territory he had conquered, but he also began to formalize plans for the establishment of the Royal Saudi Army. Meanwhile the Ikhwan, who had been forbidden to continue their raiding after 1925, began to organize again in response to Abd al Aziz' actions, which the Ikhwan interpreted as moves to modernize the newly formed country in contravention of their religious beliefs. These disenchanted Ikhwan leaders led a revolt against Abd al Aziz. After meeting with the rebel leaders and demanding their surrender, Abd al Aziz mobilized his regular troops to put down the rebellious Ikhwan.

While his troops were attempting to achieve these aims, Abd al Aziz was negotiating with the British for the purchase of four military airplanes and for British pilots to fly them. He was successful in this venture and at the same time acquired a fleet of some 200 automobiles and trucks, which he used to good advantage. He took to the field in person, and by the end of January 1930 the Ikhwan were soundly defeated, never to be a threat to the Saudi regime again.

Shortly afterward, however, the country was faced with a much greater problem—the first military intervention by a foreign force. A series of incidents in the 1931-32 period on the border with Yemen resulted in Yemeni forces occupying Najran, which lay inside Saudi territory. The invaders were thrown back in the spring of 1932, but negotiations for a settlement continued until April 1934, when Abd al Aziz decided to counterattack. He sent two army columns across the frontier into Yemen, the first commanded by Amir Saud ibn Abd al Aziz Al Saud, his oldest surviving son, and the second by Amir Faisal, his next oldest son. After successful campaigns both columns were ordered to hold their positions while a treaty was concluded at Taif (see ch. 2).

The remaining years of the 1930s were peaceful ones for Saudi Arabia, giving Abd al Aziz time to carry out his plans for the development of a military establishment. The organization of forces during this period was very similar to the arrangement in the mid-1970s. From the noble tribes, particularly of the Najd, that continued to support the House of Saud, the king recruited the manpower to build a strong national guard, the mainstay of the country's defense system (see ch. 7). These tribes also contributed men to the Royal Guard, an elite force whose sole mission was to safeguard the well-being of the royal family. The king also began recruiting from other loyal but lesser tribes to build up a regular army, and his plan was to have these two major forces complement and counterbalance each other. The Royal Saudi Army was not to achieve an equal ranking with the National Guard, however, until its reorganization and modernization was begun in the mid-1960s.

Neither of these forces saw action during World War II. Saudi Arabia remained neutral until February 1945, when Abd al Aziz declared war on Germany and Japan but made no contribution of troops to the war effort. Therefore when Abd al Aziz died in 1953, shortly after the establishment of the Ministry of Defense and Aviation, Saudi forces had had no real combat experience. The country was one of the founders of the League of Arab States (Arab League), however, and contributed a noncombatant battalion to the Egyptian section of the Arab forces during the Palestine war in 1948.

There was a great deal of skepticism throughout the Saudi population when the country's second king, Saud, succeeded his father (see ch. 2; ch. 8). But many people were worried more about the future of monarchical governments in the Arab Middle East than about whether Saud could continue to rule as well as Abd al Aziz had been able to. King Faruk of Egypt had been overthrown in July 1952; and by the time Saud took office, Egypt had a republican form of government, albeit one under military control. North and south of the boundaries of Saudi Arabia the remaining Arab royal families were in tenuous situations. The Hashimite kings of Jordan and Iraq and the royal family of Yemen (Sana) had to contend with many pressures both from within their countries and from outside agitation. These situations would produce many tense moments between Saudi Arabia and its regional neighbors during the 1950s and 1960s.

Gamal Abdul Nasser's forceful and derogatory broadcasts against the remaining royal regimes and his call for nationalist revolutions became even more inflammatory after Egypt's war with France, Israel, and the United Kingdom in late 1956. In April 1957 King Hussein of Jordan, threatened by Syrian forces on his northern border and claiming that his government was being undermined by the exhortations of Nasser, called on King Saud for direct military assistance. Saud at once sent a small armed unit to Amman to show support for Hussein's authority; the possibility of revolution in Jordan was abated through this show of force, although no armed conflict took place.

The next year, 1958, was very eventful for Saudi Arabia. In early 1958 the senior amirs of the royal family compelled Saud to transfer full executive powers to Crown Prince Faisal, who was already prime minister. Among other things Faisal began to seek ways to develop a viable military establishment (see Foreign Influence and Military Posture, this ch.). His efforts to produce a modern army took on increasing vigor in mid-1958 when King Faisal of Iraq, most of his royal family, the prime minister, and many others were killed during a violent military coup d'etat on July 14.

After the shock of these events had lessened, Saudi Arabia spent four peaceful years before embarking on the most significant military campaign in its short history as a state. In September 1962 an army coup led by Colonel Abdullah al Sallal against Imam Muhammad al Badr in Yemen (Sana) began a civil war in that country that was not resolved until 1969. Sallal was supported by Egypt and a group in Southern Yemen—in 1976 the People's Democratic Republic of Yemen [Yemen (Aden)]—called Free Yemenis. Imam Badr fled north and sought assistance from loyal tribes and from the king of Saudi Arabia. Within a short time the supporters of Imam Badr, called royalists, were fighting against Egyptian forces sent by Nasser.

Crown Prince Faisal, who had resigned all his executive powers in January 1961, decided that these events in Yemen left him no choice but to return to power as prime minister (see ch. 8). Faisal had three things in his favor as he planned what action to take concerning the civil war in Yemen (Sana): the support of the United States, the unquestioned loyalty of the Saudi armed forces and the National Guard, and the consensus of support of the royal family and religious leaders. Faisal quickly moved troops to the Yemen (Sana) border, announced his support for Imam Badr, and began assisting the royalists.

In November 1962 Egyptian aircraft penetrated Saudi Arabia and bombed some of its border villages. At Faisal's request the United States dispatched a squadron of F-100 aircraft to Saudi Arabia. Despite the strength and readiness of Saudi forces, however, Faisal favored disengagement of all forces rather than an offensive role for Saudi Arabia. Saudi-Egyptian relations reached a low point during November, and diplomatic relations were severed. Fighting between the royalists and republicans in Yemen continued until mid-1963, however, when a disengagement agreement was signed by Saudi Arabia and Egypt that provided for a United Nations truce observation mission to be sent to Yemen (Sana). Disagreement over the implementation of the agreement resulted in renewed hostilities before the end of 1963.

Because Saudi Arabia at this time faced many problems—both internal and external—King Saud was finally deposed in 1964 in favor of Faisal. Meanwhile the Soviet Union, which had been supporting the Egyptian and Yemen republican side in the war with arms and advisers, increased its commitments of military aid and assistance. One of Faisal's first major decisions as king was to modernize the military, and he began consultations with the United States and the United Kingdom as to the best means of achieving this objective.

Frustrated over the prolongation of the civil war, Faisal and Nasser again met in Jiddah. The resulting Jiddah Accord stated that Saudi Arabia would cease supplying the royalists with military aid and assistance and that all Egyptian troops would withdraw. The agreement was not immediately implemented, however, and for the next two years hostilities continued, although at a lower level.

The Saudi armed forces were not involved in armed conflicts after the Yemeni civil war, although during the June 1967 and October 1973 Arab-Israeli wars Saudi Arabia contributed some troops to support the Arab war efforts. In 1967 King Faisal sent into southern Jordan a brigade that remained there in 1976; the only other Saudi force deployed outside Saudi Arabia in 1976 was stationed at Kiswah, near Damascus, Syria, where it had been since October 1973.

When Faisal became king in 1964, he reorganized the entire military organization and named two of his half brothers to leadership posts in the area of national defense and internal security: Amir Fahd ibn Abd al Aziz Al Saud, minister of interior, and Amir Sultan ibn Abd al Aziz Al Saud, minister of defense and aviation; another half brother, Abd Allah ibn Abd al Aziz Al Saud, was retained as head of the National Guard. They organized the military and security establishment as it functioned in 1976 under King Khalid ibn Abd al Aziz Al Saud, who succeeded Faisal after the latter's assassination in March 1975.

Organization of the Armed Forces

In 1976 the mission of the armed forces in Saudi Arabia was the conventional one of safeguarding the integrity of the national boundaries (many of which were yet undefined) and protecting the country against foreign penetration and invasion. In times of severe internal disorder, however, the armed forces had the additional mission of assisting public security forces in the restoration of internal security. Furthermore the armed forces were complemented and counterbalanced, while performing these missions, by the paramilitary National Guard. Although the National Guard's primary mission was to maintain internal security, in times of grave national danger it would assist the armed forces in national defense. The National Guard, like the army, contained sections assigned to guard against possible military insurgencies.

The Military Authority

The reorganization of the Saudi government in late 1975 resulted in few changes in the areas of national defense, and the organs and functions of the numerous components of this system were much the same under Khalid in 1976 as they had been under Faisal (see ch. 8). The head (or commander) of the National Guard was Amir Abd Allah, and his half brother, Amir Naif ibn Abd al Aziz Al Saud, was minister of interior. In addition to his responsibilities in the area of public security, the minister of interior was responsible for the Frontier Force and the Coast Guard and thus an important figure also in the area of national defense (see fig. 17).

In 1976 the minister of defense and aviation was Amir Sultan, a full brother of Crown Prince Fahd and of Amir Naif (see ch. 8). The king, however, is the commander in chief of the armed forces, in keeping with a tradition set by Abd al Aziz. Other important persons in the ministry of defense and aviation included General Uthman al Humayd, the chief of staff (a position always held by a member of the Royal Saudi Army), and Vice Minister Amir Turki ibn Abd al Aziz Al Saud, another full brother of the crown prince.

The minister of defense and aviation exercises operational control and supervision over the Royal Saudi Army, the Royal Saudi Navy, and the Royal Saudi Air Force as well as control of civil aviation, including the country's national airline, Saudia. He is assisted by a vice minister, the chief of staff, and an office of military inspection. The chief of staff is responsible to the minister for the supervision of the activities of the army, navy, and air force. In a fashion similar to the organization of United States armed forces, the chief of staff is assisted by four staff directors responsible for personnel, intelligence, operations and training, and logistics.

Within the Ministry of Interior a deputy minister is directly responsible to the minister of interior for the supervision of the activities of the Frontier Force and the Coast Guard. The National Guard is an autonomous organ of government and is under the personal control of the king through a commander (head) personally selected and appointed by him.

Army, Navy, and Air Force

The Royal Saudi Army is the dominant armed force in Saudi Arabia. In 1976 it was made up of one armored brigade and four infantry brigades; each brigade contained three to four battalions and included approximately 5,000 officers and men. In addition to these major units there were six antiaircraft battalions, three artillery battalions, and one parachute battalion. Since 1965 the army has been equipped with a Hawk Air Defense System. In 1976 the system included ten surface-to-air (SAM) missile batteries.

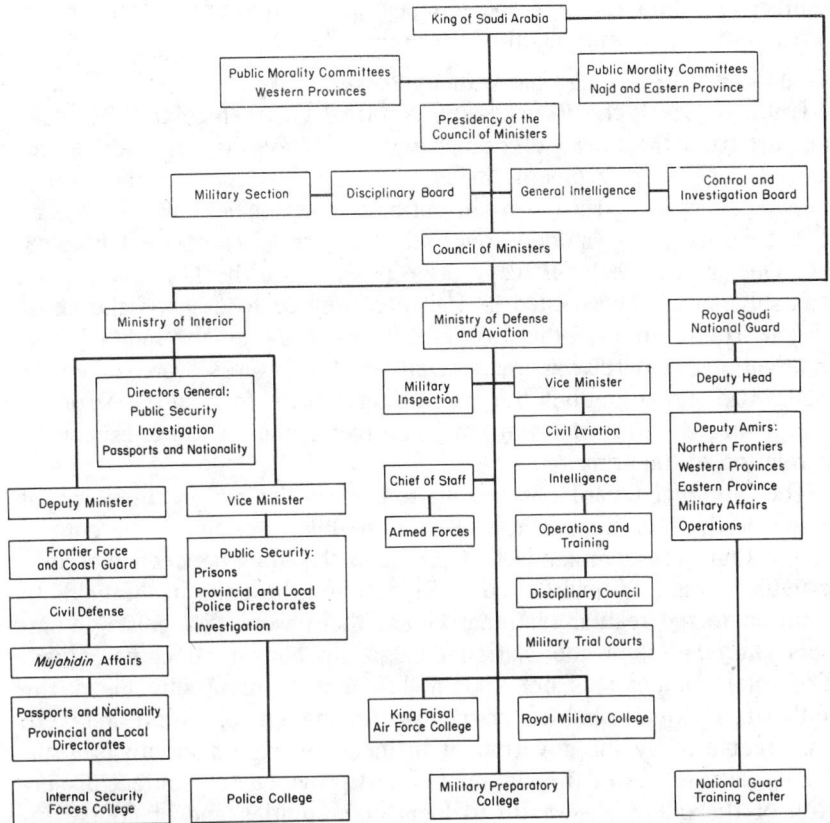

Figure 17. Saudi Arabia, Government Organization in the Areas of National Defense and Internal Security, 1975

The most visible unit of the army was the Royal Guard battalion, which had been an autonomous military unit until it was incorporated into the army in 1964. Members of the Royal Guard battalion accompany the king, as well as other senior members of the royal family, at all times. Their mission is the protection of the leadership of the House of Saud, and Royal Guard personnel are the elite of the armed forces.

The Royal Saudi Navy was the least developed of the armed forces in 1976; it was assisted in its duties by the Frontier Force and the Coast Guard. In contrast the Royal Saudi Air Force had made significant progress in both growth and sophistication since Faisal's 1965 decision to concentrate on its development. By 1976 the air force was made up of two fighter-bomber squadrons, two counterinsurgency training squadrons, two interceptor squadrons, two transport squadrons, and two helicopter squadrons.

The Saudi Arabian armed forces were divided into nine area commands, the boundaries of which were not clearly defined. Most of the military installations were located near the major cities or near the borders of neighboring countries (see fig. 18).

Royal Saudi National Guard and Auxiliary Forces

Until the 1960s the Royal Saudi National Guard received the most support from the king's office because of its role as defender of the security of the government. Its mission not only included promoting internal security and assisting in national emergencies but also meant that it served as a watchdog over all other armed forces in the country. During the 1960s, however, the position of the National Guard was substantially weakened as Faisal continued to develop the army and air force. In 1972 this loss of balance between the military and the National Guard was recognized, and measures were taken to modernize and strengthen this paramilitary force. In 1976 the National Guard seemed to be returning to its former equal standing, especially in relation to the army.

The National Guard has installations near the major cities and at many border locations. These were all mobile units under the control of the four area commands that provided the links between the commander of the National Guard in Riyadh and the units in the field. In addition to the regular National Guard there were "irregular" members (*mujahidin*) of the National Guard in almost all communities. The total number was not known, but they were usually under the authority of loyal tribal leaders (known as shaykhs or amirs) and were paid regularly by the government to meet one day a month (see ch. 7). These reserves of the National Guard provided for a direct dispersion of the country's wealth to local communities and of course increased the ability of the National Guard in times of emergency to deal with a threat to internal security anywhere in the country.

The Frontier Force and the Coast Guard, which are under the authority of the minister of interior, constitute the remaining auxiliary forces. Their assignments tend to be in such administrative affairs as managing the relations between settled and nomadic beduins, the organization of civil defense, and border and port security, including the problems of passport and nationality regulations. In 1976, however, these two units constituted a force greater in number than the Royal Saudi Navy and almost as large as the air force; hence they must be considered important segments of the whole Saudi security organization. As of early 1976 the Coast Guard had eight Hovercraft of the Winchester class (United Kingdom) and about twenty-five patrol boats.

ADMINISTRATION AND TRAINING OF THE MILITARY

Military Strengths and Overall Costs

It was estimated that in 1965 the Royal Saudi Army and the National Guard each numbered 18,000 men. By 1976 those estimates had

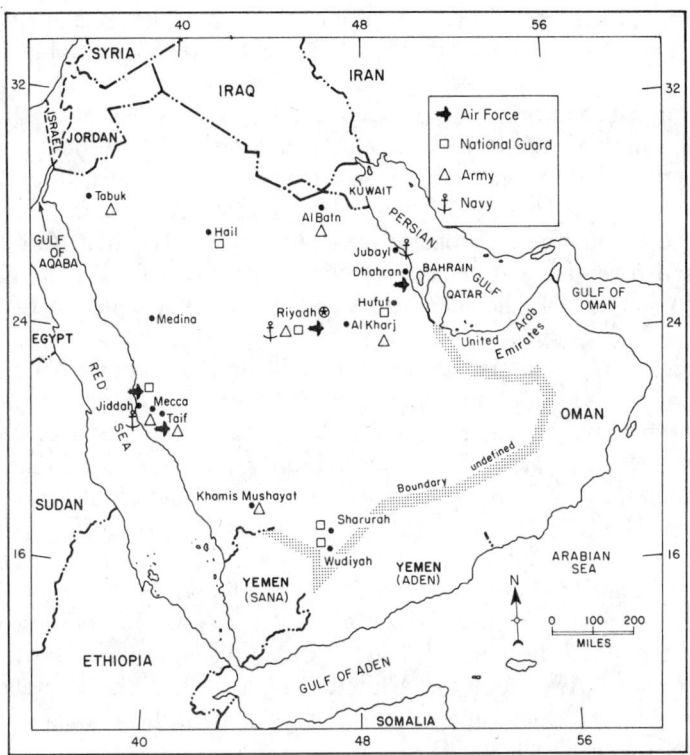

Figure 18. Saudi Arabia, Major Military and National Guard Installations, 1975

changed substantially: the army, including officers and enlisted personnel, numbered over 40,000 men, and the National Guard was estimated to have 16,000 regulars on active duty. These estimates and others used throughout this chapter (unless otherwise noted) are from the most current reports prepared by the International Institute for Strategic Studies, the Stockholm International Peace Research Institute, or the United States Department of Defense. Like many of the statistics in other chapters, those presented here should always be considered estimates, although statistics on national defense are carefully scrutinized by the organizations noted.

In addition to the army and the National Guard the remaining personnel involved in national defense and internal security in 1976 were 1,500 in the Royal Saudi Navy, 5,550 in the Royal Saudi Air Force, and a total of 6,500 in the Frontier Force and the Coast Guard. No estimates exist as to the number of reserves that are available.

In 1961 defense expenditures and purchases of arms and matériel accounted for 14 percent of total government expenditures; by 1975 they had increased to over 20 percent of a vastly enlarged government budget. It is calculated that total national defense costs increased by 306 percent from 1969 through 1974. The increase from 1972 to 1973 alone was 41.7 percent; from 1973 to 1974 it was 59.3

percent. Saudi Arabia has increased its defense budget almost to the same degree that its oil revenues have skyrocketed (see table 15; ch. 11).

A large proportion of the defense expenditures has been allocated to the purchase of massive amounts of arms and matériel, primarily from the United States but also from other countries, especially France and the United Kingdom. These purchases began after World War II and increased steadily until the mid-1960s when, through increased revenues and because of the decisions of Faisal, the country rapidly undertook the modernization of its entire military establishment.

Each of the military services, as well as the auxiliary forces, has been affected by the modernization of the national defense system. In 1976 the army had at its command numerous armored vehicles, including AMX-20 armored vehicles (France), M-47 Patton tanks (United States), M-41 Walker Bulldog light tanks (United States), and Panhard AML-60 and AML-90 tanks (France). Beginning in 1964 Saudi Arabia was most interested in installing an effective SAM system and in 1966 signed an agreement with the Raytheon Corporation (United States) to purchase their MIM-23A Hawk SAMs. In addition to this system in 1976 the country had on order the improved Hawk SAM, the Rapier SAM from the United Kingdom, and the Crotale SAM from France. Numerous other infantry and artillery weapons were part of the army's arsenal.

Table 15. *Saudi Arabia, National Defense, Strength and Overall Costs, Fiscal Years 1971-76*

Year	Budget Expenditures		Total Revenues	Armed Forces Manpower[2] (in thousands)
	Total	National Security and Defense (in billions of riyals)[1]		
1971	6.5	0.9	6.4	41.0
1972	10.8	1.1	10.8	40.5
1973	13.7	1.4	13.2	42.5
1974	22.8	1.8	39.5	43.0
1975	45.7	2.3	94.9	47.0
1976[3]	110.9	3.9	86.7	n.a.

n.a.—not available.
[1] For value of the riyal—see Glossary.
[2] Figures do not include the Royal Saudi National Guard manpower, which held stable at 16,000 regulars during these years.
[3] Saudi Arabian government estimates.

Source: Based on information from Saudi Arabian Monetary Agency, *Annual Report, 1394-1395 A.H.*, Jiddah, 1975; Saudi Arabian Monetary Agency, *Statistical Summary*, No. 2, Dammam, 1975, p. 59; and "Saudis Will Cut Spending to Cool Economy," *Middle East Economic Digest*, London, 20, No. 10, March 5, 1976, p. 29.

Saudi Arabia, however, has moved most rapidly in purchases of aircraft and had a small but modern air defense system by 1976. The aircraft available for service included Northrop F-5E Tiger II aircraft (United States), BAC-167 Strikemaster aircraft (United Kingdom), BAC Lightning F-52 and F-53 aircraft (United Kingdom), and Lockheed C-130 Hercules aircraft (United States). In addition the air force maintained a BAC Thunderbird I SAM system and two helicopter squadrons equipped with Agusta-Bell 206A Jet Ranger (Italy) and Agusta-Bell 205 Iroquois (Italy) helicopters. The annual issues of *The Military Balance* (International Institute for Strategic Studies) and of *World Armaments and Disarmament: SIPRI Yearbook* (Stockholm International Peace Research Institute) provide reliable estimates of the military equipment possessed by almost all countries, including Saudi Arabia.

The weapon strength of the National Guard in 1976 was difficult to ascertain from documents available to the public but, because of its relationship to the royal family and its function as a counterweight to the army, one can assume that the guard was adequately equipped to carry out its mission. Beginning in 1975 the United States-based Vinnell Corporation was awarded a US$77 million contract to train the National Guard in an attempt to modernize its methods. This was the first time a private contractor was publicly responsible for training, instructing, and equipping foreign troops.

Saudi Arabia is entirely dependent on foreign powers for equipment and weapons. In May 1974 the Arab Defense Council of the Arab League approved the creation of the Egyptian-proposed Organization for Sophisticated War Industries (OSWI), which in 1976 was headquartered in Cairo. The slowness with which this organization moved to establish a military weapons industry, however, caused a coalition of Arab states—Egypt, Saudi Arabia, Qatar, and the United Arab Emirates—to set up the Arab Military Industries Organization (AMIO) on May 10, 1975.

This organization was also headquartered in Cairo, primarily because Egypt was the only country that had a significant capability in military production. Because military weapons factories, experienced Egyptian labor, and ample supplies of iron and steel (produced in Egypt) were available, Cairo was seen as a natural choice. In 1976 Egypt's military production factories were manufacturing Al Zafir missiles and a variety of small arms, and AMIO was negotiating a contract to assemble British military aircraft in Egypt. Saudi Arabia's major role in the organization was probably that of its principal financial supporter, in hopes that the country would be less dependent on foreign military purchases in the future.

Manpower, Recruitment, and Training

Although manpower resources in Saudi Arabia were sufficient to meet the needs of the armed forces in 1976, many young Saudis were being attracted to private employment as a result of the country's economic prosperity, which posed a potential conflict with the plans of the armed forces to increase their size. The government had not resorted to conscription, however. All service was voluntary, and recruits enlisted for three-year periods. Recruiting stations were located in the larger towns and cities, and notices were sent to tribal communities when necessary.

Recruiting for the regular armed forces is carried out nationwide, not restricted to any particular region. As a result military personnel constitute a fairly representative cross section of the population. In contrast the National Guard is recruited from the beduin tribes in the areas in which they will serve. The four area commands (or the four brigades of the National Guard) are based on the country's four basic regions, and each is composed of recruits from the tribes within these regions.

Saudi beduin are generally characterized as tough and courageous. They are accustomed to the harsh climate of their country, make excellent desert fighters, and endure hardships stoically. After Abd al Aziz suppressed tribal warfare in the early decades of the twentieth century, the martial spirit of the tribes was lessened, but they have continued to take pride in their ability to exist in the desert and consider themselves superior to those who lead sedentary lives (see ch. 7).

Of the estimated population of 5.6 million in 1976, about 1.5 million were males between the ages of fifteen and forty-nine; it was estimated that 804,000 were physically fit for military service. Almost 64,000 reach military age (eighteen) annually, and manpower requirements for the military were being met without adverse effects on industry or agriculture.

A career as an officer in the armed forces was open to any young man who was able to meet the requirements for a commission. These were that a candidate either be a native-born citizen or have been a naturalized citizen for at least five years and be at least eighteen and in good physical and mental health. Further, he must be of good reputation and must neither have been subjected to any penalty under sharia law nor have been imprisoned for a felony within the previous five years.

Military training was extensive throughout the armed forces and was patterned after that in the United States armed forces, at least in part because of the close relationship over a twenty-five-year period between the two countries. Training was specifically a function of the training section of the operations and training office in the Ministry of Defense and Aviation. Since the beginning of each of the armed services, Saudi Arabia has depended on foreign countries for training guidance in the use of modern weapons and maintenance. Egypt, Pakistan, the United Kingdom, France, and the United States have all assisted at various times in the reorganization and training of the regular armed forces, but in 1976 the United States was the primary country giving such assistance. The National Guard, assisted in the past by the British in its training, was being modernized in 1976 with the assistance of a private corporation based in the United States (see Foreign Influence and Military Posture, this ch.).

The rank structure of the Saudi armed services corresponds generally to that of the United States armed forces, and the United States equivalents are usually used in translation into English. The Arabic names for all ranks are the same in all the services. Military officials called officer clerks (*katib*) are integrated at all staff levels of the army. They are known as "white rank officers" because their insignia of rank is white rather than the red and gold of regular army officers.

Seniority is determined from the date of commission. If the original commission is at a rank higher than second lieutenant, seniority is determined from the date of appointment but is below that of regular promotions of the same date. Newly appointed second lieutenants serve on probation for two years; if their performance has been unsatisfactory, they are transferred to another unit for an additional probationary period of one year. If they are still considered unsatisfactory officers, those commissioned from warrant officer or noncommissioned grades revert to their former ranks, and others are separated from the service.

Efficiency reports are rendered by commanding officers every six months on second lieutenants on probation and once a year on all others up to the rank of brigadier general. An officer who receives an unsatisfactory efficiency report is so informed and given two weeks in which to submit his rebuttal or explanation. The matter is then referred to the officers' committees, which have been established within the Ministry of Defense and Aviation to handle personnel affairs. The committees are responsible for appointment and promotion, retiring and recalling to active duty, recommending the granting of awards and decorations, appointments to key positions, transfers, selection of officers for chiefs of military schools, selection of candidates for military missions, and the granting of educational leaves.

The military school system is under the direction of the Army School Command. The schools in operation in 1976 offered instruction in flying, operations, communications and electronics, maintenance, logistics, administration, orientation-observer, and missiles. Most service schools offered basic and advanced courses of instruction for both officers and enlisted personnel. As the number of Saudi officers trained in the United States increased, so did the effectiveness of the instruction offered at the service schools.

Service schools frequently operated below capacity, however, because of a shortage of qualified students resulting from the generally low level of education throughout society, but this condition was improving because the number of public schools had increased since the mid-1960s (see ch. 5). In addition the government operated a number of basic military schools in the larger cities that offered a free education in elementary and intermediate subjects to prepare young men for service in the armed forces. The Military Preparatory School in Riyadh was open to young men who agreed to enter the Royal Military College and become officers. Young Saudis were attracted to these military schools because students attending them received free board, lodging, and uniforms plus a small monthly allowance in cash.

The Royal Saudi Air Force also has a school of higher education, the King Faisal Air Force College; the navy had plans for establishing an academy. Both of the military colleges offer three-year courses of instruction including academic and military subjects. As an autonomous armed force the National Guard provides training for its personnel, which includes areas of formal training offered at the National Guard Training Center.

Military Ranks, Pay, and Awards

Saudi Arabian uniforms and rank structures show the legacy of long association with the armed services of the United Kingdom and the United States. The headgear of many units throughout the armed forces identifies more accurately the roles filled by specific individuals. The Royal Guard battalion of the Royal Saudi Army, for example, wears a red beret, but all other enlisted men wear a dark green beret. Officers in the army, according to their rank, wear distinctive headgear that is styled after the British. The navy and air force wear white and blue uniforms respectively; the officer ranks of the air force have a tan lightweight uniform.

In contrast to the military dress are the traditional styles still used as optional uniforms by the Royal Guard and the National Guard; both wear the *thaub* (robe) and *kaffiyah* (headgear). These are both usually solid white in the Royal Guard; but the National Guard, who wear either a white *thaub* (from which the notion of "White Army" arose) or a simple brown uniform similar to that of the army, wear a *kaffiyah* that is red and white checkered. Special uniform items are provided for certain members of the armed forces, such as tank or aircraft crewmen, according to their special functions; these are mainly styled after those of the United States.

The armed services use a grade structure based on the superiority of the army. The chief of staff of the armed forces, a position that can only be held by the army, holds the rank of general (*fariq awwal*). There are fifteen remaining ranks open to army personnel—sixteen counting the lowest recruit entry level (*jundi*) during basic training.

The air force has the same rank structure, but the general of the air force cannot be appointed chief of staff. Saudi Arabia's very small navy has a rank structure that is equal to that of the army and air force except that the highest rank is absent (see fig. 19; table 16). In practice the ranks of General of the Army and General of the Air Force had not been used as of early 1976.

In addition to a monthly base pay, members of the armed forces receive certain allowances that make them at least as well paid as most other government services. In the mid-1970s Saudi officers and enlisted men were probably the best paid of any military personnel in the Arab countries. In addition members of the armed forces and their dependents receive free medical and dental care and hospitalization at military installations, a few of which have special military hospitals.

Pay increases are provided every two years for all officer grades from second lieutenant to colonel until a maximum for the grade is reached, at which the officer remains until promoted. All officers receive living, clothing, and housing allowances. There are also special allowances for those officers in certain positions of command or those who perform hazardous duties. Warrant officers also receive living, clothing, and housing allowances. Noncommissioned officers and other enlisted ranks qualify for special allowances, which are classified into sixteen categories according to skills.

All Saudi military awards are classified as decorations, achievement medals, or medals. Decorations carry a monetary award that is paid to the recipient for the rest of his life. Decorations include the King Abd al Aziz Al Saud Decoration and the National Military Decoration. Achievement medals include the Efficiency Medal, the Medal of Merit, and the Appreciation Medal. Medals include the Long Service and Good Example Medal, the Exceptional Promotion Medal, and the War Wounded Medal. All military decorations and medals are awarded by approval and order of the king. The same approval is required for the acceptance of a foreign decoration by a member of the armed services.

Military Justice

Military justice for the armed forces is regulated by the Code of Military Justice, decreed and published by the Ministry of Defense in 1947. It is applicable to all members of the armed forces and all retired personnel and civilians connected with the armed services who commit crimes or offenses of a military nature. In 1976 military trial courts under the authority of the Minister of Defense and Aviation had jurisdiction over military or political offenses committed by persons subject to the military code. Crimes in violation of the sharia, however, were under the jurisdiction of the sharia law courts (see ch. 8).

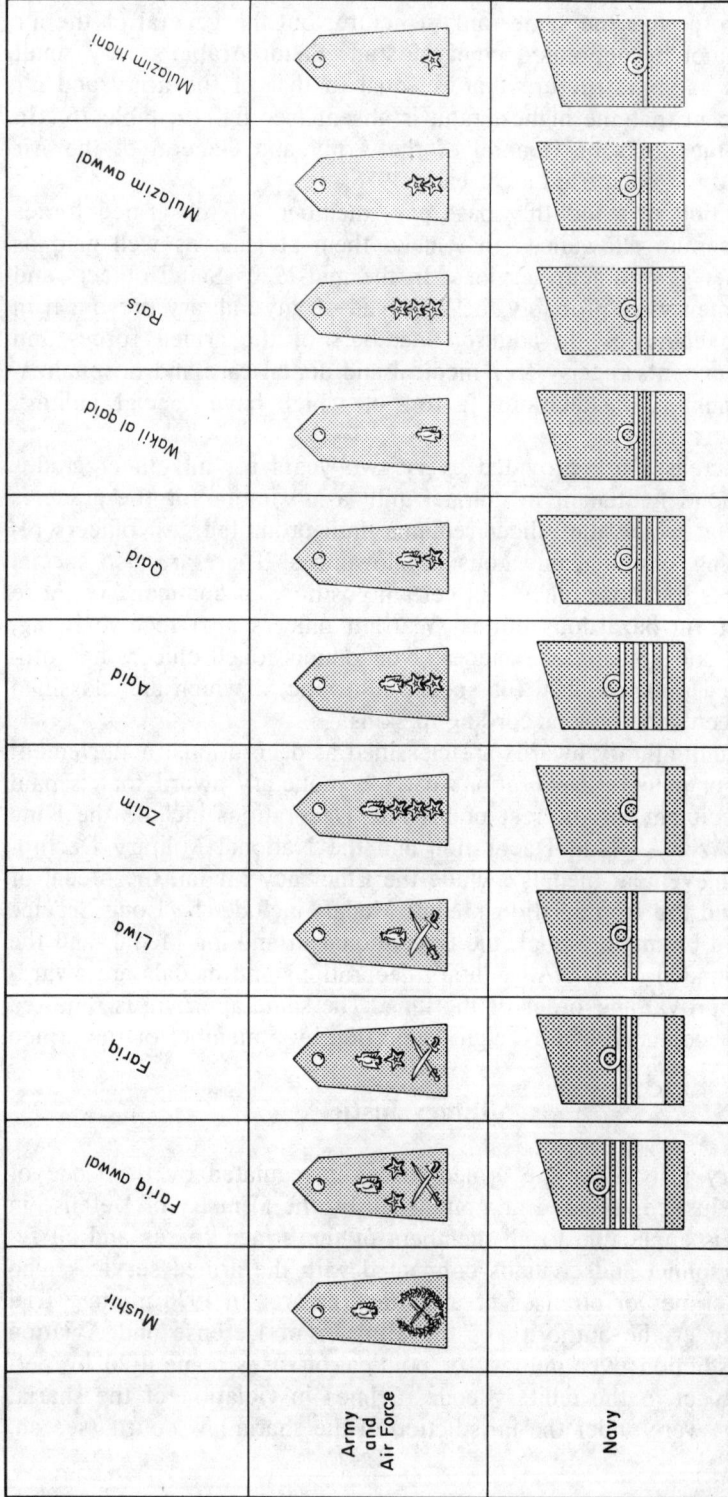

Figure 19. Saudi Arabia, Insignia of Officer Ranks, 1976

Table 16. Saudi Arabia, Titles of Military Rank, 1976

Arabic Name	Army	United States Equivalent Navy	Air Force
Mushir	General of the Army	.....[1]	General of the Air Force
Fariq awwal	General	Admiral	General
Fariq	Lieutenant General	Vice Admiral	Lieutenant General
Liwa	Major General	Rear Admiral (upper half)	Major General
Zaim	Brigadier General	Rear Admiral (lower half)[2]	Brigadier General
Aqid	Lieutenant Colonel	Commander	Lieutenant Colonel
Wakil al qaid	Major	Lieutenant Commander	Major
Rais	Captain	Lieutenant	Captain
Mulazim awwal	First Lieutenant	Lieutenant (junior grade)	First Lieutenant
Mulazim thani	Second Lieutenant	Ensign	Second Lieutenant
Wakil mumtaz	Warrant Officer	Warrant Officer	Warrant Officer
Wakil sariya	Master Sergeant	Senior Chief Petty Officer	Senior Master Sergeant
Naib	Sergeant	Petty Officer 2d Class	Staff Sergeant
Arif	Corporal	Petty Officer 3rd Class	Sergeant
Jundi awwal	Private 1st Class	Seaman	Airman 1st Class

[1] There is no rank equivalent to Admiral of the Fleet.
[2] Rear Admiral (lower half) replaces the former rank of Commodore.

A military trial court is composed of senior officers in good standing and includes a president and four other voting members, a legal adviser, a recorder, and a recorder representing the defendant. The president is the highest ranking member of the court and must be either of higher rank than the defendant or senior in grade if of the same rank. Trial procedures are direct and uncomplicated, and trials are conducted so as to give the benefit of the doubt to the defendant. A case is brought to trial only after a thorough and impartial investigation and the submission of a complete report of the alleged incident. The court's decision may be invalidated or commuted either by the minister of defense and aviation or by the king for irregularities, omissions, evidence of prejudice, or evidence that pressure was brought to bear. The king and the minister have the sole rights of review of sentences imposed by the trial court, and subject to their concurrence the judgments of the trial court are final.

Punishable offenses are classified as felonies, misdemeanors, or disobediences. Felonies and misdemeanors are subject to trial by a military court and upon conviction are punishable by severe or disciplinary punishments as prescribed. Disobediences are less serious offenses and are punishable administratively.

Military felonies include high treason against the kingdom and disloyalty to the country or the armed forces. Severe punishments are meted out to those found guilty of such offenses. The king alone has the right to execute the sentences of the court or to dismiss, commute, or mitigate punishment in conformity with the laws.

Military misdemeanors meriting the imposition of disciplinary punishment include such acts as misbehavior in wartime, misuse of authority, misuse of military funds or equipment, agitation for leaving the service, and violation of military regulations and directives. Disciplinary punishments include imprisonment for up to eighteen months and forfeiture of pay for from one to three months.

Disobediences or failures to obey orders are punished administratively. Punishments, which range from forfeiture of one day's pay and imprisonment for twenty-four hours to imprisonment for forty-five days, are scaled according to the seriousness of the offense.

FOREIGN INFLUENCE AND MILITARY POSTURE

Saudi Arabia was, until the early 1960s, a closed society often referred to as the "Islamic island." In response to the real external threat apparent in the country's involvement in the Yemeni civil war, however, the need to establish an effective system of deterrence was quickly realized. In the mid-1970s it was hard to imagine that Saudi Arabia had ever been in dire need of military assistance in the form of aid and grants, but this was true throughout the 1950s and remained so until the late 1960s. By 1976 the Saudi government had adequate funds to purchase virtually anything it desired, although other, noneconomic factors still interfered with the country's goal of expanding its military establishment.

Saudi Arabia remained dependent on foreign technical help for military training, construction of facilities (including the improvement of the country's basic economic infrastructure), and weapons supplies. This situation was compounded by such sociopolitical realities as the small size of the population on which the military depends for its manpower, the maintenance of two counterbalancing armed forces (the military and the National Guard), and the weak military position of the country vis-à-vis some of its neighbors.

There are other facets to the situation, however. First Saudi Arabia contains the two holiest shrines of the Islamic faith (see ch. 6). Further the country has achieved international power and status, particularly since the October 1973 War, because of its immense economic influence on many nations (see ch. 10; ch. 12). Finally a high degree of internal stability has existed at least since the mid-1960s (see Internal Security, this ch.). All of these facts must be considered in an assessment of Saudi Arabia's military posture in the region, its reliance on foreign assistance, and its attitudes toward military buildup and disarmament.

Military Aid and Assistance

Until the 1930s Abd al Aziz, concerned with conquest and the establishment of a country, showed little interest in developing a strong national defense system, relying instead on British support and diplomacy. With the discovery of oil and the first clash with the country's southern neighbor, Yemen, in 1934, one of the first goals of the new king was to build an army. He sought advice from Egypt, the United Kingdom, and the United States on how best to approach this problem. By the mid-1940s, however, Saudi Arabia began to rely more on the United States than on any other foreign power. This was a result of successful relations between the United States and Saudi Arabia as experienced through the Arabian American Oil Company (Aramco) as well as new tensions in Saudi Arabian-British relations over the Buraymi Oasis dispute (see ch. 10).

In June 1975 United States Under Secretary of State for Political Affairs Joseph J. Sisco told a House of Representatives subcommittee:

> In the security and defense field, we have conducted for the Saudis comprehensive surveys of their military requirements on two occasions in recent years, taking into account the threat they perceive to their national security and their limited manpower resources. Our cooperative effort has been to assist the Saudis to achieve several objectives which they see as critical to their own defense system: modernization and training of the ordnance corps; upgrading of their air force through acquisition of F-5E aircraft; building a small force of naval patrol craft; modernizing elements of the National Guard to improve its capabilities to protect key installations; and

construction of military infrastructure facilities. Our programs have been clearly related to Saudi Arabia's capacity to absorb the equipment it purchases. Because training, maintenance, and the construction of the physical plant to use the equipment are such a major portion of our defense-related activities in Saudi Arabia, and because these programs are stretched out over a period of many years, the cost figures involved are often many times higher than would be the case in a purchase of hardware.

The first United States military mission of any consequence arrived in Saudi Arabia in July 1943, but the first significant mutual defense agreement was not formalized until June 18, 1951 (see table 17). Saudi Arabia then became part of the United States government's Military Assistance Program (MAP) and by 1976 had become one of the largest participants in this program. As a result of the 1951 agreement the United States Military Training Mission (USMTM) arrived in Saudi Arabia in 1953. (Such missions were regularly known as the Military Assistance and Advisory Group (MAAG) in foreign countries but, because Saudi Arabia balked at the reference to "assistance," the United States altered the name of the group in Saudi Arabia to USMTM.)

Nevertheless the Saudi Arabian government under King Saud (reigned 1953-64) was continually faced with deficit budgets despite increasing oil revenues, and the country received both military aid and assistance from the United States during these years. Since at least the late 1960s Saudi Arabia has had no need for military aid and has paid for purchases and services in conjunction with its military imports programs. For military equipment and training Saudi Arabia in 1976 depended not on the United States alone but on a number of other countries as well—especially France and the United Kingdom.

The first major takeoff point in Saudi attempts to modernize the armed forces and the National Guard as well as the beginning of a trend toward increasing arms purchases came in 1964 when King Faisal deposed his brother, King Saud. Since that time the United States and others have effectively changed the military posture of the country through ever-growing training and construction programs; some of the training of the Saudi military personnel is done abroad, mostly in the United States. The supply of arms, which started gradually, began to increase very rapidly during the 1970s.

Three groups have been involved in the implementation of United States-Saudi Arabian military agreements: the United States Department of Defense, including the Corps of Engineers; private subcontractors to the United States government; and private corporations awarded contracts by the Saudi Arabian government. American citizens, both military and civilian, have performed important functions in the development of the national defense organizations in Saudi Arabia. It was estimated that in mid-1975 there were just over 16,000 Americans in Saudi Arabia, of whom almost 15,000 were employees and dependents of private concerns and about 1,500 were employees in defense-related occupations. In mid-1975 five major United States corporations accounted for most of the defense-related employees: Lockheed, 301; Northrop, 389; Raytheon, 346; Bendix, 166; and Vinnell, 200. In comparison were about 500 United States government employees, of whom fewer than 300 were military.

Estimates in early 1976, however, were that the number of Americans had grown to as many as 23,000 and might reach 35,000 by 1980. The relatively low number of military advisers was related to the fact that the Saudis had become competent in carrying out many of their own training functions and also that Saudi Arabia had begun awarding direct contracts to American corporations for assistance in training, construction, and maintaining necessary weapons and equipment. These direct contracts, which were intended to reduce the role of the United States government in providing training and weapons and return this role to the commercial channels more typical of the 1960s, were actually awarded to private concerns by the United States Department of Defense under the United States Foreign Military Sales Act.

The first major contract in this category was awarded to the Vinnell Corporation for a three-year (US$77 million) program to train the National Guard and to construct new facilities for the guard. In March 1976 a US$1.5 billion contract to build extensive new facilities for the Royal Saudi Air Force was awarded to the Northrop Corporation, probably the most substantial agreement ever concluded in the evolution of United States-Saudi Arabian cooperation in security affairs.

These major contracts, plus numerous others designed to modernize every unit of Saudi Arabia's security system, contributed to the close ties between the two countries. Although relations remained intact during the October 1973 War, the structure of these relations changed. Saudi Arabia feared a halt of United States assistance and arms sales, and the United States feared an oil embargo. As a result Secretary of State Henry A. Kissinger and Amir Fahd (in 1976 the crown prince) met on June 8, 1974, in Washington and prepared and signed an important document that established the Joint Commission on Security Cooperation (JCSC), which held its first meeting in Riyadh in November 1974 to review recommendations for the security needs of Saudi Arabia for the years 1975 to 1985 (see ch. 10). This time period marked Saudi Arabia's second major takeoff period for military development (the first was the previous decade, 1964 to 1974).

Although the United States has been the dominant foreign influence in the development of a modern military establishment in Saudi Arabia, the Saudi government has always felt that it should not depend solely on a relationship with a single nation and has turned to other nations as sources of arms, equipment, and training. In addition United States-Saudi Arabian relations with respect to military affairs have

Table 17. Saudi Arabia, Chronology of Saudi Arabia-United States Military Relations and Saudi Arabia's Major Arms Purchases, 1943-76

Date	United States Military Cooperation with Saudi Arabia	Date	Major Arms Purchases
1943	United States mission arrives in July to determine Saudi requirements for military equipment and training		
1944	First United States military training mission arrives in April		
1946	Dhahran airfield completed		
1951	Dhahran Air Base Agreement and Mutual Defense Assistance Agreement signed June 18		
1953	Agreement to establish United States military mission signed June 27		
1955	Saudis purchase in August first United States tanks and subsequently reject Soviet arms offer		
		1956-58	55 M-47 Patton tanks (United States)
			58 M-41 Walker Bulldog light tanks (United States)
			12 F-86 Sabre aircraft (United States)
1957	Dhahran Air Base Agreement renewed in February in exchange for continued military assistance; training starts for Royal Saudi Air Force, and first F-86 jets delivered		
1963	United States Air Force interceptors temporarily stationed in Dhahran as deterrent after Egypt bombs three Saudi towns in January; Saudis initiate discussions for acquisition of modern air defense system		
		1964	300 BAC Vigilant missiles (United Kingdom)
1965	Agreement signed June 5 for United States Corps of Engineers to supervise construction of military facilities Initial sales contract for C-130 aircraft signed in September Letter of intent signed with Raytheon in December for Hawk Air Defense System and British Lightnings	1965-67	6 Hawker Hunter FGA-9 aircraft (United Kingdom)
			9 BAC Lightning F-52 and T-54 aircraft (United Kingdom)*
			37 BAC Thunderbird I (SAM) missiles (United Kingdom)
1966	Saudi Arabian mobility program signed		

334

Year	Event	Equipment/Details
1968	United States conducts initial survey of Saudi naval expansion requirements	150 Raytheon MIM-23A Hawk missiles (United States)
		40 BAC Lightning F-53 and T-55 aircraft (United Kingdom)
1968-69		25 BAC 167 Strikemaster aircraft (United Kingdom)
		220 Panhard AML-90 armored vehicles (France)
1971	Letters of offer for F-5 aircraft signed in July and September Royal Saudi National Guard modernization request received in September	8 Hovercraft (United Kingdom)
1972	Agreement on naval modernization program signed in February	
1973	Agreement to arm and train National Guard units concluded in April	20 Northrop F-5B aircraft (United States)*
1974	Agreement to provide United States equipment and training for Royal Saudi Navy signed in April United States-Saudi Arabia Joint Commission of Security Cooperation established June 8	38 Dassault Mirage III aircraft (France)*
		30 Northrop F-5E Tiger II aircraft (United States)*
		200 AMX-30 tanks (France)
1975	Contract awarded in January to Vinnell Corporation to train four battalions of the National Guard	
1976	Contract awarded in March to Northrop Corporation to provide construction and training for Royal Saudi Air Force	

*Supersonic aircraft.

Source: Based on information from *World Armaments and Disarmament: SIPRI Yearbook 1975*, Cambridge, Massachusetts, 1975; and U.S. Congress, 94th, 1st Session, House of Representatives, Committee on International Relations, Special Subcommittee on Investigations, *The Persian Gulf, 1975: The Continuing Debate on Arms Sales*, Washington, 1976.

changed, from one solely between governments to one between the Saudi government on the one hand and the United States government and private American corporations on the other (see table 18). Past military development in Saudi Arabia had given the country a capacity for deterrence. In the future (some estimates indicate as early as 1980), however, the country may move beyond this capacity to produce an offensive capability that would be an important element in the collective security system of the entire region.

Regional and World Relations

In area Saudi Arabia is the largest country in the Middle East, but in population it is one of the smallest. The country must maintain the security of over 2,000 miles of coastline on the Red Sea on the west and on the Persian Gulf on the east (see fig. 1). In addition many of its borders were either undefined or unclearly defined and, although some of its adjacent neighbors were close allies, some were quite unfriendly.

Table 18. *Saudi Arabia, Arms Imports and United States Military Assistance, United States Fiscal Years 1950-1975*

(in thousands of United States dollars)

Date	Military Assistance	Military Sales Orders	Military Sales Deliveries	Commercial Sales Deliveries
1950-65*	31,663	2,140,494	20,450	n.a.
1966	667	8,652	12,220	856
1967	768	49,324	48,854	14,902
1968	756	4,645	36,856	33,580
1969	536	4,213	32,086	35,481
1970	520	44,878	51,937	6,253
1971	632	95,954	63,774	12,723
1972	427	227,263	49,854	8,200
1973	179	625,895	108,030	5,649
1974	173	2,539,408	216,481	18,031
1975	38	7,224,588	316,070	n.a.

n.a.—not available.
*Combined total.

Source: Based on information from U.S. Department of Defense, *Foreign Military Sales and Military Assistance Facts*, Washington, November 1975.

With military and paramilitary forces that numbered about 70,000 Saudi Arabia had much to protect but relatively little to protect it with. Therefore the development of an effective military force has not been its only device to promote regional stability. Diplomacy has tended to complement the national defense system. Saudi Arabia's great wealth and its leadership in Islamic affairs have provided the country with various other methods to protect its national security interests. For example, Saudi Arabia provides military aid and assistance to Yemen (Sana), Oman and, in particular, Egypt and supports Arab efforts in the Arabi-Israeli confrontation. Saudi Arabia has consistently maintained that the country has been in a state of war with Israel (see ch. 10).

Saudi Arabia also perceives its role regionally as one of countering communism and the influence of the Soviet Union. Saudi efforts in this regard have earned it the enmity of those supported by Soviet aid, such as Yemen (Aden), Iraq, and Somalia. Saudi Arabia's immediate concern for national security, however, is concentrated on the security of three areas simultaneously: the Red Sea, the Persian Gulf, and the whole of the Arabian Peninsula. In military strength Saudi Arabia was outranked by many of its regional neighbors, particularly Egypt, Iraq, Israel, and Iran in 1976 but, because of its developing military strength, its use of diplomacy in the region, and its quick response to any possible external threat (such as the air attacks from Yemen (Aden) during the early 1970s), the country has been able to maintain the integrity of its borders.

The long-term effects, either positive or negative, of Saudi Arabia's new international economic prominence were not clear in 1976. Saudi Arabia's changing military posture itself might determine a probable outcome. Some observers have suggested, for example, that, should Saudi Arabia attain an offensive military capacity, it would be more likely to become a combatant in a future Middle East conflict and that this would have unknown effects on the country's national security structure. Further, should Saudi Arabia reach or surpass the military strength of its neighbors, relations with those neighbors would be altered, but in what direction or to what extent could not be determined in 1976.

Attitudes Toward Military Buildup and Disarmament

When a country determines to develop a greater military capability, the decision is likely to be in response to many factors, including the country's perception of an external threat. In 1976 Saudi Arabia continued to be faced with numerous but minor border disputes, some instances of potential external threat, and the reality that revolutions against royal governments had occurred in many countries of the region. In particular the Saudi government has viewed radical regimes in the region with uneasiness; this was perhaps best illustrated by the country's continuing concern over events in Yemen (Aden), which involved a potential threat to Saudi Arabia and an immediate threat to Yemen (Sana) and Oman through subversion and military actions.

The Saudi government's decision to expand and modernize its military forces was prompted in part by the 1968 decision by the United Kingdom to terminate its military presence in the Persian Gulf area and southern Arabia. The British withdrawal was completed in 1971, when Bahrain in August, Qatar in September, and the United Arab Emirates in December became independent states. Since that time Saudi Arabia has perceived it to be part of its role to attempt to fill the void left by the British withdrawal. Foreign analysts have stated that Iran has also attempted to fill this vacuum.

Although Saudi Arabia continued to acquire arms and contribute to the general arms buildup in the Middle East, it was still in the position of a relatively minor military power. As a member of the United Nations Saudi Arabia has participated in many multilateral agreements related to disarmament, although as of early 1976 it had not signed the Treaty of the Non-Proliferation of Nuclear Weapons (NPT) of 1968. Observers noted that in 1976 Saudi Arabia's leaders continued to perceive their country as faced with a situation that necessitated the acquisition of a strong military capability.

INTERNAL SECURITY

Although the population of the country is composed of many divergent tribes that have sustained a limited degree of autonomy despite the government's efforts to develop a strong central government, the people share certain social elements that have produced a definable national identity. Foremost among these is Wahhabi Islam, which encourages social and cultural homogeneity, and this in turn is supported by linguistic homogeneity (see ch. 7).

The major negative aspect of the maintenance of internal security is the large alien population, but this did not appear to be a major problem in 1976. The initial successes at bringing together the many tribes of the Arabian Peninsula in the first half of the twentieth century must be credited to Abd al Aziz and the royal family he created. If there is a single element of Saudi society that explains the low degree of internal turmoil, it is the allegiance to the House of Saud felt by almost every member of the population.

Domestic tranquillity was not attained by Abd al Aziz immediately, however, and the Saudi government developed many methods to promote an effective internal security system. First, in establishing his authority over the tribal leaders, Abd al Aziz created a flexible administrative system that allowed a high degree of local (tribal) responsibility if the tribal leaders continued to support the king. To reinforce this idea Abd al Aziz began a process of annual subsidies to loyal tribal leaders commensurate with their importance.

Perhaps of greater significance, however, was the process by which Abd al Aziz established the country's internal security forces and a system of penalties that maintained extreme obedience to the law. At the pinnacle of the public security organization, as it was in 1976, was the National Guard. With the primary missions of protecting the country from external threat and maintaining internal security, the National Guard was always central to the plans of the Saudi government to promote the settlement of the beduin tribes, prevent intertribal warfare, and protect the king and royal family from any possible threat.

When the Ikhwan ended as a military force in the 1930s, the National Guard, known then as the White Army, was the country's primary security force, as it remained in 1976. This paramilitary force is recruited from the noble beduin tribes of the regions in which members of the guard serve. Its authority throughout the country is reportedly unquestioned by the local populations, and its allegiance to the king and his designated commander of the guard is also unquestioned. The guard's ultimate goal is the rapid resolution of any show of defiance to the authority of the state; the mobility of the force and its ability to respond to problems of internal security have been of considerable significance to the perpetuation of the Saud dynasty. For example, it was with the support of the National Guard that King Faisal was able to depose his brother, King Saud, in 1964, and foreign observers have asserted that it was the National Guard that put down a reported rebellion of Saudi air force officers in 1969.

Therefore the National Guard not only was important in the development of a security system that put an end to intertribal warfare and raids by beduin on travelers, particularly Muslims making the haj, but also continued in the mid-1970s to be an effective defender of the security of the state. It did not, however, carry out this mission alone. In addition to the practice of subsidizing tribal leaders, which has persisted, there is an extensive organization of modern security forces that reinforce and complement the goals of the National Guard. Likewise the rapidly developing legal system of Saudi Arabia has contributed to the respect shown to these security forces (see ch. 8).

Public Security Forces

The organization of the public security system in 1976 was the result of the notable achievements of Abd al Aziz, who established and maintained internal security and judicial systems in an area that had previously known little of either except on a limited, local level. Gradually modern organs became responsible for public order, but these remained similar to those devised by Abd al Aziz. Therefore the extensive, well-organized governmental public security forces are complemented by local elites responsible for public order and the units of the traditional religious police *(mutawwiun)*, who maintain the observance of the strict doctrines of Wahhabism.

In addition to the National Guard the units charged with maintaining internal security in 1976 were the Public Security Police, the Frontier Force, the Coast Guard, and various other internal security forces, all within the Ministry of Interior and organized under offices of the ministry covering public security, investigation, and passports and nationality.

In return for allegiance to the king and the maintenance of peace and security in all tribal units in their regions of the country, the shaykhs received official recognition of their authority, a minimum of government interference in their affairs, and subsidies both to maintain their local strength and to reinforce allegiance to the king. Under this system offenses and breaches of the peace are punished by the responsible shaykh, and only when this local responsibility fails is the National Guard brought in to quell a disturbance. This system of local control over public security matters within the tribes has been perpetuated, and the presence of the armed forces, including the National Guard, acts mainly as a support for these local efforts.

The modern public security forces, particularly the highly centralized Public Security Police, may also be supported in an emergency by the armed forces or the National Guard, but this is less likely to occur because the police have become a modern, well-equipped security force and need little assistance to perform their duties. The Public Security Police were recruited from among all elements of the population and were organized at two governmental levels: provincial police directorates and local police directorates. The Ministry of Interior's director general for public security had nationwide responsibility for the police units, which in 1976 included an estimated 20,000 men. In practice, however, the regional governors possessed considerable autonomy in matters pertaining to public security and probably exercised direct control over the police within their administrative divisions (see ch. 8). In addition the governors and the local shaykhs usually have their own personal guards, which supplement the regular police as needed.

Police uniforms were similar to those of the Royal Saudi Army except for the distinctive red beret, but there were no police units that could be regarded as paramilitary. According to foreign observers, police methods were not considered cruel and had not aroused any general resentment. In 1960 the government established the Police College in Mecca to train its officers. A secondary school certificate was required for entrance. The police force has continually been improved, particularly after the mid-1960s, and by 1976 was equipped with radio communications and modern vehicles and had enough equipment to maintain sophisticated mobile police units in the principal cities. Helicopters, radar, and television either were being used or were being brought into use.

The deputy minister of interior had responsibility for most of the other public security forces in the country, including the Frontier Force and the Coast Guard. A separate college, the Internal Security Forces College, provided trained officers for each of these forces. Along with the Public Security Police, the Frontier Force and the Coast Guard maintained internal security. Units of all these public security forces have specific responsibility for control of crowds during Ramadan and the Islamic pilgrimage season (see ch. 6).

Another public security force of note was the autonomous religious police, organized under the authority of the king in conjunction with the country's religious leaders, who serve on the quasi-judicial public morality committees. These religious police were charged with ensuring strict compliance of the population with the puritanical precepts of Wahhabism. Local public morality committees exist in every town and derive their central governmental authority from the office of the king as organized in two central offices: one that covers the western provinces and another that covers the Najd and Eastern Province.

The religious police, once an important element used by Abd al Aziz to maintain public order, have become something of an anomaly. Their strict conservatism is increasingly in contrast to the setting of the major urban populations, and according to some observers many Saudis consider the rigorous methods used by the religious police to enforce religious conformity unnecessary. Their power is mainly to enforce public observance of such religious requirements as the five daily prayers, fasting during Ramadan, the modesty of women, and the proscriptions against the use of alcohol and tobacco. The average Saudi citizen, although devoutly religious, prefers to manage his own religious obligations, and many have protested the continued role of the religious police in society. King Faisal confirmed the feelings of these people by promoting the reform of the public morality committees in his efforts to modernize the society.

Crime and Punishment

Sharia law encompasses two categories of crime: those that are carefully defined and for which there are specific penalties and those that are implicit in the requirements and prohibitions laid down in sharia law and for which penalties may be set at the discretion of the judge (qadi) of a sharia court. In addition a third category of crime is defined by the various governmental decrees that have specified codes and regulations necessary to maintain public order and security. This third group of crimes has been established primarily since the end of World War II. The first two categories of crime are tried by the sharia courts and the third by administrators and government officials (see ch. 8).

For numerous crimes, especially those covered by sharia law, penalties specified by the law can be extremely severe. The government, however, has directed that these extreme punishments be used only as a last resort, primarily for punishing citizens who repeat crimes or when in the government's opinion the crime clearly warrants such penalties. Because many of the severe maximum punishments, such as stoning or mutilation, are carried out in public, the effect has been to produce an abhorrence of crimes that receive such penalties. In 1976 observers reported that, although these punishments were carried out infrequently, the occasional public beheading or stoning reminded the public that these penalties remained in force.

The sharia law carefully defines homicide and personal injury, fornication and adultery, theft, and highway robbery and specifies a penalty *(hadd)* for each. Various degrees of culpability for homicide and bodily injury are recognized according to intent, the kind of weapon used, and the circumstances under which the crime took place. In Islamic law homicide is not considered a crime against society, in which the state moves against the criminal. Sharia law recognizes only the right of the victim or the victim's family to bring charges against the accused for the right to retaliation or to blood money—that is, a set payment as recompense for the crime (see ch. 7).

The right to act in self-defense is recognized as nullifying the commission of a crime. Retaliation permitted to the family of the victim—actually to the next of kin of the victim—includes killing the criminal in the case of homicide or exacting the same bodily injury on him as he committed. Retaliation, however, is discouraged in Islamic law; the acceptance of blood money is considered preferable. Unintentional homicide is invariably punished by compensation of the victim's family.

In cases involving death or serious injury the accused is usually detained by the police until his trial. The right of habeas corpus is not recognized. Although the regional governor may order the police to accept a bond in the case of minor offenses, the granting of bond lies within the discretion of the local chief of police.

At the trial of minor cases the judge hears the complaints of the aggrieved party and cross-examines the plaintiff, the defendant, and any witnesses they may introduce. The judge assigns great significance to a defendant's sworn testimony under oath, although the testimony of one man equals that of two women. All cases are heard in public by a single judge. Trial by jury is unknown in Islamic law. After determining guilt or innocence and the right to compensation, the judge attempts to arrive at a fair assessment of reparations acceptable to both parties. In more serious cases the judge may suggest appropriate punishment, but he does not pass sentence. All papers pertaining to such a case are sent to the district or provincial governor who, with the advice of members of the local ulama, pronounces the sentence.

In the case of a traffic death or injury the driver at fault is subject not only to the jurisdiction of a sharia court as regards the rights of the victim's family to indemnity but also to a penalty (generally imprisonment) under the vehicle code. The lack of distinction in decree legislation between simple and criminal negligence makes imprisonment virtually mandatory for even relatively minor violations.

Fornication and adultery are considered by sharia to be crimes against the family and public morality. As such, anyone may bring the accusation before a judge, and the accused persons are severely punished if the crime is proved. Sharia law stipulates severe penalties for adultery but has established rigorous requirements for proof. Four reliable witnesses to the act must swear to the crime. If their accusation does not hold up, they are liable to punishment themselves.

Theft is punished by cutting off the right hand of the thief but, because of the severity of the punishment, a number of qualifications have been introduced to mitigate it. Petty larceny and theft from relatives are excluded, and the theft must take place by stealth from a properly secured place. If the thief repents and makes recompense before the case is brought before a judge, the punishment is reduced, and the victim may merely demand money or may grant a pardon. Highway robbery is considered a crime against public safety and is more severely punished than theft. If it involves only the taking of loot, the criminal may be punished by having alternate hands and feet cut off and by banishment; if it involves homicide or bodily harm to the victim, the criminal is liable to execution by crucifixion. Repentance reduces the severity of the crime as it does in the case of theft.

Other crimes for which a penalty is not stipulated in sharia law include various crimes against religion and public morality, including drunkenness and gambling, the neglect of requirements on prayer, fasting, and other religious duties, and crimes against the rights of individuals, such as the use of false weights and usury. The penalties for these crimes are set by the judge after considering the case on its merits and may include public flogging, imprisonment, or the imposition of fines. Most commonly these cases are brought before the sharia court by members of the public morality committees.

Prisons in the past were reported to be crowded and unsanitary, but since the late 1960s there have been efforts to improve prison conditions. There were no estimates available in early 1976 as to the number of prisoners, but it was thought to be very small in proportion to the population. Further it was unclear how many prisons were being maintained, although it was known that there were separate prisons for men and women. Women prisoners were permitted to bring their children with them to prison, and clinics have reportedly been established at all prisons. Prisoners were believed to have access to newspapers and radiobroadcasts, and literacy programs were also available. The opportunity to learn a trade existed in most of the larger prisons and contributed to the rehabilitation of prisoners.

Public Attitudes Toward Law Enforcement

In theory all persons in Saudi Arabia, including the king and all foreigners, are equal before the law and are subject to both sharia and decree law. In practice, however, members of the royal family and other important leaders have rarely been brought to public trial, and cases involving foreigners have usually been referred directly to a governor or higher official. The penalties for crime are still applicable to all individuals, however; for example, the assassin of King Faisal was a member of the royal family but was beheaded after a formal trial and sentencing. The strict system of law enforcement supposedly serves as a strong deterrent even to these groups.

The establishment of a strong central government supporting the orthodox Islamic concept of justice, combined with the development of a dual system of harsh repression of crime and swift and impartial justice, reportedly has successfully suppressed the growth of a criminal element. The incidence of crime was not publicly known in 1976, but it was reported to be very low. The situation seemed even more stable during the reign of King Faisal than under King Saud, and in 1976 King Khalid's government continued to confirm the low incidence of crimes of all kinds.

Although Saudi Arabia has all the symbols of a modern nation-state, Saudi citizens devote their loyalties to either a smaller or a larger unit than the nation and often to both at once. Traditionally the allegiance of the Saudi people has been accorded to the tribe and the extended family (see ch. 7). One of Abd al Aziz' most significant accomplishments was to implant the concept of allegiance to the House of Saud and then by extension to the authority of the royal government and judicial system. Just as important, however, is the Saudis' allegiance to the Arab people as an ethnic identity and to Wahhabi Islam as a religious identity.

All these elements of life in Saudi Arabia have produced popular attitudes supportive of an orderly society. Each aspect of a person's day-to-day activities can be categorized according to the boundaries of acceptable behavior, and few Saudis, or foreigners for that matter, attempt to break the understood rules. Therefore, as the establishment of a public security system has evolved since the creation of the country, people have accepted to a high degree such new elements of modern security forces as the police—which after all were organized according to accepted tradition.

The public security system and the judicial process were clear in the minds of citizens, and there seemed little doubt that the general population either agreed with or at least accepted the procedures of both. In 1976 the country's prosperity and its ability to provide for its citizens reinforced the strong feeling of loyalty between the people and authorities at all levels.

External Agitation and Internal Subversion

Saudi Arabia, particularly since the 1950s, has been a primary target of propaganda broadcasts from outside its borders, originating especially from Cairo, Baghdad, and Damascus (see ch. 9). This kind of subversive activity reached its peak during the early and mid-1960s when it was orchestrated by Nasser of Egypt. In 1976, however, this form of external agitation designed to undermine allegiance to the royal government originated primarily in the capitals of Yemen (Aden) and Iraq, reportedly supported by these governments and small groups of exiled Saudis. The propaganda had had little effect on the loyalty of the Saudi people to their government.

Subversion in such other forms as assassination, sabotage, and plots has been an important element in the political dynamics of the Arabian Peninsula. Abd al Aziz, who was constantly faced with these forms of internal subversion, was able to gain the loyalty of the large majority of his people, however, and thus greatly reduced the possibility of the Saud dynasty's being overthrown during his reign (see ch. 2). After Abd al Aziz' death in 1953 and particularly after the overthrow of the monarchies in Yemen (Sana) and Iraq, subversive activities sponsored from abroad against the Saudi monarchy increased.

In the 1950s domestic turmoil was mainly a result of the discontent of Saudi employees of Aramco, which resulted in a series of riots. These grievances were further aggravated when relations between Saudi Arabia and Egypt deteriorated and labor rebellions became influenced by Nasser's promotion of Arab nationalism and Arab socialism. At first these disturbances were resolved by Aramco, but in 1960 the labor organizers were joined in their efforts by a few of the younger royal princes, who were upset by the austerity measures established by Crown Prince Faisal in 1958. These princes and a small group of sympathizers exiled themselves to Egypt to gain Nasser's support and formed the Committee for the Liberation of Saudi Arabia. After Faisal became king in 1964, the princes sought and received his forgiveness; they returned to Saudi Arabia and have reportedly remained politically inactive. Within Saudi Arabia a small underground group called the Union of the Arab Peninsula committed numerous acts of sabotage during the mid-1960s before many were arrested; some were sent to prison and others deported.

The most serious known case of internal dissidence centered on the arrest of large numbers of Royal Saudi Air Force personnel in 1969. Although this event is often spoken of as an attempted coup, those under suspicion were reportedly arrested before a coup could be attempted. Perhaps a total of 120 people were arrested during the summer and fall of 1969, not all of them military personnel. Some people were described as influenced by Nasserist ideology and others as motivated by dissatisfaction with the rate of military modernization. By 1975 all those arrested had been released.

In 1976 a number of small groups outside the country still plagued the government by their clandestine and propaganda activities, but the weakness of these groups and their lack of organization rendered them of little importance. It should be noted, however, that most forms of organization are illegal. Much of the success of the maintenance of public order and the relatively low level of internal subversion must be attributed to the tremendous increase in budget allocations to reorganize the military and public security forces. For example, the Saudi government announced in July 1975 that the public security budget for the next year would be 141 percent greater than for the current year.

One of King Khalid's first actions was the release of all political prisoners in mid-1975, probably a symbol of confidence that the government had nothing to fear in the area of internal security. There was no evidence in 1976 that the Saudi regime was seriously threatened by subversive elements. The country is, however, experiencing a period of rapid and profound social change, and the government finds itself under continuing and often conflicting pressures from divergent groups with conflicting goals—military officers, progressive youth, government officials, and conservative religious leaders. How well the leadership deals with these multifaceted pressures will determine the long-range prospects for the stability of the regime.

* * * * * * * * * * * * * *

The historical development and events that have produced Saudi Arabia's present capabilities in national defense and internal security are discussed in Mordechai Abir's *Oil, Power and Politics* and Joseph J. Malone's *The Arab Lands of Western Asia*. The most important sources for information on this subject, however, are the published hearings of the United States House of Representatives (committees on foreign affairs and international relations) for the years 1973 through 1976. The publications of the Stockholm International Peace Research Institute, especially *World Armaments and Disarmament: SIPRI Yearbook 1975*, contain substantial amounts of statistical data on arms and equipment, expenditures, and trends in relation to Saudi Arabia's national defense system. This is also an excellent source to use in comparing the military establishment in Saudi Arabia with others in the region and throughout the world, particularly if used in conjunction with the International Institute for Strategic Studies' *The Military Balance, 1975-1976*. (For further information see Bibliography.)

BIBLIOGRAPHY

Section I. Social

Abir, A. "The 'Arab Rebellion' of Amir Ghalib of Mecca (1788-1813)," *Middle Eastern Studies* [London], VII, No. 2, May 1971, 185-200.

Abir, Mordechai. *Oil, Power and Politics: Conflict in Arabia, the Red Sea and the Gulf.* London: Frank Cass, 1974.

Abu-Deeb, Kamal. "Towards a Structural Analysis of Pre-Islamic Poetry," *International Journal of Middle East Studies* [London], 6, No. 2, April 1975, 148-184.

"Ahmad b. Muhammad b. Hanbal." Pages 20-21 in H.A.R. Gibb and J.H. Kramers (eds.), *Shorter Encyclopedia of Islam.* Ithaca: Cornell University Press, 1953.

Alaki, Abdelkader Madani. "Industrial-Vocational Education in Saudi Arabia: Problems and Prospects." Unpublished Ph.D. dissertation. Tucson: Department of Business Administration, University of Arizona, 1972.

Al-Awaji, Ibrahim Mohamed. "Bureaucracy and Society in Saudi Arabia." Unpublished Ph.D. dissertation. Charlottesville: Woodrow Wilson Department of Government and Foreign Affairs, University of Virginia, 1971.

Alireza, Marianne. *At the Drop of a Veil.* Boston: Houghton-Mifflin, 1971.

Al-Marayati, Abid A. (ed.) *The Middle East: Its Governments and Politics.* Belmont, California: Duxbury, 1972.

Al-Nawaihi, Mohamed. "Problems of Modernization in Islam," *The Muslim World*, LXV, No. 3, July 1975, 174-185.

Andrae, Tor. *Mohammed: The Man and His Faith.* (Trans., Theophil Menzel.) New York: Harper and Row, 1955.

Antonius, George. *The Arab Awakening.* New York: Capricorn Books, 1965.

Aramco Handbook. Dhahran: Arabian American Oil Company, 1968.

Asfour, Edmond Y., et al. *Saudi Arabia: Long-Term Projections of Supply and Demand for Agricultural Products.* Beirut: Economic Research Institute, American University of Beirut, 1965.

Bacon, Elizabeth E. *Obok: A Study of Social Structure in Eurasia.* (Viking Fund Publications in Anthropology, No. 25.) New York: Wenner-Gren Foundation for Anthropological Research, 1958.

Becker, Abraham S., Bent Hansen, and Malcolm H. Kerr. *The Economics and Politics of the Middle East.* New York: American Elsevier, 1975.

Benoist-Mechin, Jacques. *Arabian Destiny.* (Trans., Denis Weaver.) Fairlawn, New Jersey: Essential Books, 1958.

Berque, Jacques. *The Arabs.* (Trans., Jean Stewart.) New York: Frederick A. Praeger, 1964.

Bibby, Geoffrey. *Looking for Dilmun.* London: Collins, 1970.

Bill, James A. "Class Analysis and the Dialectics of Modernization in the Middle East," *International Journal of Middle East Studies* [London], 3, No. 4, October 1972, 417-432.

Bill, James A., and Carl Leiden. *The Middle East: Politics and Power.* Boston: Allyn and Bacon, 1974.

Brice, W.C. *South-West Asia.* London: University of London Press, 1966.

Brown, Edward Hoaglann. *The Saudi Arabia-Kuwait Neutral Zone.* Beirut: Middle East Research and Publishing Center, 1963.

Brown, L. Carl (ed.). *From Medina to Metropolis: Heritage and Change in the Near Eastern City.* (Princeton Studies on the Near East.) Princeton: Darwin Press, 1973.

Bullard, Reader (ed.). *The Middle East: A Political and Economic Survey.* London: Oxford University Press, 1961.

Bulliet, Richard W. *The Camel and the Wheel.* Cambridge: Harvard University Press, 1975.

Cain, Leo F., et al. "Expansion of Higher Education: An Implementation Strategy for Saudi Arabia." (Report of the U.S. Higher Education Team's Visit to Saudi Arabia, May-June 1975.) Washington: Department of Health, Education, and Welfare, August 8, 1975 (mimeo.).

Caskel, Werner. "The Bedouinization of Arabia." *The American Anthropologist* (Special Issue: Studies in Islamic Cultural History), 56, No. 76, 1954.

Chapman, Richard A. "Administrative Reform in Saudi Arabia," *Journal of Administration Overseas* [London], XIII, No. 2, April 1974, 332-347.

Clarke, J.I., and W.B. Fisher. *Populations of the Middle East and North Africa: A Geographical Approach.* New York: Africana Publishing, 1972.

Cohen, Hayyim J. *The Jews of the Middle East, 1960-1972.* New York: John Wiley and Sons, 1973.

Cole, Donald Powell. "The Enmeshment of Nomads in Saudi Arabian Society: The Case of Al Murrah," Pages 113-128 in Cynthia Nelson (ed.), *The Desert and the Sown: Nomads in the Wider Society.* (Institute of International Studies Research Series, No. 21.) Berkeley: Institute of International Studies, University of California, 1973.

———. *Nomads of the Nomads: The Al Murrah Bedouin of the Empty Quarter.* Chicago: Aldine Publishing, 1975.

Connor, Brian. "Lord of Arabia," *Middle East International* [London], No. 33, March 1974.

Conroy, K. "Nursing Oasis in Saudi Arabia," *Nursing Times* [London], 68, September 14, 1973, 1148-1150.

De Gaury, Gerald. *Faisal: King of Saudi Arabia.* New York: Praeger, 1966.

Demographic Yearbook, 1950. New York: Statistical Office, Department of Economic and Social Affairs, United Nations, 1951.

Demographic Yearbook, 1952. New York: Statistical Office, Department of Economic and Social Affairs, United Nations, 1953.

Demographic Yearbook, 1962. New York: Statistical Office, Department of Economic and Social Affairs, United Nations, 1963.

Demographic Yearbook, 1970. New York: Statistical Office, Department of Economic and Social Affairs, United Nations, 1971.

Demographic Yearbook, 1973. New York: Statistical Office, Department of Economic and Social Affairs, 1974.

Dequin, H. "Saudi Arabia." Pages 459-468 in *World Atlas of Agriculture*, II. Novara, Italy: International Association of Agricultural Economists, Instituto Geografico de Agostini, 1973.

Dickson, H.R.P. *The Arab of the Desert: A Glimpse into Badawin Life in Kuwait and Saudi Arabia.* London: George Allen and Unwin, 1959.

———. *Kuwait and Her Neighbors.* London: George Allen and Unwin, 1956.

Di Meglio, Rita. "Il Problema dei Nomadi in Arabia Saudiana e le sue Soluzioni," *Oriente Moderno* [Rome], 50, No. 6, June 1970, 273-279.

Doughty, Charles M. *Arabia Deserta.* 2 vols. London: Jonathan Cape, 1964.

Duguid, Stephen. "A Biographical Approach to the Study of Social Change in the Middle East: Abdullah Tariki as a New Man," *International Journal of Middle East Studies* [London], 1, No. 3, July 1970, 195-220.

Duquet, Firman. *Le Pèlerinage de la Mecque au point de vue religieuse sociale et sanitaire.* Paris: Editions Pieder, 1932.

Edens, David G. "The Anatomy of the Saudi Revolution," *International Journal of Middle East Studies* [London], 5, No. 1, January 1974, 50-64.

Egbert, Robert, et al. "Education in Saudi Arabia: Findings, Recommendations, and Proposed Projects." (Report of the Education Team's Visit to Saudi Arabia, November 8-27, 1974.) Washington: Department of Health, Education, and Welfare, January 28, 1975 (mimeo.).

Eilts, Hermann F. "Social Revolution in Saudi Arabia," Pt. I, *Parameters: The Journal of the Army War College*, 1, No. 1, Spring 1971, 4-18.

———. "Social Revolution in Saudi Arabia," Pt. II, *Parameters: The Journal of the Army War College*, 1, No. 2, Fall 1971, 22-33.

El-Erris, Tarik. "Saudi Arabia: A Study in Nation Building." Unpublished Ph.D. dissertation. Washington: School of International Studies, The American University, 1964.

El-Farra, Taha Osman M. "The Effects of Detribalizing the Bedouins on the Internal Cohesion of an Emerging State: The Kingdom of Saudi Arabia." Unpublished Ph.D. dissertation. Pittsburgh: Department of Geography, University of Pittsburgh, 1973.

El-Sanabary, Nagat M. "The Education of Women in the Arab States: Achievements and Problems, 1950-1970." (Paper presented at the Annual Meeting of the Middle East Studies Association, November 6-9, 1974.) Boston: 1974 (mimeo.).

Faruqi, Ismail R. al. "Misconceptions of the Nature of Islamic Art," *Islam and the Modern Age* [New Delhi], 1, No. 1, May 1970, 29-48.

———. "On the Nature of the Work of Art in Islam," *Islam and the Modern Age* [New Delhi], 1, No. 2, August 1970, 68-81.

Field, Peter. "Saudi Arabia: How the $142,000 Million Will Be Spent," *The Middle East Economic Digest* [London], 19, No. 34, August 22, 1975, 5-32.

Fisher, W.B. *The Middle East: A Physical, Social, and Regional Geography*. (6th ed.) London: Methuen, 1971.

Fontana, Charles J. "Power Politics: Saudi Arabian Style." (Report No. 0965-74.) Maxwell Air Force Base, Alabama: Air University, May 1974 (mimeo.).

George, Alan. "Bedouin Settlement in Saudi Arabia," *Middle East International* [London], No. 51, September 1975, 27-30.

Gibb, H.A.R. *Arabic Literature: An Introduction* (2d ed.) Oxford: Clarendon Press, 1963.

———. *Modern Trends in Islam*. New York: Octagon, 1972.

Glidden, Harold. "The Arab World," *Middle East Review*, 7, No. 2, 1974-75, 43-47.

Glubb, Faris. "Saudi Arabia: The Same but Different," *Middle East International* [London], No. 49, July 1975, 15-17.

Glubb, J.B. "The Sulubba and Other Ignoble Tribes of Southwestern Asia." Pages 14-17 in Henry Field and J.B. Glubb (eds.), *The Yezidis: Sulubba and Other Tribes of Iraq and Adjacent Regions*. (General Series in Anthropology, No. 10.) Menasha, Wisconsin: George Banta Publishing, 1943.

Grant, C.P. *The Syrian Desert*. London: A. and C. Black, 1937.

Grube, Ernest J. *The World of Islam*. London: Paul Hamlyn, 1966.

"Hadjdj." Pages 121-125 in H.A.R. Gibb and J.H. Kramers (eds.), *Shorter Encyclopedia of Islam*. Ithaca: Cornell University Press, 1953.

Halliday, Fred. *Arabia Without Sultans*. New York: Random House, 1975.

Halpern, Manfred. *Politics of Social Change in the Middle East and North Africa*. Princeton: Princeton University Press, 1963.
Herst, David. "Oasis of Health," *The Guardian* [Manchester], April 22, 1975, 15.
Hitti, Philip K. *History of the Arabs*. London: Macmillan, 1956.
――――. *Islam: A Way of Life*. Minneapolis: University of Minnesota Press, 1970.
Hodges, Carl N. "Desert Food Factories," *Ekistics* [Athens], 40, October 1975.
Hogarth, D.G. "Wahhabism and British Interests," *Journal of the British Institute of International Affairs*, [London], IV, March 1925, 77-79.
Holden, David. "A Family Affair," *New York Times Magazine*, July 6, 1975, 8-9, 26-27.
――――. *Farewell to Arabia*. New York: Walker, 1966.
Howarth, David. *A Desert King: Ibn Saud and His Arabia*. New York: McGraw-Hill, 1964.
Hurewitz, J.C. (ed.) *Diplomacy in the Near and Middle East*, I and II. Princeton: Van Nostrand, 1956.
"Ibn Taimiya." Pages 151-152 in H.A.R. Gibb and J.H. Kramers (eds.), *Shorter Encyclopedia of Islam*. Ithaca: Cornell University Press, 1953.
Ibrahim, Saad E.M. "Over-Urbanization and Under-Urbanism: The Case of the Arab World," *International Journal of Middle East Studies* [London], 6, No. 1, January 1975, 29-45.
Ingrams, Doreen. *A Time in Arabia*. London: John Murray, 1970.
"Interview with Ghazi Sultan," by Abd al Aziz al Nahari, *Al-Madinah*, Jiddah: March 13, 1974. Translated by U.S. Department of Commerce. Office of Technical Services, Joint Publications Research Service (Washington). JPRS 62026, No. 1164, May 17, 1974, 4-6.
Ismael, Tareq Y., et al. *The Middle East in World Politics*. Syracuse: Syracuse University Press, 1974.
James, Preston E. *A Geography of Man*. (3d ed.) Waltham, Massachusetts: Blaisdell, 1966.
Jansen, Michael E. "An American Girl on the Hajj," *Aramco World*, 25, No. 6, November-December 1974, 30-39.
"A Jewel of a University on the Arabian Sands," *Fortune*, XCII, No. 5, November 1975, 126-133.
Johns, Richard, et al. "Saudi Arabia," *Financial Times* (Financial Times Survey) [London], January 12, 1976, 11-30.
Khouri, Fred J. *The Arab-Israeli Dilemma*. Syracuse: Syracuse University Press, 1968.
Kilidor, A.R. "The Arabian Peninsula in Arab and Power Politics." Pages 145-159 in Derek Hopwood (ed.), *The Arabian Peninsula: Society and Politics*. Totowa, New Jersey: Rowman and Littlefield, 1972.

Kimball, John T. *American Culture in Saudi Arabia*. New York: New York Academy of Sciences, 1956.

Kirimly, H.B. "Medical Aspects of the Mecca Pilgrimage." Unpublished Ph.D. dissertation. London: Department of Tropical Public Health, University of London, 1966.

Kirk, Grayson L. "Ibn Sa'ud Builds an Empire," *Current History*, 41, December 1934, 291-297.

Knauerhase, Ramon. *The Saudi Arabian Economy*. (Praeger Special Studies in International Economics and Development.) New York: Praeger, 1975.

Kraft, Joseph. "Letter from Saudi Arabia," *New Yorker*, October 20, 1975, 111-139.

Lammens, Henri. *Le Berceau de l'Islam*. Rome: Pontificii Instituti Biblici, 1914.

Laoust, Henri. *Essai sur les Doctrines Sociales et Politiques de Taki-D-Din Ahmad b. Taimiya*. Cairo: Imprimerie de l'Institut Français d'Archéologie Orientale, 1939.

Lawless, Richard. "Education Expansion" *Financial Times* (Financial Times Survey) [London], January 12, 1976, 16-17.

Lebkicker, Roy, George Rentz, and Max Steineke. *The Arabia of Ibn Saud*. New York: Russel F. Moore, 1952.

Lenczowski, George. *The Middle East in World Affairs*. Ithaca: Cornell University Press, 1962.

Leonard, A.G. *The Camel: Its Uses and Management*. London: Longmans, Green, 1894.

Lewis, Bernard. *The Arabs in History*. New York: Harper and Row, 1967.

———. *The Middle East and the West*. New York: Harper and Row, 1964.

Lewis, C.C. "Ibn Saud and the Future of Arabia," *International Affairs* [London], XII, No. 4, July-August 1933, 518-534.

Lockhard, Derwood W. "Review of 'The Central Middle East.'" *American Anthropologist*, 72, No. 2, April 1970, 398-401.

Long, David E. "The Board of Grievances in Saudi Arabia," *Middle East Journal*, XXVII, No. 1, Winter 1973, 71-75.

———. "The Hajj Today: A Survey of the Contemporary Pilgrimage to Makkah." Unpublished Ph.D. dissertation. Washington: George Washington University, February 1973.

Loya, Arieh. "The Detribalization of Arabian Poetry," *International Journal of Middle East Studies* [London], 5, No. 2, April 1974, 202-215.

Lunde, Paul. "The Ka'bah: House of God," *Aramco World*, 25, No. 6, November-December 1974, 6-7.

Malone, Joseph J. *The Arab Lands of Western Asia*. Englewood Cliffs: Prentice-Hall, 1973.

Manners, Ian R. "The Desert and the Sown," *Focus*, XXII, No. 2,

October 1971.

Mansfield, Peter (ed.). *The Middle East: A Political and Economic Survey*. (4th ed.) New York: Oxford University Press, 1973.

Marx, Emanuel. "The Organization of Nomadic Groups in the Middle East." Pages 305-336 in Menahem Milson (ed.), *Society and Political Structure in the Arab World*. New York: Humanities Press, 1974.

Melamid, Alexander. "Boundary Disputes in the Persian (Arab) Gulf." (Paper presented at Annual Meeting of Middle East Studies Association, 1974.) Boston: 1974 (mimeo.).

Melconian, Marlene. "Arab Women: In Hot Pursuit of a Feminist Oriented Economy," *The Arab Economist* [Beirut], VII, No. 79, August 1975, 18-26.

Monroe, Elizabeth. "Faisal: The End of an Era," *Middle East International* [London], No. 47, May 1975, 11-13.

———. *Philby of Arabia*. London: Faber and Faber, 1973.

Mourad, Farouk. "The Attitude of Village Population in Saudi Arabia Toward Community Development: A Study in the Social Psychology of Development." Unpublished Ph.D. dissertation. Los Angeles: Department of Sociology, University of Southern California, June 1969.

Munroe, John. "On Campus in Saudi Arabia," *Aramco World*, 25, No. 4, July-August 1974, 2-9.

Murphy, Robert T., and Leonard Kasdan. "The Structure of Parallel Cousin Marriage," *American Anthropologist*, 61, No. 1, February 1959, 17-29.

Nawwab, Ismail Ibrahim. "The Hajj: An Introduction," *Aramco World*, 25, No. 6, November-December 1974, 2-5.

Nelson, Cynthia. "Public and Private Politics: Women in the Middle Eastern World," *American Ethnologist*, 1, No. 3, August 1974, 551-565.

———. "Women and Power in Nomadic Societies in the Middle East." Pages 43-60 in Cynthia Nelson (ed.), *The Desert and the Sown: Nomads in the Wider Society*. (Institute of International Studies Research Series, No. 21.) Berkeley: Institute of International Studies, University of California, 1973.

Otkum, Galip. "Outline of Ground Water Resources of Saudi Arabia." (Paper presented at International Conference on Arid Lands in a Changing World, June 1969.) Tucson: 1969.

Page, Stephen. *The USSR and Arabia: The Development of Soviet Policies and Attitudes Towards the Countries of the Arabian Peninsula*. London: Central Asian Research Centre, 1972.

Patwardhan, Vinayak N., and William J. Danby. *The State of Nutrition in the Arab Middle East*. Nashville: Vanderbilt University Press, 1972.

Penrose, Edith. "Oil and State in Arabia." Pages 271-285 in Derek Hopwood (ed.), *The Arabian Peninsula: Society and Politics*. Totowa, New Jersey: Rowman and Littlefield, 1972.

Peppelenbosch, P.G.N. "Nomadism on the Arabian Peninsula: A General Appraisal," *Tijdschrift voor Economische en Sociale Geographie* [Leiden], LIX, No. 6, 1968, 335-346.

Peretz, Don. *The Middle East Today*. New York: Holt, Rinehart and Winston, 1963.

Perkins, George. *The Camel: His Organization, Habits, and Uses*. Boston: Gould and Lincoln, 1856.

Philby, H. St. John. *Sa'udi Arabia*. London: Ernest Benn, 1955.

Phoenix (pseud.). "A Brief Outline of the Wahabi Movement," *Journal of the Central Asian Society* [London], XVII, No. 4, October 1930, 401-416.

Polk, William R., and William J. Mares. *Passing Brave*. New York: Ballantine Books, 1973.

Population Bulletin of the United Nations Economic Commission for Western Asia [Beirut], 7, July 1974.

Rainey, R.C. *Meteorology and the Migration of Desert Locusts*. (Anti-Locust Memoir 7, Technical Note, No. 54.) London: World Meteorological Organization, 1963.

Rentz, George. "Saudi Arabia." Pages 115-125 in J.H. Thompson and R.C. Reischauer (eds.), *Modernization of the Arab World*. Princeton: Van Nostrand, 1966.

―――. "Saudi Arabia: The Islamic Island," *Journal of International Affairs*, XIX, No. 1, 1965, 77-86.

―――. "The Wahhabis." Pages 270-284 in A.J. Arberry (ed.), *Religion in the Middle East: Three Religions in Concord and Conflict*, II: Islam. Cambridge: Cambridge University Press, 1969.

―――. "Wahhabism and Saudi Arabia." Pages 54-66 in Derek Hopwood (ed.), *The Arabian Peninsula: Society and Politics*. Totowa, New Jersey: Rowman and Littlefield, 1972.

Royal Institute of International Affairs. *The Middle East: A Political and Economic Survey*. London: Oxford University Press, 1958.

Rugh, William A. "Emergency of a New Middle Class in Saudi Arabia," *Middle East Journal*, 27, No. 1, Winter 1973, 9-20.

―――. *Riyadh: History and Guide*. Dammam; N. pub., 1969.

Rustow, Dankwart. *Middle Eastern Political Systems*. Englewood Cliffs: Prentice-Hall, 1971.

Sanger, Richard H. *The Arabian Peninsula*. Ithaca: Cornell University Press, 1954.

Saudi Arabia. Central Planning Organization. *Development Plan 1395-1400 (1975-80)*. (Reproduced by National Technical Information Service, U.S. Department of Commerce, PB 246,572.) Springfield, Virginia: NTIS, 1976.

Saudi Arabia. Ministry of Education. "Bi-Annual Report of the Ministry of Education 1973 and 1974." (Presented at the Thirty-Fifth

Session of the International Bureau of Education.) Geneva: September 1975 (mimeo.).

Saudi Arabia. Ministry of Petroleum and Mineral Resources. Directorate General of Mineral Research. *Mineral Resources of Saudi Arabia: A Guide for Investment and Development.* Bulletin No. 1. Beirut: Middle East Export Press, 1965.

"Saudi Arabia: A Construction Boom," *The Arab Economist* [Beirut], VII, No. 75, April 1975, 30-35.

"Saudi Arabia Buys More U.S. Foods," *Foreign Agriculture*, XIV, No. 5, February 9, 1976, 2-4.

"Saudi Arabia Kingdom's Foreign Policy Remains Unchanged," *The Link*, 8, No. 3, Summer 1975, 1-8.

Sayigh, Yusuf A. "Problems and Prospects of Development in the Arabian Peninsula." Pages 286-303 in Derek Hopwood (ed.), *The Arabian Peninsula: Society and Politics.* Totowa, New Jersey: Rowman and Littlefield, 1972.

Schacht, Joseph. *An Introduction to Islamic Law.* Oxford: Clarendon Press, 1964.

Schieffelin, Olivia (ed.). *Muslim Attitudes Toward Family Planning.* New York: Demographic Division, The Population Council, 1967.

Schmidt, Peter. "Letter from Saudi Arabia: In the Name of Allah," *Encounter* [London], XLII, No. 6, June 1974, 48-51.

Schultz, T. Paul. *Fertility Patterns and Their Determinants in the Arab Middle East.* (Rand Corporation Series, No. RM-4978-FF.) Santa Monica: Rand Corporation, 1970.

Sebai, Zohair A. "Knowledge, Attitudes and Practice of Family Planning: Profile of a Bedouin Community of Saudi Arabia," *Journal of Biosocial Science* [Oxford], 6, No. 4, October 1973, 453-461.

Shahid, Irfan. "Pre-Islamic Arabia." Pages 3-29 in P.M. Holt, Ann K.S. Lambton, and Bernard Lewis (eds.), *The Cambridge History of Islam, I: The Central Islamic Lands.* Cambridge: Cambridge University Press, 1970.

Shamekh, Muhammad Abdul Rahman al. "The Birth of the Critical Essay in Saudi Literature," *Al-Darah* [Riyadh], 1, No. 1, February 1975, 9.

Sharabi, Hisham. *Arab Intellectuals and the West: The Formative Years, 1875-1914.* Baltimore: Johns Hopkins University Press, 1970.

Skzynear, Lynn. "The Arab Woman's Changing Role," *Christian Science Monitor*, January 30, 1975, 15.

Smalley, W.J. "The Wahhabis and Ibn Sa'ud," *Muslim World*, XXII, No. 2, July 1932, 227-246.

Smith, Wilfred Cantwell. *Islam in Modern History.* New York: Mentor Books, 1957.

Stamp, L. Dudley (ed.). *A History of Land Use in Arid Regions.* Paris: United Nations Educational, Scientific and Cultural Organization, 1961.

Stevens, J.H., and R. King (comps.). *A Bibliography of Saudi Arabia.*

(Occasional Paper Series, No. 3.) Durham, England: Centre for Middle Eastern and Islamic Studies, University of Durham, 1973.

Summary of Saudi Arabian Five-Year Development Plan. Washington: United States-Saudi Arabian Joint Commission on Economic Cooperation, 1975.

Sweet, Louise E. "The Arabian Peninsula." Pages 199-266 in Louise E. Sweet (ed.), *The Central Middle East: A Handbook of Anthropology and Published Research on the Nile Valley, the Arab Levant, Southern Mesopotamia, the Arabian Peninsula, and Israel.* New Haven: Human Relations Area Files Press, 1971.

──────. "Camel Raiding of North Arabian Bedouin: A Mechanism of Ecological Adaption," *American Anthropologist*, 67, No. 5, October 1966, 1132-1150.

Szyliowicz, Joseph S. *Education and Modernization in the Middle East.* Ithaca: Cornell University Press, 1973.

Tachau, Frank (ed.). *Political Elites and Political Development in the Middle East.* Cambridge, Massachusetts: Schenkman Publishing, 1975.

Taylor, Alice (ed.). *Focus on the Middle East.* New York: Praeger, 1971.

Thesiger, Wilfred. *Arabian Sands.* New York: E.P. Dutton, 1959.

Thomas, Alfred, Jr. *Saudi Arabia: A Study of the Educational System of the Kingdom of Saudi Arabia and Guide to the Academic Placement of Students from the Kingdom of Saudi Arabia in United States Educational Institutions.* (World Education Series.) Washington: American Association of Collegiate Registrars and Admissions Officers, 1968.

Tibawi, A.L. *Islamic Education: Its Traditions and Modernization into the Arab National Systems.* London: Luzac, 1972.

Twitchell, K.S. *Saudi Arabia, with an Account of the Development of Its Natural Resources.* Princeton: Princeton University Press, 1953.

U.N. Industrial Development Organization. *Summaries of Industrial Development Plans*, III. (IO, 109.) Vienna: UNIDO, 1973.

U.S. Department of Labor. Bureau of Labor Statistics. *Labor Law and Practice in the Kingdom of Saudi Arabia.* Washington: GPO, 1972.

Uzayzi, R.Z., and Joseph Chelhod. "L'amour et le mariage dans le désert," *Objets et Mondes* [Paris], IX, No. 3, 1969, 269-278.

Van Beek, Gus W. "The Rise and Fall of Arabia Felix," *Scientific American*, 221, No. 6, December 1969, 36-46.

Van der Leecen, Frits. *Water Resources of the World.* Port Washington, New York: Water Information Center, 1975.

Van der Meulen, D. *The Wells of Ibn Sa'ud.* New York: Frederick A. Praeger, 1957.

Van Nieuwenhuijze, C.A.O. *Sociology of the Middle East: A Stocktaking and Interpretation.* (Social, Economic, and Political Studies of the Middle East, No. 1.) Leiden: E.J. Brill, 1971.

Von Grunebaum, Gustave E. "Growth and Structure of Arabian Poetry, A.D. 500-1000." Pages 121-141 in Nabih Amin Farris (ed.), *The Arab Heritage*. New York: Russell and Russell, 1963.

"Wahhabiya." Pages 618-621 in H.A.R. Gibb and J.H. Kramers (eds.), *Shorter Encyclopedia of Islam*. Ithaca: Cornell University Press, 1953.

Wall, Michael. "The Arabs' New Frontier," *Middle East International* [London], No. 6, December 1969, 36-46.

Walton, Kenneth. *The Arid Zones*. Chicago: Aldine Publishing, 1969.

Watt, W. Montgomery. "Muhammad." Pages 30-56 in P.M. Holt, Ann K.S. Lambton, and Bernard Lewis (eds.), *The Cambridge History of Islam, I: The Central Islamic Lands*. Cambridge: Cambridge University Press, 1970.

———. *Muhammad: Prophet and Statesman*. London: Oxford University Press, 1961.

Wenner, Manfred W. "Saudi Arabia: Survival of Traditional Elites." Pages 157-192 in Frank Tachau (ed.), *Political Elites and Political Development in the Middle East*. Cambridge, Massachusetts: Schenkman Publishing, 1975.

Winder, Richard Bayly. *Saudi Arabia in the Nineteenth Century*. New York: St. Martin's Press, 1965. .

Wolf, Eric. "The Social Organization of Mecca and the Origin of Islam," *Southwestern Journal of Anthropology*, 7, No. 4, Winter 1951, 329-356.

Wright, Pearce. "The King Faisal Medical City," *Times* [London], May 13, 1975, I-X.

Zafer, Mohammed Ismail. "An Investigation of Factors Which Are Associated with Enrollment and Non-Enrollment in Teacher Education Programs of Public Education in Saudi Arabia." Unpublished Ph.D. dissertation. East Lansing: Department of Secondary Education, Michigan State University, 1971.

Zeuner, F.A. *A History of Domesticated Animals*. New York: Harper and Row, 1963.

(Various issues of the following publications were also used in the preparation of this section: *Arab Report and Record* [London], January 1972-May 1976; *Christian Science Monitor* [Boston], January 1975-May 1976; *Financial Times* [London], January 1975-May 1976; *Foreign Broadcast Information Service: Middle East and North Africa* [Washington], September 1975-May 1976; *Middle East Economic Digest* [London], January 1972-May 1976; *New York Times*, January 1975-May 1976; and *Washington Post*, January 1975-May 1976.)

Section II. Political

Abir, Mordechai. *Oil, Power and Politics: Conflict in Arabia, the Red Sea and the Gulf*. London: Frank Cass, 1974.

Adelman, Morris A. "The Political Economy of World Oil." (Paper presented at Annual Meeting of American Economic Association, December 1973.) New York: 1973 (mimeo.).

Al-Awaji, Ibrahim Mohamed. "Bureaucracy and Society in Saudi Arabia." Unpublished Ph.D. dissertation. Charlottesville: Woodrow Wilson Department of Government and Foreign Affairs, University of Virginia, 1971.

Alexander, Yonah. *The Role of Communications in the Middle East Conflict: Ideological and Religious Aspects.* New York: Praeger, 1974.

Al-Hamid, Hamad S. "The Legislative Process and the Development of Saudi Arabia." Unpublished Ph.D. dissertation. Los Angeles: Department of International Relations, University of Southern California, 1973.

Al-Marayati, Abid A. (ed.) *The Middle East: Its Governments and Politics.* Belmont, California: Duxbury, 1972.

Al-Mazyad, Sulaiman M. "The Structure and Function of Public Personnel Administration in Saudi Arabia." Unpublished Ph.D. dissertation. Claremont, California: Department of Political Science, Claremont Graduate School, 1972.

Al Tamimi, M. Amin. "The Genealogical Tree of the Al Saud Dynasty." (In Arabic.) Cairo: Department of Design, 1968.

Anderson, J.N.D. *Islamic Law in the Modern World.* New York: New York University Press, 1959.

Anderson, J.N.D. (ed.) *Changing Law in Developing Countries.* New York: Praeger, 1963.

Aramco Handbook. Dhahran: Arabian American Oil Company, 1968.

Azar, Edward E. *Probe for Peace: Small-State Hostilities.* Minneapolis: Burgess, 1973.

Azar, Edward E., and Thomas J. Sloan. *Dimensions of Interaction: A Source Book for the Study of Behavior of 31 Nations from 1948-1973.* Pittsburgh: Center for International Studies, University of Pittsburgh, 1975.

Becker, Abraham S., Bent Hansen, and Malcolm H. Kerr. *The Economics and Politics of the Middle East.* New York: American Elsevier, 1975.

Beling, Willard A. (ed.) *The Middle East: Quest for an American Policy.* Albany: State University of New York Press, 1973.

Bidwell, Robin L. *The Arab World, 1900-1972.* London: Frank Cass, 1973.

Bill, James A., and Carl Leiden. *The Middle East: Politics and Power.* Boston: Allyn and Bacon, 1974.

Borthwick, Bruce M. "The Islamic Sermon as a Channel of Political Communication," *Middle East Journal,* XXI, No. 3, Summer 1967, 299-313.

Boyd, Douglas A. "The Arab States Broadcasting Union," *Journal of Broadcasting,* 19, No. 3, Summer 1975, 311-320.

———. "An Historical and Descriptive Analysis of the Evolution and Development of Saudi Arabian Television." Unpublished Ph.D. dissertation. Minneapolis: Department of Journalism, University of Minnesota, 1972.

Bujra, Abdalla S. *The Politics of Stratification: A Study of Political Change in a South Arabian Town.* Oxford: Clarendon Press, 1973.

Chapman, Richard A. "Administrative Reform in Saudi Arabia," *Journal of Administration Overseas* [London], XIII, No. 2, April 1974, 332-347.

Cottrell, Alvin J. "The Political Balance in the Persian Gulf," *Strategic Review*, II, No. 1, Winter 1974, 32-38.

Coulson, Noel J. *A History of Islamic Law.* Edinburgh: Aldine, 1964.

De Gaury, Gerald. *Faisal: King of Saudi Arabia.* New York: Praeger, 1966.

De Tarrazi, Phillip. *History of the Arab Press.* London: Trinity Press, 1967.

Edens, David G. "The Anatomy of the Saudi Revolution," *International Journal of Middle East Studies* [London], 5, No. 1, January 1974, 50-64.

Eilts, Hermann F. "Social Revolution in Saudi Arabia," Pt. I, *Parameters: The Journal of the Army War College*, 1, No. 1, Spring 1971, 4-18.

———. "Social Revolution in Saudi Arabia," Pt. II, *Parameters: The Journal of the Army War College*, 1, No. 2, Fall 1971, 22-33.

Entelis, John P. "Nationalism, Nasserism, and the Arab World," *Arab Journal*, IV, No. 1, Winter 1967, 35-42.

Field, Michael. *A Hundred Million Dollars a Day.* London: Sidgwick and Jackson, 1975.

Fontana, Charles J. "Power Politics: Saudi Arabian Style." (Report No. 0965-74.) Maxwell Air Force Base, Alabama: Air University, May 1974 (mimeo.).

Green, Timothy. *The Universal Eye: The World of Television.* New York: Stein and Day, 1972.

Hadda, Wadi'd. "The Interaction Between Science and Society in the Arabic Press of the Middle East," *Science Education*, 58, No. 1, 1974, 35-49.

Halliday, Fred. *Arabia Without Sultans.* New York: Random House, 1975.

Hammond, Paul Y., and Sidney S. Alexander (eds.). *Political Dynamics in the Middle East.* New York: American Elsevier, 1972.

Holden, David. "A Family Affair," *New York Times Magazine*, July 6, 1975, 8-9, 26-27.

Hopwood, Derek (ed.). *The Arabian Peninsula: Society and Politics.* Totowa, New Jersey: Rowman and Littlefield, 1972.

International Institute for Strategic Studies. *The Middle East and the International System*, Pt. 2: Security and the Energy Crisis. (Adelphi Papers, No. 115.) London: 1975.

Ismael, Tareq Y., et al. *The Middle East in World Politics.* Syracuse: Syracuse University Press, 1974.

Kerr, Malcolm. *The Arab Cold War.* (2d ed.) New York: Oxford University Press, 1971.

Kraft, Joseph. "Letter from Saudi Arabia," *New Yorker,* October 20, 1975, 111-139.

Lenczowski, George. *Soviet Advances in the Middle East.* Washington: American Enterprise Institute, 1972.

——. "Tradition and Reform in Saudi Arabia," *Current History,* 53, No. 306, February 1976, 94-104, 115-116.

Levy, Reuben. *The Social Structure of Islam.* (2d ed.). London: Cambridge University Press, 1969.

Liebesny, Herbert J. *The Law of the Near and Middle East: Readings, Cases, and Materials.* Albany: State University of New York Press, 1975.

Long, David E. "The Board of Grievances in Saudi Arabia," *Middle East Journal,* XXVII, No. 1, Winter 1973, 71-75.

McClelland, Charles A., and Anne Ancoli Gilbar. "An Interaction Survey of the Middle East." Pages 149-168 in Willard A. Beling (ed.), *The Middle East: Quest for an American Policy.* Albany: State University of New York Press, 1973.

Malone, Joseph J. *The Arab Lands of Western Asia.* Englewood Cliffs: Prentice-Hall, 1973.

Mansfield, Peter (ed.). *The Middle East: A Political and Economic Survey.* (4th ed.) New York: Oxford University Press, 1973.

Maull, Hanns. "Oil and Influence: The Oil Weapon Examined." (Adelphi Papers, No. 117) London: International Institute for Strategic Studies, 1975.

Melamid, Alexander. "Boundary Disputes in the Persian (Arab) Gulf." (Paper presented at Annual Meeting of Middle East Studies Association, 1974.) Boston: 1974 (mimeo.).

Merrill, John C., Carter R. Bryan, and Marvin Alisky. *The Foreign Press: A Survey of the World's Journalism.* Baton Rouge: Louisiana State University Press, 1970.

Middle East and North Africa, 1975-76. (22d ed.) London: Europa Publications, 1975.

Mowlana, Hamid. "Mass Media Systems and Communications Behavior." Pages 584-598 in Michael Adams (ed.), *The Middle East: A Handbook.* London: Anthony Blond, 1971.

——. "The Press and National Development in the Middle East," *Intellect,* 103, No. 2371, October 1975, 38-45.

Nakhleh, Emile A. *Arab-American Relations in the Persian Gulf.* Washington: American Enterprise Institute, 1975.

——. *The United States and Saudi Arabia: A Policy Analysis.* Washington: American Enterprise Institute, 1975.

Page, Stephen. *The USSR and Arabia: The Development of Soviet Policies and Attitudes Towards the Countries of the Arabian Peninsula.* London: Central Asian Research Centre, 1972.
Polk, William R. *The United States and the Arab World.* (3d ed.) Cambridge: Harvard University Press, 1975.
Rand, Christopher T. *Making Democracy Safe for Oil: Oilmen and the Islamic East.* Boston: Little, Brown, 1975.
Rentz, George. "Saudi Arabia: The Islamic Island," *Journal of International Affairs,* XIX, No. 1, 1965, 77-86.
Rugh, William A. "Emergence of a New Middle Class in Saudi Arabia," *Middle East Journal,* 27, No. 1, Winter 1973, 9-20.
Rustow, Dankwart. *Middle Eastern Political Systems.* Englewood Cliffs: Prentice-Hall, 1971.
Sanger, Richard H. "Ibn Saud's Program for Arabia," *Middle East Journal,* I, No. 2, April 1947, 180-190.
Saudi Arabia. Central Planning Organization. *Development Plan 1395-1400 (1975-80).* (Reproduced by National Technical Information Service, U.S. Department of Commerce, PB 246,572.) Springfield, Virginia: NTIS, 1976.
Schacht, Joseph. *An Introduction to Islamic Law.* Oxford: Clarendon Press, 1964.
Shaker, Fatina A. "Modernization of the Developing Nations: The Case of Saudi Arabia." Unpublished Ph.D. dissertation. Lafayette: Department of Political Science, Purdue University, 1972.
Shamekh, Muhammad Abdul Rahman al. "Journalism in Saudi Arabia: A Historical Analysis," *Journal of the Gulf and Arabian Peninsula Studies* (in Arabic) [Kuwait], I, No. 3, July 1975, 11-26.
Sheean, Vincent. *Faisal: The King and His Kingdom.* Tavistock, England: University Press of Arabia, 1975.
Shobaili, Abdulrahman S. "An Historical and Analytical Study of Broadcasting and Press in Saudi Arabia." Unpublished Ph.D. dissertation. Columbus: Ohio State University, 1971.
Solaim, Soliman A. "Constitutional and Judicial Organization in Saudi Arabia." Unpublished Ph.D. dissertation. Baltimore: Department of Political Science, Johns Hopkins University Press, 1970.
––––––. "Saudi Arabia's Judicial System," *Middle East Journal,* 25, No. 3, Summer 1971, 403-407.
Statistical Yearbook, 1973. (25th ed.) New York: Statistical Office, Department of Economic and Social Affairs, United Nations, 1974.
Stevens, J.H., and R. King (comps.). *A Bibliography of Saudi Arabia.* (Occasional Paper Series, No. 3.) Durham, England: Centre for Middle Eastern and Islamic Studies, University of Durham, 1973.
UNESCO Statistical Yearbook, 1974. Paris: United Nations Educational, Scientific and Cultural Organization, 1975.
U.S. Congress. 92d, 2d Session. House of Representatives. Committee on Foreign Affairs. Subcommittee on the Near East. *U.S. Inter-*

ests in and Policy Toward the Persian Gulf. Washington: GPO, 1972.

U.S. Congress, 93d, 1st Session. House of Representatives. Committee on Foreign Affairs. Subcommittee on the Near East and South Asia. *New Perspectives on the Persian Gulf.* Washington: GPO, 1973.

U.S. Congress. 93d, 2d Session. House of Representatives. Committee on Foreign Affairs. *The Persian Gulf, 1974: Money, Politics, Arms, and Power.* Washington: GPO, 1975.

U.S. Congress. 93d, 2d Session. House of Representatives. Committee on Foreign Affairs. Subcommittees on Europe and on the Near East and South Asia. *United States-Europe Relations and the 1973 Middle East War.* Washington: GPO, 1974.

U.S. Congress. 94th, 1st Session. House of Representatives. Committee on International Relations. *United States Arms Sales to the Persian Gulf.* Washington: GPO, 1975.

U.S. Congress. 94th, 1st Session. House of Representatives. Committee on International Relations. Special Subcommittee on Investigations. *The Persian Gulf, 1975: The Continuing Debate on Arms Sales.* Washington: GPO, 1976.

U.S. Congress. 93d, 2d Session. Senate. Committee on Foreign Relations. Subcommittee on Multinational Corporations. *Multinational Corporations and United States Foreign Policy.* Washington: GPO, 1974.

U.S. Congress. 94th, 1st Session. Senate. Committee on Foreign Relations. *Multinational Corporations and United States Foreign Policy.* Washington: GPO, 1975.

U.S. Department of State. Bureau of Public Affairs. Office of Media Services. "Current Policy: The Palestinian Issue." (No. 8.) Washington: November 1976.

―――. "News Release: Saudi Arabia and the United States." Washington: February 23, 1976.

United States Information Agency. *Arabian Peninsula: A Communications Fact Book.* Washington: GPO, 1964.

Watt, W. Montgomery. *Islamic Political Thought.* Edinburgh: Edinburgh University Press, 1968.

Wenner, Manfred W. "Saudi Arabia: Survival of Traditional Elites." Pages 157-192 in Frank Tachau (ed.), *Political Elites and Political Development in the Middle East.* Cambridge, Massachusetts: Schenkman Publishing, 1975.

Wilkenfeld, Jonathan, Virginia L. Lussier, and Dale Tahtinen. "Conflict Interactions in the Middle East, 1949-1967," *Journal of Conflict Resolution*, 16, No. 2, June 1972, 135-154.

World Communication: A 200-Country Survey of Press, Radio, Television, and Film. New York: UNESCO Press, 1975.

Young, Oran R. "Intermediaries and Interventionists: Third Parties in the Middle East Crisis," *International Journal*, 23, 1970, 52-73.

(Various issues of the following publications were also used in the preparation of this section: *Arab Report and Record* [London], January 1972-May 1976; *Christian Science Monitor* [Boston], January 1975-May 1976; *Financial Times* [London], January 1975-May 1976; *Foreign Broadcast Information Service: Middle East and North Africa* [Washington], September 1975-May 1976; *Middle East Economic Digest* [London], January 1972-May 1976; *New York Times*, January 1975-May 1976; and *Washington Post*, January 1975-May 1976.)

Section III. Economic

Adelman, Morris A. *The World Petroleum Market.* Baltimore: Johns Hopkins University Press, 1972.

Aramco: A Review of Operations, 1975. Dammam: Arabian American Oil Company, 1976.

Aramco Handbook. Dhahran: Arabian American Oil Company, 1968.

Asfour, Edmond Y., et al. *Saudi Arabia: Long-Term Projections of Supply and Demand for Agricultural Products.* Beirut: Economic Research Institute, American University of Beirut, 1965.

Chapman, Richard A. "Administrative Reform in Saudi Arabia." *Journal of Administration Overseas* [London], XIII, No. 2, April 1974, 332-347.

Cole, Donald Powell. *Nomads of the Nomads: The Al Murrah Bedouin of the Empty Quarter.* Chicago: Aldine Publishing, 1975.

Dequin, H. "Saudi Arabia." Pages 459-468 in *World Atlas of Agriculture*, II. Novara, Italy: International Association of Agricultural Economists, Instituto Geografico de Agostini, 1973.

The Europa Yearbook, 1975, A World Survey, I. London: Europa Publications, 1975.

Field, Michael. *A Hundred Million Dollars a Day.* London: Sidgwick and Jackson, 1975.

Freeman, S. David. *Energy: The New Era.* New York: Vintage Books, Random House, 1974.

Gurfinkel, Mariano. "As Oil Prices Rise," *International Monetary Fund Survey*, October 13, 1975, 297-305.

"The Hajj: A Special Issue," *Aramco World*, 25, No. 6, November-December 1974.

Hassanain, Mahjoob Ahmed. "An Economic Review of the Saudi Arabian Planning Framework." Unpublished Ph.D. dissertation. Pittsburgh: Faculty of Arts and Sciences, University of Pittsburgh, 1971.

Hitti, Said H., and George T. Abd. "The Economy and Finances of Saudi Arabia," *International Monetary Fund Staff Papers*, XXI, No. 2, July 1974, 247-306.

Hopwood, Derek (ed.). *The Arabian Peninsula: Society and Politics.* Totowa, New Jersey: Rowman and Littlefield, 1972.

International Institute for Strategic Studies. *The Middle East and the International System*, Pt. 2: Security and the Energy Crisis. (Adelphi Papers, No. 115.) London: 1975.

International Monetary Fund. Bureau of Statistics. *International Financial Statistics*, XXVIII, No. 11, November 1975, p. 355.

Jacoby, Neil H. *Multinational Oil*. (Studies of the Modern Corporation, Graduate School of Business, Columbia University.) New York: Macmillan, 1974.

Joyner, Christopher C. "The Petrodollar Phenomenon and Changing International Economic Relations," *World Affairs*, 138, No. 2, Fall 1975, 152-176.

Katanani, Ahmad Kamal. *Policies and Models for Planning the Economic Development of the Non-Oil Sector in Saudi Arabia*. Ph.D. dissertation. Economics Department, Iowa State University, 1971. Ann Arbor: Xerox University Microfilms. 72-12562.

Knauerhase, Ramon. *The Saudi Arabian Economy*. (Praeger Special Studies in International Economics and Development.) New York: Praeger, 1975.

Kraft, Joseph. "Letter from Saudi Arabia," *New Yorker*, October 20, 1975, 111-139.

Long, David E. "The Hajj Today: A Survey of the Contemporary Pilgrimage to Makkah." Unpublished Ph.D. dissertation. Washington: George Washington University, February 1973.

McLachan, Keith, and Narsi Ghorban. *Oil Production, Revenues, and Economic Development*. (Quarterly Economic Review Special Series, No. 18.) London: Economist Intelligence Unit, 1975.

Magnus, Ralph H. "Middle East Oil," *Current History*, 68, No. 402, February 1975, 49-53.

Nakhleh, Emile A. *Arab-American Relations in the Persian Gulf*. Washington: American Enterprise Institute, 1975.

"The Oil Crisis: In Perspective," *Daedalus*, 104, No. 4, Fall 1975.

"Out of the Fire," *Economist* (Special Supplement) [London], 255, No. 6873, May 17, 1975.

Parker, John B. "U.S. Agricultural Exports to the Arabian Peninsula Soar," *FATUS-Foreign Agricultural Trade of the U.S.*, October 1975, 54-81.

Polk, William R., and William J. Mares. *Passing Brave*. New York: Ballantine Books, 1973.

Price Waterhouse. *Doing Business in Saudi Arabia*. New York: October 1975.

Rand, Christopher T. *Making Democracy Safe for Oil: Oilmen and the Islamic East*. Boston: Little, Brown, 1975.

Sampson, Anthony. *The Seven Sisters: The Great Oil Companies and the World They Made*. New York: Viking Press, 1975.

Saudi Arabia. Central Planning Organization. *Development Plan 1395-1400 (1975-80)*. (Reproduced by National Technical Information Service, U.S. Department of Commerce, PB 246,572.) Springfield, Virginai: NTIS, 1976.
Saudi Arabia. Saudi Arabian Monetary Agency. *Annual Report, 1394-1395 A.H.* Jiddah: SAMA, 1975.
———. *Statistical Summary*. (No. 2, 1393-94.) Dammam: Saudi Arabian Government Publications, 1975, pp. 62-65, 72-73.
———. *Statistical Summary*. N.pl.: n.pub., December 1969-January 1970, pp. 40-42.
"Saudis Will Cut Spending to Cool Economy," *Middle East Economic Digest* [London], 20, No. 10, March 5, 1976, pp. 6 and 29.
Stevens, J.H., and R. King (comps.). *A Bibliography of Saudi Arabia*. (Occasional Paper Series, No. 3.) Durham, England: Centre for Middle Eastern and Islamic Studies, University of Durham, 1973.
Tachau, Frank (ed.). *Political Elites and Political Development in the Middle East*. Cambridge, Massachusetts: Schenkman Publishing, 1975.
U.N. Industrial Development Organization. *Summaries of Industrial Development Plans*, III. (IO, 109.) Vienna: UNIDO, 1973, 255-317.
U.S. Congress. 93d, 1st Session. House of Representatives. Committee on Foreign Affairs. Subcommittee on the Near East and South Asia. *New Perspectives on the Persian Gulf*. Washington: GPO, 1973.
U.S. Department of Commerce. Domestic and International Business Administration. *Foreign Economic Trends and Their Implications for the United States: Saudi Arabia*. (FET-75-069.) Washington: GPO, June 1975.
———. "World Trade Outlook for Near East and North Africa." (Overseas Business Reports, OBR 75-47 and OBR 76-09.) Washington: GPO, November 1975.
U.S. Department of the Interior. Bureau of Mines. *Mineral Trades Notes*, 72, No. 7, July 1975.
Wells, Donald A. *Saudi Arabian Revenues and Expenditures*. Baltimore: Johns Hopkins University Press, 1974.
(Various Issues of the following periodicals were also used in the preparation of this section: *Aramco World* [New York], January 1970-April 1976; *Economist* [London], January-April 1976; *Financial Times* [London], January 1975-April 1976; *International Financial Statistics* [Washington], January 1975-April 1976; *Middle East Economic Digest* [London], January 1975-April 1976; *Middle East International* [London], January 1975-April 1976; *Mid East Markets* [New York], January 1975-April 1976; *New York Times*, January 1975-April 1976; *Oil and Gas Journal* [Tulsa, Oklahoma], January 1975-April 1976; *Petroleum Intelligence Weekly* [Neww York], Jnuary 1975-April 1976; *Quarterly Economic Review: Saudi Arabia-Jordan* [London], January

1972-April 1976; and *Saudi Economic Survey* [Jiddah], January 1975-April 1976.)

Section IV. National Defense

Abir, Mordechai. *Oil, Power and Politics: Conflict in Arabia, the Red Sea and the Gulf*. London: Frank Cass, 1974.

Adelman, Morris A. "The Political Economy of World Oil." (Paper presented at Annual Meeting of American Economic Association, December 1973.) New York: 1973 (mimeo.).

"Arab Military Industries a Reality," *The Middle East* [London], No. 10, July 1975, 105-108.

Aramco Handbook. Dhahran: Arabian American Oil Company, 1968.

"Arms Sales to Saudi Arabia," *International Defense Review* [Geneva], 8, No. 1, February 1975, 23.

Becker, Abraham S., Bent Hansen, and Malcolm H. Kerr. *The Economics and Politics of the Middle East*. New York: American Elsevier, 1975.

Be'eri, Eliezer. *Army Officers in Arab Politics and Society*. New York: Praeger, 1969.

Bill, James A., and Carl Leiden. *The Middle East: Politics and Power*. Boston: Allyn and Bacon, 1974.

Cottrell, Alvin J. "The Political Balance in the Persian Gulf," *Strategic Review*, II, No. 1, Winter 1974, 32-38.

De Gaury, Gerald. *Faisal: King of Saudi Arabia*. New York: Praeger, 1966.

Eilts, Hermann F. "Social Revolution in Saudi Arabia," Pt. I, *Parameters: The Journal of the Army War College*, 1, No. 1, Spring 1971, 4-18.

――――. "Social Revolution in Saudi Arabia," Pt. II, *Parameters: The Journal of the Army War College*, 1, No. 2, Fall 1971, 22-33.

Gottheil, Fred M. "An Economic Assessment of the Military Burden in the Middle East: 1960-1970," *Journal of Conflict Resolution*, XVIII, No. 3, September 1974, 502-513.

Gutteridge, William. *Military Institutions and Powers in the New States*. New York: Praeger, 1965.

Hammond, Paul Y., and Sidney S. Alexander (eds.). *Political Dynamics in the Middle East*. New York: American Elsevier, 1972.

Harrigan, Anthony. "Security Interests in the Persian Gulf and Western Indian Ocean," *Strategic Review*, I, No. 3, Fall 1973, 13-22.

Hopwood, Derek (ed.). *The Arabian Peninsula: Society and Politics*. Totowa, New Jersey: Rowman and Littlefield, 1972.

Hurewitz, J.C. *Middle East Politics: The Military Dimension*. New York: Praeger, 1969

International Institute for Strategic Studies. *The Military Balance 1975-1976*. London: 1975.

Johnson, John J. (ed.) *The Role of the Military in Underdeveloped Countries.* Princeton: Princeton University Press, 1962.
Joshua, Wynfred, and Stephen P. Gibert. *Arms for the Third World: Soviet Military Aid Diplomacy.* Baltimore: Johns Hopkins University Press, 1969.
Malone, Joseph J. *The Arab Lands of Western Asia.* Englewood Cliffs: Prentice-Hall, 1973.
Maull, Hanns. "Oil and Influence: The Oil Weapon Examined." (Adelphi Papers, No. 117.) London: International Institute for Strategic Studies, 1975.
Melamid, Alexander. "Boundary Disputes in the Persian (Arab) Gulf." (Paper presented at Annual Meeting of Middle East Studies Association, 1974.) Boston: 1974 (mimeo.).
Middle East and North Africa, 1975-76. (22d ed.) London: Europa Publications, 1975.
"The Middle East and the International System: Security and Energy Crisis." (Adelphi Papers, No. 115.) London: International Institute for Strategic Studies, 1974 (mimeo.).
Nakhleh, Emile A. *The United States and Saudi Arabia: A Policy Analysis.* Washington: American Enterprise Institute, 1975.
Naqvi, Ali Raza. "Laws of War in Islam," *Islamic Studies* [Islamabad, Pakistan], 13, No. 1, 1974, 24-43.
Narayanan, R. "U.S. Postures in West Asia: Defence Arrangements with Saudi Arabia—A Case Study." Pages 298-323 in M.S. Rajan (ed.), *Studies in Politics: National and International.* New Delhi: Vikas Publications, 1971.
Page, Stephen. *The USSR and Arabia: The Development of Soviet Policies and Attitudes Towards the Countries of the Arabian Peninsula.* London: Central Asian Research Centre, 1972.
Pranger, Robert J. "Toward Arms Control in the Middle East." (Middle East Problem Paper, No. 9.) Washington: Middle East Institute, 1974.
Pranger, Robert J., and Dale R. Tahtinen. *Implications of the 1976 Arab-Israeli Military Status.* Washington: American Enterprise Institute, 1976.
Rand, Christopher T. *Making Democracy Safe for Oil: Oilmen and the Islamic East.* Boston: Little, Brown, 1975.
Rugh, William A. "Emergence of a New Middle Class in Saudi Arabia," *Middle East Journal,* 27, No. 1, Inter 1973, 9-20.
Saudi Arabia. Central Planning Organization. *Development Plan 1395-1400 (1975-80).* (Reproduced by National Technical Information Service, U.S. Department of Commerce, PB 246, 572.) Springfield, Virginia: NTIS, 1976.
Saudi Arabia. Saudi Arabian Monetary Agency. *Annual Report. 1394-1395 A.H.* Jiddah: SAMA, 1975.

———. *Statistical Summary*. (No. 2, 1393-94.) Dammam: Saudi Arabian Government Publications. 1975.

"Saudis Will Cut Spending to Cool Economy," *Middle East Economic Digest* [London], 20, No. 10, March 5, 1976, pp. 6 and 29.

Stevens, J.H., and R. King (comps.). *A Bibliography of Saudi Arabia*. (Occasional Paper Series, No. 3.) Durham, England: Centre for Middle Eastern and Islamic Studies, University of Durham, 1973.

Stockholm International Peace Research Institute. *Arms Trade Registers: The Arms Trade with the Third World*. Cambridge: MIT Press, 1975.

Stork, Joe. *Middle East Oil and the Energy Crisis*. New York: Monthly Review Press, June 1975.

Tahtinen, Dale R. *Arms in the Persian Gulf*. Washington: American Enterprise Institute, 1974.

U.S. Arms Control and Disarmament Agency. *World Military Expenditure Arms Trade 1963-1973*. Washington: GPO, 1975.

U.S. Congress. 92d, 2d Session. House of Representatives. Committee on Foreign Affairs. Subcommittee on the Near East. *U.S. Interests in and Policy Toward the Persian Gulf*. Washington: GPO, 1972.

U.S. Congress. 93d, 1st Session. House of Representatives. Committee on Foreign Affairs. Subcommittee on the Near East and South Asia. *New Perspectives on the Persian Gulf*. Washington: GPO, 1973.

U.S. Congress. 94th,, 1st Session. House of Representatives. Committee on International Relations. *United States Arms Sales to the Persian Gulf*. Washington: GPO, 1975.

U.S. Congress. 94th, 1st Session. House of Representatives. Committee on International Relations. Special Subcommittee on Investigations. *The Persian Gulf, 1975: The Continuing Debate on Arms Sales*. Washington: GPO, 1976.

U.S. Congress, 93d, 2d Session. Senate. Committee on Foreign Relations. Subcommittee on Multinational Corporations. *Multinational Corporations and United States Foreign Policy*. Washington: GPO, 1974.

U.S. Congress. 94th, 1st Session. Senate. Committee on Foreign Relations. *Multinational Corporations and United States Foreign Policy*. Washington: GPO, 1975.

U.S. Department of Commerce. Office of Technical Services. Joint Publications Research Service—JPRS (Washington). The Following items are from the JPRS series:

Translations on the Near East and North Africa. "History and Current Status of Royal Saudi Air Force," *Aviation*, Paris, June 15-30, 1972. (JPRS 56531,No. 794, July 18, 1972.) "Inauguration of National Guard Training Center," *Al Madinah*, Jiddah, May 21, 1975. (JPRS 65287, No. 1383, July 22, 1975.) "Political Opposition Within

Nation Is Described at Length," *Swat al Taliah*, Aden July 4-5, 1973. (JPRS 60197, No. 1039, October 3, 1973.)

U.S. Department of Defense. *Foreign Military Sales and Military Assistance Facts.* Washington: Data Management Division, Comptroller, DSAA, November 1975.

Wenner, Manfred W. "Saudi Arabia: Survival of Traditional Elites." Pages 157-192 in Frank Tachau (ed.), *Political Elites and Political Development in the Middle East.* Cambridge, Massachusetts: Schenkman Publishing, 1975.

World Armaments and Disarmament: SIPRI Yearbook 1975. (Stockholm International Peace Research Institute.) Cambridge: MIT Press, 1975.

(Various issues of the following publications were also used in the preparation of this section: *Arab Report and Record* [London], January 1972-May 1976; *Christian Science Monitor* [Boston], January 1975-May 1976; *Financial Times* [London], January 1975-May 1976; *Foreign Broadcast Information Service: Middle East and North Africa* [Washington], September 1975-May 1976; *Middle East Economic Digest* [London], January 1972-May 1976; *New York Times*, January 1975-May 1976; and *Washington Post*, January 1975-May 1976.)

GLOSSARY

Al—Uppercase connotes family or belonging to, as in Al Saud (q.v.), Al Faisal, or Al Sudairi; lowercase represents the definite article *the*, as in Rub al Khali.

Al ash Shaykh—Literally the House of the Shaykh; the patrilineal descendants of Muhammad ibn Abd al Wahhab.

Al Saud—Literally the House of Saud; the patrilineal descendants of Muhammad ibn Saud.

amir (pl., *umara*)—Strictly speaking, commander. In Saudi Arabia amir often means prince.

awqaf—See waqf.

barrels per day—Production of crude oil and petroleum products is frequently measured in barrels per day and often abbreviated bpd or bd. Other measurements include barrels per year and metric tons. A barrel is a volume measure of forty-two United States gallons. Conversion of barrels to metric tons depends on the density of the specific product. About 7.3 barrels of average crude oil weigh one metric ton. Heavy crude would be about seven per metric ton. Light products such as gasoline and kerosine would average close to eight barrels per metric ton.

dhimmis—Tolerated subject peoples in Muslim realms. In exchange for the payment of special taxes and certain limitations of rights, they are permitted to practice their own religions and keep their own laws within their own communities. Dhimmis are "People of the Book," usually meaning Christians and Jews.

downstream—The oil industry views the production, processing, transportation, and sale of petroleum products as a flow process starting at the wellhead. Downstream includes any stage between the point of reference and the sale of products to the consumer. Upstream is the converse. Upstream of the wellhead includes exploration and drilling of wells.

fatwa—An authoritative legal interpretation by a mufti (q.v.) that can provide the basis for court decision or government action.

fiscal year (FY)—see table A.

flared—Much of the natural gas from Saudi crude oil production was burned in the open air from pipes at various facilities.

hadith—Tradition based on the precedent of Muhammad's words and deeds that serves as one of the sources of Islamic law.

haram—Literally both sacred and forbidden. Especially the sacred area surrounding Mecca that is closed to non-Muslims; also refers to other sacred areas.

hijra (pl., *hujar*)—Literally to migrate, to sever relations, to leave one's tribe. Used in two senses. Throughout the Muslim world hijra refers to the migration to Medina of Muhammad and his early followers. In this sense the word has come into European languages as Hegira and is usually somewhat misleadingly translated as "flight." In Saudi Arabia hijra also refers to the agricultural settlements of the Ikhwan al Muslimin (*q.v.*), which combined features of religious missions, farming communities, and army camps.

House of Saud—Al Saud (*q.v.*).

hujar—Plural of hijra (*q.v.*).

ibn—Literally son of; used before proper name to indicate descent from. *Bint* means daughter of; *banu* (or *bani*) is literally sons of and is used to mean tribe or family of.

Ikhwan al Muslimin—The Muslim Brethren; the brotherhood of desert warriors, founded by King Abd al Aziz, who were settled in the *hujar* (*q.v.*).

imam—A word used in several senses. In general use it means the leader of congregational prayers; as such it implies no ordination or special spiritual powers beyond sufficient education to carry out this function. It is also used figuratively by many Sunni (*q.v.*) Muslims to mean the leader of the Islamic community and in this sense traditionally designated the head of the House of Saud as the leader and guardian of religion in his domain. Among Shiites (*q.v*) the word takes on many complex and controversial meanings; in general, however, it indicates that descendant of the House of Ali who is believed to be God's designated repository of the spiritual authority believed to be inherent in that line. The identity of this individual and the means of ascertaining his identity have been the major issues causing divisions among Shiites.

jihad—The struggle to establish the law of God on earth, often interpreted to mean holy war.

majlis—Tribal council; in some countries the legislative assembly. Also the audience of the king or shaykh open to all citizens for the purposes of adjudication.

mufti—Religious jurist; interpreter of Muslim law. *mutawwiun*—Literally volunteers. The so-called religious police authorized to assure obedience with Wahhabi (*q.v.*) religious teachings.

qadi—Judge in sharia (*q.v.*) law courts.

Saudi riyal (SR)—Paper unit of currency that consists of twenty qurshes and 100 halalas. In March 1973 the par value of the riyal was defined with the International Monetary Fund (IMF) as SR4.28255 per one SDR (IMF special drawing rights—a unit of account made up of a basket of major international currencies), the equivalent in early 1976 of 3.20751 gram of fine gold per riyal. Saudi Arabia took advantage in September 1975 of the wide fluctuations around this SDR peg permitted by the IMF regulations in effect to link the riyal to the United States dollar for periods of time. This avoided frequent official exchange rate changes caused by the rapid changes in the value of international currencies, particularly the dollar. The history of the riyal for conversion purposes is: from 1954 to January 1960, SR3.75 per US$1; January 1960 to December 1971, SR4.50 per US$1; December 1971 to February 1973, SR4.14 per US$1; February 1973 to March 1973, SR3.73 per US$1; and March 1973 to early 1976, SR3.55 per US$1. These official rates at times differed substantially from the free market value of the riyal because of various economic factors.

Sharia—Islamic law.

sharif—Specifically descent from Muhammad through his daughter Fatima. Literally noble, exalted, having descent from illustrious ancestors. Frequently used as an honorific.

shaykh—Leader or chief. Used to mean either political leaders of tribes or towns or learned religious leaders. Also used as an honorific.

Shiite—A member of the smaller of the two great divisions of Islam. The Shiites supported the claims of Ali and his line to presumptive right to the caliphate and leadership of the world Muslim community and divided from the Sunni (q.v.) in the first great schism of Islam. Later schisms have produced further divisions among the Shiites.

SR—Saudi riyal (q.v.).

Sunni—The larger of the two great divisons of Islam. The Sunni, who rejected the claims of Ali's line, believe that they are the true followers of the Sunna, the guide to proper behavior composed of the Quran and the *hadith* (q.v.).

ulama (sing., *alim*)—Collective term for Muslim religious scholars.

Wahhabi—Name used outside Saudi Arabia to designate adherents to Wahhabism (q.v.).

Wahhabism—Name used outside Saudi Arabia to designate official interpretation of Islam in Saudi Arabia. The faith is a puritanical concept of Unitarianism (the oneness of God—Al Dawah al Tauhid) that was preached by Muhammad ibn Abd al Wahhab, whence his Muslim opponents derived the name.

waqf (pl.,*awqaf*)—In Muslim law a permanent endowment or trust, usually of real estate, in which the proceeds are spent for purposes designated by the benefactor. Usually devoted to charitable purposes.

INDEX

Abd al Aziz (1765-1803): 25, 26
Abd al Aziz ibn Abd ar Rahman Al Saud (1902-53): 28, 29-35, 46; British support, 30, 31-32, 48, 211, 313; conquests, 29-30, 31, 47-48, 160, 308, 312-314; criticism of, 35; discovery of oil and oil concessions, 7, 9, 10, 34, 142, 169, 212, 268-269; exercise of judiciary powers, 188, 190; exile in Kuwait, 29, 159-160; foreign policy, 208, 216; founded kingdom of Saudi Arabia, 1, 9, 10, 32, 76, 133, 141-142, 160, 313; generosity, 48, 87; government, 32-34, 160, 166, 173, 177, 178, 206; legal system, expansion of, 137, 143, 187, 190; lineage, 26, 141, 159, 163-164, 165; loyalty and control of beduin tribes, 3, 30, 123-124, 131, 141-142, 143, 175, 313, 338-339, 345; modernization under, 91, 96, 142, 193, 194, 311, 312, 314, 331, 339; overspending, 34-35; personal attributes, 33, 34-35, 131, 313; political marriages, 31, 33, 143, 160; World War I, 30-31
Abd al Aziz ibn Rashid, defeat by Abd al Aziz Al Saud; 160
Abd Allah (1814-18): 26, 27, 165
Abd Allah (1865-71, 1875-89): 26, 28-29
Abd Allah bin Ubayy: 22
Abd Allah ibn Abd al Aziz Al Saud: 2, 3, 158, 163, 170, 178, 205, 317, 318
Abd Allah ibn Abd ar Rahman: 162-164
Abd Allah ibn Thunayyan: 159
Abd ar Rahman (1875, 1889-91): 26, 29, 159, 160, 165
Abdullah, King of Transjordan: 31
Abdullah al Sallal: 316
Abdullah ibn Jiluwi: 33
Abdullah Sulaiman: 33
Abha: 80
Abqaiq: 52, 59, 260
Abu Bakr: 23, 118
Abu Dhabi: 12, 47, 210
Abu Hanifa (Hanafi school of law): 186
Abu Jifan oil field: 261
Abu Safah oil field: 261
Abu Sufyan: 19-20, 21
Abu Talib: 19, 20
Abyssinia: 16
Adelman, Morris A.: 252
Adham, Kamal: 216
administrative districts: viii, 48, 184-85, 340; map, 49; under Abd al Aziz, 33, 338-339
Aflaj oasis: 51
Africa, radio broadcasts: 204
Agricultural Bank: 229-230
agriculture (*see also* livestock): 50, 51, 285, 286-297; Asir highlands, 45, 289, 290, 291, 292; budget, 235, 236, 240, 241, 242; constraints, 45, 55, 286-287; credit, 229-230, 296; cropping patterns and production, 50, 55, 285, 289, 291-293; date palms, 55, 285, 288, 289, 291, 292; development projects, 34, 55, 132, 288; dune shifting problems, 55, 289, 296; employment, 224, 236, 237, 287; five year plans, 239, 288-289, 293, 296; GDP, ix, 222, 224, 287, 291; government ownership of land, 143; government role, 295-297; irrigation, 54-55, 79, 289, 293, 295, 296; landholdings, 289-291; model farms, exhibits and cooperatives, 185; subsistence level, 291; tenant farming, 290; traditional, 285, 287-288; water resource development, 54, 295; wells and oases, 285, 288, 290-291
Ahmad ibn Abd ar Rahman Al Saud: 162, 164
Ahmad ibn Muhammad ibn Hanbal: 120, 187
airfields: ix, 46, 60, 221
Al Abd Allah lineage: 159
Al ash Shaykh lineage: 4, 113, 121, 141, 144, 160, 165, 171, 188
Al-Awaji, Ibrahim: 132-133, 149
Al Bilad: 199, 200

375

Al Faisal lineage: 159
Al Kharj oasis: 51, 54, 59, 67
Al Manhal: 199, 200
Al Medina al Munwara: 199, 200
Al Murrah tribe: 135, 137, 143
Al Nadwah: 200
Al Naqrah minerals: 57
Al Nuayriyah: 67
Al Qaysumak: 67
Al Rashid lineage: 135, 143, 160, 313
Al Riyadh: 199, 200
Al Saud. *See* House of Saud
Al Tijarah: 200
Al Ukadh: 200
Al Yamamah: 201
Al Yaum: 201
Al Zazirah: 199, 200
Algeria: 36, 77; oil interests, 253, 256, 259
Ali (656): 118, 119
Ali Reza family: 306
Anayzah tribe: 135, 141
Arab cold war: 207
Arab-Israeli conflict: 207; 1967 war, 42, 209, 256, 257; 1973 war, 42-43, 169, 208; Saudi supportive role, 206, 207-208, 232, 315, 317, 337
Arab Maritime Petroleum Transport Company: 259
Arab Military Industries Organization (AMIO): 323
Arab Petroleum Investments Company: 259
Arab Shipbuilding and Repair Company: 259
Arab States Broadcasting Union: 196
Arabian American Oil Company (Aramco): 34, 264, 269-272, 301; Aramco Radio, Aramco Television, 202; construction and modernization of facilities, 35, 59, 62, 266-267, 270-271; fifty-fifty profit-sharing arrangements (tax), 255, 270; foreign workers, 36, 147; health and sanitation projects, 77, 79, 80, 83, 270-271; location of aquifers, 54; natural gas uses, 299; production, 7, 265-266; publications, 199; Ras Tanura oil refinery, 264, 267-268; relations with Saudi Arabia, 8, 37, 271, 331; Saudi government participation, 234, 257, 269; Saudi labor, 35, 36, 68, 271, 345
Arabian Oil Company: 265, 266, 268
Arabian Peninsula, Arabic name: 10
Arabian Sun: 199

Arafat: 85, 126, 127
Aramco. *See* Arabian American Oil Company
Arar: 67, 80
archeology: 11
armed forces (*see also* internal security; and Royal Saudi National Guard): ix, 311, 318-338; Army School Command, 325-326; budget, ix, 169, 235, 236, 240, 242, 321-322, 344; commander-in-chief, 157, 311, 318, 319; consensus in selection of king, 157; foreign military aid, ix, 8, 211, 312, 314, 316-317, 318, 320, 322-325, 331-337; internal security role, 311, 317; location of installations (map), 321; manpower, recruitment, and training, ix, 143-144, 311, 315, 320, 321, 323-326, 333-334, 335; military authority, 318; military justice, 327, 330; military ranks, pay, awards, 326-327; modernization, 3, 33, 39, 312, 315, 330-331, 339; National Guard loyalty to Faisal, 316, 339; posted abroad, ix, 208, 317; organization, 311, 317-320; potential offensive capability, 336, 337; potential political leadership, 171; Royal Guard, 162, 168, 315, 319, 326; Royal Saudi Air Force, ix, 3, 39, 212, 311, 319-320, 326, 327, 333, 334, 335; Royal Saudi Navy, ix, 3, 311, 319, 321, 326, 327, 334
Ash Shafi (Shafi school of law): 125, 186
Asir: 31, 33, 50-51, 54, 56; agriculture, 45, 289, 290, 291, 292; disease control, 79, 80; housing, 74; population and commercial center, 301; Yemeni refugees, 64, 132
Atayba tribe: 138
Australia, meat exports: 70
aviation, civil: 311
Awazim tribe: 134
Aws tribe: 17

Bab al Mandab: 14
Badiet ash Sham: 51
Badr, Imam Muhammad al: 316
Badr (town): 21, 22
Baghdad Pact: 37
Bahrain: 47, 209, 210, 264, 338; historic, 28; OAPEC membership, 259; oil, 267, 269
Bani Khalid tribe: 24, 25, 28
Bani Said tribe: 138
banks and banking (*see also names of banks):* 226-230, 243; banking licenses, 229; commercial, 226-228; conformity

to Islamic law, 226, 228-229; deposits, credit, 227-228, 229-230; government banking institutions, 228-230
Banu Nadir tribe: 17
Banu Quraysah tribe: 17
Banu Sinan tribe: 24, 121
Basra: 24
beduin: as unskilled labor, 147; blood feuds, 137-138, 143; contributions and disadvantages to state, 67, 148-149; courtship, marriage, family, 150-152; culture and values, 10, 16, 18, 34, 87, 93, 137-139, 143, 150, 324; definition, none, 67, 133; diet and nutrition, 71, 291; ghazw (raiding and plundering), 18, 19, 21, 23, 143, 293; government settlement projects (hujar), 30, 55, 67-68, 123, 142, 147, 293, 294-296, 313; government subsidies, 147, 294, 295; health services, 82; heroic tales and poems, 18; hospitality, 138, 139; lineage, 136-137, 138, 150; local government, 183-184; loyalty to House of Saud, 3, 30, 33-34, 123, 141-142, 143, 170, 175, 339; music and dance, 93; oil wealth, effect, 287, 297; pre-Islam, 16-19; self-perception, 11; settled communities, relationship, 134-135, 142; settlement patterns and villages, 66-68, 136, 294-295; shaykhs (amirs), selection, leadership, influence, 138-139, 148, 183, 184; social change, 147-149; social distinctions, 132, 134, 144, 148; traditional life, 16-19, 133, 134-139, 147-148, 285, 288; tribal leaders, role in selection of king, 157, 161; tribal loyalty, 67, 136-137, 288; tribal names and organization, 136-137, 150; tribal territorial limits, 47, 48, 63, 136, 148, 183, 288; tribes (map), 135; water rights, 290-291; women, 72, 152
birth rate. See health
Bishah wadi: 51
boundaries (see also names of countries): viii, 31, 41, 46-48, 210; maritime, 47; neutral zones, 31, 46, 209; oil ownership disputes, 48, 210; tribal de facto possession, 47, 48, 63, 136; undefined, indefinite, 45, 47, 63, 336
British entries. See under United Kingdom
Buraydah: 141, 202
Buraymi Oasis: 25, 35, 51, 289; dispute with British, 41, 47, 210, 211, 331
calendar: vi, 20, 75, 114; conversion of dates to Gregorian dates, vii
California Arabian Standard Oil Company (Casoc) (see also Arabian American Oil Company): 269
camels: camel raising, 134, 135-136, 285, 288, 293; domestication, 15, 16; war camels, 17-18
Canaanites: 13
capital city. See Riyadh
Chase Manhattan Bank: 230
Chelhod, Joseph: 153
China, People's Republic of: 215
China, Republic of: 215
civil service: 157, 182-183, 223, 237; non-Saudis, 182, 183
Clayton, Sir Gilbert: 31
climate: viii, 45, 53-54; early, 13; temperature and humidity, 53
Cole, Donald P.: 137, 142, 144, 149
Committee for the Liberation of Saudi Arabia: 345
Council of Ministers: 41, 157, 178-182, 185, 319; advisory role, 33, 157; autonomous agencies and public corporations, 182; consensus in selection of king, 157; executive and legislative functions, 174, 187, 217, 231, 232, 238; members of royal family, 2, 4, 170; Presidency of, 176, 178, 182, 183, 190; reorganization, 1975, 158, 170, 171, 174, 178, 181-182, 196, 298 Saudi citizenship, 182; under Abd al Aziz, 33, 160, 161, 170, 173, 174, 175, 178; under Faisal, 36-37, 38, 41, 167, 168, 173, 175, 181,
Cox, Sir Percy: 31

Dahna dessert: 45, 50, 52-53
Dammam: administrative center, 65, 87, 190; banks, 226; industry, 298, 301, 303, 304, 305; offshore oil fields, 47, 264; port, ix, 60, 61, 62; radio and television stations, 201, 202; sewage system, 77
Dariyah: 24, 27, 121; community development center, 88
Dawasir wadi: 51
death rate. See health
Dhahran: 52; airfield, ix, 60; Aramco headquarters, 65; Aramco trachoma research center, 79; College of Petroleum and Minerals, 39; railroad, 59
Dhahran Air Base: 37, 212, 333
Dibdiba plain: 52
diet and nutrition: 69-71, 79; animal protein, 67, 70, 71, 294, 295, 297; desert

377

plants and animals, 56; food preparation, 80, 85; meal patterns and mealtimes, 70-71; of infants, 71; religious food restrictions, 71, 116; subsidies (*see also* imports), 69-70, 75; Western foods, 71

disarmament position: 338

dress: 71-72; foreign women, 150; Western, 72; women, 72, 150, 341

economic aid: 214, 235, 246, 312, 331: Egypt and Jordan, 43, 206-207, 208, 232, 235, 316, 337

economy: ix, 6-7, 219-236; budget, 230-236, 240, 242; capital expenditures, 232; Central Planning Organization (CPO), 39, 64, 182, 232, 238-239; constraints, 7, 219, 239, 240-241, 243-244; foreign interests (banks), 226; GDP, ix, 6, 220, 221, 222, 241; historic, 219-220; human resources and physical infrastructure, 6, 34, 88-89, 99, 146, 178, 219, 231, 235, 236, 238, 241-244, 246; IMF stabilization plan, 1958, 225, 231, 238; inflation, 243-244; oil dominated, 7-8, 219, 220, 243, 245; planning, 238-244; private sector, 219, 223-224, 238; promotion of foreign investments, 197, 304; real purchasing power, 221; reserve funds, 232, 235, 245; traditional paternalism, 33-34, 231

Ecuador: 253

education: 91-92, 97-112, 125; adult, 106, 107, 108; brain drain, 5, 100, 145, 183; budget, 223, 240; early, 97-99; elementary, 40, 98, 104, 105, 106; extracurricular cultural activities, 77; female, 40-41, 92, 99, 102, 103, 104, 105, 106, 107, 110, 111, 154; five year plans, 92, 100, 104, 110, 111, 241; foreign teachers, 92, 98, 100-101, 145; government-subsidized education abroad, 4-5, 36, 99, 111, 144, 145, 172, 183, 212-213; higher, 5, 40, 100, 103, 105, 106, 109, 111, 144; lack of facilities, 101, 102, 103; literacy, viii, 92, 185, 194, 196, 197, 199; modernization program, 40-41, 91, 98-100, 144, 168, 219, 221; number and social origin of students, 100, 101-102, 103, 104, 106-110; religious orientation, 91-92, 98, 99, 110, 111; religious schools, 92, 99, 103, 105, 106, 107, 111; rote and other traditional methods, 97, 111-112; scientific and literary, 110, 131; secondary, 40, 99, 100, 104, 105, 106, 107; Supreme Council for Education, 103; teachers and teacher training, 98, 99, 100-101, 105, 107, 109, 112; vocational training, 40, 103, 105, 106, 107, 110, 185, 237

Egypt (*see also* Nassar, Gamal Abdul): Al Azhar University, 81; gift of Kiswah (covering of the Kaabah), 129; historic, 13-14, 23, 27-28; Middle East News Agency, 203; military aid, 312, 324-325, 331; military government, 207, 315; military production factories, 324; mutual defense pact, 37; nationals employed in Saudi Arabia, 37, 100, 146, 271; OAPEC membership, 259; radio broadcasts, 203, 345, 346; relations, 37, 38, 169, 206-207, 209, 316, 345; Saudi economic and military aid, 206-207, 232, 235, 337; Saudi sports participation, 77; Saudi students, 99; Soviet relations, 207, 317; Suez Canal, 37, 208, 211, 256, 315; Syrian relations, 208; Yemen crisis, 41-42, 209, 316, 333

Eilts, Hermann: 140

Eisenhower, Dwight D.: 37

electric power: 299-300, 305; capacity, 300; government subsidized rates, 73, 300; private companies, 299, 307

equality, principle: 139, 143, 181

Europe, Western: oil imports, 245, 248, 264; Saudi students, 5; trade, 8

Fahd ibn Abd al Aziz Al Saud: crown prince, 157, 162, 165, 170; foreign relations, 210, 213, 216; government position, 2, 43, 158, 168, 169, 178, 205, 317, 335; lineage, 26

Faisal (1834-38, 1843-65): 28, 159, 165

Faisal ibn Abd al Aziz Al Saud (1964-75): as amir, 31, 33; assassination, 1975, 9, 43, 202, 312, 344; austerity program, 38, 124, 146, 184; basic law, proposed, 168, 174-175; foreign policy, 42, 206-207, 212-213; lineage, 3, 26, 163, 166, 167; modernization program, 38-39, 40-41, 157, 168, 181, 188, 193, 195, 196, 311, 316, 317, 322; reign of, 9, 39-43, 162, 168-169, 175, 177-178, 184; reputation and respect for, 40, 168, 207; under Saud, 33, 36-37, 160-162, 167-168, 173, 216; upbringing and religious idealism, 40, 166-167, 168; wife, influence of, 154; Yemeni campaign, 314-315, 316-317

Faisal ibn Fahd ibn Abd al Aziz Al Saud: 165

Faisal ibn Musaid: 202

films, private showings: 202
First National City Bank (of New York): 226
fiscal year: vi
fish and fishing: 56, 68, 297
Five Year Development Plan (1970-75) *(see also under specific headings)*: 69, 71, 169, 235, 239-241, 300
Five Year Development Plan (1975-80) *(see also under specific headings)*: 1, 6, 46, 78, 79, 83, 86, 190, 212, 220, 221, 236, 241-243, 300
flora and fauna: 55-56
Food and Agriculture Organization, U.N. (FAO): 54, 68
foreign population: 45, 63, 64, 78, 86, 141, 144-146, 182, 237-238, 338; Americans, 144, 304, 332, 335; cafe society, 76, 150; descendants of pilgrims (ajnabi), 10-11, 64, 98, 132, 140; Egyptians, 37, 100, 146, 271; income taxes, 234; Jews, exclusion, 113, 214; law cases against, 344; Lebanese, 146, 182; oil workers, 57, 131, 145, 299; percent of population and increase in number, viii, 1, 219, 221, 223, 236, 238, 244; work permits and entry documents, 238; Yemenis, 64, 146, 236
foreign relations *(see also economic aid; names of countries)*: 205-217, 312, 336-338; accreditation to king, 177, 217; anti-communism, 8, 37, 209, 210-211, 214, 337; Arab unity, 37, 205, 207; conduct of, 205-206, 216-217; foreign broadcasting programs, purpose, 197; homeland of Islam, 197, 206; international power and status, 1, 196, 207-208, 331, 337-338; Islamic solidarity, 205, 210-211, 215-216; mediatory role, 207, 208, 209-210; Middle Eastern and Islamic states, 206-211; personal diplomacy, 206, 207, 216; purpose and focus, 205, 209-210, 211, 214-215; regional, 205, 209-210, 337-338; Saud reign, 37; Western states, 205, 211-214
France: Agence France Presse, 203; informational activities, 203-204; military aid, ix, 214, 312, 322, 324-325, 332, 334; 19th century interests, 29; relations, 39, 213-214
Gabon: 253
General Electric (U.S.): 307
General Investment Fund: 230
General Petroleum and Mining Organization (Petromin): 182, 268, 297-298

geography: vii-viii, 45-46, 48-55; Arabian Shield, 57; deserts, 45, 50, 51, 52-53; fault line (Great Rift), 45, 48-49; mountains, escarpments, 45, 49-50, 51; Najd, 50, 51; Northern Arabia, 51-52; salt marshes, 50, 51, 55; Soyuz-Apollo survey, 49
Germany, Federal Republic of: 203, 204, 214
Getty Oil Company: 250, 261, 265, 266, 268
Ghalib, Sharif: 25
Ghawar oil field; 260, 261
Glidden, Harold W.: 5
Golan Heights: 49
government *(see also* administrative districts; Council of Ministers; king): 32-34, 157-185; absolute monarchy, viii, 1-2, 175, 177, 311; administrative budget, 235, 236, 240, 242; basic law, proposed, 168, 174-175, 184; bureaucracy, 4, 149, 170, 171; centralized, autocratic, viii, 41, 157-158, 168, 172, 175, 177, 178; Constitution (Organic Instructions), of the Hejaz, 32, 173, 187; Consultative Council, 157, 160, 173, 177, 187; decision-making, 166-182, 205-206, 262; Department of Religious Research, Ifta, Missionary Activities, and Guidance, 125; internal stability, 157, 206, 331, 344, 346; legal bases, 172-175; legislation by decree, 158, 173, 174, 177, 187; local, 183-185; model of single-party system, 166; nepotism, 33, 48, 113, 145, 146, 149, 162-166, 181; personal accessibility of members *(see also* majlis), 181, 184; political influences, 158, 170-172; political parties, organized interest groups, viii, 158, 166, 346; provincial and municipal councils, 185; secular political power, 32-33, 145, 171-172, 181, 182-183, 307; state and religion indistinguishable, 32, 118, 124, 157, 172, 187; structure, 176; tradition and custom, 173, 184-185
Gulf of Aqaba: 46
Gulf of Oman: 47
Hadidim tribe: 134
Hail: 29, 31, 51, 135, 314
haj. *See* pilgrims
Hajj: 199, 200
Harad: 59, 67
Haradh, King Faisal Settlement Project: 294

Harmaliyah oil field: 261
Hasa oasis: 52, 54, 289; beduin agriculture settlements, 68, 295-296; historic, 25, 28, 29, 30, 33
Hazim tribe: 134
health: viii, 6, 77-86; armed forces, services for, 327; birth and death rates, 64, 66; birth control, 81; budget, 223, 240; dental, 71; disease, 78-81; foreign physicians and nurses, 82; government medical facilities, 41, 64, 69, 81-83, 221, 241; hajis, 83, 84-86, 308; harmful insects, 56, 79, 80, 81; infant mortality rate, viii, 6, 64, 78, 80; life expectancy, 64; private facilities, 77, 79, 80, 83; Saudi Red Crescent Society, 83-84, 86; traditional beliefs and remedies, 78-79; urban facilities, 6, 66
Hebrews: 13
Hejaz: 50-51, 54, 289, 301; Abd al Aziz proclaimed king, 31-32, 160; ajnabi (descendants of foreign pilgrims), 10-11, 64, 78, 132, 140; early government, 173; early trade routes, 15, 16; pre-Islamic conquest, 16-19; religious conversion, 21-23; Shiites, 125; urbanization, 140-141
history (see also House of Saud; Wahhahi Islam): 9-43; Al Ubaid culture, 11, 12; Arabic Felix, 12, 13-16; Dilmun, 12; Mamluks, 23-24; migrations, 13, 14, 23; 19th century, 25-29; Ottoman Turks, 24, 25-31 passim, 173, 186, 187, 313; pre-Islamic religious, 14, 15-16, 22, 24, 116-117, 120; pre-historic, 11-16; Saudi civil wars, 28-29; Sharifians, 23-24, 25; Treaty of Jiddah, 1927, 31-32, 35, 47, 317; Westernization, 9
Hitti, Philip K.: 118
Hogarth, David: 10
Holden, David: 8
House of Saud (see also Muhammad ibn Saud): 24-29, 159-166; branches of, 2, 158-160; business, professional, technological careers, 146, 165-166; Committee for the Liberation of Saudi Arabia (in Egypt), 345; economic and political power, 5, 144, 146, 162, 165, 166, 169-170; funds, budget, 235; genealogy (charts), 26, 163-164; government posts, 2-3, 145, 170, 181, 185; graft, corruption, and conspicuous consumption, 34-35, 124; intermarriages, 165; law enforcement against, 344; number of relatives, 146; origin, 4, 23, 24-25, 113, 141, 159; present senior member, 162, 164; religious leadership, 3, 4, 9, 30, 32; role in selection of king, 157, 161; secular and technical education, 4-6, 165; Sudairi Seven, 154, 165; "uncles" and "nephews," 164-165
housing: financing, 72-74, 75, 88, 230; government projects and subsidies, 73, 241; investment, 298; Mina, 85, 86; new construction, 221; shortage, 69, 72, 79, 243; urban shantytowns, 72, 73, 79, 287
Hufuf: 12, 52, 67, 291; Al Murrah tribal center, 135; camel and sheep market, 305; industries, 72, 301, 302; railroad, 59
Humayd, Uthman al: 318
Hussein (1908): 29-30, 31
Hussein, Hashimite king of Hejaz: 314
Hussein, king of Jordan: 43, 209, 315-316
Hutaym tribe: 134
Hywaytat tribe: 134

Ibn Khaldun: 131, 142
Ibn Saud. See Abd al Aziz ibn Abd ar Rahman Al Saud
Ibrahim: 27
Ibrahim ibn Muhammad ibn Ibrahim Al ash Shaykh: 188
Ikhwan al Muslimin (Muslim Brethren) (see also Royal Saud National Guard): 30, 31, 32, 123-124, 142-143, 313, 314, 339
imam: title of, 4, 29, 160; traditional chief imam, 118, 160
Imam Muhammad ibn Saud University: 105, 106, 107, 109
imports: 219, 222, 243, 246; foodstuffs, 55, 69, 70, 246, 287, 294, 296, 305; international franchises, 286, 306-307; tariff policies, 62, 75, 233, 234, 298, 304; valuation, ix
Indonesia: 253, 258
industry: 286, 297-305; construction, 6, 57, 221-222, 223, 286, 298, 299, 302-303, 305; desalination plants, 6, 299, 300, 305; electric consumption, 300; employment, 237, 238, 297, 300, 301, 302; foreign technical help, 286, 298; GDP, 222, 286, 297; growth rate, 6, 223-224, 239-240, 297, 302; hydrocarbon based, 241, 243; investment policies, 297, 298, 303, 304; local craftsmen, 286, 301; natural resources, 298-299, 303; personalized and family oriented, 149; petrochemical industries, 6,

241, 243, 299, 303, 305; planned development, 304-305; royal family members, 146; underutilization, 302
Institute of Public Administration: 182, 183
intellectual and artistic expression: 91, 92-97; Arabic language, importance to, 93-95; architecture, 93; art, 96; classical age, 91, 93, 96; Islamic constraints, 91, 92, 97, 122; music and dance, 93, 96; oral traditions, 18, 92, 96; poetry, 91, 92, 94, 95, 96; prose, 95; Quran, 95, 118; Ukaz poetry fair, 17, 18, 20, 95-96; Western forms, 91, 96-97
internal security *(see also* armed forces; national security; religious police; Royal Saudi National Guard): 185, 293, 311, 338-346; Abd al Aziz, 338-339; Arab and Middle East general insecurity and radical movements, 169, 207, 315, 337-338, 345; armed forces role, 311, 317; budget, 346; Coast Guard, ix, 318, 319, 320, 321, 340, 341; foreign propaganda campaigns, 312, 345, 346; Frontier Force, ix, 318, 319, 320, 321, 340, 341; Internal Security Forces College, 341; officers' rebellion, 1969, 311-312, 339, 345-346; political groups, prohibition of, viii, 158, 166, 346; political prisoners, release by King Khalid, 346; Public Security Police, 2, 311, 340-341; regional, tribal, 340; Union of the Arab Peninsula, 345
International Bank for Reconstruction and Development: 63, 223, 246
International memberships *(see also* League of Arab States; Organization of Arab Petroleum Exporting Countries; Organization of Petroleum Exporting Countries; United Nations): viii, 196
International Monetary Fund stabilization plan, 1958: 225, 231, 238
Iran: 210; Continental Shelf Agreement, 1968, 41, 210; oil interests, 253, 258; Shiites, 119
Iraq: 208-209, 315; boundaries, 31, 46; historic, 25, 46; Hasayn tomb at Karbala, 122; Iran, relations, 209; King Faisal, 31; military coup, 1958, 207, 208-209, 316; neutral zone, 46, 209; oil interests, 253, 256, 259; propaganda from, 209, 345; Shiites, 119; Soviet relations, 208, 337; Syrian relations, 208, 209

irrigation: 54-55, 79, 289, 293, 295, 296; early, 15
Islam *(see also* pilgrims *(haji);* sharia; Wahhabi Islam): Arabic-beduin orientation, 21-22; early Jewish rejection of Muhammad as prophet, 21-22, 117; holidays, 75-76; holy places, 113, 116-118, 126-129; jahaliyah (time of ignorance before Islam), 16, 123; Jews and Christians, "people of the book", 119; jihad (holy wars), 21, 116, 122-123; meaning, 114; messianic prophets and sages, 18-19, 114-115; Muslim, meaning, 114; origin and conquest of Hejaz, 19-23, 95, 113-118, 126; Quran, literal word of God, 114, 118, 120, 121, 122; Ramadan, 115-116, 117, 125, 201, 341, schools of religious law, 120, 125, 158, 175, 186, 187; sects, development, 118-120; Shiites (Shia), 118-119, 125, 132; Sunni doctrine, viii, 119; tenets, 21-22, 113-116
Islamic Conference: 205, 210, 215-216; Islamic summit, 1965, 39-40; Khartoum summit, 1967, 206-207; Rabat summit, 1969, 42, 215
Islamic Development Bank: 216
Islamic University: 106, 107, 109, 111
Ismaili tribe: 25
Israel *(see also* Arab-Israeli conflict): 113, 194, 226; Faisal position, 42, 214, 215; technical state of war, 214, 337
Italy: 323
Jabal Dhahran oil fields: 34
Jabal Idsas: 57
Jabal Sayid: 57
Jabal Shammar: 51
Jabal Tuwaiq: 45, 49, 50, 51, 53, 54
Jabrin oasis: 79
Jafura desert: 52
Jaham oil field: 261
Japan: 205, 214; trade, 8, 245, 248, 264, 297
Jawf oasis: 52, 68
Jayzan: 80
Jiddah: administration center, vii, 87, 174, 181, 190; agriculture, 289, 295; airport, ix, 60, 309; banks, 226; diplomatic center, 203, 217; early French and British consulates, 29; industry, 299, 301, 302, 304, 305; iron ore deposits, 299; oil refinery, 268; population and ethnic groups, 64, 65, 66; port, ix, 61, 62; press, 198, 200; private hospitals, 83; radio and television stations,

381

201, 202; schools and colleges, 39, 82, 109, 111; sewage system, 77; USIS library and information center, 203
Jiluwi: 159
Jiluwi family: 158-159, 160, 165, 185
Jordan: 100, 146, 208, 209, 315-316; boundaries, 41, 46; internal instability, 207, 209; Saudi armed forces in, ix, 208, 209, 317; Saudi economic aid, 43, 206-207, 208, 232, 235, 316
Juaymah oil terminal: 267
Jubayl: industrial complex, 299, 303, 304, 305; port, 62
Juffali, E. A., and Brothers: 307
Juraybiat oil field: 261
Juridical Institute: 41
Kennedy, John F.: 38-39
Khadijah: 19
Khalid ibn Abd al Aziz Al Saud (1975-): 3, 162, 170-171, 317; as amir, 38, 168; continuation of Faisal policies, 157, 169-170, 175, 178, 193; exercise of judicial power, 188; foreign policy, 205, 207, 210, 216, 217; genealogy, vi, 26, 163, 165; general support, 157; majlis, 181; release of political prisoners, 346; selection as crown prince, 39, 157, 162
Khalid ibn Ahmad (791): 96
Khalid ibn Musaid: 202
Khalid ibn Saud (1840-41): 28
Khaybar: 22, 51, 135
Khazraj tribe: 17
Khubar: 77, 79, 83; commercial center, 65, 299; port, 62
king: 175-178; investiture, 143, 161, 177, 184; official piety, 172; powers and limitations of, 2, 40, 157, 158, 166, 168, 175, 177-178, 187; principles of succession, 157, 161-162; selection and consensus of support, 157, 161, 162, 166, 168, 177; selection of crown prince, 161; shaykh of shaykhs, 143, 157, 175; tribal address, 139, 143
King Abd al Aziz University: 39, 82, 109, 111
King Faisal Air Force College: 326
King Faisal University: 111
Kissinger, Henry A.: 213, 335
Knauerhase, Ramon: 63
Korea, Republic of: 214
Kraft, Joseph: 63
Kuwait: 77, 209; 'Abd ar Rahman and Abd al Aziz, exile in, 29, 159-160; Al Sabah ruling family, 159; boundaries, 31, 46; neutral zone, 46; oil deposits, 262, 265; OPEC and OAPEC membership, 253, 258, 259

labor (see also civil service; foreign population): 69, 145, 236-238; agricultural, 224, 236, 237, 287; arbitration committees, 190; beduin, 147, 293, 295; construction industry, 221-222; government principal employer, 183; manpower shortage and lack of skilled workers, 6, 69, 77, 82, 92, 99-100, 144, 145, 171, 182, 183, 201, 237, 238, 243, 302; oil industry, 220, 237, 245, 260; qualified young Saudis, 57, 182-183; unionization and strikes forbidden, 35, 36; unlimited absorption ability, 171; wage and salary subsidies, 6, 75; white collar, prestige, 110; women, 69, 101, 105, 109, 154, 195, 198, 236
Lamar: 57
language: Arab official, viii; early, 13; effect on intellectual expression, 93-95; functional bilingualism, 94; homogeneity, 338; structure, 94-95
Laoust, Henri: 122
Lawrence, T. E.: 10, 30-31, 60
League of Arab States: viii, 205, 215, 315; Arab oil conference, 254-255; boycott on firms doing business with Israel, 8, 213, 304; regional military industries, 323
Lebanon: civil war, 209; Saudi students, 99
legal system (see also sharia): viii, 118, 122-123, 185-190, 339, 341-344; administrative decrees, viii, 32, 33, 124, 157, 177, 187, 190, 311, 341; Board of Grievances, 187, 189, 190; commercial disputes, 189, 190; definitions of crime and culpability, 342-344; expansion, 187, 190; ijtihad (personal reasoning), 187; incidence of crime, 344; international law loopholes in Islamic law, 48; juvenile delinquents, 88; king, judiciary powers, 177, 188; legal training, 188; military justice, 328, 330; Ministry of Justice, 181, 187, 188, 189; prisons, 343-344; public attitudes, 344-345; tribal law, 25, 137, 143
Lewis, Bernard: 95
Libya: 207, 209, 253, 256, 259
lineage: beduin, 136-137, 138, 150; major families, 135, 137, 143, 158-160; village, 139, 141
livestock (see also beduin): 70, 134, 135-

136, 287, 288-289, 293-295, 296; early camel raising, 15, 16, 17-18; experimental cattle farms, 70; horses, 18, 295; Hufuf camel and sheep market, 305; overstocking and overgrazing, 67, 148, 294, 296-297; pasture, 51-56 *passim*; sheep and goats, 134, 135, 148, 285, 288, 293-294

living conditions: 69-77; alcohol and tobacco, 74, 122, 124-125, 341; café society, 76; consumption patterns, 74; government subsidies, 75, 241; holidays, 75-76; inflation, cost of living, 69, 74-75; leisure, 76-77, 124-125; Ramadan, 76

Lockheed Corporation: 335

Maharah oil field: 261

Mahd al Dhahab: 57

majlis: 33-34, 138, 140, 169, 181, 183-184; Faisal assassination, 43

Malaysia: 210

Malik Ibn Anas (Maliki school of law): 125, 186

Malone, Joseph: 35

Mares, William: 95, 293

Marib Dam: 15

marriage: 150, 151-152, 189; divorce, 152; foreign marriages, 151-152; mother-in-law and daughter-in-law relationship, 153, 154

Marx, Emanuel (quoted): 138 .

mass communication *(see also* press; radio and television): ix, 5, 181, 193-204; careers in, 194, 198; English language, 199, 200, 202, 203; foreign audiences, 196, 197; foreign sources, 203-204; General Directorate of Broadcasting, Printing, and Publishing, 195; government and family interests, ix, 193-194, 195-196; government purposes, 193, 195, 197-198, 201; government subsidies, 194, 196; haj, 201, 308; mosque as information channel, 197-198; postal services, 33; religious proscriptions, 125, 193-194, 196, 199, 201, 202; telegraph, 33; traditional, informal channels, 193, 197-198; United States Information Service, 203; Voice of Islam, 202

Mawaali tribe: 134

Mecca *(see also* Muhammad; pilgrims): 1, 140, 289; appeal court, 190; early trading center, 17, 22; haram (sacred area), 116, 117, 126-129; historic, 23, 25, 27, 31; Kaabah and black stone,

10, 113, 114, 117-118, 126-128, 129; living conditions, 73-74, 80, 81; Police College, 340; population and ethnic groups, 64, 66; radio station and press, 194, 198, 200; religious significance, 16, 116-118; Saudi Elmi Institute, 98, 99; Ukaz poetry fair, 17, 18, 20, 95-96

Medina *(see also* Yathrib): 1, 10, 140; agriculture, 289, 291; historic, 23, 25, 27, 31; living conditions, 73-74, 80; population and ethnic groups, 64, 66; television station, 202

Mesopotamia: 12, 13, 15

Mexico: 253

Mina: *haji* center, 85, 128, 129, 309; Jabal al Nur, 126, 127; tent camp fire, 1975, 84

minerals *(see also* oil): 57, 299, 302-303; GDP, 222; natural gas, 6, 260, 266, 299, 303;

Ministries of: Agriculture and Water, 54, 179; Commerce, 179, 182, 190; Commerce and Industry, 182; Communications, 61, 179, 182; Defense and Aviation, 39, 103, 162, 179, 311, 312, 315, 319, 324, 326, 327; Education, 99, 102, 103, 106, 110, 179, 197; Finance, 231; Finance and National Economy, 179, 229, 230, 231-232, 239; Foreign Affairs, vii, 84, 179, 216-217; Health, 81-82, 85, 179; Higher Education, 103, 179; Industry and Electricity, 170, 179, 182, 298, 303; Information, 179, 181, 193, 195, 197, 201, 202, 203; Interior, 61, 98, 180, 182, 190, 311, 312, 318, 320, 340; Justice, 158, 171, 180, 181; Labor and Social Affairs, 76-77, 87, 88, 165, 180, 190; Municipal and Rural Affairs, 54, 180, 182; Petroleum and Mineral Resources, 57, 170, 180; Pilgrimage Affairs and the Awqaf, 84, 125, 126, 129, 180, 197; Planning, 170, 180, 182; Posts, Telegraphs, and Telecommunications, 180, 182, 196; Public Works and Housing, 180

Mobil Oil Company: 268, 269

modernization *(see also under* names of kings and under specific headings): 32, 74, 144-149, 172; coexistence with religious conservatism, 32, 35, 40, 172, 173, 177-178; gradualist approach, 35, 146, 158, 171, 194-196, 263; within Saudi value systems, 11, 97, 157, 243-244

money *(see also* oil wealth): ix, 219, 224-

383

226, 243; currency reforms, 228; early bimetallic standard, 224; exchange rates, 225, 226; historic coins, 224; paper currency, 224-225, 228, 229; pilgrims' receipts, 224-225, 228, 229; prohibited foreign exchange transactions, 226

Morocco: 77

motor vehicles: 59, 190

Muawiyah: 118

Muhammad (570-632) *(see also* Islam): 19-23, 95, 113-115, 116, 117-118, 126, 128; hijra, 20, 75, 114

Muhammad Ali: 27, 28

Muhammad ibn Abd al Aziz Al Saud: 162, 163, 165

Muhammad ibn Ali al Harkan: 188

Muhammad ibn Saud (1742-65): 3, 10, 24-25, 113, 121, 141, 159

Muntafiq tribe: 134

Musaid ibn Abd ar Rahman: 162, 163, 164, 168

Muscat and Oman. *See* Oman

Muzdalifah: 127, 128

Nafud desert: 45, 50, 52

Naif ibn Abd al Aziz Al Saud: 2, 170, 318

Najd: 51, 313; agriculture, 55, 291; bedouin agricultural settlements, 68; governorship of crown prince Saud, 33, 35-36; Saudi homeland, 10, 121, 160, 174

Najran: 16, 46, 48, 80, 314

name: vii, 1

names, personal, as genealogical charts: vi, 138, 151

Nasir ibn Abd al Aziz Al Saud: 162, 163

Nasser, Gamal Abdul: 37-41 *passim,* 169, 207, 315, 317, 345

National Commercial Bank: 226

National Day: 76

national identity: 193, 338, 344

national security *(see also* armed forces): ix, 311-346; national security council, 177; regional stability, 337

Nazir, Hisham Muhi al Din: 4, 170

Netherlands: 24

Netherlands Trading Society: 226

News from Saudi Arabia: 197, 199, 200

Nigeria: 253, 256

Northrop Corporation: 334, 335

Occidental Oil Company: 256

oil *(see also* Arabian American Oil Company; oil wealth; Organization of Arab Petroleum Exporting Countries; Organization of Petroleum Exporting Countries): ix, 1, 245-275; Abqaiq field, 260, 261; capital intensive, 245, 260; dependence on foreign technological and managerial skills, 200, 211, 212, 262; discovery and explorations, 48, 124, 131, 220, 248-249, 260, 264; domestic consumption, 266; employment, 237, 245, 260; exports, ix, 1, 220, 245, 248, 265; fifty-fifty profit-sharing arrangement, 255-256; foreign concessions, 7, 34, 249-250, 255-256, 268-275; GDP, ix, 221, 222, 223, 245, 260; Ghawar field, 260, 261; government, ownership of oil deposits, 260; government "participation in oil companies, 257, 262, 269; historic uses, 247; international oil industry, 248-253; locations, 47, 50, 261; 1973 oil embargo, 43, 245, 257, 266; oil tankers, 52, 256, 267, 268, 270; pipelines, 60, 256, 267, 268, 270, 305; prices, 42-43, 221, 245, 250-253, 255, 256, 257; producer-consumer interdependence, 214, 262, 263-264; production, ix, 1, 7, 42, 206, 239, 241, 245, 248, 249 (graph), 263, 264-266, 268; quality, 260-261; Red Line Agreement, 269; refineries, 241, 243, 267-268, 304-305; reserves, 1, 220, 245, 248, 249 (graph), 260, 262-263; royalties and income taxes, 234, 269; Safaniya field, 260, 261; Saudi policies, 245-246, 262-264; transportation 256, 266-268, 270; wasting asset, 262-263, world demand, 246-248, 249, 264, 265; Zararah oil field, 47

Oil Caravan Weekly: 199

oil wealth: 144-149, 206; as economic weapon, 42, 207-208, 245, 263-264; domination of economy, 7-8, 219, 220, 234, 243, 245, 337; foreign investments and deposits, 7-8, 246, 303-304; increases, 42, 232, 235, 240-241, 246, 257, 265; national prestige and stability, 169, 196, 331, 337-338; private property of ruler, 34; royal consumption patterns, 34-35, 36, 74, 96-97, 124-125; selected years (table), 233; social and economic uses, 6, 34, 39, 88-89, 97, 99, 146, 178, 219, 231-246 *passim,* 285-286

Olympic Games: 77

Oman: 12, 41, 210, 338; boundaries, 47; Saudi military aid, 337

Organization for Sophisticated War Industries (OSWI): 323

Organization of Arab Petroleum Exporting Countries (OAPEC): viii, 43, 206, 215, 259; cooperative Arab energy ventures, 259
Organization of Petroleum Exporting Countries (OPEC): viii, 7, 206, 215, 253-259; nationalization, 42, 256-257; oil policy, 254-258; oil pricing, 42, 246, 253-254, 255-256, 257-258; origin and membership, 253; regional groups, 258, 259; Saudi influence, 245, 258-259
Pakistan: 146, 210, 271; military aid, 312, 324-325; rice exports, 70
Palestine Liberation Organization (PLO): 43, 207
Palestinians: 37, 42, 100
Palmyra: 15
Persia: 16
Persian Gulf: continental shelf agreement with Iran, 1968, 41, 210; national security concerns, 210, 337; ports, ix, 61, 62; termination of British presence, 338
Petra: 15
Petromin: 182, 268, 297-298
Philby, H. St. John: 35
Phoenicians: 13
pilgrims *(haji)*: 113, 125-129; assimilation, 10-11, 64, 98, 132, 140; dress, 126; early, 23, 28, 220; from communist-controlled countries, 211; guide system, 140, 308-309; haj, duty of all Muslims, 115, 116, 206; Haj Affairs Directorate, 86; haj rites, 126-129; health and living conditions, 83, 84-86, 308; High Committee for the Haj, 84; income source, 34, 141, 224, 307-308; Jiddah Quarantine Center, 85; logistical and administrative support, 60, 61, 126, 226, 286, 308-309, 341; number of, 309; pan-Islamic conference, 1929, 32; pilgrims' receipts, 224-225, 228, 229; ports of entry, 61, 62, 309; Saudi Red Crescent Society services, 83-84, 86
police. *See* Public Security Police; religious police
Polk, William: 95, 293
population *(see also* foreign population): viii, 1, 45, 62-68; age, sex, and ethnic composition, 64; census inaccuracies, 63, 104, 133; distribution, 45, 64-67; Najd, 51, 65; urban, 65, 66
ports: 61-62; congestion, inadequacy, ix, 6, 62, 69, 219, 223, 243; new construction, 42, 62, 221

Portuguese, historic: 24
postal service: 33; stamps, 97
press: 36, 96, 195-196, 198-201; cartoons, 199; circulation, 198, 199; Egyptian influence, 198; English language, 199, 200, 203; "literary journalism," 198-199; news agencies, 203; press establishments, 195; private ownership, 193, 194, 195; Saudi citizens', requirement for press concessions, 195
Public Security Police: 2, 311, 340-341
Qafilat al Zaft: 199
Qahtan tribe: 138
Qatar: 209, 338; boundaries, 41, 46-47; historic, 28; OAPEC and OPEC membership, 253, 259
Qatif: 65, 79, 289
Qizan: 62, 295
Quraysh tribe: 17, 19-20, 116, 117, 119,
Qusaibi, Ghazi Abd ar Rahman al: 4, 170
radio and television: 194, 196-197, 198, 201-203; government owned, 193; television, 92-93, 154; women announcers, 154, 195
railroads: ix, 59-60
rainfall: 45, 50, 51, 53, 54, 285, 287, 289, 298-299
Ramadan. *See* Islam
Ramlah oil field: 261
Ras al Mishab: 46
Ras Tanura: oil field, 260, 264; oil port, ix, 52, 61, 62, 267
Rashid, Muhammad ibn: 29, 51
Raytheon Corporation: 333, 334, 335
Real Estate Development Fund: 230
Red Sea: boundary, 46; geology, 48; national security concerns, 337; navigation, early, 15, 24; ports, ix, 50, 61, 62
religion. *See* Islam; Muhammad; Wahhabi Islam
religious police (mutawwiun): 115, 340; enforcement of morals, 72, 123, 125, 202, 341
Rentz, George: 124
Replica: 199, 200, 203
Ribyan oil field: 261
Rimthan oil field: 261
Riyadh: 51, 65; administration center, 87, 174, 181, 190, 217; agriculture, 289, 295; airport, ix, 60; appeal court, 190; capital, vii, 27, 33; commercial center, 226, 268, 302, 304, 305; Damman-Riyadh railroad, ix, 59; growth, 141; historic, 25, 160; King Faisal Specialist Hospital and Research Center, 6, 82;

land prices, 69; living conditions, 72, 80, 101; Military Preparatory School, 326; population, 65, 66; press, radio, television, 198, 200, 201, 202; school of Islamic law and religion, 30; USIS English-language center, 203

Riyadh Bank: 226

roads: ix, 57-59, 296; construction, 221, 241; load limits, 59; roads tax, 234

Romans: 15

Roosevelt, Franklin D.: 212

Royal Saud National Guard: allegiance to royal family, 171; establishment, 314, 339; maintenance of public order, 311, 317-318, 320, 339, 340; *mujahidin*, 320; National Guard Training Center, 326; Saud officers, 2, 158, 311, 318; Saud White Army, 36, 39, 168; size, ix, 320-321; tribal recruitment and shaykh leadership, 3, 143-144, 171, 315, 320, 324, 339; uniforms, 326; U.S. equipment and military advisers, 8, 212, 323, 324-325, 331-336

Rub al Khali (Empty Quarter): 45, 47, 50, 52, 53; oil deposits, 260

Rugh, William: 125, 145, 149

Rumma wadi: 51

Ruwala tribe: 134

Saad ibn Abd al Aziz Al Saud: 162, 163

Sadat, Anwar al: 207

Sakaka oasis: 52, 68

sanitation: 77-78, 79, 80, 221; *haji* tent cities, 85-86

Saud (1803-14): 25, 26, 159

Saud (1871-75): 26, 28-29

Saud, House of. *See* House of Saud

Saud ibn Abd al Aziz Al Saud (1953-64): 33, 35-39, 184, 195; deposed, 1964, 39, 161, 162, 171, 317, 339; judiciary powers, 188; lineage (chart), 26; overspending and lack of leadership qualities, 9, 35-36, 87, 124, 160-162, 167-168, 231; Saud-Faisal power struggle, 37-39, 161-162, 167-168, 175, 177, 316; selection as crown prince, 160, 161; Yemeni civil war, 41, 314-315

Saud ibn Faisal ibn Abd al Aziz Al Saud: 2-3, 165, 205, 216

Saudi(s) or Saudi Arabian(s), term for nationals: vii

Saudi Arabia: derivation of name, vii, 1, 9; model of medieval Islamic state, 40

Saudi Arabian Broadcasting Company: 197, 201

Saudi Arabian Fertilizer Company: 230

Saudi Arabian Mining Syndicate: 57

Saudi Arabian Monetary Agency (SAMA): 182, 228-229, 230, 231, 232

Saudi Arabian Television Service: 202

Saudi Credit Bank: 230

Saudi Economic Survey: 199

Saudi Gazette: 199

Saudi Government Railroad Organization: 59

Saudi Industrial Development Fund: 230

Saudia: 61, 318

Schacht, Joseph: 5

settlement patterns: accidental settlements, 66-67, 148; beduin traditional, 66-68, 136, 294-295; government beduin settlement projects (hujar), 30, 55, 67-68, 123, 142, 147, 293, 294-296, 313; natural, 66; oases, 47, 64, 65, 136; villages, 139-141

Shammar tribe: 51, 134, 135

sharia (sacred Islamic law): viii, 124, 143, 173, 311; administration by king, 157, 158; court system, 188-190, 327; definitions of crime and culpability, 341-344; grand mufti, 181, 188; Hanbali school of religious law, 120, 121, 158, 175, 187; historic, 25, 120; *ijma*, 120, 186, 187; major schools of jurisprudence, 120, 158, 186-187; qiyas, 186, 187; Quran, hadith, and Sunna, viii, 120, 186, 187; revealed by God, 186

Sherarat tribe: 134

Shobaili, Abdulrahman: 198

Sisco, Joseph J.: 331-332 (quoted)

size: vii, 45

slavery, abolition: 5, 38, 168

society *(see also* beduin): 5-6, 131-155; allegiance to House of Saud, 338, 344; births and birthdays, 63, 153-154; cultural uniformity, 132, 338; descent and family membership, 133, 139, 140, 149, 150-152; ingroup solidarity *(asabiyah)*, 5; men and women, 152-154; middle class, 4-5, 36, 73, 145, 146-147, 149, 150-151, 171; primacy of traditional values, 5, 9, 11, 92, 97, 131-132, 146, 147, 149-152; privileged classes, 36, 124, 146, 148; religion and, 2, 5, 113, 117, 118, 122-123, 124-125, 146, 185, 338, 344; shame-oriented, 5; social changes, 132, 144, 146, 171-172, 346; social cliques, 149, 171; social distinctions, 123, 139, 144, 146, 148, 183; social life, 140, 152; television, effects of, 202; Western-style social behavior,

5, 11, 146
Socony-Vacuum. *See* Mobil Oil Company
Socotra: 14
soil: 45, 50, 51, 52, 54-55; salinity, 55, 296, 297
Somalia: 337; historic Point, 14
South Africa: 215, 226
Southern Rhodesia: 215, 226
Soviet Union: 337; informational broadcasting, 204; oil production, 248, 250
sports: 76-77
Standard Oil Company of California (SOCAL): 34, 212, 269
Standard Oil Company of New Jersey (Exxon): 269
Sudairi family: 160, 165
Sudan: 146
Sultan ibn Abd al Aziz Al Saud: 2, 39, 43, 168, 170, 205, 317, 318
Sulubba tribe: 134
Sumeria: 11, 13
Summam plateau: 52
Supreme Council for Youth Welfare: 77
Surra wadi: 51
Syria: Egyptian relations, 208; historic, 13, 23; Iraqi relations, 208, 209; nationals in Saudi Arabia, 119, 146, 182; OAPEC membership, 259; propaganda broadcasts, 345; Saudi armed forces in, ix, 317
Szyliowicz, Joseph: 98
Taha el-Farra: 143
Taif: 17, 20, 31; treaty, 1934, 314
Taimiya, Taki al Din Ahmad ibn: 24, 121
Talal ibn Abd al Aziz Al Saud: 38, 174
Tathlith wadi: 51
taxation: 34, 234-235; income, 234; jihad tax (1971), 234; roads tax, 234; zakat (annual alms tax), 22, 30, 87, 115, 125, 234
territorial sea, limits: 47
Texaco: 269
Tibawi, A. L.: 99
Tihamah Lowlands: 50, 79, 295
tourism abroad: 76
trade: commercial agents, payments, 243, 307; domestic, 285, 286, 305-309; early, 12, 14-16, 24, 52, 219-220; foreign exchange reserves, ix, 1, 7; frankincense and myrrh, 12, 14, 15-16, 56; GDP, 222; local markets (suq), 135, 220, 297, 305-306; merchant houses, 145, 146, 306-307; private investment, 298
TransArabian Pipeline (Tapline): 256, 267, 270; seminomadic settlements, 66-67, 77, 148
transportation: ix, 46, 57-62, 64, 182, 198, 285; budget, 235, 240; camel, 287-288; employment, 61, 237, 238; GDP, 222; government subsidies, 59-60, 61; inadequate, 6, 34, 46, 60, 62, 223, 243, 266-268; map, 58; taxies and private buses, 59; trucks, 148, 223, 285, 286, 293, 294
Treaty of Jiddah, 1927. *See* history
Tunisia: 77
Turkey, historic: 23-31 *passim*
Turki: 33
Turki ibn Abd al Aziz Al Saud: 2, 170, 205, 318
Turki ibn Abd Allah (1824-34): 26, 27-28, 159
Tusun: 27
Uhud: 21, 22
ulama: consensus in selection of king, 157, 161; conservatism, 181, 194; *ijma* (consensus of ulama), 186, 187; political influence, 171, 198; relationship to House of Saud, 3; senior, members of Al ash Shaykh, 4; social position, 144, 146
Umar ibn al Khattab: 20, 75, 118
Umm al Qura: 199, 200
Unayzah: 51, 141
United Arab Emirates: 41, 209, 210, 338; boundary, 47, 210; OAPEC and OPEC membership, 253, 259
United Arab Republic: 37
United Kingdom: Eastern and General Syndicate, 269; informational activities, 203; Joint Commission, 212; military aid, ix, 211-212, 312, 314, 317, 322, 323, 324-325, 331, 332, 333, 334; 19th century interests, 24, 29; relations, 39, 210, 211-212; Reuters, 203; support of Abd al Aziz, 30, 31-32, 48, 211; termination of Middle East military presence, 208, 209, 212, 338
United Nations: Dariyah community development center, 88; membership, viii, 215; truce observation mission to Yemen (Sana), 215, 316; voting record, 215
United States: Americans in Saudi Arabia, 100, 271, 332, 335; Associated Press, 203; financial and other advisers, 8, 212, 228; Joint Commission of Security Cooperation, 211, 213, 304, 334, 335; military aid, ix, 8, 211, 312,

316, 317, 322, 323, 324-325, 331-336; moon landings, 92-93; oil imports (needs), 248; relations, 8, 37, 38-39, 205, 211, 212-213, 304, 335; Saudi students, 5, 212-213; trade, 297, 304
United States Information Agency (USIA): 203
University of Petroleum and Minerals: 92, 101, 109, 111
University of Riyadh: 82, 109, 111, 145
urban centers: 65-66, 132, 140-141, 184; living conditions, 66, 72, 73-74, 77-78, 287; movement to, 11, 66, 147, 224, 236-237, 285; real estate values, 223
Uthman (646): 118
Uyaynah: 24, 121
Uzayzi, R. Z.: 153
vegetation: 54-56; forest, 50, 289
Venezuela, oil production, pricing: 252-256 passim
Vinnell Corporation: 334, 335
Voice of America: 203
Voice of Islam (Sawtaal Islam): 197
Voice of Israel: 203
Wadi Fatima: 57, 302
Wadi Shuwas: 57
Wadi Sirhan: 51-52, 68
Wahhab, Muhammad ibn Abd al (al Shaykh, the imam): 3, 4, 10, 24-25, 26, 96, 113, 121-122, 141, 159, 187
Wahhabi Islam (see also sharia; Wahhab, Muhammad ibn Abd al): viii, 121-124; and society, 2, 113, 117, 118, 185, 338, 344; as early nationalistic movement, 28; Christian enclaves, 113, 119; Committee for Encouragement of Virtue and Discouragement of Vice, 32, 38, 123, 125; origin, 24-25, 121-122; pragmatism, 124; religious intolerance, 113; revival under Abd al Aziz, 30, 123-124, 313; tenets and forbidden innovations (bida,) 121-124; Wahhabi, meaning, usage, 3-4, 120-121
Wasia: 54
Water Desalination Organization: 54

water supply: 53, 54-55, 295, 298-299; improvement projects, 68, 77-78, 295, 296-297; quality, 54, 77; tribal water rights, 134, 136, 288, 290-291; urban, 66, 77
welfare: 69, 86-89, 168, 241; child care, 88; physically and mentally handicapped, 87, 88; social security, 87-88, 241; traditional, 86-87, 117, 136, 138
Well of Zamzam (Hagar): 86, 126-128
Westernization. See modernization
White Army. See Royal Saud National Guard
wildlife: 56
women: 152-154; employment, 101, 105, 109, 154, 195, 198, 236; influence and role, 153-154; leisure activities, 76; medical treatment, 78, 82; prison conditions, 343-344; public worship, 115; seclusion of, 69, 72, 146, 150, 152-153, 154, 341; tribal, 152
World Bank (IBRD): 63, 223, 246
World Health Organization: 79, 84
World War I: 30-31
World War II: 211, 212, 215, 264, 315
Yamani, Ahmad Zaki: 170; dress, 72; international prestige, 4; oil negotiations, 205-206, 257
Yanbu: industry, 268, 299, 304; port, ix, 61, 62
Yathrib (see also Medina): 17, 20-21, 114
Yemen: 28, 48, 119, 314-315
Yemen (Aden): boundary, 47; relations, 210, 337, 338, 345; Yemeni (Sana) civil war, 316
Yemen (Sana): boundary, 46, 50; civil war, 1962, 38, 41-42, 207, 209, 215, 312, 316-317, 330; relations, 210, 315, 338; Saudi military and economic aid, 210, 337; workers in Saudi Arabia, 64, 146, 236

Zararah oil field: 47
Zazirat al Arab: 10
Zuluf oil terminal: 267

PUBLISHED COUNTRY STUDIES
(Area Handbook Series)

550-65	Afghanistan	550-151	Honduras
550-98	Albania	550-165	Hungary
550-44	Algeria	550-21	India
550-59	Angola	550-154	Indian Ocean
550-73	Argentina	550-39	Indonesia
550-169	Australia	550-68	Iran
550-176	Austria	550-31	Iraq
550-175	Bangladesh	550-25	Israel
550-170	Belgium	550-182	Italy
550-66	Bolivia	550-69	Ivory Coast
550-20	Brazil	550-177	Jamaica
550-168	Bulgaria	550-30	Japan
550-61	Burma	550-34	Jordan
550-83	Burundi	550-56	Kenya
550-50	Cambodia	550-81	Korea, North
550-166	Cameroon	550-41	Korea, South
550-159	Chad	550-58	Laos
550-77	Chile	550-24	Lebanon
550-60	China	550-38	Liberia
550-63	China, Republic of	550-85	Libya
550-26	Colombia	550-163	Malagasy Republic
550-91	Congo	550-172	Malawi
550-90	Costa Rica	550-45	Malaysia
550-152	Cuba	550-161	Mauritania
550-22	Cyprus	550-79	Mexico
550-158	Czechoslovakia	550-76	Mongolia
550-54	Dominican Republic	550-49	Morocco
550-52	Ecuador	550-64	Mozambique
550-43	Egypt	550-35	Nepal, Bhutan & Sikkim
550-150	El Salvador	550-88	Nicaragua
550-28	Ethiopia	550-157	Nigeria
550-167	Finland	550-94	Oceania
550-155	Germany, East	550-48	Pakistan
550-173	Germany, Fed. Rep. of	550-46	Panama
550-153	Ghana	550-156	Paraguay
550-87	Greece	550-185	Persian Gulf States
550-78	Guatemala	550-42	Peru
550-174	Guinea	550-72	Philippines
550-82	Guyana	550-162	Poland
550-164	Haiti	550-181	Portugal

550-160	Romania	550-53	Thailand
550-84	Rwanda	550-178	Trinidad and Tobago
550-51	Saudi Arabia	550-89	Tunisia
550-70	Senegal	550-80	Turkey
550-180	Sierra Leone	550-74	Uganda
550-184	Singapore	550-97	Uruguay
550-86	Somalia	550-71	Venezuela
550-93	South Africa	550-57	Vietnam, North
550-171	Southern Rhodesia	550-55	Vietnam, South
550-95	Soviet Union	550-183	Yemens, The
550-179	Spain	550-99	Yugoslavia
550-96	Sri Lanka (Ceylon)	550-67	Zaire
550-27	Sudan	550-75	Zambia
550-47	Syria		
550-62	Tanzania		

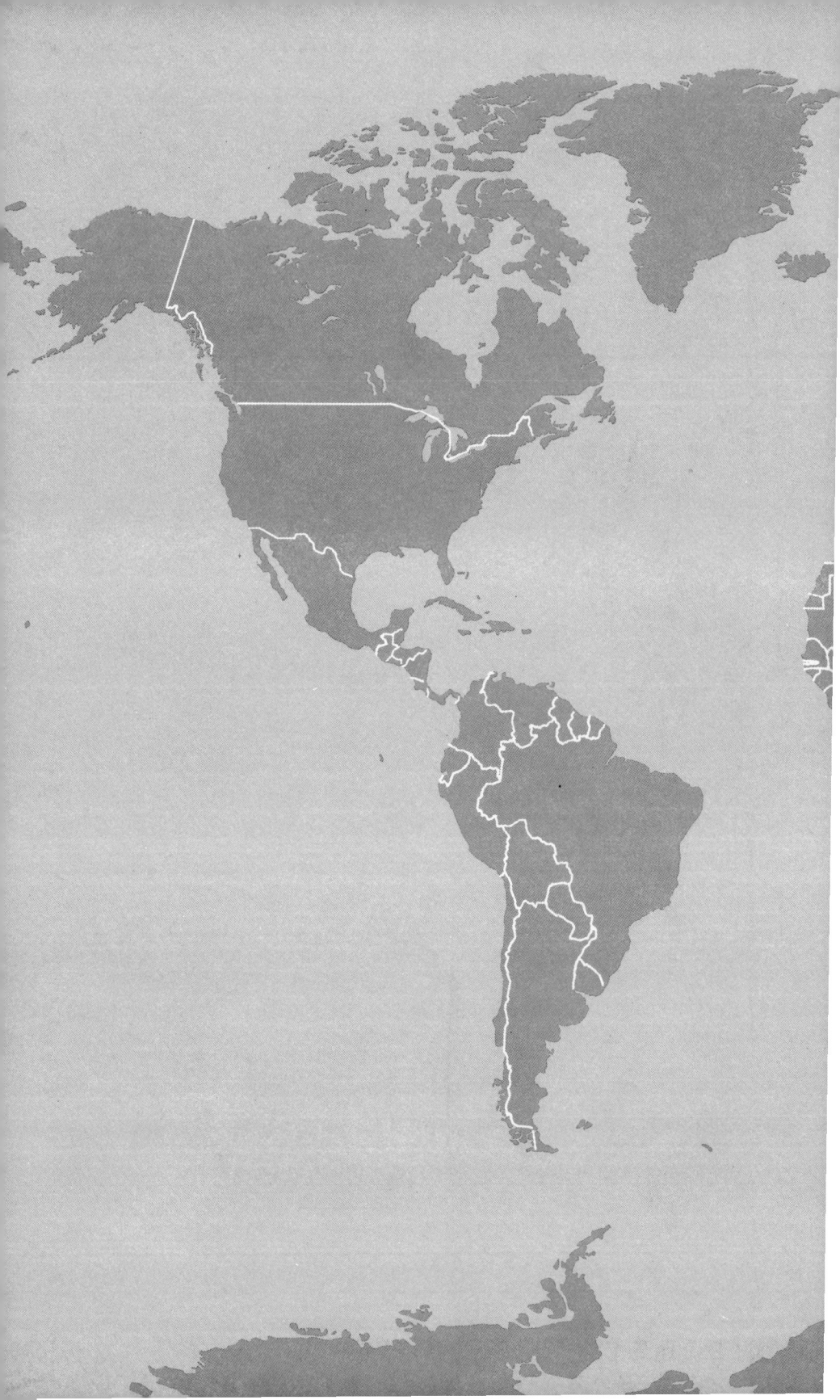